A Transactional Approach to Early Language Training

James E. McLean

Lee K. Snyder-McLean

The University of Kansas
Bureau of Child Research
Parsons Research Center

Charles E. Merrill Publishing Company
A Bell & Howell Company
Columbus   Toronto   London   Sydney

**Merrill Communication Development and
Communication Disorders Series**
James E. McLean, Consulting Editor

Published by
Charles E. Merrill Publishing Company
A Bell & Howell Company
Columbus, Ohio 43216

This book was set in Helvetica.
The production editor was Linda Hillis.
The cover was prepared by Will Chenoweth.
Cover photo by Carl Williams.

This work was developed under a grant from the U.S. Office of Education, Department of
Health, Education and Welfare. However, the opinions and other content do not necessarily
reflect the position or policy of the Agency, and no official endorsement should be inferred.

Library of Congress Catalog Card Number: 77-90784
International Standard Book Number: 0-675-08400-8
    3 4 5 6 7 8 9 10/ 85 84 83 82 81 80

Printed in the United States of America

Preface

This book presents the rationale, findings, and conclusions of a two-year federally supported project. This project was designed to develop a model of natural language and to derive from that model perspectives that would be productive in designing assessment and treatment procedures for young handicapped children with severe language delays or deficits.

The work on this project extended across two professional work settings for the authors. The main body of the project was carried out at George Peabody College for Teachers in Nashville under a contract (OEC-0-74-9185) between the federal government and George Peabody College. Prior to the completion of the project and its final reporting, the authors accepted appointments with the Bureau of Child Research of the University of Kansas. The final analyses and preparation of the report on this project, therefore, were carried out at the Parsons Research Center, a component of the Kansas Center for Research in Mental Retardation and Human Development, established as a cooperative unit between the Bureau of Child Research and the Parsons State Hospital and Training Center, a state institution for retarded persons.

Any undertaking of this size and scope requires the efforts of many people and we would like to identify here many of those who have contributed to this project through the course of its development and eventual completion.

Gerald Mahoney, now at the University of California at Los Angeles, was a Research Associate on the project at its initiation. We are heavily in debt to Jerry, for it was he who first found and assessed the importance of Bruner's recent conceptualizations regarding the nature of language and the relationship between language and the conditions of its acquisition. Jerry's own work in developing more ethological perspectives on language has also been both provocative and productive in shaping our views.

Mary Beth Branston, now a doctoral student at the University of Wisconsin, was vital in her contributions throughout this project. Her early literature abstracts, her unabashed enthusiasm for Piagetian constructs in early cognitive development, and her work designing curriculum applications of the "transactional model" in the Kennedy Center preschool helped us greatly in developing an appreciation for the overall constructionist position reflected in our perspectives.

Linda McCormick, now at the University of Alabama at Birmingham, provided additional insights important to our understanding of the sensorimotor developmental stages. The characteristics of the sensorimotor stages, discussed in Chapter 2, were part of a manuscript she prepared during her tenure on this project.

In the middle stages of the project, Francine Holland, a doctoral candidate at Peabody, contributed significantly to our convictions that cognitive perspectives lend an important reality to clinical procedures. Guided by these constructs, her work with children was both artful and empirically productive for us.

In the final stages of the project, Gloria Austin, another graduate student at Peabody, provided invaluable help in organizing and detailing perspectives in assessment which complemented the transactional model. Linda McCormick also made contributions to our perspectives on assessment, as did Rebecca Dubose, another Peabody faculty member.

We would also like to acknowledge the most significant substantive contributions of the many professionals and students who, through their positive reactions to presentations of the various ideas and positions represented in this transactional approach to language, gave us the courage of our convictions that such views were indeed productive from a clinical/educational perspective.

On the more technical side of projects like these are the people whose considerable skills make it possible to keep things going with some order and those who make it possible to report finally what has been done. We have had the best of such support. At Peabody, Patti Haggarty served as an Administrative Assistant and kept things (and people) organized—clearly an invaluable and unenviable task. Also at Peabody, Helen Thomas, an Administrative Assistant to the Programs for Special Education, managed the fiscal aspects of the contract with such skill and commitment that she deserves to be considered a prime contributor to any and all of its products. Stan Roit of the Media Support Services of the Parsons Center used both skill and imagination in the cover design and figures of the final report of the project. Finally, we wish to acknowledge our debt to Ruth Staten, Administrative Assistant of the Parsons Center, for her skill and commitment in the production of the final manuscript of this work. She gave us a written product of which we could be proud.

Lastly, we would like to acknowledge our debts to the major "systems" which provided the overall bases for our excursions into this exciting area of the language and communication of children. These systems include both George Peabody College for Teachers and the University of Kansas which, through their respective facilities of the John F. Kennedy Research Center and the Parsons Research Center, supported us in excellent fashion. In addition to the functionality of their physical settings and the overall vitality of their ongoing programs, both George Peabody College and the University of Kansas provided another kind of support which is probably as important. Both of these institutions have provided us with a rich history of inquiry into the problems and the solutions of problems which are represented in a population of human beings labeled "handicapped." We have no doubt that the fact of these histories has made contributions to our work in ways that are impossible to quantify here but which are, nevertheless, as important as any specific body of data. We acknowledge our debt to all of those who have contributed to the development of these histories.

A WORD ABOUT GENDER . . .

In preparing this text for publication, the authors have devoted much time and thought to the issue of *gender* and have concluded that there is no completely satisfactory resolution of this controversial problem. We are, of course, particularly sensitive to the role of language as a mirror and, to some degree, a shaper of our concepts and intentions. However, we are also sensitive to the primary function of language as a means of effective communication between speaker/writer and listener/reader. Thus, our dilemma: to take the more egalitarian, "he/she"-"him or her" route, thus adding further to the cumbersomeness of this already difficult material; or to adopt the more efficient and conventional (if chauvinistic) policy of using exclusively male gender throughout the text. Originally, the male member of this writing team had carefully adhered to the former, egalitarian policy in all of his chapters, while the female author had opted for the latter, more conventional use of male gender in her chapters. That is, he used *he/she* while she used *he*. Ultimately, it was agreed to do it her way and use *him* throughout. In short, the reader is assured that the use of the male gender in this book to refer to nonspecific human referents is merely a matter of convenience and is in no way intended to connote any sexual discrimination or limitations.

J.E.M. (he)
L.K.S. (she)

Contents

part 1   Background Perspectives   1

   1   Rationale and Objectives   3

part 2   Deriving a Model of Early
          Language Acquisition   11

   2   Cognitive Bases of Language Acquisition   13

   3   Social Bases of Language Acquisition   47

   4   The Sequence of Early Linguistic Development   79

   5   A Transactional Model of Language Acquisition:
        Summary   111

part 3   The Transactional Model and Early Language
          Intervention   119

   6   Assessment Implications   121

   7   Implications of the Transactional Model
        for Treatment Programs   175

part 4   Conclusions and Summary   233

   8   Implications for Research   235

   9   Summary   249

Appendix   Language Sample Data   257

References   265

Index   275

part 1

Background
Perspectives

chapter 1

Rationale and Objectives

Throughout history, human attempts to lessen the effects of handicaps which can beset the human organism have often been focused on the human communication system. A rich and generative language system, in all of its standard modes of speech, writing, and reading, is a strong indication that a person is functioning within the normal range of behavior as defined in most modern cultures. Conversely, a deficient language system is often among those deviations from behavioral norms deemed significant enough to deny an individual full access to the culture's activities and benefits. It is both logical and practical, then, that any special clinical educational efforts which are designed to attend to the problems of human handicaps should include pervasive programs directed toward the language systems of their various target populations. As the constructs and the delivery systems of special educational services are expanded and modified, language intervention programs must be appropriately modified to meet the demands of new educational designs.

The Problem

The recently intensified national commitments to provide education for young handicapped children and the more severely handicapped older children have required concentrated attention to the problems involved in clinical intervention into early language-acquisition products and processes. Because of new accountability standards and new demands by the delivery system, these problems have reached crisis proportions. Even though research and intervention in early language acquisition have been relatively productive, a completely satisfying, comprehensive intervention program in language acquisition has yet to be devised. Ironically, despite a recent abundance of theory and data pertaining to nontalking or severely language-deficient young children, most service delivery systems in the area of special educational services are not benefitting from the radical modifications of

3

language theory which are emerging worldwide. Direct-service personnel are still faced with a morass of isolated and sometimes contradictory language-training materials and programs. There are programs directed by sequential syntactic structures (Gray & Ryan, 1973; Stremel & Waryas, 1974) and programs directed by sequential semantic forms (MacDonald, 1976; Miller & Yoder, 1972, 1974). There are other programs whose goals focus on a construct of attaining functional utterances (Buddenhagen, 1971; Guess, Sailor, & Baer, 1974). Still other programs targeting on the basis of now-rejected linguistic constructs, such as the "pivot-open" structure (for example, Bricker, 1972), are still in wide circulation and wide application.

In addition to the problem of selecting programs appropriate for specific language-training targets, service personnel in special education and clinical speech are faced with the problem of selecting programs which are also appropriate for the children they serve. Some language programs are aimed at the "cognitively disorganized" child (Marshall & Hegrenes, 1972), the "young developmentally delayed" child (Bricker & Bricker, 1974), the "language and learning disorders of the pre-academic child" (Bangs, 1968), or the "disadvantaged" child (Bereiter & Engelmann, 1966). These are certainly not inadequate programs. Rather, from this inventory of programs for specific categories of children, there comes no adequate perspective about the overall process of language learning needed for the entire heterogeneous population of handicapped children.

Thus, in spite of the availability of many language programs, clinical educators still find themselves in need of more effective perspectives to help them cope with the language problems present in various levels of populations of mentally retarded, autistic, or multiply handicapped children. Without a basic and comprehensive model of language acquisition and treatment and appropriate programs directed toward that model, designers of service delivery systems in special education too often must choose an existing program or two and make these serve all children as best they can.

McLean (1972) has emphasized that language-intervention programs must be directed by constructs of language and the language-learning process, not by categorical labels. Such a view does not preclude individualized programming for specific child needs. It does, however, require a commitment to identifying targets in terms of specific language needs—not generalized categories of children. Although programmatic research abounds, a pervasive theoretical base for intervention in the various language problems of young, handicapped children of various etiological types and degrees of severity does not exist.

The absence of language-intervention programs which integrate and accommodate all of our knowledge concerning language acquisition is attributable to a number of causes. The first of these is the number of theoretical bases from which language-training programs are generated. Perhaps more critical than just the number per se, is the apparent incompatibility of these generative bases. The theoretical positions which have spawned language-training programs are often polarized (for example, behavioral versus nativistic). Along with such polarization comes an incompatibility between programs which have been generated from various theories. By the very fact of their theoretical bases, existing language programs tend only to grow in number—not to sum in their valid coverage of the language needs of children.

As a result of the proliferation of language-training programs from disparate theoretical bases, designers of early education and special education programs must consider a widely varying collection of such programs. These programs vary in terms of the specific training objectives which they project as a function of differences in the general characteristics of the handicapped populations which they target and as a function of their specific theoretical biases regarding what language is and what it does.

The problems attacked in this investigation, then, are those attendant to the plethora of language-training programs generated from a variety of theoretical positions. These programs present widely varying perspectives of desirable targets and procedures for early language training of the heterogeneous population of young handicapped children. The differing targets and procedures offer ample testimony to the disparateness, nonadditiveness, and mutually exclusivity of the available theoretical models of language. Such theoretical fragmentation in turn testifies to the need for an overall perspective of language as optimally inclusive of all available knowledge as it can be, while maintaining both logical and empirical rigor. It is such a comprehensive perspective which is sought as a product of this book and was the goal of the project upon which this book is based (see Preface).

Operational Perspectives

The direction of the operational processes needed to attain a more comprehensive and integrated perspective on language has been strongly suggested by the very nature of the research and theorizing occurring in the overall area of children's language. First, recent work in language concentrates on attempts to understand better the early language of children by analyzing it more from the perspective of its child users than by its comparison to language models derived from the analysis of mature language systems. Secondly, recent research, with its child-centered perspectives, has begun to suggest that more knowledge about the process of normal language acquisition by children could perhaps tell us more about the actual nature of language forms and functions than had previous theoretical models.

It is our conviction, then, that the results of these more empirical approaches to child language may provide the bases for far better overall models of the language and language-acquisition processes of children than has been possible previously. It is further our opinion that a richer understanding of normal language and language acquisition could provide important perspectives about both the target behaviors and the manipulable variables which are appropriate for severely language-delayed handicapped children.

Until the work of Bloom (1970), Schlesinger (1971), Slobin (1973), and Bowerman (1973a), language-intervention programs for handicapped children were based on theoretical models which described the language system but which did not describe either the acquisition of that system or the communicative use of that system, even for normally learning children. Upon entering the project upon which this book is based, we concluded that the more recent research and theoretical focus on both the products and the process of normal language acquisition could be productively analyzed and utilized in the derivation of new models from which language intervention with handicapped children could be generated. Therefore, the original rationale was based heavily upon literature from the areas of language research which initiated and reflected these newer perspectives. The essence of that original rationale is presented in the following section.

Statement of Rationale

In the early 1970s, data from the research of several developmental psycholinguists (Bloom, 1970; Bowerman, 1973a; Slobin, 1973) indicated that the emerging language of children has a similar semantic intent across children and across cultures. Such a universality of semantic intent implies that most children, regardless of their language or culture, operate from a similar "view of the world." This inferred universal conceptual base for early language utterances assumes critical importance, since the authors cited above, as well as others (Miller & Yoder, 1972; Premack, 1970; Ruder & Smith, 1974), interpreted their data to conclude that a child's emerging language "maps onto" his existing knowledge. This view in linguistics, psychology, and speech pathology integrated extremely well with the views of cognitive psychologists which held that thought precedes and serves to structure language (MacNamara, 1972; Piaget, 1971; Sinclair-deZwart, 1969).

It had thus been proposed that children's cognitive knowledge determines emerging language forms and that children's early utterances are attempts to "map" this knowledge for their listeners (MacNamara, 1972; Schlesinger, 1971). This position was antithetical to the structuralist view originated by Chomsky (1957, 1965) that innate predispositions toward syntactic rules dominated the entire language-development process. Chomsky's position underemphasized the roles of experience, social interaction, situational context, and most important perhaps, the various functions of language in the language-acquisition process. It led to an extremely pessimistic view of any attempts at intervening in the language-acquisition process (McNeill, 1970). The then-emerging cognitive/semantic position was particularly appealing to clinical disciplines, because it asserted that language acquisition results from children's interactions with their environment, and it allowed the view that language acquisition is amenable to intervention.

The overall effect of the revised perspectives regarding the form and functions of children's early language was significant in a number of ways. Among the major implications were:

1. A more intensive awareness of the nature and substance of early cognitive development.
2. A renewed commitment to theoretical and empirical consideration of the relationship between cognitive organization and emerging language, that is, the cognitive bases of language.
3. A revised view of linguistic structure as controlled more by intended meaning than by innate structural representations.
4. A renewed appreciation of a basic transactional process by which language is acquired and through which it functions in a social context.

These implications from theory and research seem representable in a more comprehensive and integrated system of treatment which could be directed toward the overall language rules of handicapped children. While each of these implications may have been represented in some form in one or several of the existing language programs, no one language-intervention program existed then, or exists presently, which integrates all four elements into a functional treatment model.

Our original project was initiated with all these considerations in mind. The general nature of the project's activities was straightforward. First, we conducted in-depth explorations and analyses into the emerging theory and data relating to the cognitive/semantic and the social/environmental bases for language performance. Second, we related the findings in these areas to synthesize a more integrated and pervasive perspective on the process of language acquisition at its earliest levels. Third, we compared both the process and the products of the derived integrated model of acquisition with the process and products of currently available language-intervention programs for young handicapped children. The fourth and final activity was to analyze any disparities between the derived model of the acquisition process and the current clinical models of this process. This final activity included the projection of recommendations for research and development activities which would show promise for improving the assessment and treatment of severe language delays among handicapped children.

Specific
Objectives

The ultimate goal for this overall line of investigation has been to develop a model of the process and products involved in the acquisition of early language forms and functions by young children. Such a comprehensive model would serve to specify the requirements of any language-intervention program designed to facilitate language acquisition among children who are severely language-delayed. Such an ideal model needed to be one which would meet the following requirements:

1. Identify the appropriate *cognitive bases* of language learning.
2. Provide an appropriate representation of the *transactional processes* which lead to the effective acquisition and productive contextual generalization of target behaviors.
3. Specify and sequence appropriate *linguistic target behaviors* in terms of their forms and functions.
4. Provide the basis for a criterion-referenced measurement system with an empirically derived continuum of language acquisition ranging from no proficiency to ideal performance. Criterion levels would be established at many points on this continuum where it is desirable to obtain reliable and explicit information about the adequacy of the child's language functioning.

It was our contention in 1974 that at least the rudimentary aspects of this ideal system were becoming available in the theoretical and applied literature of this area of study. It was our further contention, however, that representations of this ideal model were neither complete nor adequately synthesized in language-training programs currently available.

The cognitive bases of emerging language, for example, were well identified (Bloom, 1970; Olson, 1970; Slobin, 1973). The form and content of linguistic targets in emerging repertoires were, to a large part, also documented (Bloom, 1970; Miller & Yoder, 1972; Slobin, 1973; Smith, Ruder, & Stremel, 1973). Even the transactional operations which facilitate the acquisition of appropriate linguistic topographies controlled by appropriate cognitive structures were broadly represented in some excellent clinical teaching procedures (MacDonald & Blott, 1974) and in excellent theoretical perspectives (Blank, 1974; Nelson, 1973a; Olson, 1970). We argued that there was an important need for all of the above factors, as well as other relevant information, to be represented fully in a more comprehensive, integrated, and sequential clinical training model.

Our specific objectives, then, were to provide the service delivery network of special education with (a) a model for language acquisition which would synthesize the most contemporary and productive perspectives about language prerequisites, language targets, and optimal teaching strategies for application to the language training of young handicapped children and (b) a related system for the assessment of language and prelanguage repertoires which would serve both to identify a child's appropriate entry point into a training program and to evaluate the effectiveness of that training program. Finally, it was the goal of the original project to (c) specify those parts of an idealized system which appeared ready for application and empirical validation. The project was also committed to identifying gaps in the system which would require further research and development activities. In order to achieve the final goal of this investigation—the specification of a comprehensive model language-intervention system—three general activities were set for the project:

1. The development of a *conceptual framework* for language intervention based on a review of the literature pertaining to normal language development and the effect of various handicapping conditions on the acquisition of language.
2. An inventory of existing intervention techniques, materials, and assessment instruments to delineate those resources which are most congruent with the model conceptual framework.
3. The specification of the components of a *comprehensive treatment model,* based on the derived conceptual framework and encompassing appropriate available resources, which would be capable of accommodating a wide range of handicapping conditions.

These objectives and activities, then, generated the material presented in this volume.

Organization of Content

This book is organized in terms of the general activities and specific objectives presented above. Part 2, which immediately follows, includes chapters 2 through 5 and covers those activities designed to produce the overall derived model of normal language acquisition. In part 2, we present our review and synthesis of the *cognitive* bases of language, the basic elements of the *social* bases of language, and the *linguistic* elements of normally developing early language. As the final chapter in that part, we offer a transactional model of language and language acquisition derived from the theory and data reviewed to that point. It is our contention that language acquisition reflects the effects of a complex set of transactions between the language-learning child and his environment. This set of transactions involves those related to the development of the child's knowledge of the physical world and the social world. Further, we see this transaction as involving a complex reciprocal relationship between the child and a mature language user who is basic to the child's environment.

In further analysis of the derived model of language acquisition in part 2, we will present a schematized version of what we think this model means in terms of the operational elements involved in children's expressive and receptive performances in language.

Part 3 of the book includes chapters 6 and 7. These chapters detail what we see as the major implications of the transactional model for both the assessment and treatment of language deficits among young or severely delayed children. In this part, specific intervention targets and procedures indicated by the conceptual model are described and the clinical treatment and assessment instruments congruent with this model are identified and discussed.

Within part 4, suggestions for research in both basic and applied areas of language and language acquisition are offered, and a brief summary of the book's major points is presented.

The perspectives and models offered in this book are highly theoretical at this time. They do seem to be valid syntheses and extensions of the empirical data available. As they are translated into ongoing clinical and educational applications with handicapped children, clinicians and teachers will provide data on their adequacy or inadequacy.

part 2

Deriving a Model of Early Language Acquisition

chapter 2

Cognitive Bases of Language Acquisition

Any definitive consideration of language must begin with the construct that it is an arbitrary system by which humans communicate their thoughts and ideas. Whether these thoughts or ideas reflect needs, observations, or feelings, there remains a tacit realization that language has *content* and that this content is related to its users' mental or cognitive processes. Obviously, these mental processes underlying language are both complex and, when considered at the level of individual language learners, somewhat idiosyncratic. Obviously too, determining the specifics of these processes is complicated by the covertness of such activities within the activities of the human mind. Thus, even though there is the awareness that cognitive functions and their resultant organization of schemas and concepts are basic factors in both the process and the products of language acquisition, the specification and full exposition of these functions are proving to be a difficult, if not impossible, task. In fact, the dominant theoretical bases of most language treatment and research activities have taken forms which completely avoid any need to consider cognitive functions per se. The transformational grammar base which undergirds much treatment and research is based on a reductionistic system developed by Chomsky (1957, 1965) that considers language only in terms of its structural grammar rules. On the other theoretical pole, the behavioral analysis base for research and treatment applications in the language acquisition process draws on the constructs of Skinner (1957) that consider language only in terms of its quantifiable controlling factors, such as antecedent and consequential stimuli.

It should be clear that both the transformational grammar approach and the behavioral approach represent not so much a denial of the cognitive bases of language and language acquisition as they do a reaction to the difficulties involved in understanding and specifying the nature of such a base. Both Chomsky and Skinner developed systems which avoid dependence on what, in different ways, both consider unknowable or, at least, unquantifiable.

Despite the dominance of these two powerful ideational bases, many psychologists and psycholinguists have continued to explore the issues and problems regarding the relationship between cognition and language. In recent years, the work of many of these professionals has produced new perspectives and revitalized old perspectives in the whole area of cognition and its relationship to and manifestations in language and language acquisition. This body of knowledge is still far from definitive, nevertheless, it offers both provocative and productive perspectives for the applied professional in language. It was one of the commitments of this project to attempt to make this body of knowledge more pertinent to the task of designing effective language treatment programs for young, handicapped children.

Importance of Cognitive Bases to Language Intervention Practices

Theory and practice are often thought of as independent of each other and, often, as mutually exclusive worlds. In the sense that some theories have no practice arm, this might sometimes be true. Yet, it would be difficult to imagine a practice that does not have a referent theory responsible for either its goals or its procedures. Indeed, in the area of language intervention, the relationship between theory and practice seems to be almost linear; one's practice is usually an extremely accurate reflection of his theory. For example, if one's theoretical view of language is based on transformational grammar, one's intervention practices are directed toward the coin of that realm—base grammatical structures and their transformations. On the other hand, if one's theoretical base in language intervention is radical behavioral theory, one's clinical targets are expressed within the constructs of that theory, such as "manding" responses or appropriate "tacts" of antecedent stimulus objects (Skinner, 1957).

One of the more important ramifications of this isomorphic relationship between current theory and practice in language intervention is that the two most dominant theories in the field are basically *adult-centered* models. Transformational grammar (Chomsky, 1957, 1965), for example, is a reductionistic system which allows one to describe the structure of all possible utterances in a mature language system and specify the derivation of the structure in terms of its relationship to a finite number of "base" structures in the language. With such a theoretical base, child language has been compared to mature language systems and "explained" from the point of view of that reference. On the other theoretical pole, behavioral theory is a similarly reductionistic system which allows one to describe all possible utterances in terms of their observable antecedent stimulus controls or consequences.

We are applying the term *reductionistic* to refer to attempts to describe, explain, or quantify language in ways that attain universal applicability. Chomsky's (1957) transformational grammar system is a reductionistic process aimed at being able to describe language structures of any type. Skinner's (1957) analysis of language as a collection of verbal behaviors controlled by certain types of antecedent or consequential stimuli might also be considered reductionistic within the context of this discussion.

These examples show that attempts at universally consistent systems for discussing language necessarily require the assumption of a single unit or system of analysis. Thus, Chomsky chose the syntactic structure and ignored meaning and/or function, whereas Skinner chose function in a narrow sense and ignored grammar rules. Inherent in the applications of such systems is the fact that they have superimposed a limited, adult perspective on the interpretation of the structure and the functions of child utterances. In this sense, both of these theories encourage intervention practices which ignore the child subject both in terms of the child's reality regarding the structure of an utterance and/or the child's reality regarding the function of an utterance. While still far from complete, the amplification of the cognitive theories reflected in the recent literature is allowing far more consideration of children's perspectives in considering both the structure and the function of their language utterances.

The importance of reflecting child perspectives more completely in language intervention programs is extremely far-reaching in its specific implications. One should see that such perspectives would have impact on all aspects of intervention from the targets of intervention to the nature of the teaching variables used and the patterns of manipulation applied to such variables. In short, changes in the *theoretical* perspectives for intervention design will modify both the content and the context of language intervention programs. Thus, the discussion of new perspectives on the cognitive bases for language acquisition which follows these introductory remarks should be anticipated as highly productive of constructs which will have direct reflections in the treatment model developed for young, handicapped children. As noted above, these reflections will involve both targets of intervention and the procedures and/or processes utilized to attain such targets.

At this point, we will move into the specifics of the theoretical and empirical dimensions which have brought about changes in our view of the cognitive bases of language and language acquisition. These dimensions are several and they are complex. We shall begin our expositions on them by providing an overview of the issues and perspectives from which they have emerged.

Issues and Perspectives in Cognition and Language

As suggested in the introduction to this section, when we set out to explore the relationship between cognition and language, we are, essentially, exploring the relationship between language and the other higher-order, but nonlanguage, operations of the human mind. Clearly, close and interactive relationships exist. Just as clearly, however, their detail, mechanics, and lineal properties in regard to one another are not well understood. We know that humans perceive and organize their experiences within the world. We know that humans store these percepts and concepts and that they are able to retrieve them for applications in other, highly varied experiences within the world. We know further that humans can translate these thoughts into codelike structures composed of strings of articulated sounds and traffic them within a large group of other humans who share that particular code. But, when it comes down to explaining this overall process (or, for that matter, any part of it) we are reduced to dreadfully *flat-plane* perspectives of a marvelously complex and dynamic process or set of processes.

In many ways, the degree and depth of knowledge necessary to attempt explanations of this process contribute to the "flat-plane" nature of our available perspectives. Attempts to explain the phenomenon of human language very often follow an inductive process which starts with some specific piece of knowledge, insight, or perspective and proceeds from this point to develop the whole. Although general judgments about the value or productivity of the inductive reasoning approach to such problems are inappropriate here, it can be said that the prevalence of such an approach in this area weighs heavily on attempts to integrate and sum the vast store of theoretical and empirical knowledge concerning the relationship between cognition and language. One seems always to be adding (or subtracting) apples and oranges.

The purpose of our establishment of this point here is to help the reader to prepare for and then to accommodate the wide range of perspectives which require coverage within this section of the text. Each of these perspectives takes a slightly different view of the "elephant" and then proceeds to describe it from that vantage point. Thus, our process here must be to include all of these inductive views before any attention is given to a composite view which might be useful in application to the specific questions involved in language intervention with young, handicapped children.

As we have analyzed the issues and perspectives important to applied questions, we have concluded that there are four major areas for discussion:

1. Semantic relationships in developing language
2. The "universal knowledge base" for early language
3. Representational and/or symbolic behaviors
4. Mechanics of communication—reference

Following the discussion of these specific topics, we will attempt to integrate and summarize the implications of these specific perspectives as they coalesce in regard to the earliest stages of language acquisition by children.

Semantic Relationships in Developing Language

As we have observed previously, one of the theories which has dominated our perspectives on language intervention has been one based on Chomsky's (1957, 1965) construct of transformational grammar. In this construct, Chomsky posits that all sentences have a "deep structure" and a "surface structure." In the deep structure, Chomsky hypothesized the meaning desired by the speaker to exist in the form of the basic syntactic structures consistent with that meaning. In the actual utterance of the sentence (surface structure), these basic grammatical structures would be maintained even though the surface structure of a sentence might be considerably different in form from its *deep structure* representation. For example, although the two sentences, "The boy hit the girl," and "The girl was hit by the boy," are different in surface structure, their deep structure is considered to be the same and the so-called passive transformation maintains the relationship of the boy as the agent of the action and the girl as its object even though their grammatical forms (as subjects of the sentence) have been reversed. Thus, by using a transformational rule which maintains the deep structure of the sentence, the two sentences say the same thing.

The most important characteristic of Chomsky's theory in the context of the intervention procedures it generates is its insistence that grammatical relationships like subject of sentence and/or predicate object of sentence are the basic units from which language utterances are constructed. This insistence has led to the view of language learning as the acquisition of these rules. As a consequence, intervention practices based on transformational grammar theory make grammar structures their goals. While certainly everyone can accept that language has structure and that any program which would target language must target its structure, many theorists and interveners alike have not found Chomsky's view of language structure to be particularly appropriate as a productive base for either describing natural language acquisition or for generating effective clinical or teaching procedures. For example, his view of language structure as independent of meaning leaves those who would intervene in child language unsure and undirected about the contexts in which these structures might be sought. In fact, as Chomsky himself attempted to face this problem of "how" children might acquire language of the structure form he describes, he was forced to assume that a child has an "innate" knowledge of grammatical structure (Chomsky, 1965, p. 37).

Despite this rather obvious lack of fit between Chomsky's theories of both the product and the process of language acquisition and any attempts to intervene in defective and/or deficient language systems among children, his ideas have persisted for over a decade as a prime mover both in research on children's developing language and in the development of intervention programs. Thus, many researchers have analyzed young children's utterances in terms of the emergence of syntactic rules. Since the primitive utterances of young children did not yet seem to match the rules of a mature language, most of these investigators identify and formulate the rules which seemed to them to be used by children. Thus, the results of careful observations of the emerging language of children were being reported in terms of the "grammars" written to describe such language (Braine, 1963; Brown & Bellugi, 1964; Brown, Cazden, & Bellugi, 1969; Brown & Fraser, 1964; McNeill, 1970).

The Semantic Revolution

An important change in the perspectives being applied to the study of language acquisition among children began when developmental psycholinguistics began to supplement Chomsky-based grammatical descriptions of the emerging language of children with descriptions of the semantic content of such utterances. Sometimes called the "semantic revolution," this trend began for most of us with the publication of Bloom's (1970) landmark study. In this study, Bloom's analysis of the utterances of three children in early stages of multi-word structures included an interpretation of the meaning of the utterance as it could be ascertained by observing carefully the context in which it occurred. She found, in accordance with previous observations by Brown and Bellugi (1964), that early childhood language can be described as "here and now" in that it is directly related to the immediate context of its occurrence. Further, Bloom found that by attending to the context of a child's utterance, she could deduce a child's meaning quite consistently. In this process of relating meaning to children's ill-formed grammar structures, Bloom discovered that the prevailing descriptions or characterizations of children's utterances attained by means of only "writing" their grammar rules failed rather completely to describe accurately the structure of these utterances. In other words, grammars written independently of the semantic intent or meaning of the child often missed grammatical relationships which were present in the utterances.

For example, Bloom recorded two occasions of the utterance "mommy sock" from Kathryn, one of her subjects. Bloom points out that both these utterances would, by then prevailing child-grammar rules, be described as identical, that is, pivot word + open-class word (Braine, 1963). In her data, however, this utterance occurred in two different contexts and, from her interpretation within these contexts, meant two different things. In one context, Kathryn was picking up her mother's stocking, while in the other context her mother was putting Kathryn's sock on Kathryn. Thus, the grammatical relationship manifest in Kathryn's utterance "mommy sock" in one case was judged to be genitive (possessive) and in the other a subject-object grammatical relationship with the semantic relationship of Agent-Object of action. The implications of this observation led Bloom (1970), who was still operating under the perspectives of the transformational grammar model generated by Chomsky, to state:

> Generative transformational grammar could be used in a more powerful way to account for children's language than it has been if semantic information were available in order to make inferences about underlying structure. (p. 9)

Bloom's investigation of the semantic content of her subjects' language revealed that they talked rather consistently about the relationships among the people and things in their immediate world. Further, as children talked about these relationships, their utterances manifested word-ordering rules which were rather consistently related to the relationships they marked.

Table 1 presents the semantic categories identified by Bloom's work and also shows her analysis of the grammatical structure of children's utterances, as well as examples of this structure. Early childhood language among Bloom's subjects included three categories specific to the relationships of objects, people, and events-as-entities in the child's context of time and space. These categories were the *existence* of things, the *nonexistence* of things whose presence had previously occurred or was expected, and the *recurrence* of things. It is important to note that these relationships are marked not just for objects, but might also be applied to actions ("no fall," "fall again"), to people or animates ("here doggie," "doggie allgone"), and/or to events ("no bye-bye," "more horsie-ride").

These data and Bloom's interpretation of them also indicated that relationships of *possession*, perceptual *attributes,* and *location* of objects, people, and events were consistently expressed in the early utterances of her subjects. In addition, the language of Bloom's subjects also revealed that children talked specifically and often about the elements of dynamic events involving actions among people and/or people and objects. Thus, children talked about the instigator of actions, the actions themselves, and the receivers or benefactors of such actions. The semantic relationships involved in these contexts related to agents, actions, and objects of actions.

Bloom's work included many additional insights about the substance and nature of child language that will be discussed later in this book. There are two additional

TABLE 1

Bloom's Meaning Categories
from Children's Utterances

Meaning	Grammatical structures	Examples
Nomination	that +Noun (N)	that book
	it +N	it car
Notice	hi +N	hi belt
Recurrence	more +N	more milk
	Verb (V) + 'gin	fall 'gin
Nonexistence	no+N	no doggie
	all gone+N	all gone milk
Attributive	Adjective +N	big train
Possessive	N +N	mommy lipstick
Locative	N +N	sweater chair
Locative	V +N	sit chair
Agent-action	N +V	Eve read
Agent-object	N +N	mommy sock
Action-object	V +N	read book
Conjunction	N +N	umbrella boot

NOTE. Adapted from *Language Development: Structure and Function* by P.S. Dale. Copyright 1972 by Dryden Press. Reprinted by permission.

rather basic contributions she provided to specification of the meaning dimensions demonstrated in a child's early utterances. She identified three distinct forms of negation in her subjects' language: *nonexistence, rejection* (of proferred object), and *denial* (of a proferred proposition). On a broader scale, she observed that children's language shows clearly the substantive versus relational aspects of language which is required to apply *different semantic* functions to *identical lexical* entities: for example, "mommy" as an agent, a possessor, a possessed entity, and so on.

Implications of Bloom's findings. In the context of the prevailing linguistic theory of that time, Bloom's findings had extremely important implications. Chomsky had rather completely rejected the need for semantic interpretation to explain syntax. Bloom, on the other hand, suggested that an analysis of the meaning of child utterances contributed much to an understanding of the child's structural grammar rules. Even though she still considered the syntactic structure as described by Chomsky the appropriate structure for language analysis, Bloom did offer rebuttal to a basic assumption of Chomsky's transformational model, namely his hypothesis that language structure was the base of language acquisition and that it most probably was a product of a child's innate predisposition toward human language structure. In this specific context, Bloom (1970) offers her opinion that:

It appears that the results of this study would cast some doubt on the view of language development as some innately preprogrammed behavior for all children. The emerging grammars proposed for the three children studied were different; a single grammar would not have accounted for the language of all three in any adequate way. (p. 227)

and following this, her judgment that:

The difference among them must reflect the importance of individual differences in the interaction between cognitive function and experience, which could not be assumed to be the same for any two children. (p. 227).

Other contributions to the semantic revolution. Bloom certainly was not alone in her identification of the important role of semantic intent in language acquisition. In fact, a review of other work shows Bloom's position to be rather conservative in that it attempted to maintain constancy with Chomsky's transformational grammar theory. For example, at the same time that Bloom's work emerged on the semantic side of the acquisition controversy, Schlesinger (1971) was circulating a paper in which he was putting forth his notion that not only was semantic intent the precursor of a child's utterances, but that such intent was also the basis of the *units* in which children generated their grammar. According to this view, instead of semantic relationships being encoded into syntactic units like subject-verb, they were directly realized through grammar rules which stated, for example, that *agent* precedes *action ("Boy hit")*. In other words, Schlesinger was proposing that grammar was *semantic* not *syntactic*. (If this statement is confusing, remember that any grammar for any language is simply a description of that language as it has been constructed by a linguist's analysis. Such an analysis comes only after a language's development and use by a group of people. Thus, the "grammar" of a language can be whatever rules one can demonstrate to account for the particular structures a language manifests.)

The notion of a *semantic* grammar was consonant with other trends in the overall field of linguistic analysis. For example, Fillmore (1968) and later Chafe (1970) were attracting much attention to their "case" grammars. In these case-grammar systems, the apparently universal semantic relationships among nouns and other parts of an utterance were identified, allowing analysis of the structures by which these relationships are marked in a language. Table 2 offers an example of "case" relationships as developed by Fillmore (1968).

While, as Table 2 shows, the structural realization rules for case relationships in English can involve rather complex word-ordering rules and the use of certain prepositions, Brown (1973) points out that such complex rules are only manifest in *adult* utterances and that, when the case relationships are applied to a *child's* utterances, they seem to be appropriately represented by the simple word-ordering rules which have been identified for such utterances as in Bloom (1973). Along this line, Brown (1973) points out that child grammars might well be appropriately analyzed as case grammars. In fact, Brown applies Fillmore's case relationships to a previously analyzed corpus of utterances for one of his early subjects and finds that indeed, the case relationships do provide a relatively good explanation of the grammars used by this particular subject.

Similar support for the relatively good fit of case grammars to children's early utterances came in the subsequent work of both Bowerman (1973a) and Greenfield

TABLE 2

Fillmore's (1968) Case Grammar Relationships

Case name	Definition	Example (italicized noun as in designated case)
Agentive (A)	The typically animate, perceived instigator of action	John opened the door. The door was opened by John.
Instrumental (I)	The inanimate force or object causally involved in the state or action named by the verb	The key opened the door. John opened the door with the key.
Dative (D)	The animate being affected by the state or action named by the verb	Adam sees Eve. John murdered Bill. John gave the book to Bill. Daddy has a study.
Factitive (F)	The object or being resulting from the state or action named by the verb	God created woman. John built a table.
Locative (L)	The location or spatial orientation of the state or action named by the verb	The sweater is on the chair. Chicago is windy.
Objective (O)	The semantically most neutral case: anything representable by a noun whose role in the state or action named by the verb depends on the meaning of the verb itself	Adam sees Eve. The sweater is on the chair. John opened the door.

NOTE: From "A First Language: The Early Stages" by R. Brown. Copyright 1973 by Harvard University Press. Reprinted by permission.

and Smith (1976). In fact, the latter pair of investigators found that case grammar particularly facilitated the study of one-word utterances and their relationship to later-developing grammatical structures. Thus, with Bloom's work came the era of interpretation of children's utterances only in terms of the grammatical structure independent of meaning. Further, the trend began to consider early language as directed by children's intent to "mean" something. As this trend has continued in the perspectives of such people as Bowerman (1973b), Schlesinger (1974), and Greenfield and Smith (1976), one sees the obvious move away from the model of transformational grammar as posited by Chomsky toward a model of language which views structure as inexplicably related to the meaning of an utterance intended by a speaker. This view integrates well with other views being generated from sources other than developmental data per se. We will return to a discussion of case-grammar later in the book.

Summary views emanating from semantic views. Even without further detail on the semantic perspectives outlined in the previous section, we can outline some important and productive contributions they have made toward the development of a better understanding of the overall relationship between cognitive functioning and language acquisition. These contributions can be outlined in near syllogistic form:

1. Children's early language utterances appear to be expressions of perceived *semantic* relationships as opposed to being expressions of innately prepro-grammed syntactic relationships among language elements.
2. Semantic relationships necessarily reflect the perception and understanding of certain relationships between and among the entities and the actions which are present in a child's environment.
3. Such perception and the subsequent development of an understanding of the relationships among and between the elements of a child's environment must be considered the products of the cognitive domain of human functioning.
4. The products of the cognitive domain in the form of the perception and understanding of relationships among elements in the environment can be considered to be a child's *knowledge* of his world.
5. Therefore, a child's language utterances reflect his knowledge of the relation-ships among and between the entities and the actions which make up his world.
6. Thus, language "maps" onto or encodes a child's existing knowledge.

The reader will have no difficulty seeing that each element of this sequencing of the contributions of the semantic revolution in psycholinguistic theory and data has a direct referent in the several key publications already cited in this general area of discussion. Similarly, the reader will have little difficulty in seeing the reflections of these summary perspectives from the area of semantics in the other areas we have already identified and will be discussing subsequently as important contributors to an overall understanding of the relationship between cognitive functions and lan-guage acquisition. Another of these major areas of contribution is discussed in the following section.

Universal Knowledge Base Reflected in Children's Language

Following the emergence of empirical evidence that children's language "mapped" their knowledge about the entities and relationships within their immediate world, there came a major body of empirical data which probed further into the nature and the scope of that knowledge base. Led by cross-linguistic studies by Slobin (1973) and Bowerman (1973a), these data demonstrated that the emergent language of children of many cultures reflected essentially the same semantic relationships. The conclusion of both Slobin and Bowerman was that, not only did these data support the primacy of semantic intent in structuring children's early language, but further the similarity of semantic relationships across the language of several highly varying cultures and highly varying grammar forms suggested that there was a *universal quality about the cognitive bases* for the content of child language. This led Slobin (1973) to "sketch-out" what he hoped could be evolved into a model for language acquisition. In this hypothesized model, Slobin views a child as developing a body of semantic intentions by virtue of *general patterns of cognitive development* and thus, "equipped with an inherent definition of the general structure and function of lan-guage, [he] goes about finding the means for the expression of those intentions (semantic) by actively attempting to understand speech" (p. 208).

The implications of this short excerpt are made more explicit by Slobin's suggestion that the developmental order of language encoding of various semantic structures can probably be keyed to the developmental order of the cognitive structures which underlie them. Slobin clearly considers linguistic development to be parallel to and dependent on cognitive development. From such a view, he stresses the need for those interested in language acquisition to become informed about the nature of the growth of the child's knowledge.

We will be applying many more of Slobin's ideas in other parts of this text to emphasize the strong direction his ideas gave to analysis of basic cognitive development theory and data as a key to tracking the emergence of so-called linguistic universals. Obviously, Slobin considered linguistic universals to be *cognitive* universals first and linguistic universals only after that fact of cognitive development. As indicated above, the other major cross-linguistic study surfacing at this time (Bowerman, 1973a), although not as expansive in its pronouncements, nevertheless confirmed Slobin's findings and corroborated his most basic perceptions of the relationships between cognitive development and linguistic development. Later, Bowerman (1974) hypothesized further about the relationship among semantic, cognitive, and language structures. We will be emphasizing these excellent perceptions of hers in other portions of this section on the cognitive bases.

Early Cognitive Development at Prelinguistic Levels

For those involved in language intervention who were not already knowledgeable about general cognitive development products and processes, the semantic data in general, and Slobin (1973) and Bowerman's (1973a) work in particular, provided a strong impetus for becoming knowledgeable in that area. With this interest concentrated on children's early language, attention inevitably turned to the early cognitive development theories of Piaget and his followers. Prominent among the Genevan group which interpreted Piagetian constructs in this context was H. Sinclair (de-Zwart). Although cautioning against any adoption of Piagetian constructs as direct "handbooks" of eventual linguistic development, Sinclair (1969, 1971, 1973) nevertheless provided the evidence to support an assumption that the products of what Piaget (1952, 1954) called the *sensorimotor* period of development had an amazing logical isomorphism with the semantic relationships observed in children's early language utterances. Some simple examples will suffice to demonstrate this general assumption.

If we recall Bloom's (1973) semantic categories, we see that the semantic relationships of *existence, nonexistence,* and *recurrence* were prominent in a child's early utterances. If we review the basic products of sensorimotor development, we find Piaget's construct of *object permanence* a prominent universal in a child's development at periods which correspond to the late prelinguistic and early linguistic stages of language development. "Object permanence" refers to a child's development of the cognitive basis for "knowing" that an object which has been removed from his immediate perception still exists somewhere and thus can be made to recur. Similarly, the sensorimotor schemata relating to *cause-effect* and *means-ends* relationships can be seen to parallel almost all of the categories applied in the case-grammar systems (Chafe, 1970; Fillmore, 1968) which have proved so appropriate in describing children's early utterances (Bowerman, 1973a; Brown, 1973; Greenfield & Smith, 1976). One should remember that case grammars are based on the relationships between nouns and the other elements of a sentence and therefore reflect relationships between the entities of a child's world and the actions in that world. Such relationships, obviously, would be strongly disposed to reflect *cause-effect* and/or *means-ends*. In fact, the overall *action* orientation of early child language has been noted by Nelson (1973a) and Bruner (1974/75). While both Nelson and Bruner's data and constructs will be explored more fully later in this book we wish here to relate this action orientation of children's language to the more general observations of Piaget. Piaget finds the sensorimotor period of cognitive development not only to be characterized by *action* and *interaction* between a child and the environment, but also to be *dependent* on such action schemata for the very attainment of its products. The isomorphism between early cognitive development and early linguistic development may exist as much in their similar *interactive behavioral bases* as in the similarity between their respective products. The dynamics and the products of the sensorimotor period described in the next section will clarify this point.

Sensorimotor interaction. Bruner (1973) differentiates two forms of infant competence—people skills and thing skills. In this section we will be concentrating on the development of thing skills, assuming this competence to be basic to the formation of both the object concept and the action schemata which appear to be "mapped" by the semantic categories that are prominent in children's early utterances. The development of people skills, another critical dimension of the process of acquisition of language, will be discussed in those sections of this report concerned with the role of social transactions in language development.

In developing thing skills, children seem to pass through a fairly orderly set of functional stages of sensorimotor interactions which are marked by increasing sophistication in the strategies and processes appropriate for acquiring perceptual and motor information. At first the child is little more than a sensory detection device, but as motor abilities develop the child becomes an explorer and a manipulator and begins discovering the multiple properties of objects in the environment. They roll, bounce, make noise, change shape, and so on. As the child comes to see himself as separate from these objects and the actions he performs, he begins to explore different means to the same or different ends. His interest shifts from *what* the object can do to what he can do *with* it.

This theme of *intentionality* appears to pervade and unify all the research in this area. Hunt (1965), for example, discusses the motivational character of the infant's first stimuli-orienting responses, efforts to maintain perceptual contact with familiar objects and interest in exploring novel objects. Matheny, Dolan, and Wilson (1974) and Yarrow and Peterson (1976) find such motivational characteristics as persistence, attentiveness to objects, and desire to interact with and elicit feedback from objects to be highly correlated with mental development (as measured by the Mental Development Index of the Bayley Scales).

The infant is not passively impinged upon. He is rather, an active explorer busily investigating the objects and relations in the environment. If an object or toy provides feedback (makes sounds or changes shape when manipulated), it becomes the focus of more attention and the feedback-evoking responses are usually repeated.

These are intentional, motivated, and goal-directed behaviors seemingly controlled by neither a need to reduce physiological tensions nor particular caretaker variables, but rather by the infant's inherent need to interact with and have an effect on the environment, reconcile discrepancies, and repeat perceptual and motor activities that produce interesting and desirable results. If the nature of an environment matches the normal infant's apparent motivational needs, we can assume that a self-reinforcing, self-perpetuating interaction process will evolve.

While many investigators have been largely concerned with charting those perceptual and motor behaviors that seem to indicate progressive approximation of adult action patterns or that have "psychological reality" from an adult's perspective, Uzgiris (1976) has concentrated on forms of functioning characteristic of infancy itself. Specifically, in her most recent research, she focuses on the unique progression of the infant's actions. From observation of 12 infants from one month to two years old, Uzgiris outlines four distinct levels of observable actions during the sensorimotor period. At the first level of simple undifferentiated actions (roughly analogous to Piaget's stages II and III), actions lack differentiation. The infant applies a limited repertoire of schemata rather indiscriminately with little apparent knowledge of or concern with object properties. At this early level, the infant's predominant actions on objects (mouthing, looking, shaking, and banging) are not combined or in any way coordinated with each other, but are applied one at a time to one object at a time. There are three parallel developments near the end of this period which appear to indicate a readiness for transition to the next higher level. First is the application of different schemata, in close succession or simultaneously, to the same object. Uzgiris notes that this transition development may be assessed by the appearance of the "examining" schema. A second development which appears to signal readiness for transition is interaction with responsive objects and persons. Third, the infant begins to "join" or coordinate actions on different objects.

The second level of organization is characterized by differentiated actions (approximately 8–12 months of age). The infant now applies his repertoire of schemata more discriminately in accord with a diverse range of object characteristics. Means-ends differentiations lead to the selective joining of schemas. These developments can be observed in sequences of actions directed toward removing obstacles, using intermediaries to attain goals, exploring object properties, and exploring spatial and causal relationships between objects. Action sequences are first coordinated with respect to single objects and then, somewhat later, with multiple objects. Joint action activities become prominent at this level as the caretaker begins to play an important role in facilitating action sequences. For example, the infant drops objects with the expectation and anticipation of retrieval by someone else to complete the action sequence. Toward the end of the period represented by this level, infants are imitating familiar sound patterns and attempting to imitate action sequences. This level also marks the beginning of the differentiation of actions from goals and two-part actions. Interestingly, this is roughly the age when Bruner (1970) observed the infant strategy of setting one object in reserve while picking up another.

At the third level—the level of regulation by differentiated feedback—the beginning of regulation of actions by their outcomes becomes evident. This level is roughly analogous to Piaget's stage V (12–18 months of age). Instead of continuing simple repetitions, the child initiates behavioral changes which produce variations. Several changes in behavior toward objects can be observed: there are fewer (and more appropriate) actions applied to particular objects and the actions begin to reflect culturally approved modes of object interaction. At this level, infants imitate unfamiliar visible gestures more readily when they are performed in relation to an object than when simply presented as gestures.

The fourth level—the level of anticipatory regulations—presumably characterizes the infant's readiness for language. The infant conserves an object through a series of inferred displacements (object permanence), while also indicating awareness of its identity and nonidentity. A number of parallel achievements in other domains are also noted by Uzgiris. Infants engage in more social activities, directly and accurately imitating novel sounds and gestures, and use foresight in some problem solving at this level.

These four levels of organization described by Uzgiris represent a first attempt to document parallel achievements empirically within the cognitive domain. When fully validated, these data will allow the assessment, with convergent methods, of achievement stages across task series and identification of individual differences in attainment of specific concepts across diverse tasks. The descriptive approach being taken by Uzgiris should be considered an essential preliminary step prior to documentation of relationships among the various sensorimotor attainments. In addition to asking the question *when*, however, we must continue to ask *how*. What are the processes underlying these observed behavior changes which Uzgiris describes so elegantly?

Bruner (1973), considering how early skilled action develops and the context in which it emerges, emphasizes two related requisites—intention and "mastery play" (p. 6). He analyzes intention into five constituent measurable features. (Note that Bruner's analyses of intention would seem to be as appropriately applied to communicative intention as action intention.) The initial measurable feature of intention is anticipation of the outcome of the act. This can be observed, for example, in the development of visually guided reaching when a desired object first produces prolonged looking, followed by mouth action, and if the intent persists, activity of hands, arms, and shoulders. While these subroutines do not initially occur in a correct order allowing the infant to capture the desired object, they are nevertheless evidence of the infant's intention and desire to perform the action. The subsequent features of intention are: the selection among appropriate means to attain the desired end, sustained direction of behavior toward the means, termination of the action as defined by attainment of the end state, and finally, some correction of the action if not totally appropriate to the desired outcome. Thus, in time and with feedback and adequate practice in the presence of the desired object, or the "releasing stimulus" (p. 3) as Bruner terms it, the action is successfully executed.

This skilled action mastery occurs in the context of, and is most readily observable in, the infant's mastery play routines. This mastery play is different from the reciprocal play Bruner refers to in later papers. It is strictly infant-object play which can be facilitated by an adult but is not dependent on caretaker reciprocity. Mastery play provides the infant with opportunities to experiment with a range of possible routines on a variety of objects. It also provides an opportunity for the child to model various object play patterns demonstrated by an adult for incorporation into other routines. Bruner makes a generalization about a child's ability to profit from adult action models which is most often made in relation to utilizing linguistic input: The child's skill at a complex construction task per se, determines to what extent he is capable of taking advantage of skilled behavior being modeled by the experimenter" (p. 8). This emphasizes the importance of matching input to a child's developmental level.

While Bruner emphasizes the "release" (p. 9) of skilled action behaviors by appropriate objects in the environment, he does not speculate about the properties of objects which might lead to their being selected by the infant for action construction routines. McCall (1974) offers some pertinent data on the differential saliency of various object and toy stimuli. He found manipulative exploration in infants 8½ to 11½ months of age to be an increasing function of sound potential and plasticity of the stimulus objects, a finding consistent with numerous earlier studies involving human infants (Goldberg & Lewis, 1969; Jacklin, Maccoby, & Dick, 1973) and animals (Sackett, 1965; Welker, 1961). Another pertinent finding was the tendency of infants to evidence a denser and richer (more concentrated) form of manipulation and play with the more complex stimuli, playing longer and evidencing significantly higher rates of manipulation, including visual regard and circular responses. The more complex objects and toys are obviously more responsive, allowing the infant to experience more feedback from the consequences of active manipulations. Although almost half of the infants in McCall's series of studies manifested idiosyncratic multivariate styles of play at 10 months, the others clustered into three homogeneous groups, indicating a development sequence. One group (presumably the most advanced) spent long periods of sustained object interaction characterized by mature, businesslike, and at the same time creative styles of play. A second group seemed to respond to the primitive sensory properties of the objects with a more superficial and physical play style. A third group played for only a short time with each object or toy in an even more superficial and unimaginative manner.

McCall's data suggest a number of implications for the selection of objects and toys for assessment purposes and training. The most appropriate object would have the following intrinsic properties: (1) functional complexity; (2) sizes and shapes which lend themselves to such activities as bouncing, rolling, and stacking; (3) creative and/or sound potential (clay, xylophone); and (4) social familiarity sufficient to elicit delayed imitation (telephone, tea set). If the perceptual and functional characteristics inherent in some objects make them more susceptible to selection for attention and interaction, these characteristics should be given serious consideration in the selection of stimuli both for assessment and programming purposes. Nelson and Bonvillian (1974) found that maternal variables, such as reinforcement for manipulation and naming and total number of utterances, had negligible association with their children's object manipulation. This finding certainly strengthens the premise that various properties of the objects themselves, rather than other environmental variables, affect object manipulation behaviors.

In this section, we have considered Uzgiris' observations of action pattern development, Bruner's observations of the intention features and context of action pattern development, and McCall's research on salient properties of the objects of these action patterns. From these considerations, we have a picture of an interactive young child intent on understanding the properties and the relationships among these properties or entities within the environment. Piaget characterizes this activity as a child's *construction* of his knowledge (or schemas) relating to the things of the world. This characterization of children as constructionists, actively *working* on their environment toward the construction of knowledge about it, seems to be a particularly valuable perspective to hold onto. It is this same perspective which would seem to describe and account for the continued labor a child must manifest in order to "connect" new knowledge about the world with that specific system of noisemaking and noise-stringing rules that allows him to "talk" about this knowledge.

Sensorimotor Development and Language Acquisition

Without taking sensorimotor development to be a "handbook" to language development, the following two sections will look further at the relationships between the sensorimotor cognitive processes and products and those processes and products which now seem apparent in children's earliest language utterances. The preceding overview has drawn only the broadest conclusions about the parallelisms which exist between the products of the sensorimotor stages of cognitive development and the products of the earliest stages of linguistic development (e.g., object permanence, cause-effect, and means-ends cognitive schemas as they parallel semantic categories like existence, nonexistence, recurrence, agentive, instrumental, and dative). The following sections will move to a slightly finer-grain analysis of early, emerging *elements* in children's language.

This finer-grain analysis of some aspects of children's early language learning is made possible by Nelson's (1973a) empirical investigation of the conceptual features underlying the entities and/or events "named" in children's first words and her subsequent (Nelson, 1974) theorizing about the findings of that study. At this point, it would seem unlikely that one could overestimate the contribution that these two presentations make to the better understanding of the relationship between cognitive functions and language acquisition—Nelson's perspectives are, at once, basic, innovative, and generative in nature.

Nelson's conceptual model for language acquisition. Nelson's conceptual framework accounting for a child's organization of the world in the apparently "universal" semantic relationships expressed in children's language (Slobin, 1973) was generated by her findings about the first words that children acquired (Nelson, 1973a). After analyzing the first 50 words acquired by a population of 18 subjects between the ages of 9 and 24 months, Nelson (1974) offers the following summary observations, as well as their translation into more general "principles":

> 1. There is a small set of words that are learned at the outset by a large number of children. These consist largely of names for food, people, animals, and things that move or change in some way (Nelson, 1973a). The one outstanding general characteristic of the early words is their reference to objects and events that are perceived in dynamic relationships: that is, actions, sounds, transformations—in short, variation of all kinds. This characteristic dynamic base results from principles utilized by the child rather than being adult imposed. Such a conclusion is supported by the obvious fact that the child selects from among those words spoken to him by adults those that he will use (Leopold, 1948; Nelson, 1973a).
>
> 2. In addition, it has been widely observed by students of child language that when a word that expresses his meaning is not available, the young child from the very beginning of language acquisition will frequently invent one (e.g., Leopold, 1949; Lewis, 1951; Nelson, 1973a, 1973b). Similarity may be based on many different dimensions, of which the static perceptual dimension of shape or form is only one; others include function,

action, or affect. Piaget (1962), Leopold (1948), and Werner and Kaplan (1963) among others have provided extensive examples of this early propensity for generalization, and Clark (1973) has recently analyzed some of the overextensions of word meanings found in early language diary studies. Bloom (1973) has suggested that there are stages of generalization reflecting the use of different cognitive principles at different ages, but the evidence for this hypothesis is, at present, slight. Furthermore, the child's meanings may also be under-extended or simple "different from" adult meanings. "Over-extension" oversimplifies the generalization phenomenon.

In summary, the above properties of early word learning express the following general principles of concept-word relations: (a) selectivity from a larger set of parent words on the basis of the dynamic properties and relations of the referents, (b) generation or the production of concepts to which the child will attach his own word if none is available, and (c) generalization of word use to new concept instances along as yet not understood dimensions of similarity. A theory that attempts to explain the acquisition of words and meanings must therefore take these principles into account. (p. 269)[1]

After presenting the general principles which must be accounted for in any conceptual model for language acquisition, Nelson underscores the inadequacy of some current theories of concept formation and outlines one which she deems more adequate to the task. Specifically, Nelson (1974) rejects the prevalent theory which equates a concept with a *class* whose members are determined by the presence or absence of certain "features." According to this construct, concepts are created by the abstracting of relevant features and discriminating them from those features which are not relevant to the particular concept and/or class. In rejecting this "abstraction theory" of concept formation, Nelson applies Cassirer's critique of this construct (Cassirer, 1953, cited in Nelson, 1974, p. 270). Both critiques observe that the abstraction theory essentially presupposes the basis of its explanation, that is, it defines a concept as an abstraction of features which is developed by an abstraction of features. This critique of one of the theories of concept formation is not unlike those criticisms directed at linguistic explanations of language development: language is grammar, thus it is acquired by virtue of innate preprogramming of grammar forms.

The importance of Nelson's work, however, lies not in her rejection of one theory, but rather in the identification of a view of concept formation which has a far better validity in language contexts. This revised construct of concept formation is Cassirer's relational concept theory, which proposes:

The essence of a concept is defined in terms of logical relationships (or logical acts) rather than in terms of common elements. Thus concept acquisition involves the attempt to comprehend the exemplars of the concept within a functional or relational rule rather than through the specification of a set of critical attributes. (Nelson, 1974, p. 274)

In applying this construct to language, Nelson recognizes that it may describe an overall cognitive process which adequately represents the principles now viewed as underlying early language development. Specifically, a relational concept theory seems to incorporate the same processes and products that Nelson observed in the child's development of semantic concepts, both in early word learning and underlying the structures of multiword utterances. For example, many of the early words of children seem to be used to name entities which either afford certain dynamic actions upon them or provide the child with dynamic feedback properties upon manipulation. Both of these "attributes" are essentially relational attributes as opposed to being abstractions of fixed features.

As Nelson continues her analysis of a concept-formation theory which fits language learning, she points out that the basis of Piaget's sensorimotor schemata development demonstrates a relational concept development theory in that children investigate the appropriate functions of things through manipulation and form classes of things according to these functional use features. Accepting that sensorimotor schemata cannot (or should not) be directly projected onto language acquisition, Nelson instead makes the highly productive observation that, if the products of these sensorimotor interactions cannot be applied to language, the *principles* of cognitive organization they imply can certainly be so applied. Indeed, she points out, the semantic features that controlled her subjects' early words were based on function and/or other relational attributes determined by experience with the named elements. Thus, Nelson sees a child forming an eventual *semantic concept* of an entity in much the same process as a child forms a *sensorimotor scheme* of that object. When a child utters "ball," the concept underlying the word is *not* to be interpreted in terms of standard *semantic feature* theory, for example, + round + rollability + bounciness. Rather, it is a *semantic concept* which might include all sorts of relationships and functions, such as + rollability + bouncability + throwability + takes actor + can be located in many places and + allows possession. A semantic concept based on relational attributes as opposed to abstract attributes is the basis by which one can explain a child's utterance of the single lexical item "ball" in many, almost obscure, semantic relationships:

Mother drops an orange and it *rolls*.
Child observes another child *throwing* a stone.
Father throws and *catches* a coin.
Child wants mother to play *reciprocally* (agent/receiver).

In all of these contexts, the child's semantic concept is quite specific, and yet each of them is also a relational feature of the semantic concept of *"ball."* This observation is essentially a representation of Bloom's (1970) statement that a child learns to use identical lexical items in various semantic relationships. The observation also provides the primary data to describe the *nature* of a child's cognitive organization processes. The reader will also see, in a forthcoming discussion on *communication reference,* how this construct of relational concept formation fits with one's *use* of the language in communicative acts.

Implications of Nelson's theoretical position. Nelson's work has moved current research beyond simple correlational relationships between cognitive development and language acquisition and into a stage of hypothesizing and testing the notion that language is a rather *direct* reflection of the child's cognitive processes themselves. Thus, instead of looking for the elusive "deep structure" link between a child's knowledge and the form and structure by which it is realized in language, theorists may now begin with the assumption that children talk the way they do because that's the way they think. The final acceptance of such a relationship would have profound implications about language and language intervention. Researchers will first need to test this hypothesis.

Generalizations about a Universal Knowledge Base

In the previous discussion of children's knowledge base for language, we have examined research related to the overall cognitive development of children. The research, as summarized in the following generalizations, supports the view of language as a system of behavior that is so closely related to basic cognitive processes that it cannot be productively viewed or modified as separate from these processes.

1. Semantic universals in children's language appear to be well documented. The basis for these universals seems only to be accounted for by the fact of existing, general *cognitive* universals among child language learners.
2. Basic theories of early cognitive development among children recognize sensorimotor interactions with the elements of a child's environment as the universal process by which certain cognitive schemata are organized.
3. The formalized cognitive schemata which appear to be universally attained in the sensorimotor period show a direct correspondence to the *substance* of early semantic categories.
4. The interactive nature of the process of cognitive development in early childhood describes a child who is "constructing" a knowledge base. This characterization of an interactive, constructionistic child is highly consonant with the process hypothesized to be required for language learning by a young child.
5. The characterization of a child's knowledge as being strongly *relational,* which is inherent in the sensorimotor construct of cognitive development, appears strongly paralleled in the similarly *relational* bases of the semantic features represented in early child language.
6. The apparent correlation of relational bases for both cognitive schemata and semantic concepts signal, at the least, that common processes may be functional in the realization of both types of concepts.

Representational and Symbolic Behavior

In the previous section, we viewed the cognitive bases for language from the perspective of language *content.* In this section, we will briefly discuss the pertinence of another dimension of cognition by analyzing it from the perspective of language as *representational* or *symbolic* behavior.

By definition, language is a system of arbitrary, symbolic representations of both concrete and abstract referents. In attempts to translate this definitive construct into its earliest conceptual or cognitive elements, researchers have again been drawn to the work of Piaget. Prominent in the Piagetian hypotheses regarding early cognitive development of children is one which suggests that the symbolic functions of language are the upper end of a *continuum* of representational behaviors. As Morehead and Morehead (1974) interpret Piaget's postulate, "the symbolic function includes all mental behavior capable of re-presenting reality when it is not immediately present, including deferred imitation, imagery, symbolic play, language, drawing, and dreaming" (p. 159).

Piaget considered that the roots of symbolic functioning lay in imitation (Flavell, 1963; Sinclair, 1969), an accommodative routine in which some perceived event is "re-presented" in the presence of the model and then later in deferred imitation after the event has ceased to exist. Similar re-presentations of a motor scheme are eventually projected into a child's play and serve to allow the child to play "symbolically" by an "assimilative" (Piaget, 1952, 1954) routine. Through application of such internalized schemata, the child can attain such reality transformations as turning a piece of facial tissue into a doll blanket or a wooden block into an airplane. These same motor schemata can also become gestures for communicative representations of actions or objects. At this stage of Piaget's hypothesized continuum, the representation of objects or events is now removed in both time and space from its referent through some covert processes of internalization of the referent in imagery or some other indexing mode. Finally, the young child is able to represent objects or events through symbols which share common properties with the referent and/or "true signs" in which the relationship between the representation and the referent is an arbitrary, socially determined one. On the receptive side of the process, children seem to follow an analogous process of perceiving and decoding various types and levels of "signifiers" as they represent their "significates" (Morehead & Morehead, 1974). In this process, children react to "signals" (for example, peek-a-boo action by mother evokes anticipation or peek-a-boo action scheme from child), "indexes" (sees mother put on her coat, goes to the door to go bye-bye), "symbols" (sees drawing of ball, goes and gets ball), and "true signs" (that is, responds to "word" in totally novel context).

While such analyses of symbolic behaviors seem to match both logic and empirical reality, a process for teaching such movements along the symbolic continuum by functional means is certainly not known at this time. Indeed, although we might conceive of such behaviors being modeled or demonstrated to children, the process seems so dependent on a child's internalized operations that it is not easily manipulated by outside events. Thus, the child's ability to behave "symbolically" is his to determine on the basis of unknown properties of mental functioning.

General sensorimotor schemata development seems similarly unresponsive to any known intervention procedures. The symbolic language behaviors developed by children seem to closely parallel the elements and processes involved in empirically identified early cognitive schemata reported by Piaget. There is nothing in this observation which implies that such development is specifically viable to external manipulations. Rather, if children can and do develop sensorimotor constructs, these constructs would appear to be highly related to achievements in symbolic development. In sum it would appear that children who do not have the internal structures necessary to attain sensorimotor functions would most probably lack the structures for attaining symbolic behaviors. The converse, however, would not appear to be true; that is, it is conceivable, and probably demonstrable, that children might have intact sensorimotor schemata and still not be able to perform symbolically at even some of the lower levels of representation.

Implications of Symbolic
Functioning Levels

Perhaps the most salient implications of the continuum of symbolic function levels lie in the use of "alternative" modes for communication training. In the majority of applications, the alternative-mode options have been between speech and nonspeech modes, like manual signs, written symbol systems, or arbitrary-form symbols similar to those used by Premack (1970) in his work teaching a chimpanzee to use a language system. While in many of these cases the alternative mode has been an accommodation to a speech production problem (such as cerebral palsy, dysarthria, profound hearing loss), there is also much potential in some modes and mode forms because they require lower levels of actual symbolic functioning. For example, it is possible that some symbolic modes might allow for more iconic representation of the significate within their signifier form. A manual system of gestures which demonstrate many of the properties of their significates might be communicative when other manual signs with more arbitrary forms might not be interpretable. Similarly, pictographs might be decoded in cases where arbitrary written forms might not be. While there is much consideration being given to the use of alternative modes of many forms and for many different reasons (see, for example, chapters by Vanderheiden & Harris-Vanderheiden, Kopchick & Lloyd, Carrier and Clark & Woodcock; in Lloyd, 1976), definitive data–specifying properties of the symbolic continuum are yet to be compiled.

Exploring the relationship between cognitive functions and *language* assumes a symbolic ability adequate to attain the properties of language. Such symbolic abilities seem properly considered cognitive functions. These particular abilities (or continuum of abilities) are of such uniqueness and apparent independence from other cognitive functions, however, that they should be considered prerequisites of language from quite a different perspective than are other cognitive bases. Specifically, symbolic behavior is, by definition, the sine qua non for language, thus it must be perceived more narrowly as a prerequisite than are other cognitive functions.

We shall, of course, again consider this particular continuum of behavior when we discuss assessment of cognitive functions in the context of language intervention and when we look at the treatment implications of all of these variables we are discussing in this first section of the book.

Mechanics of Communication: Reference

The fourth (and last) source of perspectives which appear to us to be pertinent to cognition and language lies in the analysis of the properties inherent in the process we call *communication*. It should be of considerable interest and perhaps some appropriate chagrin, that children's utterances have been recorded and analyzed extensively in terms of their grammatical structure—both syntactic and semantic—while little attention has been directed toward the effect that the *communication act* itself has on the form and content of children's utterances. While the work of the semanticists (Bloom, 1970; Bowerman, 1973a; Slobin, 1973) has, at least, redirected attention back to the *content* of child language as it is related to the entities and relationships about which children talk, nevertheless, these data and hypotheses do not quite explain why these apparently universal entities and relationships are the ones which are "mapped" in such utterances. Like the transformational grammar approach which preceded them, semantic grammar approaches still take a rather unilateral approach to explaining children's utterances. Moreover, again like those methods which preceded, these semantic approaches are still vulnerable to the distortion inherent in an *adult perspective* as opposed to a *child perspective*. Thus, while semantic approaches seem to have made a most productive move toward the latter perspective and are more cognizant of the underlying processes of existing child knowledge and environmental interaction, they still seem to lack some definitive dimensions which are critical to a fuller understanding of early language acquisition. Some aspects of these missing dimensions may be identified through a closer examination of the context of such utterances as they function as communicative utterances *directed toward a listener*.

Psychological Aspects of Communication

This section discusses the cognitive aspects of communication and their effect on the nature, form, and content of a child's utterance. It focuses on the mechanisms of communication as they reflect upon the semantic and syntactic forms used. This topic has been identified as the area of *reference* (Brown, 1976).

In 1974, Bowerman observed that semantic relationships like *agent, instrumental,* or *benefactor* may *not* be anymore psychologically "real" to a child language user than syntactic constructs like subject or predicate object. Bowerman's perspective of psychological reality seems particularly productive. In fact, recent research by Leonard (1975) indicates that children might not differentiate between the various case relationships of nouns which take the normal subject slot in simple declarative sentences (for example, agent, instrumental, dative, or objective). It would appear premature then to assume that the semantic relationships now being described by analyzers of child grammar are the full or direct basis for the utterance forms used by the child. The alternative to this assumption of *semantic grammar* rules, such as those suggested by Schlesinger (1971, 1974; see also Fillmore, 1968, and Chafe, 1970), would be that there are still other aspects of a child's psychological perspective which may serve to determine his choice of the form and content of an utterance. Current semantic grammar systems are, like the syntactic systems before them, after-the-fact-of-language explanations. In other words, they are *descriptive* of child language—not necessarily *explanatory*.

This is not to dismiss the possible important contribution of semantic relationships to children's utterances nor their importance to the overall acquisition process of language. It is intended, however, to avoid the seeming error of assigning *explanatory* status to *descriptive* systems. Bowerman's criterion of psychological reality, more than anything else, suggests again the need to force our data and theories through some "child perspective" filters in order to arrive at an initial validity check on our working hypotheses. If we do this with children's utterances, we must conclude that some of the current case relationships seem a bit obscure in terms of their potential reality for children; particularly that is, if we maintain our past conditioned ideas about children's utterances being controlled, primarily, by a *grammar* system. This holdover from Chomskian influence that assumes an utterance is necessarily controlled only by a set of word relationship rules whose requirements are being met in each utterance may be acting as an inhibitor to the discovery of alternative ways of explaining the form of children's (or adult) utterances. It is important, then, to look at the differences which might be suggested by another view of what controls the form and content of utterances.

Communication realization. Many ideas about the form and content of utterances are essentially one-dimensional views in that they consider only the speaker's determination of his utterance. Although it seems indisputable that the final account-ability for an utterance is properly placed on the speaker, the fact that there is also a listener cannot be ignored as a potential variable in the speaker's design of an utterance. Tailoring an utterance for a particular audience is a common experience. We all have many languages, for many audiences, and these audiences cause us to alter not only our syntax, but our morphological forms as well. It might be argued that such changes are simply accommodations at the surface level, and in mature speakers this is true to some degree. There is, however, evidence that these alterations for an audience are not just *stylistic* but instead represent something inherently real in the "game" of communication. Olson (1970) gives a cogent and provocative representation of the influence of communicative intent on utterance form and content.

In his analysis, Olson starts where many of our semanticists stop in that he starts with an assumption that a person can only encode into language that which he already knows. In addition, it is Olson's important point that not only can one not talk about that which he does not know, but also a person has difficulty attaining communication if he is talking about something of which the *listener has no knowl-edge*, as in this illustrative dialogue:

"Is this the attenuator you want?"

"No, the attenuator is that coil of wire."

"This one?"

"No, it's the tightly wound coil with the knob on it—the knob that turns the pointer that makes contact with the coil."

"This one?"

"Yes, that's it."

Olson's analysis of language supports a position that language utterances are designed to communicate the speaker's referent to a listener, as the sample dialogue illustrates. Whatever the referent of a speaker might be (a specific object, a desired response, or even a perceived relationship between two entities), the language utterance is designed to communicate it (the referent) to the listener. Further, Olson posits (as in the example) that the actual form of the utterance finally used by the speaker not only is controlled by the speaker's knowledge about the referent, but also is, to whatever degree possible, an attempt to anticipate the listener's knowledge of the referent.

Olson's perspectives also include many other realizations which contribute to the overall awareness of speakers' cognitive control of the specific form and/or structure of their utterances. He points out, for example, that not only the lexical elements of an utterance are determined by a speaker's chosen referent and knowledge of the referent, but even that the correct grammatical structure for a particular referent might be overridden by a speaker's knowledge. For example, a person might violate grammatical subject-verb agreement in number when discussing a grammatically singular subject which has cognitive properties of plurality: "The *crowd* voiced *their* disapproval." The meaning of a particular utterance is only interpretable in terms of its communicative intent. Bloom supports this statement with her "mommy sock" example. In this regard, Olson points out that words might mean many things, depending on the speaker's intent. Thus, a child's "milk" might mean "That's milk," "Give me milk," or "Ugh, that's milk, I thought it was orange juice." On the same basis, a referent "thing" might have many names depending on the speaker's or the listener's knowledge about it. Thus, a particular man might be "Daddy," "Jim," "that tall one," "the professor," and so on. This point has been made strongly in previous considerations of reference by Brown (1958), corroborating Nelson's (1974) views about relational concepts underlying lexical choice at another level.

The overall implications of Olson's conclusions are summed in the many characterizations of language as a communication game. The *meaning* of words or structures used is determined by their use in the particular language game being played (Brown, 1958; Olson, 1970; Wittengenstein, 1958). As Olson (1970, p. 263) begins, "We draw boundaries between events for some special purpose. That purpose specifies our language game." Olson continues that, since language reference (meaning) varies according to the particular language game being played, a descriptive account of the structure or surface content of an utterance cannot represent the true facts of such an utterance. For example, when Bloom's subject, Kathryn, picks up her mother's stocking and says "Mommy sock," Bloom describes the utterance as a noun + noun utterance with the underlying semantic relationship of possessor and possessed. Applying Olson's basic point, Kathryn is primarily intent on specifying mother's stocking as a referent in a language game designed to attain a joint reference with mother. We can hypothesize then that Kathryn searches her body of knowledge about this particular referent and finds that she knows that it is a "sock." In addition, Kathryn might find that not only is it a sock, but also it has properties that many other socks do not have and, as such, can be marked supplementally by the fact that this sock has a relational property of association with mommy. According to this hypothesis, Kathryn could be marking her referent as a sock with a relational attribute of "momminess." If this were the case, "mommy" in this reference might better be described as an attribute of the sock and, as such, more adjectival than possessive. From this perspective, Bloom's adult categorization of the utterance is slightly off the mark. While, of course, we cannot say that the above hypothesis is true, neither can anyone say for sure that it is not. In fact, given Nelson's (1974) statements about "relational" semantic features, either "explanation" could be correct and additional explanations are even possible.

As this example shows, the possible (or even probable) psychological reality which underlies a child's utterance can be very different than that being described by adult analytical systems—be they syntactic or semantic. Bowerman emphasized this (1974) when she questioned whether semantic relationships, as described by adults, are truly representative of a child's reality. Indeed, following the persuasively logical analyses of Olson and the others who have pointed up the relativity of language content in the context of its "game" goals, we would have to begin to consider that the form of an early utterance may be dictated more by its communicative function and its sociophysical context than by any "grammar" system per se. Bruner (1975) corroborates this point in his considerations of the ontogenesis of speech acts within mother-child interactive routines.

In discussing this ontogenesis, Bruner (1975) identifies two primary routines in the interaction process: learning the segments of *joint actions,* and constructing routines to assure *joint reference* between speaker and listener. In the segmenting of joint actions which are usually carried out by mother and child, Bruner identifies parallels between the attributes of such routines and the primitive case-grammar categories involving agents–actions–receivers–locations, and so on. Not only does he note the isomorphism between the segments of action routines and the grammatical cases, but also he notes that the predominant order of linguistic elements, as they are applied to these action segments, is also isomorphic with the order in which these segments are observed in physical experience; for example, agent–action–object of action (Greenberg, 1963, cited in Bruner, 1975, p. 4). Thus, Bruner suggests that a segmenting of the elements of action routines is a child's reality. Case grammars like those of Fillmore (1968) and Chafe (1970) based on noun relationships with other parts of sentences make for a good fit between a child's action segmenting utterances and case-grammar relationships. But rather than hypothesizing that the utterance was guided by "case-grammar rules," one might just as easily assume that the utterance was guided by the segmented elements of a perceived action sequence and that case grammars are well designed to describe this child reality.

It should be established that all formal grammars may simply be *describing* the products of rule systems for child language products and are essentially independent from the units used in a child's creation of the grammar. Therefore, the "boy" in the utterance "boy push truck" may be neither the subject, nor the agent, but rather, to the child, may be simply the first element in a perceived physical event as suggested by Greenberg.

Bruner (1975) suggests another possible source for the rule system which underlies child utterances—that of a sequence which represents a child's reality of *Topic + Comment* or *Subject + Predication.* According to this rule, the subject is the child's subject and may or may not qualify as the sentence's subject. Thus, a child may say, "me push," "push car," or "car push" and be structuring his perception of subject + predication or topic + comment. In the third utterance, "car push," for example, the child may actually be implying an action-object relationship but, by choosing his own "topic," creates a *passive* construction ("car is being pushed").

Bruner's (1975) two possible controlling systems—segmentation of action elements and Topic + Comment—seem extremely logical and attractive explanations for early child utterances. First, they represent plausible constructs for child reality. Second, as Bruner shows, they seem to fit the contexts in which much child language learning occurs (child-adult interactions). Third, both of these systems produce utterances which match the rules codified by the case-grammar categories and the other semantic relationships which seem appropriate to describe early language forms.

A fourth and important support for the validity of Bruner's observations is that such childhood realities as action segmenting and topic-comment are totally accepting of the speaker/listener knowledge requirements demanded by Olson's (1970) cognitive/semantic base for utterance forms. A child may choose his *topic* by virtue of his knowledge of a particular referent and arrange his *comment* according to an action segmentation process (for example, "go bye-bye, car"). Another child may, on the other hand, choose his topic by virtue of its importance to his "game" and his comment in terms of its further specifications of an important referent to identify the desired game ("mommy [read] book").

While a full acceptance of Bruner's and Olson's hypotheses may seem rather precipitous at this point in our knowledge, one must appreciate the fact that both of these perspectives represent important commitments in developing an understanding of the psychological bases of children's language by moving directly to the child language user's reality. As we discussed in the earliest parts of this section, current theories which apply adult perspectives to children's language have seemed less than ideal when translated into intervention programs.

Implications of Reference Theory

The foregoing discussion has been guided by various views of language utterances as *communication units*. Particularly, it has reflected the recent attention to the form and content of utterances as they are related to a speaker's perspective in constructing an utterance. Olson's (1970) point that a speaker attempts to transmit information about his particular communicative referent to a listener implies that the final realization structure reflects the knowledge the speaker has of the referent as well as the speaker's assumptions about the listener's knowledge of the referent. With the speaker's cognitive control of an utterance emphasized, Olson considers the psychological bases of a language utterance in contrast to the linguistic bases. Thus, again we are led to differentiate between theories and quantification systems that describe and those that explain a particular utterance.

Once we view language, as Olson does, as an exchange of information to the point that a communicative referent has been successfully transmitted between speaker and listener, we realize that most grammar rule systems, either syntactic or semantic, cannot be translated into strictly communicative or referential terms. While it is true that such systems can be used to quantify or analyze the units used to transmit this information, they do not describe the communicative basis which the information was chosen for transmitting. Thus, it seems inappropriate to think of language utterances as being generated as grammar. Rather it would appear more logical to think of utterances as being generated by a speaker's choice of referent with the grammar relationships being dictated by the nature of the referent and the information required to "map" it for effective communication.

Bruner (1975) suggests that many grammar forms observed in children's language seem to fit certain psychological processes observed in children's interactions with their environment. As Bruner (1975) observed, these interactions include the dynamic interactions with objects in the environment as characterized by Piagetian, sensorimotor, and social interactions with mothers or other primary caretakers. As Bruner sees it, children's utterances are generated to accomplish *joint references* or *routines of joint action* (Bruner, 1974/75, 1975). Their language utterances reflect the *information* needed to accomplish these purposes—namely, the segmenting of action or the presentation of relevant referent-element information in utterances structured by Topic-Comment relationships. Bruner concludes that both of these types of information are realized in the child's utterance through psychologically determined *Topic-Comment* structures.

Bruner's (1975) observations may be interpreted as saying that a child's psychological reality for language utterances is isomorphic with his overall psychological processing mechanisms. This recalls Nelson's (1974) perspectives in which she also suggests that children's linguistic patterns are reflections of their overall cognitive processing patterns in that both seem strongly based on the perception and organization of entities in their world in terms of the relational attributes of such entities. While taking quite different approaches to the overall problem, Bruner and Nelson seem to come to conclusions which corroborate one another. Particularly, both of them represent views of language in which child utterances are viewed as reflections of psychological perspectives and general cognitive processing styles instead of as representations of certain linguistic rule systems. However, both Bruner (1975) and Nelson (1974) find semantic relationships, particularly those represented in case-grammar systems (Chafe, 1970; Fillmore, 1968) more appropriately descriptive and quantifying of these psychological processing elements than Chomsky's (1957, 1965) transformational grammar system seems to be.

In summary, the view of language structure and content generated by communication perspectives strongly militates against purely linguistic analyses of language. Specifically, these views hold that a strictly linguistic analysis misses the true content of a language utterance which they conclude is the rather direct encoding of a child's psychological processing products and perspectives. These products and perspectives are cognitive holdings related to all aspects of the utterance—from its required communicative content to the relationships best suited to represent this content. In this view, the best test of a linguistic grammar system is not how it might describe the rule system of a language utterance, but how accurately it describes the communicative and referential reality of an utterance. Those most prominent in this area of study—Olson (1970), Bruner (1975), and Nelson (1974)—indicate that no grammar system is truly adequate to this task but that the semantic, case-grammar units seem closest to describing the reality that exists for a child speaker.

Synthesizing the
Cognitive Bases of Language

As we anticipated in the introductory statements in this topic area, the cognitive bases for language and language acquisition can be seen to be both complex and multifaceted. In addition, the perspectives offered within this area are broadly productive in their implications for existing theoretical and applied bases for language intervention programs. The following section will be an attempt to synthesize much of the foregoing discussion into perspectives which are more focused and therefore more definitive in their form and their implications. This synthesis will focus on three areas:

1. The perspective which suggests that children's language has a psychological reality that is not adequately represented in either transformational grammar systems or functional analysis of behavior systems.

2. The perspective which suggests that the isomorphism between cognitive and language development comes as a result of similar developmental processes underlying each—namely, a constructionistic/interactional process.
3. The perspective which suggests that neither the content nor the structure of children's language can be adequately described in isolation from either its cognitive bases or its communicative function.

We shall discuss each of these areas of focus in turn with an emphasis on applying the material to development of an intervention model.

Psychological Reality of Language

Certainly, one of the most immediate problems in planning a language intervention program for young, severely delayed, handicapped children is the selection of the targets to be sought through such intervention. Decisions regarding the targets of intervention are influenced by many variables at many different levels. The issue of psychological reality is one such level, and it is a level which seems extremely underrepresented in today's intervention programming. Further, it appears to us that the underrepresentation of this level is one cause of significant problems in language intervention programming.

For example, both transformational grammar and behavioral models of language and language acquisition are basically *adult realities*. Furthermore, these systems are highly abstract models which have no specific contact with the internal world of the child language user. Skinner (1957) eschews any consideration of "inside" events and deals only with observable behaviors. Chomsky (1957, 1965) considers the inside events associated with language utterances to be either innately a part of the human cognitive structure or inculcated at unspecifiable levels and/or forms which can only be described (or labeled) as "deep structures."

However, to a language clinician or teacher who must select targets for language training, such targets must take on specific form and content. The Noun Phrase + Verb Phrase structure of Chomsky must be translated into specific nouns and verbs as well as specific function words which can complete the structural relationships between the nouns and verbs. Thus, the clinician or teacher must select and implement a reality for the targets. What nouns and what verbs and, indeed, what prepositions, articles, and adjectives?

The same problems face the behavioral modifier intervening in language. The categories suggested by Skinner (1957) offer only the grossest of functional contexts. Again, the fine grain of a speaker's specific intent or functional need is left to the intervener to specify and target. Again, we see adult perceptions of what children should be taught to talk about as the determiner of the language intervention target. In this behavioral area, it is even more ironic that, as some behavioral modifiers have sought resources to determine specific language exemplars to be trained, they have moved to structural grammar systems rather than cognitive bases—e.g., Gray and Ryan (1973), Carrier (1974), Carrier and Peak (1975). In their move to grammar structure, the behaviorists seem to be in great danger of missing the entire point of the function of language which is, theoretically at least, their focus.

At both of the theoretical departure points which have dominated language intervention programming, then, we see that the teacher or clinician has had little help in determining the specific targets or contexts of intervention as they might be related to a child's psychological reality. Instead, these interveners have had to operate from descriptive constructs of language which are, at least, one abstraction level away from any specific utterance which might be targeted.

As psycholinguistic data and theory began to reflect the individually idiosyncratic, yet collectively universal, semantic content of child utterances, a move began to look again at the bases from which such content could be generated by children. Obviously, the only possible source for semantic intent had to lie in the child's cognitive organization of the entities and relationships which were part of his world. As the cognitive organization of children was more fully analyzed, the specific nature of the entities and the relationships among these entities as they are perceived by children seemed to have linear representation in both the general and the specific elements of children's utterances. In other words, not only did children's utterances "map" the entities and relationships present in their environment, but the relationships and entities in their world directed the content and form of their utterances. Thus, language and language use seem no longer to be adequately or productively viewed as separate from meaning or communication. Quite the contrary, the analysis of the cognitive bases of language which supplemented the "semantic revolution" has generated a view of language which insists that the early language of children cannot be viewed except as it represents an after-the-fact reflection of children's cognitive organization and holdings. Importantly, it must also include the basic nature and purpose of children's communicative transactions within the social compact in which they reside or function. This view holds that it is children's perceptions of both the physical and social environment which generate language specifically in both form and function. Thus, it is this child reality which must be used to determine the form and function of intervention targets and the intervention contexts in which such targets can be most clearly and accurately discovered by children.

It is time, then, that psychological reality of child language be used to at least supplement the previous descriptive bases for determining both the targets and the procedures for language intervention among young, handicapped children. The currently hypothesized constructs have many dimensions which appear productive in designing both the substance and the procedure of language intervention with these children. Included in a child's reality is a most important social dimension which will be examined in depth in the next chapter of this text. The social dimension plus the cognitive bases reflected in this chapter combine to provide a view of child language which is far richer and more clinically "real" than any programs generated from the previous linguistic or behavioral bases. The section of this text directed toward clinical treatment implications will attempt to make this new richness more specific by suggesting new models for treatment of young, severely language-delayed children.

Table 3 identifies some of the major positions regarding the reality of child utterances. Such psychological bases are clearly beyond explanation by grammatical rules or behavioral descriptions alone.

TABLE 3

Some Recent Hypotheses on the
Psychological Bases of Children's Language Utterances

Bloom (1970)	Semantic relationships based on knowledge of the world are encoded.
Schlesinger (1971)	Semantic relationships are used to structure utterance rules.
Slobin (1973)	Semantic intentions stemming from general cognitive development are encoded.
Olson (1970)	Cognitive information about a referent is transmitted to a listener.
Nelson (1974)	Cognitive information about a communicative referent is transmitted by marking of the relational properties of the referent.
Bruner (1975)	The various elements of action events are segmented and marked. The properties of joint referents are marked.

Isomorphism in Cognitive and Language Development

We have observed that a child's earliest utterances manifest primitive semantic relationships which are isomorphic with those earliest sensorimotor cognitive schemata identified in the work of Piaget (1952, 1954). This supports the perspective that, at the least, language development is a product of the same human processes and strategies that underlie general cognitive development. This same observation is used to support a stronger hypothesis: a child's early language is a rather direct manifestation of his cognitive holdings.

Whether one subscribes to the weakest or the strongest of the basic cognitive hypotheses in regard to language, one cannot consider language without also focusing on cognitive development—both in its products and in its process. The Piagetian characterization of an active child, manipulating the environment and constructing knowledge about that environment as a result of the information derived from such manipulations, has appeal in its inherent logic for any program which would "teach" a child anything. Such logic is specifically important when it comes to teaching a repertoire of behavior which is as complex and basic as is language.

These characterizations of a manipulative and constructive child learner militate against intervention procedures which would target language responses through procedures which do not involve a child in the most dynamic representations of a constructive process. Yet, if we look at the procedures suggested by our two most dominant current theoretical bases, we see programs aimed at essentially abstract linguistic structures or utterance forms to be imitated in the presence of an adult-constructed representation of their "referent." (article + noun + copula + adjective—"The ball is red.") If the child subjects of such programs indicate that they can construct the appropriate structures or representational functions from such procedures, there is no problem. If, however, some children cannot make progress through the complex matrix of sequentially presented syntactic structures, or if they cannot learn and appropriately generalize the imitative response in accordance with its designated referent, the procedures should be reconsidered. The perspectives offered by the observed relationship between the products and processes of both cognitive development and language development offer specific directions for procedural redesign. The direct clinical or intervention directions obtained from this perspective will be detailed in Chapter 7.

Structure and Content of Language Described in Isolation

The third area of focus which has been generated by the cognitive perspectives of language is, naturally, another facet of all of the foregoing observations. As with other such facets of the overall perspective, however, this one also has a productivity of its own which supplements the others. The final perspective states that since human language encodes what is communicated among humans, language forms and content cannot be considered apart from the psychological processes and the communicative needs of humankind. Thus, Nelson (1974) and Bruner (1975) emphasize that language is an observable manifestation of the human cognitive and social condition. This perspective is also strongly supported and supplemented by Slobin (1973), MacNamara (1972), Luria (1974/75), and Olson (1970). The focus that this view adds to those already discussed is simply that language form, content, and function are highly related. Consequently, these researchers essentially reject descriptive systems of language which are purely linguistic, because such systems ignore the physical and psychological bases of language and communication. Instead, they point to language as an integrative behavior which not only has its unique form and function but which, within its form and function, carries the products of many other human behavioral domains. By the nature of its content, language carries within it the products of the cognitive developmental domain; by nature of its function, language carries within it the products of human social development; and, by nature of its form, language carries within it the complex products of all of the inputs identified above plus the effect of the nature and functions of the human physiological and neurological systems.

In a recent article, Mason (1976) explores the representational processes in primates and man. In his introductory section, Mason states:

> All behavior that is guided by sensory information, that is, most of the behavior that interests us, implies some type of schema or functional "image" of the environment. Behavior is the endpoint of an information processing sequence. (p. 284)

We take this observation as a nice statement of the basis of our current rejection of a continued view of language as a behavior which can be appropriately considered separately from other higher human functions. To paraphrase Mason's point, it appears most obvious that language behavior implies some type of schema of the environment and that, indeed, it is the endpoint of a multifaceted information processing developmental sequence. Language does not have its totally separate determiners in human knowledge or reality. Rather, it is a product of the knowledge and reality which is developed and subsequently communicated to other humans who share in a potential for similar knowledge or reality. That language behavior has a dependence on some special symbolic capabilities which are unique to it seems not to negate its relative integration of other human behaviors and psychological realities.

As we have seen and as we will explore further in succeeding sections, language and language acquisition include and depend on all of the human processes. It requires sensory processing; organization of the environment's sensory information into discriminable schemata, constructs, or concepts; and an awareness of the nature and function of human social compacts. Language, therefore, seems well considered, with other complex human behaviors, as an integrative, constructed behavior. Further, by virtue of the critical ecological organization that we see evident in all complex systems, it would seem naive indeed to imagine that any one part of such a complex human system can be considered without considering its relationships with other parts of the system.

Currently dominant perspectives which isolate language structures from meaning or from "inside events" are, literally, unproductive. They obscure the directions and inhibit the motivations for further work toward attaining better understandings of language and its acquisition by both natural and clinically contrived means. It is for this reason that this chapter has focused on the most recent perspectives on the cognitive bases for language. It is also for this reason that the next chapter will examine the recent perspectives on language which are related to the *social bases* for language and language acquisition. Finally, it is toward the overall purpose of constructing a perspective on language acquisition that is appropriately representative of its dynamic and integrative properties that we will sketch-out a derived model of language development which incorporates these cognitive and social properties more completely than do current transformational and/or behavioral models.

Summary

The following summary statements are derived from this chapter's review of the literature on the cognitive bases of language.

1. Language *content* has its primary bases in the child's knowledge about the entities and the relationships among and between these entities in his environment. As such, then, language content represents the products of a child's processing of the sensory and social information gained through interactions within the environment. A child's language seems appropriately considered to reflect the psychological reality of the environment which he has constructed.

2. Language *structure* has its primary cognitive bases in three distinct, yet highly related areas. First, the structure of a child's utterance is determined in part by the *nature* of the relationships contained in the content of the utterance (that is, the structure of an utterance "maps" the relational attributes of its referent(s)). Consequently, the structure of an utterance is not independent of meaning.

   Secondly, the structure of a child's utterance seems to reflect its speaker's psychological perception of the *relative* values of the utterance's elements—in other words, the psychological topic and the predication (or commenting) on the topic.

Thirdly, the structure of a child's utterance seems to depend primarily on *word-ordering* rules which represent both the referential relationships and the psychological relativity identified above.

3. Language *function* seems to have been underestimated or inadequately considered in previous analyses of children's language. While it is generally accepted that children's language is communicative in function, the details and the mechanics of communication have not been sufficiently represented in current theory and application. The functions of language to (a) establish joint or common referents and referential relationships and (b) establish joint or cooperative social routines have not been adequately treated as to their influence on both the content and the structure of children's language. Neither have these functions of language been adequately analyzed as to their implications for language acquisition or intervention strategies and contexts. This latter area will be treated in more depth later in the book.

chapter 3

Social Bases of Language Acquisition

Just as researchers and clinicians have recently become sensitized to the critical role of cognitive development as a base for language acquisition, so have they shown a renewed interest in the social bases of language. It is to this parallel component of the language acquisition process that we will now direct our attention. In actuality, of course, the processes of cognitive and social interaction which underlie the emergence of language cannot be neatly separated. Thus, the reader is asked to remember that the products and processes of social learning to be discussed in this chapter are intertwined with the parallel cognitive achievements described in the preceding chapter.

There has long existed a general awareness of the close relationship between social interaction and language usage. Traditionally, when pressed to describe the function of language, lay people and academicians alike have responded with statements such as: "We use language to communicate thoughts and ideas." Implicit in such a statement, of course, is the recognition that language is a social tool—that is, we communicate to someone else. In 1927, DeLaguna (republished, 1963) scrutinized this historical view of language's basic function as the communication of thoughts or ideas from human to human. While not disputing this view, she points out that this perspective might not adequately represent the function of language. Rather, it might only describe the *means* for attaining a function which is even more basic:

Once we deliberately ask the question: *What does speech do? What objective function does it perform in human life?*—the answer is not far to seek. Speech is the great medium through which human cooperation is brought about. It is the means by which the diverse activities of men are coordinated and correlated with each other for the attainment of reciprocal ends. Men do not speak simply to relieve their feelings or to air their views, but to awaken a response in their fellows and to influence their attitudes and acts. It is further the means by which men are brought into a new and momentous relationship with the external world, the very relationship which makes the world for them an objective order. (pp. 19–20)

Supporting DeLaguna's emphasis on the nature and importance of language function in the context of human social compacts, Bruner (1974/75) states that "neither the syntactic nor the semantic approach to language acquisition takes sufficiently into account what the child is trying to do by communicating. As linguistic philosophers remind us, utterances are used for different ends and use is a powerful determinant of rule structures" (p. 283).

This perspective is also reflected in Miller and Yoder's (1972) statement that, in order for a child to use language, the child must have not only something to say and a way to say it, but also a reason to say it. This realization is extremely basic and is reflected even in the common-sense wisdom of parents who explain the later emergence of language among their younger children by noting that the older sibling's tendency to interpret and respond to nonverbal communicative efforts alleviates the younger child's need or reason for using language.

Unfortunately, this perspective of language as a means for achieving social/ communicative functions has generally not been reflected in the developmental linguistic literature until quite recently (perhaps due to the reductionistic tendencies discussed in the introduction to this book). During the past two years, however, researchers from the fields of both psychology and linguistics have begun to examine this aspect of early childhood language and have added greatly to our understanding of the role which social interactions play in the young child's acquisition of language. From the linguistic research has arisen a growing body of literature dealing with what is called the "pragmatics" (as opposed to "semantics") of language. The study of language pragmatics has focused on the specification and delineation of the specific communicative functions realized through language and how these functions change over the course of development from emergent through adult linguistic forms.[1]

From research in developmental psychology has come an understanding of the actual dynamics of very early social interactions. This research has indicated that such interactions provide not only the basis for communication which will later be achieved linguistically, but also the vehicle through which the child acquires the linguistic structures and much of the semantic content of the language system. Further, this research has objectified and quantified many of the specific behaviors exhibited by both the adult and the infant/child in such interactions. Such objectification has led to much exciting theoretical speculation concerning the specific functions these behaviors serve in maintaining a productive language-learning social context.

---

[1]For present purposes, the authors have chosen to use the term *pragmatics* in a rather restricted and simplified sense; i.e., to refer to the study of communicative functions realized through language. In actuality, the study of pragmatics is a highly specialized branch of linguistics with a terminology and taxonomy of types all its own. Thus, the broad term "communicative intent" used in this book is most closely related to the *performative* component of language pragmatics, while the referencing strategies and mechanisms referred to in Chapter 2 are associated with the pragmatic construct of *presupposition*. A third aspect of pragmatics, the conversational postulate, is not reflected in the current treatment because it is associated with levels of language development beyond the scope of this work. The reader interested in a more complete treatment of the pragmatics (in the fullest linguistic sense of the word) of child language is referred to Elizabeth Bates' text, *Language and Context* (1976).

In this chapter, we will describe the new perspectives on the social bases of language acquisition in more detail. The major developments in the study of pragmatics will be described first, followed by the specific preverbal communication development which seems to underlie this aspect of language. Finally, we will examine the dynamic social interactive processes which seem critical to the transmission of the linguistic code and identify the specific behavioral contributions to these interactions by both adult and child.

The Pragmatics of Language

As noted above, there has been a recent resensitization among researchers and clinicians to the fact that people talk for a reason. That is, language does not exist as an end in itself but as a means to the achievement of some specific social/communicative function. It seems probable not only that people use language as a means to achieve such functions, but also that children first acquire language as a more effective means to achieve their communicative objectives. The linguistic realization of these social and communicative functions is referred to as the "pragmatics" of language and has been the subject of much recent study. Bruner (1974/75) has defined "pragmatics" as the "directive function of speech through which speakers affect the behavior of others in trying to carry out their intentions" (p. 283). It should be pointed out that the concept of pragmatics is a linguistic one and that most of the work in this field has been aimed at providing a taxonomy or classification system which accounts for the range of observed functions served by language. As such, these systems are descriptive, in the sense that transformational grammars describe the syntax of a language and case grammars describe the semantics of a language. Such taxonomies are highly useful in generating targets but are not to be taken as explanations of the process by which the classified behaviors are constructed or generated.

Global Accounts

For the sake of establishing an overall perspective, we will consider first two relatively global accounts or descriptions of the social functions achieved by language. A good example of such an account is that cited previously from DeLaguna's 1927 text: "Men do not speak simply to relieve their feelings or to air their views, but to *awaken a response in their fellows and to influence their attitudes and acts*" (p. 20, italics ours). Similarly, Bruner (1975) argues: "Language is acquired as an instrument for *regulating joint activity and joint attention*" (p. 2, italics ours).

In both of these accounts, two broad functions of language are identified. First, both specify the regulation or influencing of a listener's actions. This function is perhaps the most intuitively obvious and most readily explained. Thus, we have little doubt concerning the intended function of such utterances as "Please pass the salt," "Would you please write up the report for this committee?" or even "What do you know, my glass is empty already!" Although these sentences vary greatly in semantic content, syntactic structure, and even intonation and stress patterns, we have little trouble recognizing the intended function of each and can classify all as attempts to affect the actions of the listener. Because such utterances are designed to evoke overt behavioral responses from the listener, it is relatively easy to determine not only the speaker's intent in producing the utterance, but also the efficacy of the utterance in actually achieving that intent.

A second very broad class of communicative function is that of "influencing attitudes" or "regulating joint attention." Again, it is not difficult to identify exemplars of these functions regardless of the semantic and syntactic form used to achieve them. Within this category, we would identify such utterances as "I think Harry Jones would make an excellent chairman," "Isn't that music lovely?" or "Now I understand what you mean by pragmatics." While it is not difficult to recognize examples of this second function, it is often very difficult to specify the speaker's underlying purpose or intent. Therefore, it would be difficult to determine when that intent has been successfully achieved. While in some cases the listener may be able to infer a specific motivation for a particular utterance of this type, often it seems that such utterances serve primarily to maintain the speaker's role in a social interaction.

It is not our purpose here to delve into the underlying motivations or hidden meanings conveyed by much language—particularly among adults. Suffice it to state that these two broad categories do differ in terms of the ease with which motivation and efficacy can be specified. We will return to this issue later in our discussion of implications for clinical intervention. Obviously such a global account of the functions of language masks many finer-grained and potentially productive discriminations of more specific functions commonly served by language. Two more in-depth analyses and descriptions of the pragmatics of early childhood language follow.

Pragmatics of Emerging Language

In 1975, two major treatments of the functions of emergent language appeared (Dore, 1975; Halliday, 1975). Halliday, who focused on earlier stages of development, argued for a functional, child-centered approach to the study of how children acquire language. He began his investigation with a set of hypotheses concerning the child's earliest intentions or uses of language. He then tested these with one subject, Nigel, by observing and documenting this child's linguistic development from the age of nine months through two years. On the basis of these data, Halliday has proposed three phases of development: Phase I—the child's initial functional language system; Phase II—the transition from Phase I to Phase II; and Phase III—the learning of adult language. For our purposes, Phases I and II are most relevant.

The following are the functions which Halliday hypothesized would be reflected in early (Phase I) language. Their associated translations or "glosses" are listed below:

Instrumental	("I want")
Regulatory	("Do as I tell you")
Interactional	("Me and you")
Personal	("Here I come")

Heuristic	("Tell me why")
Imaginative	("Let's pretend")
Informative	("I've got something to tell you")

Phase I, covering the period of 9 months through 16½ months, was broken down into five one-and-one-half-month observation periods. During the first two periods (through 12 months), Nigel's language consisted of idiosyncratic but consistent sounds used to serve the first four functions (instrumental, regulatory, interactional, personal) and contained no standard grammatical or lexical forms. Throughout the remainder of Phase I, of the other three functions (heuristic, imaginative, informative), only imaginative was clearly represented, but only by 5 of the total of 145 utterance types produced during this phase. An additional characteristic which marked this phase was that each function was isomorphic with specific forms used to map it—that is, the idiosyncratic protowords used by Nigel were each associated with one specific function. For example, the protoword "nanana" was used only in a general instrumental demand function which could be glossed as "give me that," while "bø" was used only in a specific instrumental demand function which could be glossed as "give me my bird."

Phase II, the phase of transition to adult language (for Nigel the period from 16½ to 24 months) was marked by several important developments. In this stage, the child's language for the first time consisted primarily of standard lexical items. Initially, as these were acquired they were isomorphic (that is, in one-to-one correspondence) with specific functions, as had been the protowords of Phase I. However, during Phase II, Nigel learned to use the same word to serve different functions and in different grammatical contexts.

A second development which Halliday ascribes to this period is the appearance of two clearly distinct functionally defined types of utterance which subsume and extend the specific functions of Phase I. Halliday identifies these two broad functions as *pragmatic* and *mathetic*. The pragmatic function is described as "language as doing" and is supposed to derive from the earlier instrumental and regulatory functions. This function is reflected in such utterances as "mummy come," "help juice," and "more meat." The mathetic function, on the other hand, is defined as "language as learning" and is supposed to derive from the Phase I personal and heuristic functions. Examples of mathetic functions in Nigel's corpus include "green car," "two book," and "tiny red light." One indication that these functions were, in fact, functionally discrete was that Nigel very consistently produced mathetic utterances with a falling intonation and pragmatic utterances with a rising tone. This early indication of intonational or paralinguistic marking will be relevant in later discussions and has specific clinical implications.

A final development noted by Halliday in Phase II is the ability to participate in a dialogue. By this accomplishment, Halliday means the ability to adopt and assign communication roles in the context of a verbal exchange. This development suggests more than the reciprocity or turn-taking behavior often noted in early mother-infant protodialogues in which the members produce vocalizations in alternating order. Instead, Halliday is referring to the ability to participate in a true dialogue in which each speaker's response is controlled by the semantic and pragmatic content of the other speaker's previous utterance. For Nigel, this skill was considered to be mastered during a two-week period around 18 months when he developed the ability to respond to a Wh- question, respond to a command, respond to a statement, respond to a response, and initiate dialogue with a Wh- question.

While Halliday's study traced the development of pragmatics from the period immediately before the child's production of standard, socially defined language through the production of multiword grammatical utterances, Dore (1975) has concentrated specifically on the period of one-word utterances. Dore suggests that the early one-word utterance—which he terms a "Primitive Speech Act" (PSA)—be viewed "not merely as an elliptical adult speech act, but a qualitatively different entity which possesses only some features similar to full speech acts" (p. 32). He suggests that PSA's can be described in terms of a "rudimentary referring expression" (that is, the lexical/semantic component of the utterance) and a "primitive force-indicating device" (here "force" refers to the illocutionary force or communicative function of the utterance). This primitive force is most commonly realized as an intonational pattern overlaid on the rudimentary referring expression. For example, in the PSA "doggie↑" the rudimentary referring expression is "doggie," a word which is probably adequate for establishing joint reference with a listener. The utterance is overlaid with a rising intonational pattern (shown here by an arrow) indicating the illocutionary force of the utterance which in this case might be requesting a confirmation of the label or an indication of the dog's location. Within this framework, Dore has analyzed the one-word PSA's produced by two children in the one-word stage of language development. On the basis of these data, he has identified nine types of speech acts, shown here with examples:

Labeling	("eyes" while touching doll's eyes)
Repeating	("datə" after hearing mother say "doctor")
Answering	("bow wow" after mother points to picture of dog and asks "What's this?")
Requesting (action)	("uh? uh? uh?" after trying to push pegs in hole, mother responds by helping)
Requesting (answer)	("buk↑" after picking up a book)
Calling	("mama" said loudly with distinct intonation while mother is across room)
Greeting	("Hi" when teacher enters room)
Protesting	("no" while resisting mother's efforts to put shoes on)
Practicing	("daddy" when daddy not present and with no response from mother)

Each of these types is defined by Dore not only in terms of the phonemic features of the child's actual utterance but also in terms of the child's nonlinguistic behavior (such as focus of attention), the relevant contextual features, and the usual or anticipated adult response (see Table 1).

Functions of Early Child Language:
Summary and Conclusions

In reviewing the perspectives on language function offered in the more global accounts of Bruner and DeLaguna and the specific delineations of the pragmatics of emerging language offered by Halliday and Dore, we find much consistency. This

TABLE 1

Dore's Primitive Speech Act Types

Primitive speech act	Child's utterance	Child's nonlinguistic behavior	Adult response	Relevant contextual features
Labeling	Word	Attends to object or event; does does not address adult; does not await response.	Most often none; occasional repetition of child's utterance.	Salient feature focused on by child; no change in situation.
Repeating	Word or prosodic pattern	Attends to adult utterance before his utterance; may not address adult; does not await response.	Most often none; occasional repetition of child's utterance.	Utterance focused on; no change in situation.
Answering	Word	Attends to adult utterance before his utterance; addresses adult.	Awaits child's response; after child's utterance, most often acknowledges response; may then perform action.	Utterance focused on; no change in situation, unless child's response prompts adult reaction.
Requesting (action)	Word or marked prosodic pattern	Attends to object or event; addresses adult; awaits response; most often performs signaling gesture.	Performs action.	Salient feature focused on by child and adult; change in condition of object or child
Requesting (answer)	Word	Addresses adult; awaits response; may make gesture regarding object.	Utters a response.	No change in situation.
Calling	Word (with marked prosodic contour)	Addresses adult by uttering adult's name loudly; awaits response.	Responds by attending to child or answering child.	Before child's utterance, adult is some distance away; adult's orientation typically changes.
Greeting	Word	Attends to adult or object.	Returns a greeting utterance.	Speech event is initiated or ended.
Protesting	Word or marked prosodic pattern	Attends to adult; addresses adult; resists or denies adult's action.	Adult initiates speech event by performing an action the child does not like.	Adult's action is completed or child prevents action.
Practising	Word or prosodic pattern	Attends to no specific object or event; does not address adult; does not await response.	No response.	No apparent aspects of context is relevant to utterance.

NOTE. From "Holophrases, Speech Acts and Language Universals by J. Dore. *Journal of Child Language*, 1975, **2**, p. 33. Used by permission.

53

consistency is not surprising and, in fact, is mutually supportive, since all of these investigators have been dealing with the same general phenomenon. Further, comparison of the slightly different perspectives offered by each provides a total perspective of early language function which promises to be highly productive in terms of implications for clinical intervention. In Table 2, the accounts of function discussed in this section are juxtaposed. Terms used by the different authors which appear to refer to similar functions are placed horizontally parallel in the table. The conclusion that becomes most clear in examining this table is the existence in all accounts of the two broad types of functions described at the outset of this section—those which specifically serve to affect the actions of the listener and those which serve to join speaker and listener in some joint reference towards an ultimate objective which, at best, can only be inferred. The reader may recognize this gross distinction as being very similar to Skinner's (1957) constructs of "mand" and "tact" and, at a surface level, these terms are quite analogous to the two broad functions indentified here.[2] To avoid further proliferation of terminology, we have chosen to identify these two broad functions as Type I and Type II and define them behaviorally as follows:

Type I functions: The functions of requesting or demanding some overt behavioral response from the listener. Communicative acts of this type, therefore, specify their own reinforcer and provide a means of assessing the effectiveness of the communication in achieving that reinforcer through direct observation.

Type II functions: The functions of establishing joint reference with a listener where the ultimate intent or function is not specified by the content of the communicative act. While a response may be expected from the listener, the nature of this intended response is not specified in the communicative act and thus its effectiveness cannot be judged directly by an outside observer.

In Table 2, the specific types or categories of function presented are designated as being either Type I or Type II. Looking at this table, the reader will note a general consensus regarding the nature of Type I functions. Further, Dore's specific identification of the functions "protesting" and "calling" and Halliday's distinction between instrumental and regulatory functions seem to offer a fine-grained specificity which has particular value in targeting for clinical assessment. One point which should be made about Type I functions (and which may be surprising to those with behavioral leanings) is that Halliday found this type of function to be consistently the least common in the corpora of Nigel's early utterances.

In contrast to Type I functions, the Type II functions identified in Table 2 show a greater disparity among the functions identified by different authors. This disparity most certainly is due to the very nature of these functions—that is, the ambiguity regarding the speaker's underlying intent or objective. To avoid the trap of inferring intents, we should look at the consequences which typically attend certain types of communication and the apparent functions these serve for the child.

Perhaps the two broadest functions which seem to be served by Type II utterances are the acquisition and organization of knowledge about the world and the

---

[2]Skinner's complete functional analysis has not been discussed because, although his "mand" construct is defined in terms of communicative function—in terms of the effect on a listener—his "tact" is analyzed only in terms of the relationship between an antecedent stimulus and the speaker (for example, an object in the environment evokes a verbal label or tact).

TABLE 2

Communicative Functions of Children's Language

Bruner	DeLaguna	Halliday Stage I	Halliday Stage II	Dore
I Regulating joint actions	Influence a listener's acts	Instrumental	Pragmatic	Requesting action
		Regulatory		Calling
				Protesting
II		Interactional		Greeting
		Personal	Mathetic	Labeling
Regulating joint attention	Influence a listener's attitudes	Heuristic		Requesting answer
		Imaginative		Repeating
		(Informative)		Answering
				Practicing

acquisition and organization of knowledge about language itself. The former function would include Halliday's "heuristic" function and Dore's "requesting answer" (when used to test a hypothesis concerning the extension of a concept). The second function, which has been called metalinguistic (Premack, 1971), would presumably include Dore's "repeating," "practicing," and again "requesting answer" (when used to acquire or test a linguistic label for a known referent).

Another apparently basic function, referred to by Dore's "greeting" and Halliday's "interactional" categories, is signaling the initiation or termination of a social interaction. In adult interactions, this function is highly conventionalized and its omission is typically regarded as a sign of rude or asocial behavior. It is not surprising, therefore, that this function appears early in communication development. In fact, this may be the type of language behavior which is most consistently and directly trained by parents—It is common to see even the smallest infant being held aloft by a mother who, while waving the child's hand, urges "Wave bye-bye" or "Say hi." It would seem that this ability to signal the initiation or termination of an interaction in some conventionalized manner may be essential in assuring the child's opportunities for participation in the social interactions which are so critical to early development.

Dore's category "answering" points to an important consideration in any analysis of communicative function: the function of language produced in response to a question or directive from another individual may well be simply to indicate some willingness to comply or cooperate with the other speaker and may not reflect any autonomous intent. For example, it is probable that the young child who admits guilt for a missing cookie under direct questioning may well not have offered the information of his own volition. The implication of this point for clinical practice—particularly assessment—is that direct questioning and prompting for linguistic output from a child may produce data on the child's structural competence—and even compliance—but such data should not be interpreted as indicative of the communicative functions the child typically achieves through language.

A final function not reflected specifically in Table 2 is one which these writers have found from experience to be frequently reflected in children's language from the earliest stages. This is the function we will refer to as "entertainment." From the earliest ages, children seem to delight in the sheer sound of nonsense words and their power for evoking laughter from a listener. Nelson (1973a), in describing the type of language she calls "expressive," provides many examples of early utterances which were associated with ritualized games between the child and care giver (for example, "row row," "peek a boo," "up"). We are suggesting that the function of entertainment, including not only play with words but also words which specifically mark or signal social rituals or games, is one which is probably common in most emerging language repertoires and further, seems to be an important indicator that the child's emerging language is a truly social behavior system.

At this point, the reader should have a perspective of language as a vehicle through which we achieve specific communicative functions. Further, it has become evident that these functions are directly related to our interactions and integration within a social world. In the remainder of this chapter, we will examine the social-interactive bases which seem to underlie the child's acquisition of a functional communicative language system. We will first consider the social bases for the preverbal communication behaviors which, in turn, underlie later linguistic communication. Then we will examine the dynamics of social interactions as the vehicles through which a culture's linguistic structural code is transmitted to the young child.

Social Bases for
Preverbal Communication

During the early stages of development, nearly all language produced by the normally developing child is social in nature. Although adult language is often used for nonsocial covert functions (such as verbal mediation, problem solving, and so on), the very young child's language seems to be largely overt and closely related to social contexts. Vygotsky (1962) reports that even the self-imperative type of speech (for example, Billy says, "Billy push car" while pushing his toy car, but does not address the utterance to any listener), often thought of as egocentric, decreases greatly in the absence of a comprehending listener. Furthermore, several writers have argued that before the young child acquires linguistic structures for achieving pragmatic functions, he must already have established these communicative functions through nonverbal means in the context of social interactions (Bruner, 1974/75; Lewis & Freedle, 1972; Mahoney, 1975).

A Reason to Talk:
The Infant as a Social Being

The most basic implication of all this is that language acquisition, so conceptualized, requires and assumes that the child is a social being. If all the pragmatic functions of early language ultimately serve to effect cooperative interactions between the child and others in his environment, then the child must first have some basic desire or even "drive" to enter into such relationships. In other words, the child must have a *reason* to communicate.

This argument, of course, leads to the question, "How does the infant arrive at this level of socialization?" While it is impossible to answer this question definitively and while there may well be a significantly innate component in this process, recent analyses of mother-infant interactions have shed some light on this question.

Learning theory. One approach to the task of explaining how the human infant becomes a social being has been to analyze this process in the framework of behavioral learning theory. As the reader is surely aware, this theory suggests that all behavior can be accounted for in terms of the consequences which maintain or increase these behaviors—in other words, the reinforcers of the behaviors. Such reinforcers may be of two types—primary or secondary. Primary reinforcers are those consequences which directly satisfy a basic desire or need (such as food, or escape from pain). Secondary reinforcers, on the other hand, are initially neutral stimuli which are associated with the primary reinforcement until, through the process of stimulus generalization, they acquire reinforcing properties in themselves.

According to the principle of stimulus generalization, the feeding situation may be the basis for the infant's learning that the mother or caretaker is rewarding. Considered within the context of modeling principles (Bandura, 1972), this caretaker reinforcement property can subsequently be expected to contribute to the caretaker's behavior being more readily imitated. A feeding infant studies the face of his caretaker as he feeds and experiences simultaneously the alleviation of hunger, tactile contact, kinesthetic stimulation (from the cradled posture), and olfactory and auditory stimulation. In the context of feeding, the infant learns to associate comfortable, pleasant sensations with the sensory stimulation provided by his mother and to make the responses of visual scanning, babbling, smiling, and body adjustments in response to the feeding person.

This explanation of the socialization process seems to have some validity. However, other recent work in the study of early social development indicates that the process may be more subtle and complex than this behavioral approach would suggest. These new perspectives have grown out of the study of early infant attachment to significant adults.

Attachment theory. The concept of infant-mother "attachment," first set forth by Bowlby (1958, 1969), has received considerable attention in recent years and has generated much productive research. Although some of the interpretation and conclusions which were drawn on the basis of Bowlby's early work have since been disputed, the growing body of data documenting the attachment phenomenon is impressive. "Attachment" has been defined as:

> An affectional tie that one person or animal forms between himself and another specific one—a tie that binds them together in space and endures over time. The behavioral hallmark of attachment is seeking to gain and maintain a certain degree of proximity to the object of attachment, which ranges from close physical contact under some cir-

cumstances to interaction or communication across some distance under other circumstances. (Ainsworth & Bell, 1970, p. 50)

The key aspects of attachment which should be emphasized are that it is specific to one or a few persons and that it is enduring. Bowlby (1958, 1969) has argued that the tendency to form attachments and the behaviors by which this is accomplished have evolved as adaptive behaviors which function to assure the protection necessary for the relatively helpless human infant. It is generally argued that the infant is innately or genetically predisposed towards interactions with other humans and that many neonatal reflexes (such as rooting and sucking) provide the newborn infant with a repertoire for promoting and maintaining physical contact with adults (Ainsworth, Bell, & Stayton, 1974).

While this basic tendency is argued to be innate, research has indicated that environmental variables are also important in this process. In normal developmental environments (family units), the infant has opportunities to interact with one or a few adults who are consistently available to him and develops attachment bonds by about six months. There is some empirical indication that these attachments are formed with the figure(s) with whom the child has had the most interactions.

It has been found, however, that there are "striking and stable individual differences" in the quality and realization of the attachment bonds between infants and their mothers (Ainsworth et al., 1974). While suggesting that some of these variations may be accounted for by differences in the infants' innate behavioral tendencies, these authors were able to document four specific dimensions of maternal behavior which related to the nature of the attachment formed. It was found that behaviors which were associated with more stable attachment bonds were also significantly correlated with the child's compliance or obedience to maternal commands or prohibitions. On the other hand, more traditional "disciplinary" behaviors were not significantly related to the child's tendency to comply. The four critical dimensions of maternal behavior identified by these investigators are represented in the accompanying table.

Stable attachments and infant compliance		Unstable attachments
1. Sensitivity	←————————→	Insensitivity
2. Acceptance	←————————→	Rejection
3. Cooperation	←————————→	Interference
4. Accessibility	←————————→	Ignoring

Overall, then, the theory and data on attachment formation suggest that the consistent presence and accessibility of one or a few adults who are sensitive to and accepting of the infant's own behavioral tendencies—rather than being instrusive and insisting upon controlling all of the child's behavior—are critical environmental requirements if the child is to form successfully the attachment bonds which will serve as the basis for social interactions with the world of adults. Ironically, the environmental factors described here are precisely those which are most typically lacking in institutional settings. In fact, the implications of attachment theory for institutional care of young children have been the subject of recent study (Tizard & Tizard, 1974), but this is an area of concern which awaits much further empirical work. We will return to this issue in our discussion of implications for intervention.

Summary. At a theoretical level, the two theories of infant socialization described here—learning theory and attachment theory—represent almost diametrically opposed perspectives of the process, one treating the infant as a *tabla rasa* which must become socialized and the other viewing the infant as innately predisposed to social interactions from birth. In terms of clinical implications, both perspectives offer potentially productive insights for intervention with young, severely delayed children. Although these insights will be discussed in more detail later we will mention here that the data on attachment provide a model for structuring early living environments to the extent possible and that the learning theory model suggests an alternative means for developing social bonds where such environmental structuring is not feasible or sufficient.

As noted earlier, probably the most basic prerequisite for a child's acquisition of a functional language system is that he be a social being. In the preceding part of this chapter, we have examined some perspectives on the process by which the child attains this status. In addition to this general socialization, of course, it is also necessary for the child to learn the basic "communication game" and to develop preverbal means of communicating with the adults in the environment.

Function, Form, and Development of Preverbal Communication

The importance of preverbal communication in the child's language development appears to be two-fold. First, at the most general level, the child must learn to play the "communication game." That is, he must learn that through taking a role in the cooperative social exchange process we call *communication,* he can affect his environment and the people in it. This very general realization, which may at first seem trivial, assumes significance if we analyze the responsiveness of many institutional environments to the severely handicapped child's communicative signals. In highly regimented environments where the child's actions and interactions are controlled by noncontingent scheduling rather than being contingent upon the child's signaling, this realization may not develop.

The second important role of preverbal communication is to provide a basis for linguistic communication. Just as the child can only learn to talk about what he already knows, so too it seems that he can only learn to convey liguistically those functions which he already intends or accomplishes nonlinguistically. This notion that language maps existing communicative functions has been expressed repeatedly in the developmental literature (Bruner, 1974/75; Halliday, 1975; Mahoney, 1975) and appears to have particular clinical significance in designing an intervention model for severely language-delayed children. This section will consider the probable function, form, and development of the child's preverbal communication abilities.

Function. Before discussing the functions of preverbal communication, we should clarify the terms to be used. Although we frequently use the term "communicative intent" in describing function, the term "intent," if taken literally, is problematic. For example, while the infant's early crying most surely is communicative, it may not be appropriate to impute conscious intent to the infant in producing the cry. Similarly, the Type II functions discussed previously, in which the desired response from a listener is not specified, may or may not reflect any specific conscious intent from the young child. Thus, as Bruner has pointed out (1974/75), it has become customary to use the term "function" in discussing the pragmatic aspects of communication and to describe function in terms of the actual effects of a particular type of communication, rather than inferring underlying intent on the part of the speaker.

In identifying the functions of preverbal communication, we have two sources. First, the documentation of very early nonlinguistic realizations of these functions may be found at the preverbal level. Thus, we may infer, particularly from Halliday's (1975) Phase I data, that the four functions which he identified as being the first to be mapped linguistically (instrumental, regulatory, interactional, and personal) are probably those which the child has already achieved prelinguistically. Secondly, we may examine the data on infant-caregiver interactions and note the communicative functions which seem to be accomplished. From this perspective, it appears that infants communicate effectively in achieving: (1) relief from discomfort (such as wet diapers, hunger), (2) attainment of desired objects (for example a toy which has fallen from the infant's hand), (3) re-establishment of proximity with attachment figures (for example, when mother has walked out of the room), and (4) maintenance or initiation of an interaction with an adult through establishing joint reference (for example, a child indicates or attends to a preferred toy or game).

In Table 3, these two sets of hypothesized preverbal communication functions are juxtaposed. At the theoretical level, it is confirming to note that there appears to be a definite parallel between these two sets of differentially derived functions. (At this level, we cannot make our Type I and Type II distinction since the reinforcer of a nonverbal communicative act cannot be directly specified by semantic content.)

TABLE 3

Probable Preverbal Communicative Functions

Source I: Halliday's first four functions of early language	Source II: Analysis of mother-infant interactions
Personal function Description of a personal state, including notice or reaction	*Referencing* Routines established for assuring joint reference
Interactional function "Me and you"	*Establishment/re-establishment of proximity* Behaviors which serve to bring the mother to the infant
Instrumental function "Get me _____"	*Reaching routines* Reaches toward desired object out of reach
Regulatory function "Do this _____"	*Discomfort signals* Signals for relief from discomfort when hungry, diapers wet, etc.

While this analysis of the "pragmatics" of preverbal expressive communication remains to be empirically validated, the "face validity" of this close parallel suggests that these four broad functions are potentially productive as initial targets for assessing and intervening in the communication repertoires of nonverbal, language-delayed children.

Form. A second question regarding the nature of preverbal expressive communication concerns the forms through which this is carried out. Bruner (1974/75) posits a developmental sequence of four types of infant signals in the first year. The earliest infant intention-imputing signals are in the *demand mode* (primarily crying to express discomfort). Demand signals usually function quite effectively for the infant as they bring the mother into contact, or at least proximity. If demand mode signals are responded to appropriately, an expectancy of response is established and demand signals become request signals. *Request mode* signals are neither as intense nor as insistent as demand signals and the infant often pauses to ascertain whether the anticipated caretaker response is forthcoming. Both Bruner (1975) and Dore (1975) have noted that even at this early stage the infant has begun to mark communicative functions differentially with the stress and intonational patterns which will form the paralinguistic component of his expressive language. The third signaling mode is the *exchange mode* which begins with the infant gesturally indicating demands for objects and progresses to verbal requests for the receipt of objects. At this stage, role reversal is observed with the infant receiving, then handing back, then requesting again, receiving again, and so on. A *reciprocal mode* then gradually replaces the exchange mode. Mother-child interactions and signaling begin to revolve around a joint task format which has a "taking turns" rule (among other standardizations). This developmental progression in types and quality of signaling over the first year appears to be of central importance both for the development of speech acts and the establishment of interaction rules for later grammatical structures.

In considering the form of these early communication exchanges, it is important to note that the child is also developing receptive communicative abilities. In other words, the child is learning to respond differentially to the communicative input he received from the environment. The next section will analyze the form of this input more fully. Note here, however, that the aspects of input form to which the preverbal infant responds include not only contextual and gestural cues, but also adult intonation and stress patterns (Bruner, 1975; Lewis, 1936; Menyuk, 1974).

Development. Finally, and perhaps most importantly, we must address the question, How does the infant develop expressive communication abilities? (We will look at the development of receptive abilities in a later section.) Most basically, it appears that the infant learns to communicate intentionally, and refines his communicative repertoire as a result of environmental responsiveness to his earliest, almost reflexive communicative behaviors.

There is evidence that caregivers are able to respond differentially to an infant's signals (smiling, fretting, and even different crying patterns) almost from the moment of birth (Richards, 1974; Wolff, 1963, 1969), conferring the status of social communication on some infant behaviors as early as the first weeks of life. This apparently inherent caregiver sensitivity and skill in decoding and adding to signaling patterns seem to be critical to the infant's entry into the "communication game," for it is presumably through these early experiences that the child first realizes the value of human communication.

The dynamics of maternal responsiveness to infant crying were examined by Bell and Ainsworth (1972) in a longitudinal observational study of 26 mother-child dyads which spanned the infant's first year of life. In this study, promptness of maternal responsiveness was found to be associated with a steady decrease in both rate and duration of crying in the last quarter of the infant's first year. Of particular interest was the finding that infants for whom crying was most functional in terms of evoking caregiver responsiveness developed the most adequate and varied range of more sophisticated communication signals, such as facial expressions, gestures, and vocalization in their second year. In a more recent study, Ainsworth, Bell, and Stayton (1974) point to four essential components of maternal sensitivity: (1) awareness of the infant's signals, (2) accurate interpretation of these signals, (3) appropriateness of response, and (4) promptness in responding.

Another line of recent infant research which appears particularly relevant here is the transitional analysis of responding patterns in mother-child interactions. Those studying vocal interactions (Bateson, 1971; Strain, 1974; Vietze & Strain, 1975) consistently report a reciprocal or alternating pattern which Bateson (1971) has described as constituting "protoconversations." Similar procedures have been used in analyzing gaze patterns in mother-infant interactions by Stern (1974), who concluded that three- and four-month-old infants can regulate social interactions through the control of gaze behavior, and by Kendon (1967) who characterized the gaze interactions of the infant as an early form of "dialogic exchange." Summed, these findings seem to add credence to the notion of an evolving set of reciprocal or conversational communicative behaviors.

Bruner (1975) points up the critical function of caregiver-infant play rituals in aiding the infant to further elaborate his signaling system. Maternal sensitivity now takes the form of inferring the infant's communicative intentions rather than simply his physiological state. Bruner traced the development of various forms of mother-infant interaction by observing six dyads from the time the infants were 7 months old until 13 months. Mothers tended to interpret their infant's intentions in one of two ways. Some mothers interpreted their child's intentional behavior in terms of intended actions and seemed to see their own role as supporting the child's attempts to achieve action outcomes. Other mothers interpreted their child's intentional behavior as information seeking. The latter interpretation resulted in such maternal facilitating responses as handing the child an out-of-reach object at which he was gazing or simply following the infant's gaze to note where he was looking.

These data are compatible with Ryan's (1974) classification of cues used by mother/caretakers to interpret their infant's communicative intent (adapted from Austin, 1962). Successful mothers used the following cues to decode infants' nonstandard sounds: (1) aspects of the utterance (intonation patterns), (2) accompaniments of the utterance (pointing, searching, refusing, etc., and the physical state of the infant), and (3) circumstances of the utterance (context).

Finally, Escalona (1973) also studied the question of how communication first develops. In her study, Escalona identified 17 categories of social responses in the two infants she observed for 24 months. She calls these "social input responses" and defines them as occasions when the baby responded to an alteration in the perceptual field initiated by the other person. In both of the children she observed, 13 of the 17 social responses showed the same order of emergence. Most had emerged by the age of six or seven months, although the forms in which they occurred appeared to change with advancing age. By five and one-half months, infant social signals such as showing things, initiating reciprocal games, and expressing wishes and demands were observed, and like the caretaker-initiated responses, they emerged in a distinguishable sequence. Particularly noteworthy is Escalona's observation that a given signal emerges in the infant's expressive repertoire about three months after he gives evidence of having discriminated that particular input—presumably evidence of the commonly observed receptive-expressive time lag.

Summary. It is apparent that in the process of natural child development, the ability to achieve a variety of specific communicative functions effectively through nonverbal means appears very early and is highly refined by the end of the first year of life. While this remarkable achievement may to some extent be attributable to the sort of innate predisposition to social interactions posited by attachment theory (discussed previously), there appear to be critical environmental factors which are essential to the child's actual realization of this ability. Specifically, it seems that the environment must provide: (1) responsive adults (usually caregivers) who interpret and respond to the infant's communicative behaviors and (2) frequent opportunities for participation in play rituals with adults. In a later chapter, we will consider the implications of these findings for clinical assessment and intervention with young, severely language-delayed children.

Having considered the pragmatics of early language and the social bases for preverbal communication, we now turn our focus to the final topic of this chapter: social bases for the acquisition of linguistic structure.

Social Bases for the Acquistion of Linguistic Structure

Although there is much controversy among developmental linguists regarding the degree to which a child may be innately predisposed for language acquisition, there is a consensus that the infant must learn the specific linguistic forms and structures of his culture through some process of social transmission. This final section examines data on the specific aspects of the child's interactions with mature speakers in his social world which seem to be essential to this transmission process.

The Learning Process

Over the years, several theories have been advanced regarding the nature of the structural learning process. These can be discussed in terms of four major approaches: reinforcement, expansion, imitation, and comprehension. As will become evident, all of these accounts assume the learning process to be transactional or interactional in nature—that is, all suggest that the child acquires linguistic structure in the context of some interaction with a mature speaker. However, the level of contribution posited for each member of these interactions varies as does the general reciprocity ascribed to the process. We will first consider the data on reinforcement, expansion, and imitation and then examine the apparent role of comprehension in the language acquisition process. Finally, we will suggest a model of this process as a reciprocal transaction.

Reinforcement. One explanation of the way children acquire linguistic structure is that they are selectively reinforced for producing utterances which are increasingly correct structurally. While this theory has intuitive appeal, it has not been supported by the data. Brown and his colleagues have specifically tested this hypothesis by examining the nature of response-consequence contingencies which actually operate in parent-child verbal interactions (Brown, Cazden & Bellugi, 1969; Brown & Hanlon, 1970). These investigators found that "there is not a shred of evidence that approval and disapproval are contingent on syntactic correctness" (Brown et al., 1969, p. 70). What this study did show was that when adult approval and disapproval were given, they were contingent upon the truth value of the child's utterance rather than its structural correctness:

> Thus, *Her curl my hair* was approved because the mother was, in fact, curling Eve's hair. However, Sarah's grammatically impeccable *There's the animal farmhouse* was disapproved because the building was a lighthouse. (Brown et al., 1969, p. 70)

Dale (1972) notes that the reinforcement theory is also contraindicated by the common parental practice of responding to the communicative intents of their children rather than to their syntactic correctness. (As we noted earlier this tendency is critical to the development of communication behavior in general.) Thus, Dale suggests that the child who says "mi" will be given milk by his mother, but that a short time later he will begin to produce a more advanced form of the request—for example "want milk"—although his mother would still be willing to reinforce the more primitive "mi."

Thus, it seems that reinforcement learning theory does not adequately account for the young child's acquisition of structure or even the refinement of existing structures. We should not, however, totally reject the value of reinforcement in the child's acquisition of language. Rather, it seems that reinforcement should be defined in terms of the realization of some communicative function or intent and that it probably serves more to increase the general class of communicative behavior than the more specific subclass of correct linguistic structure.

Expansion. A second and more widely accepted account of the structure-learning process is that parents teach correct structure through providing an expanded model of the child's own utterance (for example—Child: "Daddy shirt." Father: "Yes, Daddy put on his shirt."). While there is no question that this type of verbal exchange does occur in parent-child interactions, the actual frequency and value of such expansions remain subjects of controversy.

Supporting this theory, Brown and Bellugi (1964) reported that middle-class parents expanded 30% of their children's utterances. For example:

Child: "Baby highchair" ⟶ Mother: *"Baby* is in the *highchair"*

Child: "Eve lunch" ⟶ Mother: *"Eve* is having *lunch"*

Child: "Sat wall" ———————————————————→ Mother: "He *sat* on the
                                                        wall"

(Brown & Bellugi, 1964, p. 141)

Furthermore, Slobin (1968) noted that when children imitated the expanded models provided by adults, their imitative utterances were most often more linguistically correct than the original utterances had been. For example:

Child: Pick 'mato
Adult: Picking tomatoes up?
Child: Pick 'mato up.
(Slobin, 1968, cited in Dale, 1972, p. 117)

On the other hand, several recent studies in which the nature of parental speech directed towards a language-learning child was observed and quantified revealed that, in fact, such expansions represented only a very small proportion of such speech acts (Friedlander, Jacobs, Davis, & Wetstone, 1972; Ling & Ling, 1974; Nelson, 1973a). Furthermore, Brown, Cazden, and Bellugi (1969) found that the order of emergence of five regular inflections in the speech of their subjects correlated with the frequency with which those inflections were used by the parents in free speech, rather than with the frequency with which these inflections were provided in expansions for the child. Finally, in a study in which expansions were employed as an intervention procedure, Cazden (1965) found that this procedure was less effective in improving the language structure of toddler-aged children in a day-care setting than was a procedure in which well-formed sentences relevant to the substance of a child's utterance were provided in response to each child utterance.

Thus, it seems that the role of expansions in the transmission of linguistic structure is far from clear. At best, it seems that this behavior, when exhibited by adults, is only useful when: (1) the child is already producing at least two-word utterances which afford grammatical expanding, (2) the expansion includes structures which the child is "ready" to begin producing, (this point will become clearer when we discuss imitation), and (3) the expansion remains within the child's receptive competence.

Imitation. Perhaps the most controversial theory of structure acquisition is that the child learns his culture's linguistic code through imitation. Again, although this approach has some intuitive appeal in that it is consistent with most adults' experiences with very young children, empirical scrutiny has generally failed to support this theory. Basically, two broad types of evidence are cited in refuting this account of structure acquisition. First, it is obvious that many of the structures found in early language repertoires would not have been learned from an adult model. Thus, we assume that such child utterances as "All gone sticky," "Mommy blouse on," "Eating mommy cookie," and "Put away Allison bag," were constructed by the child and not learned through imitation.

A second line of argument against the imitation account of structure learning is identified by Dale (1972). He cites the evidence that children who could never imitate an adult utterance nonetheless may manage to attain the highest level of syntactic competence in their receptive language. Here he notes the case reported by Lenneberg of a boy who, due to neuromuscular disability, was unable to produce an articulated speech sound but who was able to comprehend language and thus had learned, without benefit of any imitation, to decode linguistic structure.

Although imitation may not account for the child's acquisition of linguistic/syntactic structure, there are still other reasons for which we should consider this process in looking at the total process of language learning. First, despite the fact that imitation may not be an essential component of the natural syntactic acquisition process, it does have empirically demonstrated value as a language-training procedure in cases of delayed or deviant development.

Secondly, it seems entirely probable that imitation is functional in the development and refinement of the phonemic and paralinguistic expression of language. The articulation of speech sounds is a complex motor act and, like other motor acts, is probably learned through overt practice and, in the case of a conventionalized behavior like speech, this practice must strive towards matching an observed (heard) model. If this is the case, we would expect to see imitation particularly evident at the one-word stage, when the child adds new words (and thus new phonemic entities) to his lexicon at a geometric rate. In fact, two studies do lend support to this view of the function of imitation in mastering new words.

The language development of 18 children was studied longitudinally from the age of 12 months to 24 months by Nelson (1973a), who measured, among many other variables, the verbal imitation behaviors of each child. Nelson found a significant (p < .01) positive correlation between the amount of imitation at 21 months and both the size of vocabulary and the Mean Length of Utterance (MLU) at two years. However, imitation at two years was slightly negatively correlated with these other measures of language development at that age. In addition, Nelson reports that very little imitation occurred before a child was spontaneously producing at least a few words. In discussing her findings, the investigator suggests that imitation may be an important strategy during the early stages of language development, when the child's primary task is the acquisition of lexical items. However, the strategy ceases to be functional, or may even be counterproductive, at a later stage when the child's primary task is the acquisition of syntactic structures.

Further support for the function of imitation, at least during the lexical acquisition period, comes from Dore's (1975) analysis of children's speech during the one-word, or "holophrastic" stage. Dore characterized the children's utterances in terms of the communicative intent or function which they mapped. In so doing, Dore identified nine distinct types of speech acts common in these early language samples. One of these nine categories is imitation or, as Dore labels it, "repeating." It is illustrated by the following example from Dore's data:

> M, while playing with a puzzle, overhears her mother's utterance of "doctor" (in a conversation with the teacher) and M utters "datə"; mother responds "Yes, that's right honey, 'doctor,'" and then continues her conversation; M resumes her play with the puzzle. (p. 31)

It seems highly probable, at least on an intuitive basis, that this child's imitation, paired with the resultant confirmation from mother, served as a means for the child to confirm and rehearse her own production of a supposedly familiar word. It must be realized, however, that the actual significance of this imitation could only be analyzed in light of a knowledge of the child's previous experience with and knowledge of the referent situation associated with "doctor."

Further, although imitation may not be essential to natural development, there is evidence that when it does occur it is closely related to the child's existing level of linguistic competence and specifically to his ability to comprehend the utterance. Dale (1972) has noted, for example, that when children do imitate adult utterances, they will paraphrase and reduce the model in their imitation so that the imitative version retains the meaning of the adult utterance, but the structure more closely reflects the child's own productive level. This common finding in turn suggests that children imitate only that which has some meaning for them. Another example comes from Bloom's (1974) report of Peter's use of imitation. She recorded Peter's utterances in a free-play context and then later, in a different setting, read the utterances back and asked Peter to imitate them. Without the supporting context which originally gave the utterances meaning, Peter was unable to imitate his own utterances. Finally, in a recent in-depth treatise on the role of imitation, Bloom, Hood, and Lightbown (1974) have concluded that imitation is not random but highly selective when it does occur. These investigators conducted an in-depth analysis of the spontaneous verbal imitation behavior of six children and the changes which occurred in this behavior as the children developed from an MLU of 1 to an MLU of 2. To greatly simplify their findings, these investigators reported that:

1. During the period studied, each child's rate of imitation tended to remain constant or decreased.
2. These children tended to imitate only those words and structures which they had begun to produce spontaneously.
3. As a child became more proficient in the spontaneous production of a particular lexical or structural type, he tended to imitate this type of utterance less.

Thus it appears that there is some systematic selection process operating in the child's verbal imitation, at least during these early stages. Further, this selective imitation may represent the process by which the child perfects the ability to map those linguistic forms and structures orally which he already comprehends and is beginning to produce spontaneously.

Finally, an interesting result reported by Shipley, Smith, and Gleitman (1969) further testifies to the selective and strategic nature of verbal imitation. These investigators found that children speaking in two- and three-word "telegraphic" utterances were increasingly likely to imitate a verbal command as the linguistic complexity of that command increased. The presence of a nonsense (and thus unfamiliar) word also increased the probability of imitation. Perhaps more significantly, the imitated commands were most likely to be responded to correctly. Again, then, there is evidence that early verbal imitation is selective and serves in some way to help the language learning child lock-in the linguistic information appropriate to his level of development.[3]

We can conclude, then, that both expansion and imitation may contribute to the child's refinement of his expressive language, but that both depend to a large extent upon the child's ability to comprehend the utterances being expanded or modeled.

[3]Since the writing of this report, the authors have prepared a paper in which the role of imitation in early language acquisition is treated in more depth. Interested readers should write to the authors at the Parsons Research Center, Parsons, Kansas 67357, and request Working Paper #332.

Consequently, comprehension occupies a critical role in any account of how language is acquired.

Comprehension. Having considered the process of language development and noted that all roads eventually lead us back to the child's comprehension of language, we now address the most difficult question of all: How does the human infant first come to comprehend the language which he hears? By "comprehend" we are referring to the ability to derive meaning—more specifically, to derive the speaker's intended meaning—from a perceived communicative act. The answer to the question of how this ability first develops is, then, derivable only through an inferential process. We are asking a question about the infant's internal cognitive/linguistic processing of incoming stimuli and thus have no direct means of observing or analyzing the process.

In our review of the literature, the most viable and cogent attempt which we found to explain this initial acquisition is that offered by MacNamara (1972). To simplify, MacNamara concludes that the infant initially uses known meaning as a clue to language form. In other words, the child learns the linguistic code by inferring the meaning of a perceived linguistic input as it co-occurs with a referent which already has meaning within the child's own cognitive/conceptual system. This explanation, of course, is consistent with the perspectives on cognitive bases for language acquisition outlined earlier in this book.

Such an explanation of initial acquisition as a process of decoding an incoming linguistic stimulus on the basis of an already established and known referent suggests clearly that this first stage in language learning is receptive in nature. This conclusion is consistent with the commonly held view that reception/comprehension precedes production (Fraser, Bellugi, & Brown, 1963; Lovell & Dixon, 1967) as well as the findings by Escalona (1973) reported earlier that communicative intents were expressed only after they were responded to as input-stimuli. In recent years, there has been some controversy and reevaluation of the reception-precedes-production theory and it is now clear that this relationship is not as simple as it seems. (This issue will be addressed in a later chapter when we look at the sequence of linguistic development.) At these earliest acquisition stages, however, all data seem consistent with MacNamara's account.

The most basic conclusion to be drawn from this perspective of comprehension as the critical key for the child's entry into the language system is that there are two elements which must be present in early child-adult interactions if the child is to achieve this entry. First, the adult must provide appropriate input in co-occurrence with known and established referents; and second, the child must decode that input by associating it with the appropriate referent.

Transactional model. On the basis of all the perspectives discussed to this point regarding the process of language acquisition and development, we have arrived at a transactional model of this process. Specifically, we have concluded that language learning occurs as a product of dynamic reciprocal partnerships established between the child and the mature speakers in his environment. Further, this partnership demands contributions from both members—and most basically, the partnership demands mutual responsiveness between adult and child. Thus, it seems to be critical for the adult to be sensitive to and to respond to the child's specific efforts at communication, as well as to the child's general level of communicative/linguistic functioning. For his part, the child must attend, process, and respond to the linguistic/communicative models provided by the adult.

In the following pages, we will look at the evidence which is available concerning the specific nature of both the adult and child behaviors which seem to function in natural interactions to assure that these mutually responsive roles are fulfilled.

Facilitating Adult Behaviors

One way in which adults assist the child in learning to play the communication game is by responding to the intents expressed in early child signaling behaviors. We will now look at behaviors manifested by adults in interactions with language-learning children which serve more specifically to assist such children in mastering the linguistic structure of their culture's language. The data indicate that these facilitating adult behaviors serve two primary functions: to demonstrate the parsing or segmenting of dynamic events and relationships which is reflected in the semantic component of language, and to provide appropriate models of the lexical and syntactic structures by which this semantic component is "mapped."

Semantic segmenting. Bruner (1975) has dealt extensively with the role of dynamic interactions in the child's formation of basic concepts which underlie semantic roles and relationships. He notes that mothers seem to set up standard interaction routines (usually in play) to provide their infants with an opportunity to learn to predict their mother's behavior and essentially calibrate their attention with hers. The principal form of signaling observed by Bruner was "marking the segments of action" (p. 12). The infant, for example, offers back a toy which mother has handed him and she says "Thank you;" or she says "Aboom" after he removes a ring from a ring-and-peg toy.

In another paper, Bruner (1974/75) further expands his notion of the critical importance of mother-child interaction variables. He contends that caretakers systematically train their children in the procedures of reference (differentiation among a set of objects and subsequent tagging of a single object) within joint action sequences. Three specific reference training strategies are elaborated. The first, "indicating," can be observed as the caretaker follows the infant's "line of regard" to infer the child's attention focus and subsequently his demands. The tendency of mothers to follow their infants' line of regard has been demonstrated by Collis and Schaffer (1975), who also reported that such establishment of a visually shared referent was followed by a maternal utterance directly relating to that referent. "Marking" by the mother/caretaker of a target object is another early form of indicating. The mother shakes an object or exaggerates an action in some way to attract the child's attention or to reestablish joint attention. "Deixis" (the use of spatial, temporal, and interpersonal contextual features as joint reference cues) is the second aspect of early reference observed in mother-child interacting routines. At a prelinguistic level, deixis takes the form of such reversible role games as peek-a-boo. The third aspect of early joint reference is "naming" which facilitates the child's acquisition of linguistic tags for the objects in his environment. From these three reference training routines, then, we have some basis for inferring the joint-action experiences which lead ultimately to the child's construction of an early cognitive map.

Further confirmation for Bruner's perspective is provided by Wells (1974) who also points up the critical importance of the caretaker's ritualized structuring of the infant's physical and verbal environments. According to Wells, the meanings which the child constructs prelinguistically are heavily dependent upon the direction of his focus of attention by caretakers. A study by Clarke-Stewart (1973) lends further support to the argument with her finding that children's cognitive development (as measured by the *Bayley Scales of Infant Development*) and the complexity of their play with objects (observational data) are highly correlated with the amount of time spent in joint object-play routines between mother and child. The fact that cognitive development was not related to the general level of stimulation available in the physical environment points up the critical importance of the caregiver as object/ event mediator.

Thus, it seems appropriate to conclude that the child's development of the cognitive structures and organization which will provide the basis for semantic decoding and encoding of language derive in large measure from his interactions with adults—particularly those with the primary caregiver. Specifically, it seems that the adult's contribution to this process consists of three interrelated "teaching strategies": (1) linguistic and extralinguistic marking of the segments of the interactions (for example, mother raises her eyebrows, throws up her hands and says "aboom!" after a stack of blocks has tumbled to the floor); (2) establishing joint reference or directing the child's attention to relevant elements of an event or relationship; and (3) demonstrating, encouraging, and providing opportunities for the child to explore, manipulate, and discover the relational and dynamic properties of objects in his world.

Structural modeling. In addition to and concurrent with the semantic facilitation provided by the adult in interactions with the young child, a second type of "teaching strategy" appears to be the provision of linguistic models which will facilitate the child's task of mastering the syntactic and lexical code of his language.

Evidence of the importance of such antecedent verbal modeling or stimulation is provided in monograph by Clarke-Stewart (1973), who measured a wide variety of maternal and child variables over the period when the infants were between 9 and 18 months of age. A considerable number of correlations between specific mother and child variables were found. For example, children's language ability was found to be more related to the mother's nonresponsive speech (initiating/eliciting speech) than to responsive verbalizations, which confirms Cazden's (1965) observation that the young child needs a language model more than a language reinforcer. Similarly, the number of vocalizations (by the child) directed to the mother was significantly related to maternal verbal stimulation, confirming the findings of a substantial number of previous studies (Bateson, 1971; Bing, 1963; Goldberg & Lewis, 1969; Gordon, 1969; Irwin, 1960; Kagan, 1971; Lewis & Freedle, 1972; Milner, 1951; Schaefer, Furley, & Harte, 1968).

Probably the most obvious device used by adults to assist the young child in comprehending an utterance is the exaggeration of normal stress and intonation. It seems probable that this paralinguistic support facilitates the child's efforts to parse out the discrete phonemic elements contained in an utterance and to recognize those elements which are most important. Brown (1973) has noted that the meaning-carrying or substantive elements of a sentence (such as the subject and verb) are typically more heavily stressed than the function elements (such as articles, auxiliary verbs) and suggests this may account for the child's exclusive use of substantive words and omission of function words in early utterances. In addition, certain intonation patterns which are consistently paired with specific communicative functions probably provide the child with an additional clue to the meaning of the incoming linguistic stimulus.

A second type of facilitating behavior by adults is the reduction of length and complexity of utterances addressed to language-learning children. Thus, it has been found that, although parents tend to direct as much speech to preverbal children as to those who have already begun to use language (Ling & Ling, 1974), the utterances addressed to younger children are typically reduced in terms of both length (Nelson, 1973a) and complexity (Baldwin, 1973; Broen, 1972). When Phillips (1973) compared mothers' speech to children of different ages with that to an adult, he found that the adult-directed utterances were longer, contained more verbs and a greater variety of verb forms, more modifiers, more function words, and fewer concrete nouns. A closely related finding is that adults tend to use less complex language when addressing lower-level retarded persons (Siegel & Harkins, 1963). In fact, Shatz and Gelman (1973) recently reported that even 4-year-old children use such reduction strategies in "talking down" to less linguistically mature 2-year-old children.

In addition to reducing syntactic complexity, it seems that adults typically reduce the conceptual or semantic complexity of the lexical content of utterances spoken to a young child. Brown (1958, 1965) was one of the first investigators to study systematically the word choices which parents make when verbally interacting with their young children. Without conscious thought, parents selectively apply labels at the level of generality which they judge to match their child's cognitive development. For example, at one developmental level a mother would not select and label a dog as "collie," because she knows that such a discrimination would not be meaningful to the child. However, she would not label it as "animal" either, because she is aware that this categorization would be too broad for the child to understand. The data from a more recent study confirm Brown's findings. Anglin (1975) asked mothers to label a set of object pictures, first as if they were naming them for their 2-year-old children and then as if they were naming them for an adult. In agreement with the findings of the previous two studies, Anglin's mothers applied quite different nouns to the same set of objects depending upon the population for whom they were labeling. Though there do not appear to be any data demonstrating that this parental selectivity phenomenon occurs for other than object labeling, an assumption that it might also occur for other word classes would seem to be justifiable.

The importance of matching linguistic input to cognitive development is expanded by Nelson (1973a). She points to the critical importance of matching linguistic input to the child's conceptual *style*. In her study of children's acquisition of their first 50 words, Nelson found that mothers who use language in a way that is consonant with their children's cognitive style facilitate more rapid vocabulary acquisition than mothers whose language style contrasts with their child's. In particular, "great difficulty seems to arise when the mother uses language primarily in a R [reference] mode [for naming and describing objects and events] while the child has organized the world primarily in an active or social mode or the reverse" (p. 103).

In addition to providing language models which are reduced in both length and complexity and appropriate to the child's conceptual organization, there is evidence that mature language users provide further assistance to listeners who have not yet mastered the language code through paraphrasing and frequent repetition of utterances directed toward such listeners (Friedlander, Jacobs, Davis, & Wetstone, 1972; Phillips, 1973; Snow, 1972). Furthermore, Snow (1972) found that nonparents are just as likely as parents to demonatrate this type of modeling behavior and that it occurs quite unintentionally. Baldwin (1973) also noted that parents reported being unconscious of the seemingly systematic modifications which they made in their speech when addressing young children. This is not surprising if we think back to our own encounters with infants or toddlers and imagine a transcript of our utterances during those encounters. Such a transcript might include many redundant statements such as: "What do you see? Huh? What is that? What is it? Is it a flower? Flower? Yes, it's a flower. Look at the pretty flower." Unless we are psycholinguists or language clinicians by trade, we probably do not make a conscious effort to provide an optimal language model for the child in accordance with both learning theory and validated teaching practices. However, it seems quite likely that this is just what the mature language user does in natural (one is tempted to say "almost instinctive") verbal interactions with those who are just learning the language.

Mahoney (1975) has suggested that all of these modifications conform to Hunt's (1961) theory regarding the critical importance of a minimal discrepancy between the learner's present knowledge level and the difficulty level of a stimulus input. According to Hunt, if this discrepancy is either too large or too small the result will be, respectively, either total frustration or total boredom. It is Mahoney's (1975) contention that adults are actualizing this principle when they effortlessly provide language input which is just slightly more sophisticated or complex than that currently being produced by the child.

Similarly, the common tendency of adults to paraphrase and repeat utterances which they address to a child is consonant with the clinical and educational practice of providing multiple stimuli in slightly varying forms and contexts for the purpose of promoting concept formation and learning generalization. Thus, we must agree with Snow (1972) when she concludes that a major value of "the modifications which mothers produce for young children . . . is that simplified speech is admirably designed to aid children in learning language. This makes it somewhat easier to understand how a child can accomplish the formidable task of learning his native language with such relative ease" (p. 564).

Summary. After reviewing the adult behaviors which seem to facilitate the child's mastery of the semantic, lexical, and syntactic components of his language, we concur with Bruner (1975), who suggests that at these early stages of acquisition the natural language teacher is "an interpreting adult who operates not so much as a corrector or reinforcer but rather as a provider and idealizer of utterances while interacting with the child" (p. 17).

The Child's Role
in the Process

The adult-facilitating behaviors described above are only functional in assisting the language acquisition process to the extent that the child also contributes to the partnership. Specifically, the child must attend and respond to (as well as process) the linguistic models provided if he is to benefit from them. In this section, we will look at some of the child behaviors which seem to serve this function.

Selective listening. It seems probable that one critical element in the language acquisition process is the learner's success in gathering only that linguistic information which is useful at a particular point in his language development. An intuitively logical and appealing procedure for assuring such success would be to provide each child with some sort of filtering or censoring device which would screen out all linguistic input judged too complex or too basic to be of value to the child in his current stage of language development. In fact, it appears that a process of this type may exist in the natural interactions between young children and the mature language users in their environment. The child's contribution to this hypothesized process will be referred to here as "selective listening."

It is apparent, from the preceding review of adult facilitating behaviors, that mature language users facilitate this "filtering" process through their a priori modifications of the language which they address to linguistically immature listeners. Thus, the child's task is not to screen out the irrelevant components of every utterance to which he is exposed. Rather, the task (only slightly less formidable) is to take in only those utterances which have been modified for the child and to filter out those which are intended and appropriate for more sophisticated receivers. Such a process would constitute a child's discrimination of utterances as functional or nonfunctional for his particular language-learning needs.

Thus, we hypothesize that children who are successful in learning their native language through natural interactions must bring to these interactions some type of selective listening strategy. In fact, several investigators (Huttenlocher, 1974; Nelson, 1973; Snow, 1972) have speculated, somewhat parenthetically, on the importance of the "child's own ability to attend selectively to simple, meaningful and comprehensible utterances" (Snow, 1972).

Tentative support for this hypothesis can be derived from the results of a study conducted by Lewis and Freedle (1972). These investigators analyzed the vocalization patterns of 80 mother-infant dyads when the infants were three months old and found that, for many of the infants (especially the females), there was a significant difference between the infant's vocalizing response when the mother's utterance was addressed to the infant and when her utterance was addressed to another adult in the room. In other words, these infants were discriminating themselves from others as the objects of mother's verbalizations. Even more intriguing, though not so statistically impressive, is the initial follow-up data which were collected from three of the subjects when they reached the age of two years. For these three subjects, the rank ordering of their ability to discriminate themselves as the object of mother's utterance at three months predicted the rank ordering of their performance on a variety of language measures at two years of age. If these findings prove replicable, and if it can be demonstrated that the critical predictive variable is discriminative attending to utterances which are modified in accordance with the adult-facilitating behaviors described earlier, these findings may represent a direct demonstration of selective listening at work even in the first few months of life.

Further support can be found in the results of the Shipley et al. (1969) study in which the investigators analyzed the responses to controlled verbal commands of

11 subjects between the ages of 18 and 33 months. Briefly, the data from this experiment indicated that children who spoke primarily in one-word utterances were most apt to respond to commands consisting of one or two words, while children whose speech was characterized by two- and three-word "telegraphic" utterances were most apt to respond to well-formed grammatical commands. This finding can be interpreted as a demonstration that the children were responding discriminatively to utterance forms which were optimally discrepant from (that is, slightly more complex than) their own production level. In discussing their results, the investigators speculate that "if. . .the child does not 'tune in' to excessively complex or unfamiliar speech, this selective listening may provide him with a tractable corpus . . . To this extent, the child's effective linguistic environment is not the total indefinitely variable corpus of adult speech, nor a haphazard sample of that total" (p. 338).

The possibility that even young infants attack their linguistic environment with an efficient and systematic selective listening strategy is less incredible than it may seem at first. In recent years, researchers interested in the parameters of infant speech perception have repeatedly demonstrated that even in the first few months of life human infants do discriminate speech from nonspeech sounds in their environment and familiar from unfamiliar voices (Friedlander, 1968; Turnure, 1971); that they discriminate between contrasting phonemic or segmental features (Eimas, 1974; Moffitt, 1971); and that they discriminate between different suprasegmental or intonational patterns (Kaplan, 1969). Given this type of early discriminative repertoire, it seems reasonable to suggest that the infant has the capability to listen selectively on more functional, communicative levels.

Establishing joint reference. In addition to gathering only the most appropriate linguistic input, the language-learning child must also have some strategy for identifying, from the myriad of available objects and events which may co-occur with a given child-directed utterance, that referent which is intended by the speaker. To some extent, this task of matching a referent to its linguistic map is assured through the maternal behaviors designed to establish joint reference, as described previously. However, by its very nature, joint reference requires mutual attending, and it is thus critical that the child be able to obtain from the interaction some perceptual information regarding the immediate contextual referent of the utterance to be "decoded." Bruner (1975) has suggested that this is accomplished in mother-child interactions through what he has described as "the elaborate construction of routines for assuring joint reference" (p. 9) which, he further suggests, originate in the establishment of eye-to-eye contact. It would seem that in order to function as an active partner in establishing these routines, the language-learning child must have a class of referencing behaviors most likely consisting of such behaviors as maintenance of eye contact, following a line of regard and/or following the physical movement of mother's hand or body.

Again, available empirical evidence clearly demonstrates that infants have the capabilities required to employ these behaviors toward the establishment of joint reference. Several studies of visual behavior of infants have documented the existence of eye contact between mother and infant (or at least gazing at the eye region of the mother's face) in the first few months of life (Bruner, 1973; Greenman, 1963; Stone, Smith, & Murphy, 1973; Wolff, 1963). One way the child could assure joint reference would be to follow the mother's line of visual regard. This behavior has in fact been found in infants as young as four months (Bruner, 1975), as well as in children approximately one year old (Nelson, 1973a). An equally effective strategy, although one which seems intuitively to be somewhat less sophisticated, is visually following mother's body. This behavior has been documented by Murphy (1973), who reported that before the age of eight weeks an infant would visually follow his mother as she left a room. Thus, it does appear that a class of behaviors which might well function for the establishment of joint reference is manifested at a very early age by the normally developing child.

Feedback mechanisms. Mahoney (1975) has speculated on the critical importance of a postulated set of behaviors by which the normal language-learning child somehow signals to an adult speaker when the adult's utterances are either comprehensible and appropriate for the child or inappropriate and thus requiring some modification. Mahoney reasons that, in order for a mature language model to regulate the complexity, length, and redundancy of an utterance in the systematic fashion discussed earlier, the adult must receive some type of nonverbal feedback from the receiver which indicates whether the utterance falls within the appropriate linguistic and conceptual range for that listener. It seems likely that this type of signaling behavior is critical to the child's success in obtaining appropriate linguistic input and thus is considered here as an important part of the child's contribution to the language-learning/teaching partnership.

A study reported by Snow (1972) provides some empirical support for the reality and importance of this type of behavior in mother-child interactions and indicates that the physical presence of the receiver is directly related to the adult's language modification. In this investigation Snow examined the speech of mothers when addressing their 2-year-old children. Each mother was asked to (1) make up and tell a story to her child, (2) instruct her child how to sort a set of toys in several ways, and (3) explain a physical phenomenon to her child. These tasks were performed by each mother under two conditions: first, speaking into a tape recorder with the child not present; and next, speaking directly to the child. Even on these structured tasks and addressing their own children (a task at which they had presumably had a considerable amount of experience), these mothers employed significantly ($p < .01$) shorter and less complex utterances, as well as a greater total number of utterances, when the children were physically present than when they were only present in the mother's imagination. Snow speculates that these findings indicate "that the children played some role in eliciting the mothers' speech modifications" (p. 549).

Given that normally developing children do, then, bring to the language-learning partnership some type of active feedback mechanism, the question we must ask is: What is the nature of this feedback? Mahoney (1975) has noted that at present there are no empirical data available which directly answer this question. He suggests that there is evidence, however, of a potential disruption of the signaling or feedback system between child and caregiver for three populations of handicapped children who traditionally manifest language-learning deficits: (1) severely and profoundly retarded infants were reported to be delayed in the onset of smiling behavior (Schmitt & Erickson, 1973), (2) brain-damaged children were found to have abnormal crying patterns (Fisichelli & Karelitz, 1963), and (3) autistic children were reported by their mothers to have severely impaired signaling systems during infancy (Schaffer, 1971). At this point, the significance of these findings in terms of the feedback mechanisms which appear to operate in successful natural language learning remains at a purely speculative level.

Metalinguistic devices. In addition to the abilities to listen selectively, establish joint reference, and provide feedback, the child who has begun to produce words typically brings to interactions with mature speakers a class of verbal behaviors which may be referred to as "metalinguistic devices." This term is defined here to encompass any process by which expressive language is used to acquire further linguistic knowledge. As such, these behaviors probably represent the most direct and linguistically sophisticated strategies employed by language-learning children for gathering information about the language code from the more mature speakers in their environment. During the early stages of development, in which we are primarily interested, these devices probably occur in two, often indistinguishable forms: hypothesis testing and question asking.[4]

The suggestion that children formulate hypotheses about the linguistic code and then test these through production was originally made by Brown (1958), who postulated a type of "word game" through which young children acquire language. Recently, Nelson's (1973a) study, described earlier, has provided empirical data which may constitute correlational evidence of such a strategy. In this study, Nelson found a significant ($p < .01$) positive correlation between the total quantity of a child's verbal output at the age of 20 months and that child's vocabulary size and Mean Length of Utterance at 24 months. Interpreting these results, Nelson suggests that language production may serve as a language-development strategy by allowing the child to test his hypotheses regarding the meanings associated with particular lexical and grammatical structures on the basis of their acceptance by the more mature language users in his environment.

A second form of productive language which seems to function toward the child's mastery of the language code is question asking. The development of this type of verbal behavior was analyzed by Bellugi (1965) using language-sample data collected from three children. This investigator found that even during the early stages of language development, when these children were between 18 and 27 months with Mean Lengths of Utterance between 1.8 and 2.0, two forms of interrogative structures were already within their verbal repertoires. One form was the simple addition of rising intonation to the ends of declarative utterances already produced by the child. (It should be noted that this type of question—for example, "doggie↑"—may actually be more accurately characterized as hypothesis testing than as question asking, although of course this can only be determined in reference to both the immediate context as well as the child's previous linguistic experience.) The second form of early interrogative structure found by Bellugi was the wh-question, particularly two forms of this: "What (*NP*)" (including "What that?") and "Where (*NP*)."

The potential value of this type of verbal ability seems intuitively obvious. More empirically, however, Nelson (1973a) found a significant ($p < .05$) positive correlation between the number of questions contained in a child's language sample

---

[4]Since the writing of this report, the authors have prepared a paper in which the nature of these metalinguistic utterances is discussed more fully. The interested reader should write to the authors at the Parsons Research Center, Parsons, Kansas 67357, and request Working Paper #332.

gathered at the age of two years and the size of that child's vocabulary at the same age. In her interpretation of these results, however, Nelson cautions us that these data are only correlational and that the actual role of question asking as a language acquisition strategy is still open to question.

Looking at children in an earlier stage of language development, Dore (1975) found that one of nine communicative intents expressed by children in "holophrastic" (one-word) utterances was what he labeled "requesting answer." This type of speech act was illustrated by the following example:

M picks up a book, looks at her mother and utters "buk↑";
Mother responds "Right, it's a book."

Again, we would suggest that this type of question asking may actually function more as a procedure for hypothesis testing. However, a more open-ended type of question which might function for the acquisition of new words was found by Nelson in the earliest speech of many of her subjects. She reported that question words such as "what" and "tha" were among the first 50 words uttered by 12 of her 18 subjects and were even among the first 10 words for 6 of the children.

On the basis of the research reviewed above, we may draw several conclusions. First, we see that from the time the child first begins to produce words, he has the ability to evoke lexical labels and confirmations of his own linguistic hypotheses from the mature language users in his environment. Second, Nelson's data demonstrate that there is some relationship between the child's manifestation of this ability and his relative language maturity by the age of two years. Finally, we must conclude that the exact function and importance of this type of verbal behavior remain to be empirically demonstrated.

Summary. As described here, then, the process by which the linguistic structure of a culture is transmitted to the young child requires the active participation of that child. No matter how facilitating an environment is, or even how much structured training is provided, it would seem that language acquisition will not occur unless the child actively contributes to the endeavor. In this section, we have identified several specific behaviors which seem to represent at least part of the child's contribution to this process. These behaviors have included selective listening to appropriate linguistic input; establishing joint reference through locating and attending to a referent indicated visually (or otherwise) by an adult; providing some feedback to the adult speaker that the language model provided is or is not at an appropriate level of linguistic complexity; and, with the emergence of word production, the metalinguistic devices of hypothesis testing and question asking.

Social Bases for Language Acquisition: Summary

In this chapter, we have examined the social bases for language acquisition from three perspectives: (1) the pragmatics of language, (2) social bases for preverbal communication, and (3) social bases for the acquisition of linguistic structure. In the course of this examination, we have traveled down many diverse theoretical and empirical paths to arrive at an understanding of the social dynamics which affect and effect the language acquisition process. The danger, of course, in such a multifaceted review, incorporating many perspectives, is that the global lessons to be learned may be lost in a sea of detail. Therefore, a brief reiteration of five major conclusions we have drawn from this review follows:

1. Language is acquired because, and only if, the child has a reason to talk. This, in turn, assumes that he has become "socialized" (very possibly through some attachment process) and has learned that he can affect his environments through the process of communication.
2. Language is first acquired as a means of achieving already existing communicative functions. These preverbal communicative functions seem to be directly related to the functional or pragmatic aspect of later language.
3. Linguistic structure is initially acquired through the process of decoding and comprehending incoming linguistic stimuli. At later stages of development, the processes of imitation and expansion may serve to help the child refine his emerging language system.
4. Language is learned in dynamic social interactions involving the child and the mature language users in his environment. The mature language users facilitate this process through their tendency to segment and mark the components of the interaction and to provide appropriate linguistic models.
5. The child is an active participant in this transactional process and must contribute to it a set of behaviors which allow him to benefit from the adult's facilitating behaviors.

chapter 4

The Sequence of Early Linguistic Development

In the preceding chapters, we have repeatedly noted that language maps semantic intents toward the achievement of pragmatic functions. For this reason, we have discussed in some depth the bases for the semantic and pragmatic components of language as these may be identified in the early stages of cognitive and social development respectively. We have also examined the transactional process by which the human infant seems to acquire the linguistic structure of his culture. In the present chapter, we will turn our attention to the actual nature of this linguistic structure and attempt to trace its development from the neonatal period through the production of utterances with a mean length of 2.50 morphemes. It should be noted that this sequence has been derived from developmental literature for normal children and thus reflects acquisition of an aural/oral language system. In applying this sequence clinically, therefore, some translations will have to be made if one is working in an alternative mode (for example, manual signs). (This point will be discussed further in Chapters 6 and 7.)

The Nature of Linguistic Structure

This chapter traces the emergence and development of behavioral responses which reflect the child's growing mastery of the linguistic code through which meanings are conveyed in his culture. Most basically, this code consists of a finite set of elements which may be combined in an infinite number of ways. These elements must be combined, however, in accordance with the conventionalized rules of the particular code (or language) if they are to be effective in conveying the speaker's referent or intent. To provide a background for an account of the young child's mastery of this linguistic structure, the next seven subsections will provide a summary of the basic structural elements of a language system and of the levels at which linguistic structure may be analyzed.

Basic Components
of the System

Any oral/aural language system consists of three basic, interrelated components or levels of analysis: phonology, morphology, and syntax. Here we will briefly examine these components as they are manifested in the English language.

Phonology. Phonology refers to the sound system of a language. Specifically, it refers to those speech sounds employed by native speakers of a language (Stageberg, 1971). Phonology is most commonly analyzed in terms of the sound families which are functional for speakers of the language in signaling different meanings (for example, the difference between *can* and *pan* is signaled by a functional difference in initial consonant sounds). Such meaning-carrying sound families are called *phonemes,* and the standard American dialect consists of 38 such phonemes. Each phoneme may be pronounced in different ways depending on the verbal context as well as on a speaker's particular dialect or "accent." Such slightly varying pronunciations of a phoneme are referred to as *allophones.* Thus, the ability to discriminate between phonemes is important because these signal differences in meaning, whereas allophone discriminations are not functional for decoding meaning.

Morphology. Morphology refers to the system of meaning units in a language. A *morpheme* is a meaningful element which cannot be broken down into smaller units without violation of its meaning or without leaving meaningless parts (Stageberg, 1971). While the analysis of morphology can become extremely complex, for our purposes a few distinctions will suffice. A "free morpheme" is a morpheme which can be used in isolation (such as "look"), while a bound morpheme carries meaning but must be connected to another morpheme (for example, "tele-", "-ing"). Suffixes make up one particularly important subset of the bound morphemes. Specifically, there are two types of English suffixes: inflectional, which signal such things as plurality, tense, person, or possession (-s, -ing, -ed, -'s, and so on); and derivational (-ment, -ary, -ly).

It is important to understand these basic distinctions because utterances are often analyzed or quantified in terms of their length in morphemes. Thus, the sentence "She was looking at Tom's book," has a length of six words but eight morphemes (note that the inflectional suffixes "-ing" and "-'s" are bound morphemes). Frequently, however, when young children produce such words as "looking," there is evidence that they do not understand the meaning conveyed by the inflectional suffix. Consequently, although the word represents two adult morphemes, it may only really represent one morpheme in the child's emerging system. Because of this difficulty in assigning true morpheme status to bound morphemes found in early language, many investigators and clinicians often opt for an analysis of utterance length in terms of number of words. This form of analysis has implications for assessment that will be discussed later.

One additional definition should be provided here. Although words may be discussed in terms of morphemes, it is convenient to have a terminology which refers to words in the more conventional sense. For this purpose, linguists often use the term "lexicon" to refer to the set of words within an individual's vocabulary, and they refer to individual words within that vocabulary as "lexical items" or "elements."

Syntax. Most basically, syntax may be thought of as the system of rules which governs how words may be combined to form meaningful sentences. Stageberg (1971) notes that within the framework of syntactic analysis, a word may be defined in terms of its form (noun, verb, etc), its function (subject of the verb, object of preposition, etc.), or by position (for example, a nominal may be a word or phrase of many different forms and functions, but it is defined because its place in a sentence is one most typically occupied by a noun). It seems that the young child very early learns the association between different positions and the types of form, class, and function which normally occur in those positions. This association, referred to as a "slot-class correlation," has traditionally been thought to be a powerful strategy in the child's early syntactic development. Recent semantic theories suggest that such associations may in fact involve the correlation between a particular position and the semantic case which is typically mapped in that position. Thus, perhaps we should now speak in terms of a "slot-case" correlation.

Descriptive Grammars

Descriptive grammars may be thought of as systems analyses applied to the morphological and syntactical components of a language system. The perspectives reflected in such grammars have changed over the course of the past 20 years, reflecting a trend toward greater emphasis on the meaning of language as this relates to its structure.

Adult grammars. Traditionally, grammars have been written to account for the linguistic structures found in the speech of adult language users in a culture. Tracing the development of adult English grammars, Dale (1972) notes that the prevalent approach prior to 1957 was the "phrase structure" grammar. In phrase structure grammar, a sentence is analyzed in terms of its constituent phrase structures (a process which may sound painfully familiar to those who remember diagramming sentences in high school English). Thus, most basically, a sentence is described in terms of a noun phrase and a verb phrase, each of which in turn may be described in terms of its constituent structures.

Recognizing that such an approach dealt only with the surface-level structures of a language and failed totally to reflect the fact that many very different phrase structure arrangements may map the same meaning, Chomsky (1957) proposed a new approach to grammatical analysis. In his "generative transformational grammar," surface structures are treated as oral/verbal representations of underlying "deep structures" which are represented linguistically as simple, declarative "kernel" sentences. Thus, several sentences which vary greatly in the form and complexity of their surface structure may actually all be derived from the same kernel sentence. (For example, "John hit the ball" and "The ball was hit by John" both derive from the kernel or deep structure "John hit ball"). The process by which the deep structure is modified and/or expanded into the surface structure consists of one or a sequence of several transformations. Chomsky's grammar consists of the set of specific transformation rules which are necessary to account for the variety of syntactically correct forms which are evidenced in adult English.

While transformational grammar took us one step closer to understanding the relationship between meaning and syntactic structure, it still failed to probe the depths of deep structure—that is, the meaning or semantic intent reflected in the kernel structure—and it has been argued that this approach offered little more psychological reality than had phrase structure.

The most recent approach to grammar writing seemed to evolve in response to this dissatisfaction with transformational grammar and may be referred to as "semantic" or "case" grammar. The reader will recall from the discussion of semantics presented in Chapter 2 that such a semantic case grammar analyzes sentence structure in terms of such constructs as "agent," "instrumental," "dative," (Fillmore, 1968). Thus, a semantic case grammar describes and analyzes an assumed direct relationship between underlying semantic meaning or intent and linguistic structure.

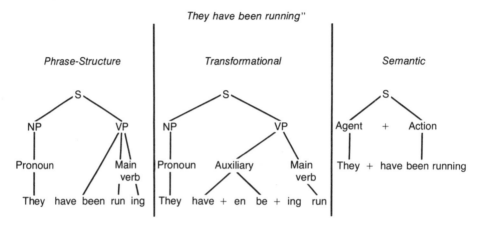

FIGURE 1. A Comparison of Phrase-Structure, Transformational, and Semantic Grammar Analysis for One Sentence.

In Figure 1, the three approaches to grammar construction and analysis are illustrated for comparison purposes. When we discuss the selection of specific linguistic targets for clinical intervention in a later chapter, the reader will note that each of these approaches has added to our ability to understand and describe the language system which we wish the handicapped child to acquire.

Child grammars. Although some followers of Chomsky have viewed early child language as merely a poor approximation of the adult system which it is innately destined to become, many developmental linguists contend that child language can be more productively studied as a system with its own grammatical rules and regularities (Bloom, 1970; Braine, 1963, 1976; Brown, 1973). Over the years, a number of such child-language grammars have been proposed, accepted, and eventually rejected (for example, pivot + open; topic + comment). In most recent years, applications of the semantic grammar approach to the specific forms and meanings found in early language have resulted in many productive new insights (Bloom, 1970, 1973; Braine, 1976; Brown, 1973; Schlesinger, 1971). In the present discussion of the sequence of early linguistic development, we will not rely solely on one approach or one type of grammatical analysis. Instead, we will describe this development in the grammatical terms which seem to reflect most accurately and adequately the forms and structures found in the corpora available for different stages of development.

Receptive vs. Expressive Language

In the previous chapter, it was noted that langue acquisition seems to occur first at the level of comprehension. We suggested that the infant first decodes the language by noting the association between an established, known joint referent and a perceived linguistic stimulus. In the present chapter, we will examine more closely the nature of receptive language, or comprehension, and its relationship to language production.

The Nature of Receptive Language

In the present context, the terms "receptive language" and "language comprehension" will be used interchangeably. A first step in understanding the nature of comprehension is to understand how it differs from other related processes.

Receptive language vs. sensation and perception. In an aural/oral language system, comprehension is most basically considered to be the deriving of a speaker's meaning through decoding a heard linguistic stimulus. This process thus requires the ability to hear and to perceptually discriminate meaningful units of sound. Note that the emphasis here is on meaningful sound units, since it is possible for a child to have some hearing loss and still be able to discriminate enough of the critical phonemes and paralinguistic patterns to derive meaning from an utterance. Conversely, it is equally possible for a child to have intact hearing or sound detection abilities and even the ability to discriminate perceptually between very similar phonemes and still not develop receptive language skills. This is not surprising if we remember that comprehension learning involves not only the perception of a linguistic stimulus, but the association of this with a known referent. Thus, reception differs from sensation and perception in that the former involves not only the ability to hear and segment incoming stimuli, but also the ability to integrate and associate meaning with those stimuli.

Receptive vs. expressive processes. The most obvious difference between receptive and expressive language is that the former involves listening and the latter involves speaking. This seemingly simplistic distinction has several more subtle implications which shed light on the qualitative differences between these processes, and also on the task of designing research and intervention procedures appropriate to each.

One important difference between the speaking and listening behaviors involved in these two types of language performance is that speaking is an overt, and thus directly observable behavior, whereas listening is a covert behavior which must be inferred on the basis of some overt manifestation. This distinction affects not only the nature of the tasks designed to evoke and assess receptive as opposed to productive language, but also the confidence with which the results of such analyses can be interpreted. It will be seen, in fact, that this problem has recently been cited in reexamining earlier conclusions drawn from data concerning the relative order of receptive and expressive development.

If we now indulge briefly in a little speculation regarding the apparent mental processes which would seem to be involved in language comprehension and production, we again note some qualitative differences between the two processes. First, we note that the structure and content of an utterance are under the speaker's control. Thus, early language production is child-controlled, whereas comprehension is other-controlled. Considering this distinction in light of the discussion of cognitive bases in Chapter 2, it would seem that, in language production, the young child is free to select the referent for his utterance on the basis of his own knowledge and experiencing of the immediate context. In comprehension, however, the child must attend to an adult utterance which may map an aspect of the context which is not known or not immediately salient to the child.

It would seem then that comprehension requires that the child be able to *recognize* incoming linguistic stimuli and then *recall* from memory of past language experiences the objects, events, or relationships which are associated with those linguistic forms. In speech production, conversely, the child must *recognize* and select from the context an understood object event and/or relationship which will serve as the referent for his utterance and then *recall* the linguistic forms which he has learned are associated with those referents. Certainly the relative difficulty of these two processes depends on many factors, the most obvious being the amount of contextual support available. That is, it would seem that comprehension might be simpler than production in a context where the child is sitting with a ball in hand and facing his mother who is sitting with outstretched hands saying "Roll the ball to me." However, the child might have more difficulty decoding that same utterance if the context contained no ball or if he were attending to a different referent. This phenomenon of contextual support or redundancy is an important aspect of early language development and one to which we will return later.

Finally, in speculating on the differential demands which language reception and production may place on the child's mental abilities, the question of memory requirements seems relevant. It would seem that in reception, the fleeting nature of the incoming stimulus (speech sounds) demands that the child be able to hold that stimulus in short-term memory until he has successfully decoded it through a search of his long-term memory stores of knowledge. On the other hand, if the child's task is to produce an utterance mapping a referent situation which remains within his perceptual field, it would seem that his short-term memory ability may be less critical. This issue of the fleeting nature of linguistic stimuli will be raised again later when we discuss the use of alternative modes.

In summarizing this brief consideration of the nature of receptive language, we may draw three conclusions. First, comprehension requires the abilities to detect and discriminate meaningful units of linguistic input, but these abilities in themselves are not sufficient to assure comprehension. Secondly, because we cannot observe comprehension directly, our analyses of this process must be inferential and will demand great caution in interpretation. Finally, it would seem that there are some qualitative differences in the nature of the mental processes which underlie comprehension and production. Consequently, we should not infer that the child's development in one is a direct index of his development in the other. Rather, we must track and target the child's early development in both of these language abilities. In the following section we will look at the issue of precedence in these two tracks of development.

Reception Precedes Production?

Traditional wisdom has held that reception precedes production in the course of normal language development. This assumption certainly has logical appeal since it stands to reason that a child cannot produce language which he does not yet understand. Further, this statement seems consonant with the theory and data on normal initial acquisition described in earlier chapers. Recent data and perspectives, however, have led to some reexamination of this precedence assumption and have resulted in a greater appreciation for the complex nature of this relationship. Because it has implications for clinical intervention, we will digress briefly here to look at this issue.

Evidence supporting receptive precedence. The assumption that receptive language precedes expressive language has a high level of face validity. Further, it is consistent with our transactional model which posits that language is first acquired through a decoding or comprehension process. In fact, even at preverbal levels, we noted earlier that Escalona (1973) found communicative intents responded to before they were expressed by infants.

The question of precedence, however, is really twofold. First, there is the argument that the child learns to comprehend language and functions at a receptive level before he begins to produce meaningful words. On this point there seems to be little debate. The second aspect of this issue is reflected in the question, does the child come to comprehend each of the specific forms and structures of his language system prior to the time he produces these in his own utterances? In a classic study of this question, Fraser, Bellugi, and Brown (1963—later replicated by Lovell & Dixon, 1967) presented 12 subjects, who were approximately 3 to 3½ years in age, with a series of three linguistic tasks which were designed to test the subjects' abilities to deal with 10 different grammatical contrasts. The three tasks were: imitation (reciting the sentence immediately after the experimenter), comprehension (pointing to one of two pictures to indicate which one matched the meaning of a sentence spoken by the experimenter), and production (after hearing the two possible sentences, using the correct one to describe a picture held up by the experimenter). The results of this study indicated that, for these children, the imitation task was consistently the easiest and that receptive performance consistently exceeded productive performance. This study is frequently cited as evidence that reception precedes production.

Conflicting evidence. In the last few years, evidence has emerged which indicates that the precedence assumption may have been overly simplistic. Recent reanalysis of the Fraser et al. (1963) study (Bloom, 1974; Fernald, 1972) has indicated that the procedures used to analyze and interpret the data were misleading. The latter writers have noted that in the comprehension task, consisting of a two-choice discrimination, there was a much greater statistical probability of responding correctly on just a chance level. After correcting for this chance factor and recomputing the results from the original data, these writers have concluded that the subjects in the Fraser study did not perform significantly better receptively than they had productively.

A more direct contradiction of the precedence assumption comes from a recent study by Chapman and Miller (1975). These investigators used 15 subjects who ranged in age from 1½ to 2½ years and within this sample defined three levels of linguistic maturity on the basis of each subject's mean length of utterance (MLU, in morphemes). The linguistic structure studied was the subject-verb-object sentence construction. Each subject was presented with both a comprehension task (in which the child was to act out with toys each of 12 sentences read by the experimenter) and a production task (in which the experimenter acted out the event with toys and the child was asked to describe it). The critical variable here was the correct assignment of the subject and object roles. The data indicated that situations in which the expected roles of animate and inanimate objects were reversed (such as "the table pushes the boy") tended to be described expressively by these children just as accurately as those which conformed to normal expectations (such as "the boy pushes the table"). In comprehension, however, there was a strong tendency for children at all three linguistic levels to act out an event in which the animate object was the agent of action, regardless of whether or not it was the subject of the experimenter's sentence. Thus, these data suggest that young children may use linguistic word-order rules to convey at least some meanings expressively before they are using those rules to decode the meanings of heard utterances. This finding, of course, relates to the point made earlier that much of the apparently sophisticated linguistic decoding demonstrated by young children may, in fact, be heavily dependent upon contextual and experimental cues rather than on the actual linguistic structures heard.

Two other types of data bear at least tangentially on this precedence issue. First, some data from intervention work with retarded children suggest that training receptive mastery of a linguistic structure does not facilitate subsequent training of the same structure expressively (Guess, 1969; Guess & Baer, 1973). Secondly, in tracing the development of comprehension in infants prior to the emergence of expressive language, Huttenlocher (1974) found that the first words comprehended were not the first words produced by a child. Thus, it is evident that whatever the relationship is between receptive and expressive development, it most certainly is not a direct linear or one-to-one type of correspondence.

A resolution. The apparently conflicting evidence regarding the precedence assumption suggests that the relationship or interaction between reception and production is at best complex and that broader perspectives are required if we are to resolve this question. One possible resolution is offered by Meadow, Seligman, and Gelman (1976). In a study of linguistic development in children from 21 through 26 months old, these investigators found two stages in the development of noun and verb forms. The first stage they call "receptive," because the ratio of words comprehended to those produced within a form class is relatively high (3+ : 1). The second stage they call "productive," because the ratio of reception to production for a form class has dropped to 1+ : 1. These authors found that their six subjects progressed from the receptive to the productive stage for nouns during the period of study. Verbs were generally not comprehended at all until after the child had progressed out of the receptive stage for nouns and, at this point, a high-ratio receptive stage for verbs emerged.

While the findings of this study remain to be replicated and the specific findings may be unique to the subjects in this small sample, it does seem that Meadow et al.

have offered a valuable perspective. Specifically, they offer the notion that reception may exceed production during the early stages of acquisition of a particular form, but that once the class is mastered, production and comprehension abilities will be approximately equal for that class. This theory would offer a possible resolution of the conflicting evidence cited here by suggesting that the different classes of behavior studied may have been in different stages of development.

Perhaps the best resolution of the precedence issue available at this point is that offered by Bloom (1974), when she suggests that comprehension and production

represent mutually dependent, but different underlying processes, with a resulting shifting of influence between them in the course of language development. In short, it will be suggested that the developmental gap between comprehension and speaking probably varies among different children and at different times and may often be more apparent than real. (p. 286)

Receptive vs. Expressive Language: Summary

In this section we have discussed the nature of receptive language and noted how this relates to stimulus detection and perception abilities. We have also compared comprehension with production and examined the issue of precedence in the relationship between these two aspects of language ability. At this point, we can draw several conclusions. First, it seems probable that reception and production represent two qualitatively different processes. Secondly, although comprehension seems to be the first step in the language acquisition process, the actual temporal or sequential relationship of receptive to expressive language development appears to be a function of many variables and seems to vary over the course of development. Thus, in designing clinical language-intervention programs, we must be sensitive to the child's development in both of these areas and not assume that one will occur or has occurred on the basis of a measure of the other. In the sections which follow, therefore, we will trace separately the apparent sequence of linguistic development in the receptive and expressive areas.

Sequential Development of Linguistic Abilities

In the following pages, we will attempt to outline briefly the sequence of major steps or milestones which seem to typify the natural linguistic development process. At the outset, let us make several points about the nature and purpose of this sequence. First, as noted in the preceding section, the development of receptive and expressive abilities will be described separately. However, these two aspects of development are always occurring concurrently within the context of each early social transaction in which the child is engaged. Secondly, the stages of development will be described somewhat eclectically. Thus, this sequence will not be described solely within the framework and terminology of one particular theoretical perspective. Rather, each stage will be described in terms of the theory and data which seem to represent most accurately that level of development.

Thirdly, where possible, the approximate chronological ages at which these developmental stages are generally noted will be identified. There is, of course, a great deal of variation in the ages at which children achieve these levels in natural development; so the reader is cautioned not to treat these ages as norm references. Rather, these ages are presented solely to provide some perspective of the relative latency or lag time which is typically required for transition from one stage to the next.

Finally, the purpose of presenting this natural developmental sequence is to provide some basis for generating a high-probability sequence of targets for clinical intervention. We do not suggest, however, that the apparent natural sequence be translated directly into a clinical sequence. Obviously, the realities of clinical contexts, procedures, and priorities, as well as the realities of specific needs and problems presented by children who require such intervention, will necessitate some departures from the natural sequence. We believe, however, that such a sequence does provide an essential perspective and framework within which clinical sequences can be established and analyzed.

Development of Receptive Linguistic Abilities

In reviewing the literature, we have identified three major stages of receptive development, within each of which a fairly consistent developmental progression can be traced. The covert nature of comprehension requires that these stages be defined in terms of overt discriminative responses, which can be interpreted as evidence of underlying receptive ability. Therefore, we have identified these stages as: discriminative responding to phonemic and paralinguistic features of linguistic stimuli (I), discriminative responding to lexical-semantic features of linguistic stimuli (II); and discriminative responding to syntactic or grammatical features of linguistic stimuli (III). This general sequence is presented graphically in Figure 2.

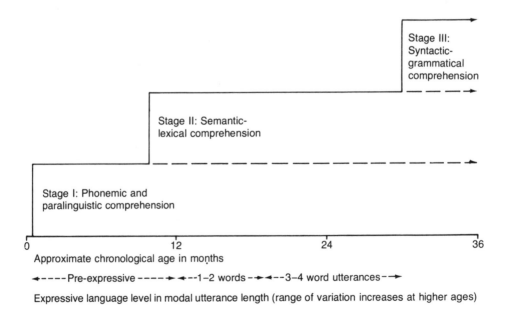

Stage III:
Syntactic-
grammatical
comprehension

Stage II: Semantic-
lexical comprehension

Stage I: Phonemic and
paralinguistic comprehension

0   12   24   36
Approximate chronological age in months

◄ - - - - Pre-expressive - - - - ► ◄ - -1–2 words - ► ◄ - -3–4 word utterances - ►

Expressive language level in modal utterance length (range of variation increases at higher ages)

FIGURE 2. Three Stages of Receptive Linguistic Development.

Stage I: Responding to phonemic and paralinguistic features. In the past five years, a growing body of research has focused on the infant's perception and discrimination of speech sounds. The most basic conclusion which can be drawn from this research is that the human infant at a very early age (at least by one month and possibly from birth) is able to discriminate between speech sounds (Eimas, 1974; Eimas, Siqueland, Jusczyk, & Vigorito, 1971; Morse, 1972; Trehub, 1973; Trehub & Rabinovitch, 1972). Specifically, the data indicate that the infant discriminates between the phonemes of his language more readily than between allophones of the same phoneme (Eimas et al., 1971) and that the ability to discriminate applies to both vowel and consonant sounds (Trehub, 1973). Further, Morse (1972) reports that infants as young as two months old could discriminate between steady and rising fundamental frequencies (pitch) of synthetic speech sounds. This latter ability would seem to be a prerequisite for the child's later discrimination of intonation contours in incoming speech stimuli.

In addition to discriminating between contrasting phonemes and fundamental frequencies, it seems that the young infant is also able to respond differently to the extra- and paralinguistic features of a speaker's voice. In his classic diary study, Guillaume (1927) reported that his child began to smile differently to a familiar voice at one and a half months. More recently, Kaplan and Kaplan (1970) have reported that two- to four-month-old infants will respond differentially to three seemingly important voice feature contrasts: angry vs. friendly, familiar vs. unfamiliar, and male vs. female.

It seems that the next ability to develop in this stage is that of discriminative responding to different intonation contours. Perhaps the most interesting example of this development comes from Meumann's 1902 diary study of his son's early development (cited in Lewis, 1936). Meumann reported that during the period from six to eight months, his son had learned to look at a window when his parents asked, "Wo ist das fenster?" One day, Meumann asked the same question using the same intonation contour in French (a language his son did not know). "Ou est la fenetre?" His son unhesitatingly looked to the window. Lewis suggests that Meumann's son was responding to the familiar intonational pattern.

A related finding is reported by Nakazima (1962), who found that infants at eight to nine months would vocally imitate an intonation pattern—an ability which we may take as evidence that the infant was discriminating such contour patterns. Finally, in a study comparing the discrimination abilities of infants at different ages, Kaplan (1969) found that infants first showed evidence of discriminating stressed intonation patterns at eight months.

The final discrimination which seems to develop in Stage I is that in which utterances are discriminated in terms of both their phonemic and their intonational features. This ability is illustrated by an anecdote from Schaffer's 1922 diary study. He reports that his 10-month-old child had learned to play a ritualized game in which the father would say, "Mache bitte-bitte" and the child would clap his hands. Schaffer found that the child would give the same response to "Mache kippe-kippe" but not to "Mache la-la," even though both were pronounced with the same intonational pattern as that which marked the original utterance. Thus, it seems that this child was attending not only to the intonation contour, but also to the phonemic pattern of the utterance, since "kippe-kippe" is phonemically very similar to "bitte-bitte," whereas "la-la" is a distinctly different set of phonemes. We may speculate that the same process may have been at work in Meumann's experiment since "Wo ist das fenster?" is quite similar in its phonemic features to "Ou est la fenetre?"

Thus, in Stage I, which spans the period from birth to approximately ten months, the infant progresses from the ability to discriminate speech sounds to the ability to respond differentially to specific phonemic-intonation patterns. Further, and more importantly, the responses themselves become differentiated, indicating that by the end of this stage the infant is truly comprehending in the sense that he is deriving some specific meaning from the linguistic input received. This stage is summarized in Figure 3.

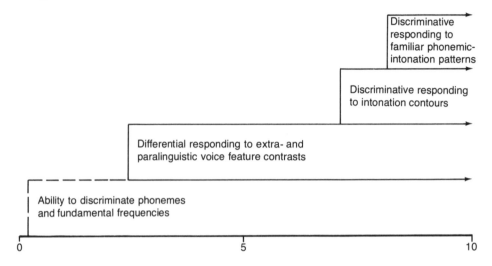

Approximate chronological age in months

FIGURE 3. Stage I (Receptive): Phonemic and Paralinguistic Comprehension.

Stage II: Responding to lexical-semantic features.   As the child enters the level of receptive development we have defined as Stage II, he is responding differentially to familiar or ritualized words and phrases. It is important to note that this responding is dependent upon the total gestalt of the linguistic event, including associated contextual, gestural, and/or intonational cues. Thus, at this level it seems appropriate to suggest that the child is comprehending the communicative essence of a social linguistic event, rather than comprehending specific linguistic structures per se. Probably the earliest common example of this type of comprehension is the inhibitory response manifested in response to an adult's prohibitive "No! No!" (Leopold, 1939; Spitz, 1957). One can easily envision the gestural and intonational cues which almost invariably accompany this utterance when it is addressed to the young child. Other examples of this type of early comprehension might include the infant's looking at or reaching for a toy when mother says the name of the toy while pantomiming a ritualized game associated with that toy or while indicating the toy through pointing or visual regard. This type of communicative comprehension is usually noted before one year of age and may be noted as young as eight months.

Up to this point, we have suggested that the child depends heavily on intonational or suprasegmental cues for determining the meaning of a heard utterance. Evidence from two related studies (Friedlander, 1967; Kagan & Lewis, 1965) indicates that this pattern changes after about 13 months. These investigators found that after this age, infants showed higher levels of attention to and a preference for nonintonated (monotonic) speech rather than normally intonated speech. Menyuk (1974) interprets these findings as possible evidence that the infant may be shifting from attending to suprasegmental to attending to segmental aspects of incoming linguistic stimuli. That is, it seems that the infant is beginning to focus attention on the specific lexical segments of utterances heard, rather than on the gestalt patterns of those utterances. This shift of focus marks the child's entry into a second level of performance within this general stage. At this level, the young child is capable of responding differentially to individual words without any contextual or paralinguistic supporting cues.

The most complete analysis of this level of receptive development known to these authors is that reported by Huttenlocher (1974). This investigator traced the receptive and expressive development of four children from 10½ to 19½ months. She saw the children approximately once every two weeks in their own homes. On the basis of each mother's report of words she thought her child could understand, Huttenlocher assessed the ability of each child to respond systematically and differentially to those words when they were presented without supporting cues. She also recorded words which the child was producing at the time of the visit. Her data show a somewhat surprising consistency across these four children in terms of the nature of the first words comprehended. In Table 1, we have summarized her data on the first words or phrases for which each of these subjects showed reliable receptive control. Huttenlocher notes that these early words were usually associated with one specific referent, rather than a whole class of objects.

Several conclusions can be drawn from Huttenlocher's data regarding early lexical comprehension. First, we may identify several categories of words which have a very high probability of being among the first a child will understand. These include the names of household pets and family members, body parts, objects related to food or eating, manipulable toys, and ritualized social or play actions. On a more general level these early words seem to share the properties of salience to the child and affordance of dynamic interaction with the child. This finding is consistent with the discussion in Chapter 2 of cognitive bases for language acquisition. Further supporting this point is Huttenlocher's observation that, although the words "kitchen," "den," and "refrigerator" were frequently used by one of the mothers in her study, these words had not appeared in her child's receptive vocabulary even as late as 19 months. It seems that such words map referents which are too large to be either highly salient to or manipulable for the child. One additional point should be made about the nature of this very early receptive vocabulary. On the basis of Huttenlocher's data it seems that most of the words which are first comprehended are nouns or words which serve as labels. This finding is supported by data from other studies of early receptive language (Carrow, 1968; Meadow, Seligman, & Gelman, 1976). We shall see, in fact, that verb forms emerge primarily in the next stage of receptive development. A final conclusion to be drawn from Huttenlocher's study is that there was considerable variation, even among these normally developing children, in both the quantity and rate of acquisition of early receptive vocabulary.

After the child has acquired a basic receptive lexicon, the next step in his comprehension development is differential responding to multiword linguistic stimuli. At this stage, we see the emergence of simple direction-following and the apparent ability to comprehend relationships indicated in a sentence. However, in this stage

TABLE 1

First Words Comprehended by Huttenlocher's Subjects

	Name of family member or pet	Label for game or social ritual	Manipulable object/toy	Body parts	Food-related	Other
Child #1	"Mommy" (10, 24)[a] "Danny" (10, 24) (brother) "Fish" (13, 20)	"Bye-Bye" (10½) "Peek-a-Boo" (10½) "Bang-Bang" (10½) "Dance" (13,6) "Stand up" (14)	"Blanket" (20,24) "Ball" (11, 11) "Pat-the-Bunny-Book" (12½) "Teddy Bear" (12½) "Dog" (toy) (13)	"Hair" (13,6) "Belly-Button" (13,20) "Teeth" (14½)	"Cookie" (10½) "Bottle" (10, 24)	
Child #2	"Cora" (dog's name) (10½)	(No other receptive or expressive language was exhibited before study terminated at 17 months)				
Child #3	"Candy" (14) (dog's name) "Mommy" (15)	"Sit down" (15½) "Patty Cake" (15½) "Peek-a-boo" (15½)	"Washcloth" (16) "Pen" (16) "Telephone" (17) "Jolly Jalopy" (17) "Shoe" (18½)	"Hair" (16) "Nose" (18½)	"Apple" (14½) "Bathe" (14½) "Cookie" (14½)	"Show (give) Mommy (me) your (the baby's) bottle" Discriminated all elements correctly at 16 months
Child #4	"Mommy" (10,24) "Canterbury" (10,24) (Cat's name)	"Whistle" (13,20) "Make a wind" (13,20) (blows)	"Pink Bunny" (12) (names for 6 stuffed animals) (13,20) "Your shoe" & "Mommy's shoe" (14)	"Your nose" and "Mommy's nose" (14)		"Mirror" (13, 6) (attached to wall)

NOTE. Data from "The Origins of Language Comprehension" by J. Huttenlocher in R. Solso (ed.), *Theories in Cognitive Psychology.* Copyright 1974 by Halsted Press.

[a] Numbers in parentheses indicate age in months and days at which child first demonstrated comprehension of each item.

the child seems to be operating purely on a lexical-semantic level, rather than on a syntactic level. For example, although the child in this stage may respond correctly when asked to "Show me the doggie," he is probably only responding to the word "doggie" (and possibly the word "show") and would be just as likely to point to the correct picture if asked to "The doggie me show." In fact, this is just the sort of task devised by Wetstone and Friedlander (1972). These investigators presented their subjects with a series of commands, half of which were in correct syntactic form and half of which were scrambled in word order so that they made no syntactic sense (for example, "Where is the truck?" vs. "Truck the where is?"). Those subjects who had been identified as fluent speakers (speaking in utterances of five or more words) were less apt to respond correctly when the key words of a sentence were misplaced than were children who were speaking in only one- and two-word utterances. Thus, it seems that the more linguistically mature children were trying to process the commands syntactically—in which case they made little sense—whereas the less mature speakers were apparently responding only to the lexical and semantic properties of the key words in the sentence.

A related finding is that reported by Chapman and Miller (1975). This study indicated that Subject-Verb-Object sentences were responded to differently by subjects grouped according to their level of linguistic development (as indicated by Mean Length of Utterance). Specifically, it appeared that only the highest level group (MLU: 2.94; Chronological Age: 2 yrs., 6 mos.) used syntax (word order) in processing the meaning of S-V-O sentences and understood that the word in the first position was the agent of the action and the word in the last position was the object. The children in the two lower level groups (MLU: 1.77 and 2.37; CA: 2 yrs. and 1 yr., 11 mos.) tended to respond not according to this syntactic rule, but according to the semantic relationship most commonly associated with the key lexical items in the sentence. Thus, these children would respond identically to the two sentences "The boy is pushing the car" and "The car is pushing the boy"—in both cases assuming that the animate word refers to the agent of action and the inanimate word to the object of that action.

To summarize, we have identified the second stage of receptive development as that in which the young child comes to comprehend linguistic input on a lexical-semantic level, but still does not comprehend syntactically. We have noted that this stage of development subsumes several developmental steps, from the child's first receptive word to his responding to multiword utterances. This stage is summarized in Figure 4.

Stage III: Responding to syntactic-grammatical features. On the basis of available developmental data, we have identified a third stage of receptive language development marked by yet another qualitative shift in the nature of the child's ability to respond to linguistic stimuli. In the first stage, we noted that the infant comes to respond appropriately to the meanings associated with ritualized phonemic and paralinguistic patterns, particularly as these occur in familiar contexts. In the second stage which we identified, the one- to two-year-old child responds increasingly to the meaning conveyed first by specific lexical items and eventually by the lexical-semantic relationships associated with the major substantive words in a multiword utterance. In the third and final stage of receptive development, the young child attends increasingly to the meaning cues provided by the syntactic and morphemic elements of a heard utterance, as well as to the "little words" (such as prepositions and auxiliaries) which carry relational and linguistic information. Whereas Stage I generally occupies approximately the first 10 to 12 months of development and Stage II may last for some 15 or 20 months, the linguistic developments of Stage III, which typically begin at around 30 months, will continue until sometime past the child's seventh birthday. Since, however, we are concerned here primarily with the early stages of language development—specifically with the period from birth to

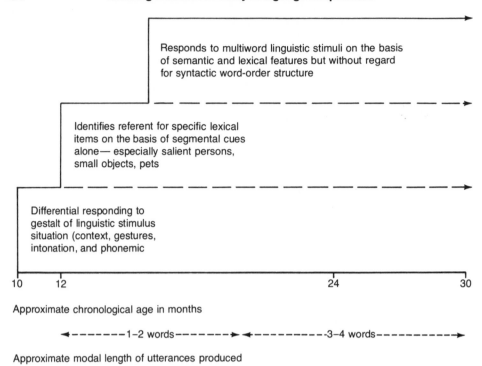

Responds to multiword linguistic stimuli on the basis
of semantic and lexical features but without regard
for syntactic word-order structure

Identifies referent for specific lexical
items on the basis of segmental cues
alone— especially salient persons,
small objects, pets

Differential responding to
gestalt of linguistic stimulus
situation (context, gestures,
intonation, and phonemic

10   12   24   30

Approximate chronological age in months

◀ – – – – – – –1–2 words– – – – – – – ▶ ◀ – – – – – – – –3–4 words– – – – – – – ▶

Approximate modal length of utterances produced

FIGURE 4. Stage II (Receptive): Lexical-Semantic Comprehension.

approximately three years, or until the child is regularly producing three- and
four-word grammatical utterances—this section will focus on only the initial
achievements of Stage III.

Although Stage III is primarily identified as the period when the child learns to
derive meaning from grammatical features, it is important to note that lexical development also continues and represents an important aspect of this stage. Whereas
the receptive lexicon of Stage II consisted primarily of labels for highly salient
objects, people, and activities, the young child entering Stage III has begun to add
more descriptive adjectives and adverbs to his receptive lexicon, thereby allowing
more accuracy in identifying specific referents intended by a speaker. A major study
of the receptive abilities of young children was reported by Carrow in 1968. In this
study, Carrow assessed the linguistic comprehension of many different lexical,
morphemic and syntactic contrasts in 159 subjects (ranging in age from 34 months
to 93 months). Her task consisted of presenting a word or phrase orally to a child and
then asking the child to select the corresponding picture from a group of three
black-and-white drawings. In terms of early lexical comprehension, Carrow's (1968)
data suggest that by 36 months, most normally developing children (at least 60% of
her sample) were able to comprehend the verbs "jump," "run," and "eat," but did not
comprehend the verbs "hit," "catch," and "give" until the ages of 42, 48, and 54
months, respectively. Thus, is seems that as the child's realm of activity increases
during the preschool years of Stage III, verb forms, as well as adjectives and
adverbs, represent significant additions to his receptive repertoire.

Another characteristic of the child in early Stage III is that he is beginning to differentially respond to a few of the "little" or function words. Specifically, the comprehension of several relational prepositions seems to be an early Stage III ability. Carrow (1968) reports that at least 60% of the 36-month-old children in her sample comprehended the prepositions "in," "on," and "under." (This was the youngest group Carrow tested. Thus, it is very possible that these abilities may exist prior to 36 months.) Similarly, the norms for the Bayley Scales of Infant Development (Bayley, 1969) indicate that at least two or three such prepositions are normally comprehended by about 30 months.

Carrow's (1968) data indicate several other lexical and morphemic distinctions which most of her children comprehended between 36 and 42 months. These include the changes in meaning signaled by:

1. "Not," following an auxiliary verb—for example, "The baby is crying" vs. "The baby is not crying";
2. Pronoun gender and number—for example, "he" vs. "she" or "they"; "her" vs. "him" or "them";
3. Tense-verb—"is riding" vs. "rode" or "will ride";
4. Noun-verb number—"the cat plays" (as opposed to several cats playing).

It is important to note that the distinctions described in numbers 2, 3, and 4 above were demonstrated by the children only on certain items, but not on related items until a later age, indicating that a general class of morphemic distinction is probably not fully mastered by the age of 42 months. For example, although the 42-month group could correctly select the picture of a boy (as opposed to a girl or a group of children) for a sentence in which "he" was the subject, and the 36-month group correctly selected the group picture for the subject "they," the correct picture for the subject *she* was not selected by most of the children until 66 months. Similarly, at least 60% of the 36-month-old children responded correctly to the item "The cat plays," but the same level of performance was not exhibited on the sentence "The boys play" until 60 months, even though the critical distinction in both sentences is the noun-verb number. In short, for the early period of Stage III with which we are concerned, we can conclude that the child is beginning to note and distinguish the differential meanings signaled by morphemic changes in gender, plurality, and tense, but that this ability is probably limited to specific cases. Furthermore, the specific distinctions first learned by any individual child may be a factor of individual experience.

Finally, the development which most clearly marks the child's entrance into Stage III, as we have defined it, is the ability to respond to the meaning conveyed by the syntax or word order of a sentence. This level of receptive responding was assessed in two studies which we discussed previously. In the Wetstone and Friedlander study (1972), it was found that only those children who were speaking "fluently" (that is, primarily in utterances longer than three or four words) were confused by scrambled word order when this affected the key substantive words in a sentence. Thus, it was only these highest level subjects who were attempting to use syntax as a guide to sentence meaning. In the Chapman and Miller (1975) study, only those subjects with an MLU of approximately 2.94 (mean CA of 30 months) attended to syntactic word order rules in designating the agent and object roles when asked to act out sentences of the subject-verb-object construction. This level of receptive performance was also manifested by most of Carrow's 36-month-old subjects, who were able to discriminate the meanings associated with the sentences "The car bumps the train" vs. "The train bumps the car" and "The boy pushes the girl" vs. "The girl pushes the boy." (Note that in Carrow's sentences, however, there is no instance of an inanimate subject acting upon an animate object.) Carrow's data also indicate that the ability to identify the subject and object in passive sentences (such as "The dog is chased by the boy") does not develop until almost six years of age. Thus, the early Stage III child seems to operate on the rule "First noun = subject; second noun = object," a rule which allows the child to respond correctly to the common S-V-O construction, but results in incorrect performance when a sentence incorporates the passive verb form.

Thus several developments occur in the early phases of Stage III. First we noted the continuing expansion of the child's receptive repertoire—particularly to include more adjectives, adverbs, and verbs, as well as a few prepositions. Further, the child begins to respond to a few simple morphemic rules as these mark distinctions in tense, gender, and/or number. This ability is not fully developed, however, until much later in Stage III. Finally, the child in early Stage III understands the importance of word order or syntax as a cue to meaning and assigns the status of subject to the first noun in a sentence and the status of object to the second noun. Again, it was noted that the comprehension of more complex constructions, in which the basic S-V-O sentence has undergone one or more transformations, does not develop until much later in Stage III. An overview of this stage is presented in Figure 5.

Development of Expressive Linguistic Abilities

In this section, we will trace the development of expressive linguistic abilities. Since this sequence is derived from the data on normal development, it will be stated in

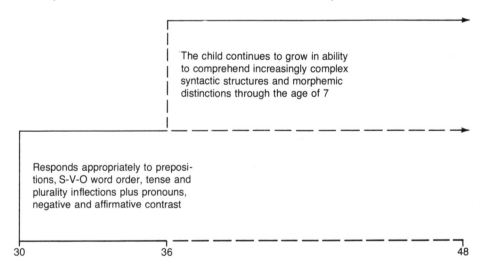

The child continues to grow in ability to comprehend increasingly complex syntactic structures and morphemic distinctions through the age of 7

Responds appropriately to prepositions, S-V-O word order, tense and plurality inflections plus pronouns, negative and affirmative contrast

30   36   48

Approximate chronological age in months

FIGURE 5. Stage III (Receptive): Syntactic/Grammatical Comprehension.

terms of oral language production. Further, although the child's ability to communicate expressively to the adults in his environment is present from earliest infancy, we are concerned here specifically with the sequence of development of conventionalized linguistic forms and structures. Thus, this section will not deal with the development of preverbal communication (see Chapter 3).

Prelinguistic vocal development. In tracing the growth of oral linguistic performance, it is common to begin with the sound production behaviors which characterize the prelinguistic period. The normally developing infant typically progresses from reflexive neonatal sound production through a period of babbling, in which the child produces a growing repertoire of both vowel and consonant sounds. During the babbling period, the infant will produce sounds repetitively in an autistic circuit (self-imitation) and will refine and reduce his sound production towards the finite set of phonemes which characterize his language. Toward the end of this prelinguistic phase of sound production, the infant typically enters a period of what seems to be vocal play. At this stage, the infant seems to be experimenting or just playing games with the sounds he can produce, uttering strings of sounds with distinctive intonational and phrasing patterns which carry no apparent meaning. Some infants go through a "jargon" period when they will produce whole strings of such utterances which sound very much like speech, except that again there are no identifiable, consistent meanings attached to the sounds being produced.

While this period of oral/vocal development is interesting, it will not be treated in further depth here for three reasons: (1) the focus in this chapter is specifically the development of linguistic structures; (2) since our ultimate concern is deriving a model for clinical intervention with severely handicapped children, for whom the oral mode may well not be appropriate in the initial stages of language acquisition, this aspect of development is probably of relatively little concern for our immediate purposes; and (3) the natural sequence of vocal development does not seem to be particularly appropriate for clinical training of articulation. (This latter point is treated in detail elsewhere—see McLean, 1976.) The issue of language mode and the appropriate place of sound production training will be discussed in Chapter 7.

In tracing the development of expressive linguistic performance, then, we will begin with the child's production of single words and identify the period of one-word utterance production as Stage I. Within the developmental period of interest in this text, we have identified three additional stages of expressive development: Stage II—the transition to grammar; Stage III—two- and three-word grammatical utterances; and Stage IV—extension and syntactic refinement of multiword grammatical utterances. An overview of this developmental sequence is presented in Figure 6.

Stage I: One-word utterance production. The child's expressive use of linguistic structure begins with the production of his first word, a celebrated event which usually occurs somewhere between the ages of 10 and 14 months, but which may occur considerably later even in normally developing children. With the appearance of this first word, the young child enters a period of one-word utterance production which will typically last for another 6 to 12 months. Within this period, his utterances will each consist of one word, but the speaking vocabulary of words which can be used in these utterances will grow dramatically. It should be noted that at this level, a string of two or three adult words may function as one child word—such as "Pat-the-Bunny-Book," produced by one of Huttenlocher's (1974) subjects at 12 months.

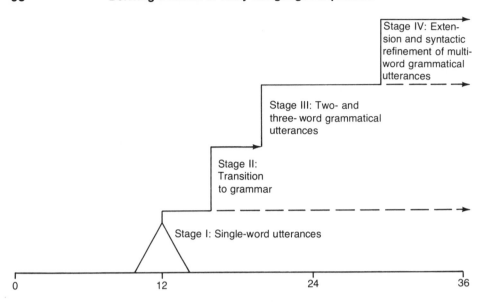

Approximate chronological age in months (at each successive level, the range of variation for corresponding chronological ages increases)

FIGURE 6. Overview of Expressive Linguistic Structure Development.

It was noted earlier that linguistic structure consists of such elements as syntax, phonology, morphology and—a special subset of morphology—lexicon. If syntax is thought of primarily as the system of rules for ordering words in a sentence, then there are some obvious problems in attempting to analyze this aspect of one-word utterances. However, through such procedures as the "rich interpretation" employed by Bloom (1970) and explained previously, efforts have been made to analyze single-word utterances as though they were in fact constituents of more complete sentences which could be inferred from nonlinguistic aspects of the utterance—such as context and the child's accompanying gestures or intonation (DeLaguna, 1927/1963; Ingram, 1971; McNeill, 1970, 1971; Menyuk, 1969). This treatment of one-word utterances as *holophrases* has led to some controversy and raises many seemingly unanswerable and somewhat esoteric psycholinguistic questions about the nature of a sentence. The functionality of this approach has since been convincingly refuted by Bloom (1973). Thus, we will not analyze single words in terms of their supposed positional class (such as subject or object) or even their apparent semantic case, in the sense that this refers to the role of a word in relation to the other words in a sentence (for example, assigning the case "agent" or "instrument" assumes an action performed by that person or object). Instead, we can most validly describe single-word utterances in terms of their form class (noun, verb, etc), their relationship to the immediate context, and their actual or apparent communicative function. This latter issue of communicative functions of one-word utterances was discussed in some detail in Chapter 3 and therefore will not be reiterated here in detail. Suffice it to remind the reader that one-word utterances serve a wide range of communicative functions, ranging from the direct requesting of an action or answer to such things as labeling or indicating a joint referent and signaling the initiation or termination of an interaction.

Probably the most complete analysis of early single-word utterances—and certainly the one which represents data from the largest number of subjects—is that reported by Nelson (1973a). In this study, the investigator documented and analyzed the first 50 words produced by each of 18 children between the ages of 12 and 24 months. This study has been discussed in some detail elsewhere (see Chapter 2) and for purposes of this chapter we will look only at the data provided by this study on the frequency of occurrence for different word classes. Rather than translating directly into terms of adult grammatical form classes, Nelson devised a system of word classes on the basis of the words her subjects actually used. Table 2 lists these classes, with the definitions and examples provided by Nelson and the frequency with which these occurred in the first 50 words produced by her 18 subjects. Also listed are the frequency of occurrence for these classes in the first ten words produced by her subjects.

TABLE 2

Summary of Nelson's Analysis of
First 50 Words Produced by 18 Children

Word category	Example	% of first 10 words	% of first 50 words	
I. Nominals—Specific (total)		24%	14%	
People	"mommy"			12
Animals	"Dizzy" (name of pet)			1
Objects	"car"			1
II. Nominals—General (total)		41	51	
Objects	"ball,"			31
Substances	"milk," "snow,"			7
Animals & people	"doggie," "girl,"			10
Letters & numbers	"e," "two,"			1
Abstractions	"good," "birthday,"			1
Pronouns	"he," "that"			3
III. Action Words (total)		16	13	
Demand-descriptive	"go," "bye-bye," "up,"			11
Notice	"look," "hi"			2
IV. Modifiers (total)		8	9	
Attributes	"big," "red," "pretty,"			1
States	"hot," "dirty," "all gone,"			6
Locatives	"there," "outside,"			2
Possessives	"mine"			1
V. Personal-Social (total)		5	8	
Assertions	"no," "yes," "want,"			4
Social-expressive	"please," "ouch"			4
VI. Function words (total)		6	4	
Questions	"what," "where,"			2
Miscellaneous	"is," "to," "for"			2

NOTE. Data from "Structure and Strategy in Learning to Talk" by K. Nelson, *Monographs of the Society for Research in Child Development*, 1973, 38, No. 149.

On the basis of these data, it seems that the most common form of early words is the "general nominal" and that the next most common is the "specific nominal." Further, it can be seen that, as the child develops his vocabulary from 10 to 50 words, the relative proportion of specific nominals decreases while general nominals increase. Action words (which, in terms of adult grammatical form-classes include not only verbs but prepositions such as "up" and "out" and even social greeting words) represent the next most common class of early words, with modifiers, personal-social, and function words all being only minimally represented.

Two broad conclusions can be drawn from Nelson's data concerning the nature of early one-word utterances. First, even in the earliest stages of expressive development, when the child has a vocabulary of 50 words or less, he has already learned to map, through a variety of form classes, many different aspects of the world around him and his relationship to it. Secondly, as Nelson states, these early words tend to be those which name "objects exhibiting salient properties of change, whether as the result of the child's own action (e.g., *ball*) or independent of it (e.g., *car*)" (Abstract). This second point, of course, relates directly to the importance of dynamic properties in the conceptual development underlying language acquisition, which was discussed in Chapter 2.

In addition to the data on early word form-classes provided by Nelson's (1973a) study, Bloom's (1973) analysis of the one-word utterances produced by her daughter Allison provides further insight into the nature of this level of expressive language development. Bloom has analyzed Allison's one-word utterances in the light of their relationship to the immediate contexts in which they occurred. Through the process of "rich interpretation," she has identified and defined several different semantic-functional classes of words which seem to be predominant in this early stage.

Before describing Bloom's analysis, two points should be made. First, we have referred to "semantic-functional classes," since at this stage it is often difficult to separate the semantic and functional aspects of an utterance. In other words, as we look at Bloom's analysis, we see that many words exhibit an early isomorphism between meaning and function—the word means what it does. Secondly, as Bloom herself and others note (Greenfield & Smith, 1976), it is often impossible to ascertain clearly the actual semantic intent underlying a child's word. Thus, the assignment of words to semantic-functional categories is a matter of subjective judgment reflecting the adult's best interpretation of what aspect of a context or event is represented by an utterance in the child's mind. In looking at the available accounts of one-word utterances, Bloom's appears to us the most cautious in that she generally assigns meanings or intents in relatively "child-sized" terms and avoids as much as possible the assignment of cognitive-semantic constructs beyond those expressed by the single word analyzed. Thus, it seems that Bloom's may be the most "psychologically real" interpretation of the meanings expressed by one-word utterances and, therefore, the most functional analysis for clinical purposes.

In her analysis of Allison's early one-word utterances, Bloom (1973) has looked specifically at the referential functions of these early words—that is, at the specific aspects of the child's universe to which specific words seem to refer. Through this process, Bloom has identified two broad kinds of early word forms: substantive and functional. These are defined by Bloom as follows:

Substantive forms: Word forms "which make reference to classes of objects and events that are discriminated on the basis of their perceptual features or attributes"

Functional or relational forms: Word forms "which make reference across such perceptually distinguished classes of objects and events" (1970, p. 70).

Substantive forms, then, are those words which serve as labels for objects and actions in the child's world (such as "ball," "dada," "jump," "kiss") and function words are those which describe some relationship which might apply to any of these substantive words (such as "more," "allgone," "there"). Most basically, Allison's

TABLE 3

Major Function Words and Their Apparent Meanings
as One-Word Utterances

General relationship	Word	Function/meaning
Existence	"there"	To point out objects
	"uh-oh"	To point out objects—particularly those which startled A
Recurrence	"more"	First to request and later to comment on the recurrence of an activity or object
Disappearance	"away"	To comment on the disappearance of object which had existed in context
	"A' gone"	(Same as above)
Nonexistence	"no"$_2$	To comment on nonexistence where existence had been expected
Cessation	"stop"	To comment on the cessation of an activity
Rejection	"no"$_1$	To protest undesired action or comment on forbidden object (e.g. stove)
Action	"up"$_1$	To request the action of being picked up
Location	"up"$_2$	To comment on spatial location

NOTE: Data from "One Word at a Time: The Use of Single Word Utterances Before Syntax" by L. Bloom. Copyright 1973 by Mouton.

function words tended to mark either the existence/reoccurrence or the cessation/ nonexistence/disappearance of objects, people, and events. In addition, the function words "up" and "no" were first used for regulatory functions—to either request to be lifted up or to reject an activity or object suggested by the adult—and only later were used to mark the more relational functions of spatial "upness" and nonexistence. This analysis of early function words is presented in Table 3.

In looking at Allison's substantive words, Bloom notes that these were primarily noun forms, a finding which is consistent with Nelson's (1973a) data presented previously. Further, these substantive words were most often used for the apparent purpose of naming or labeling aspects of the child's environment. (This type of labeling function was discussed in Chapter 3 and assigned to the broad category of Type II communicative functions.) In tracing Allison's use of the names of specific people (such as "Mommy," "Dada") Bloom notes that these were used initially for the purposes of either "announcing"—noting the presence of—or "greeting" the person named. The second function of proper names was to mark a relationship of possession or association. For example, Allison, seeing a hat usually worn by her mother, might say "Mommy" while indicating the hat. The final function or meaning which Bloom ascribes to Allison's use of person names is that of designating the agent of an ongoing or imminent action. For example, Allison said "Daddy" while handing a broken toy to her father to be mended, thus suggesting that Daddy was to be the agent of the desired action. Here Bloom notes the problem of inferring an intended semantic relationship and does not press this development further until the child's production of multiword utterances allows more confident analysis of intended semantic relationships.

It is interesting to note that although Allison's first words were names of people in her daily environment, the predominant forms in her single-word period were not substantive but functional. Bloom notes, however, that with increasing development Allison's vocabulary came to include more and more substantive words and that the tendency for individual words to recur frequently in a particular language sample decreased. Of course, Bloom's data reflect the development of just one child. Thus, the highly functional nature of Allison's early vocabulary may suggest that she was one of those children described by Nelson (1973a) who approach language acquisition with an expressive rather than a referential strategy. Therefore, rather than conclude that functional forms are generally dominant in early one-word vocabularies, it would seem more appropriate to conclude that both substantive and functional forms are evidenced and that the relative proportions of each form in any one child's early vocabulary may be a matter of individual style or experience.

A final comment should be made regarding lexical and semantic development in Stage I. This is a period in which the child's expressive lexicon is expanding not only in terms of the numbers of words he can produce, but also in the numbers of meanings he can convey with each of those words. For example in Bloom's data the words "no" and "up" and the names for particular people were first used in only one semantic function, then later used to map additional functions. Greenfield and Smith (1976) note the same expansion of both content and semantic function in their study of single-word utterances. They suggest that this characteristic of early expressive development is in accordance with the more general principle of language acquisition stated by Slobin (1973) and originally noted by Werner and Kaplan (1963): "New forms first express old functions and new functions are first expressed by old forms" (pp. 184–185).

Thus, by the end of this stage in the child's development of expressive linguistic structures, he has acquired a rapidly expanding vocabulary and is less and less redundant in the words he uses in conversations with adults. Further, the words in this early vocabulary represent a variety of form classes and many of them have begun to be used for mapping more than one semantic-functional relationship. We will now turn to the second stage in the child's development of expressive language—the transition from single- to multiple-word utterances.

Stage II: The transition to grammar. After the child is expressing multiple functions in his one-word utterances and before he is producing grammatical utterances, there is typically a transition period in which the child begins combining words presyntactically. Until recently this transition period has been largely glossed over in traditional accounts of expressive development, which often suggest that the child moves directly from the single-word utterance to two-word grammatical utterances. Recently, however, several investigators have focused attention on the sequence of linguistic steps that occur between these two types of early speech (Bloom, 1973; Braine, 1976; Greenfield & Smith, 1976). It is this transition which constitutes the second stage in our sequence of expressive linguistic structure development.

This level is characterized by the child's increasingly frequent production of multiple-word utterances which do not yet conform consistently to the syntactic rules of word order. For example, in this stage a child may say "Juice drink" rather than the more grammatically correct "Drink juice." It should be noted that not all word combinations produced in this stage are incorrect grammatically. Rather the defining characteristic of this level is the *inconsistency* of word order patterns which suggests that the child has not yet acquired a general knowledge of the grammatical rules which link the word order of surface structure to the underlying semantic relationships expressed in an utterance.

By closely examining the earliest multiple-word utterances produced by her daughter Allison, Bloom (1973) discovered that these were not actually two-word utterances but rather two one-word utterances pronounced in temporal proximity. In other words, by analyzing the intonation and timing of these early two-word utterances, she noted that they in fact consisted of two single words, each pronounced in a falling intonation with a slight pause between the two. Thus, we might actually discover that our "Juice drink" should more accurately be written as "Juice. Drink." Bloom labels this first step in the child's move to multiple-word utterances the "successive single-word utterance." It is important to note that these successive single-word utterances differ qualitatively from a string of single-word utterances which might have been produced in Level I. This qualitative difference is the relationship which exists between the two words spoken in succession. While the child at Level I may well rattle off a string of words labeling the objects in his immediate environment, the child at Level II combines words which refer to persons, objects, and/or events which are components of a specific relationship in the immediate context or recalled from the child's experience. Words are not just randomly paired up but rather combined in such a way as to provide evidence that the child now has an "awareness of the intersection of different aspects of a situation" (Bloom, 1973, p. 45).

At the same time the child is first producing such successive single-word utterances, he may already be producing two words in more fluent juxtaposition (Bloom, 1973—for example, "More cookie," "Uh oh down"). This type of juxtaposition appears to be learned as an associated unit and, as such, is not really a manifestation of the child's utilization of grammatical word-order rules. This type of utterance is described by Braine (1976) as a "positional-associative" pattern, as opposed to a "positional-productive" pattern. He distinguishes the associative patterns as those in which a particular word always occurs in the same position but actually reflects different semantic relationships to the words which are paired with it. Thus he suggests that these patterns are learned through straight association and that each two-word combination is learned as a separate entity—for example "all broke," "all done," "all shut." The positional-productive pattern is similar in that one word is learned in a consistent position, but the semantic meaning of that word applies to all words paired with it and thus the child may create or produce novel word combinations with that word—"more car," "more cereal," "more cookie," and so on. Whether or not it is valid to attribute semantic productivity to "more" and not to "all" seems to depend on one's knowledge of the child's internal definition of each of these terms. However, the general distinction appears valid; some word combinations do seem to have been learned through a process of rote association and some through a more generative process.

It seems that Braine's "positional associative" patterns are very similar to Bloom's juxtapositions and that this type of word combination may well be represented even before the child begins to produce successive single-word utterances. An important distinction here would seem to be that the positional-associative/juxtaposition pattern occurs only within a specific and relatively limited set of words and relations, whereas in the successive single-word utterance the child is at least capable of crudely marking any relationship which exists in his conceptualization by naming the components of that relationship in succession.

Bloom notes that there are two types of successive single-word utterances: *chained* and *holistic*. A chained utterance is one accompanied by the performance of some action. The word order seems to be related to the temporal order of the dynamic event, with each word often accompanied by a shift in the child's movement. The "chaining" account of early word order is somewhat difficult to apply to those utterances which do not occur within a dynamic action sequence. In these cases, it seems that the "topic-comment" account first proposed (1970) and later rejected (1973) by Bloom may be appropriate. The term "topic-comment" suggests that the child first pronounces the *topic* of an utterance—the element which has primary salience in the child's own mind—and then adds the second word as a comment or clarification of this topic. Reviewing this issue recently, Greenfield and Smith (1976) suggest another rule for early word order which seems closely related to Bloom's original topic-comment theory. They suggest that children first mark the referent which is most critical or salient, in that there is some degree of uncertainty about it—that is, it is not redundant with the context—and then add a second word which is related to the first but dispensable in that it is more likely to be already understood by the listener. This issue of topicalization is discussed in Chapter 2 under "Mechanics of Communication—Reference."

The second type of successive single-word utterance defined by Bloom is the holistic utterance, typically uttered in anticipation or at least independent of the actual carrying out of an action. This type of utterance seems to reflect the child's mental representation of the complete action or relationship. Bloom notes that both types of successive single-word utterances—chained and holistic—are present throughout this stage of development but that the chained form is more dominant initially and gradually comes to be overshadowed by the holistic form. It seems, then, that as the child becomes able to represent internally all of the elements of an action or relationship and to mark two or more of these in succession, he is moving closer to the ability to form truly grammatical constructions. Further, it seems that this increasingly dominant holistic group of utterances may well include (or at least reflect a level of development parallel to) Braine's positional-productive pattern. In both cases the child is combining words in a consistent order and pronouncing them as a single entity.

A final aspect of this transition process is suggested by Braine (1976). He argues that after a child begins to form successive single-word utterances, there are some instances in which the child attempts to express a meaning for which he has not yet acquired the rules for grammatical expression. According to Braine, this is the situation in which the child shows inconsistent and often "incorrect" word-order patterns for a particular two-word combination. Braine labels this type of utterance a "groping pattern" and notes that it is a temporary pattern which is soon replaced by the correct grammatical form in a positional-productive pattern. Braine suggests this brief period of groping-pattern production occurs for only a relatively small proportion of the grammatical utterances which the child eventually comes to produce.

Thus, in Phase II the child first combines successive single words in a chaining or topic-comment pattern, indicating that he knows that the elements of his utterance are related to one another. Following the period of predominantly chained/topic comment successive single-word utterances, the child's multiword utterances become increasingly holistic or position-productive. In some instances, this type of utterance may be preceded by a brief period in which the child seems to be "groping" for the appropriate word order to express his meaning. At the conclusion of this stage, the child is combining two words according to consistent rules of word order and is pronouncing them with a phrasing and intonation pattern which suggest a single sentence, rather than a succession of separate words. At this point, we can say that the child has begun to produce two- and three-word *grammatical* utterances and thus enters Stage III of our expressive development sequence.

Stage III: Two- and three-word grammatical utterances. The child's first production of two-word grammatical utterances usually occurs somewhere between 18 and 24 months. With this development, it becomes possible to analyze the semantic and syntactic aspects of the child's linguistic structures with a degree of confidence which was impossible during the previous two stages. In fact, much of the data available on early language acquistion has been derived from studies of children's early grammatical utterances. Thus, in looking at both this stage and the succeeding Stage IV, we find a relative wealth of empirical documentation and several semantic-based grammars which have been written to describe this level of language performance. Probably the most comprehensive of these treatments is that provided by Brown (1973) in *A First Language*. In this book, Brown summarizes most of the data available in 1973 and presents a stage theory of language acquisition in which he defines each stage by the mean length of utterances produced by the child at a particular point in time. (The MLU measure is increasingly used as an indicator of the child's relative stage of development rather than CA, because there is a wide range of variation in the ages at which children normally acquire specific linguistic abilities, whereas these developments correlate quite consistently with MLU levels.) Brown's MLU is computed on the basis of total morphemes in each utterance produced by a child within a particular language sample. (The exact procedures for computing MLU are rather complex and will not be described here. For more detail, refer to Brown [1973, p. 54] or to Slobin's [1967] *Field Manual for Cross-Cultural Study of the Acquisition of Communicator Competence*. A simplified MLU computation procedure will be discussed in Chapter 6.)

While Brown identifies five stages, his 1973 book treats only the first two of these: Stage I—MLU 1.5 to 2.0, approximately, and Stage II—MLU 2.0 to 2.5, approximately. It is important to note that all of us produce many very short, often one-word utterances in our everyday conversations ("Do you have the car keys?" "Yeah." "Where?" "Right here.") and this is certainly true of the child who is just beginning to produce multiword grammatical utterances. Therefore, if a child's Mean Length of Utterance is 2.0, we must assume that he is producing many utterances considerably longer than two words in order to balance out the many one-word utterances which he most certainly is also producing. Brown notes that children in his Stage I produced utterances up to five *morphemes* in length and in his Stage II this "upper bound" was seven morphemes. Brown's Stage I corresponds almost exactly to our Stage III and his Stage II to our Stage IV. Therefore, we will refer heavily to Brown's analysis in describing these last two stages (for our purposes) of expressive linguistic development.

As noted in earlier chapters there has been an increasing trend in recent years toward the analysis of early child language in terms of case or semantic grammars. In light of our present transactional view of language as the map of a child's knowledge of his world and his reasons for communicating with that world, such a semantic grammar approach certainly seems the most potentially productive for generating intervention implications. Therefore, we will describe the child's expressive language in Stage III in terms of the semantic relations most typically expressed by children in those stages. Further, since for clinical purposes we will need to target not only semantic relationships but also specific classes of word forms, we will also note here the form classes associated with each semantic relationship.

The most prevalent syntactic form in Stage III is the two-word utterance, a form which has been analyzed semantically by several investigators (Bloom, 1970; Brown, 1973; Schlesinger, 1971). Using the categories identified by these investigators, MacDonald and Nickols (1974) have analyzed the frequency of occurrence of particular semantic-grammatical rules in the conversational speech of 25 normal preschool children. Using data from all these sources, we have arrived at a set of two-word grammatical utterance types which seem to be most prominent in the speech of Stage III children. These utterance types, with descriptions of their associated syntactic structures, are presented in Table 4. Toward the end of this stage of expressive development, the child also begins to produce a small set of three-word utterances with increasing frequency. These are also listed in Table 4.

Analyzing the utterance types presented in Table 4, we might note four basic characteristics which seem to describe the speech produced by children at this stage of expressive development. First, many of these early utterance types seem to be extensions of the one-word utterances produced in Stage I. Particularly, the reader will recall Bloom's (1973) data indicating the prevalence of one-word utterances which marked the existence, recurrence, rejection, and nonexistence rela-

TABLE 4

Stage III: Grammatical Utterance Types*

Utterance type—semantic	Syntactic structure	Example**
Two-word utterances		
1. Agent-action	Noun + verb	"Eve read"
2. Action-object	Verb + noun	"Read book"
3. Demonstrative entity		"That book"
Nomination	that/it/etc., + noun	"It book"
Notice	hi/see/etc., + noun	"Hi belt"
4. Possessor—possession	Noun + noun	"Mommy lipstick"
5. Entity—attribute:	Verb + more	"Fall 'gin"
Recurrence	More + noun	"More milk"
Nonexistence	No/allgone + noun	"No doggie" "Allgone milk"
Attribute	Adjective + noun	"Big train"
6. Entity—locative	Noun + noun	"Sweater chair"
7. Action—locative	Verb + noun	"Sit chair"
8. Agent—object	Noun + noun	"Mommy sock"
9. Conjunction	Noun + noun	"Umbrella boot"
Three-word utterances		
1. Agent-action-object	Noun + verb + noun	"Mommy spill juice"
2. Agent-action-location	Noun + verb + noun	"Daddy sit chair"
3. Action-object-locative	Verb + noun + noun	"Throw ball here"
4. Agent-object-locative	Noun + noun + noun	"Daddy ball chair"

*Two-word utterance types are listed in *approximate* order by frequency of occurrence from most frequent (agent-action) to least frequent (conjunction). This order is derived from the data presented by Brown (1973) and MacDonald and Nickols (1974).
**Examples of two-word utterances are from Bloom, 1970.

tions which continue to be important in the early phases of Stage III. Second, the child's language at this point remains highly immediate and concrete. Most of these utterance types serve to describe specific objects and events or relationships which are salient to the child in the immediate context. Third, the child's utterances at this level consist of substantive, high-information words—such as nouns and verbs. He has not yet added the smaller, function words—articles, prepositions, auxiliaries, and so on—which are essential to adult syntax. As Brown (1973) points out, the child who is communicating within the constraints of a two- or three-word utterance must set the same types of priorities set by those who communicate by telegrams in which every word costs money—that is he selects to include only those words which are essential to convey his meaning. Finally, the syntactic form of these utterances is basically the simple declarative sentence. We do not yet see the convoluted or transformed word orders which are used in such formats as the interrogative and the passive sentence.

Stage IV: Extension and syntactic refinement of multiword grammatical utterances. Within the period of *early* language acquisition, which is our present concern, the final stage of expressive linguistic structure development is the one we have identified as Stage IV. As noted earlier, this stage correlates closely with Brown's (1973) Stage II, and we will rely primarily on his data analysis in describing this stage. Of course, one aspect of expressive language which distinguishes this stage from the previous stages is that the child is beginning to speak in longer utterances—typically three and four words but often even more. We must also remember that concurrent with the other aspects of linguistic development which mark this stage, the child is continually adding new items to his expressive lexicon. This addition in itself probably accounts for some of the increase in utterance length—particularly as the child acquires descriptive terms which allow him to expand noun and verb phrases (for example "dolly" becomes "pretty dolly").

The most significant aspect of Stage IV utterances, however, is their increasing completeness or refinement in terms of syntax and morphology. In fact, it seems that the addition of function words and inflectional morphemes probably accounts for a significant amount of the increase in utterance length which characterizes this stage. In reviewing available data, Brown has identified a set of 14 grammatical morphemes which are acquired and manifested in the speech of children at this stage. Further, by collapsing and comparing the data reported by several investigators, he has been able to rank these morphemes in terms of their order of acquisition by the children studied in these investigations. Acquisition was defined as use of the morphemes in sentences where they are required syntactically. Perhaps one of the

TABLE 5

Brown's Fourteen Grammatical Morphemes
and Their Order of Acquisition

Order of acquistion	Morpheme	Specific form(s)
1	Present progressive	-ing
2–3	Prepositions	in, on
4	Plural (regular)	-s, -es, etc.
5	Past irregular	came, ran, etc.
6	Possessive	-'s
7	Uncontractible copula	is, am, are (as in "she *is* pretty")
8	Articles	a, the
9	Past regular	-d, -ed, -/t/
10	Third person regular	-s, -/z/, etc. (as in: "She runs")
11	Third person irregular	does, has (as in: "They do" vs. "She *does*")
12	Uncontractible auxiliary	is, am, are (as in: "They *are* running")
13	Contractible copula	-'s, 'm, 're (e.g., She's pretty")
14	Contractible auxiliary	-'s, 'm, -'re (e.g., They*'re* running")

NOTE. Data in columns 1 and 2 are from *A First Language: The Early Stages* by R. Brown. Cambridge: Harvard University Press, 1973.

most fascinating findings reported by Brown was that this order of acquistion varied little among the children represented in this analysis. In Table 5, we have listed these morphemes in the mean order of their acquistion by these children and have explained the specific syntactic forms referred to by each.

We see, then, that the child in Stage IV supplies many of the function words omitted in Stage III utterances (articles, prepositions, auxiliaries, and copulars). Further, he marks several morphemic/syntactic distinctions of tense and plurality and uses the inflectional morpheme 's to mark possession. At this stage, the child's utterances are still primarily of the simple declarative type of construction. Although many children may be producing one or two specific interrogative forms by this stage (such as "What's that?"), they do not yet exhibit the ability to generate a large number of what Brown refers to as "modalities of the simple sentence"—that is variations or transformations of the normal declarative word order to produce inter-rogatives and imperatives. These abilities characterize Brown's Stage III, and go beyond the developmental scope of this book. Thus, the final stage of expressive language development within our sequence is characterized by the increasing length of the child's utterances and, more importantly, by the ability to use many function words and inflectional morphemes within the simple declarative sentence construction.

The Development of Linguistic Structure: Summary

This chapter has very briefly summarized the data and theory which seem to offer the most productive account of linguistic structure development. We considered first the nature of linguistic structure, noting that this most basically consists of the systems of phonology, morphology, and syntax. Next, we noted the different types of grammars which have been developed to describe both adult and child language and suggested that each of these efforts has been productive in adding to our overall understanding of the language behaviors we hope to assess and modify. Another issue raised and discussed in this chapter was that of receptive vs. expressive language. Noting the qualitative differences in these two dimensions of language and reviewing the literature on the question of precedence (Does receptive lan-guage precede expressive?), we concluded that these two dimensions of language development should be described separately. Finally, we have attempted to briefly trace the developmental sequence of linguistic abilities, both receptive and express-ive, in young children from birth to approximately three years of age.

At this point then, we have reviewed for the reader our perspectives, derived from two years of project activities, on the cognitive bases for language acquisition, the social bases for language acquisition and the development of linguistic structure, per se. We have noted that all of this sums in what we have called a transactional model of language acquisition. In the following chapter, we will present a graphic model, or visual representation, of this overall perspective. In the remaining chap-ters of this report, we will consider the implications of this model for clinical assess-ment and intervention, as well as for future research priorities.

chapter 5

A Transactional Model of Language Acquisition: Summary

The literature review and synthesis, reflected in the perspectives set forth to this point, finally culminate in what we will call a *transactional model* of language acquisition. In this chapter, we will briefly summarize the components of this model and present a visual model which portrays these components graphically.

Summary of Model Components

This transactional model consists most basically of three major interacting components—cognitive, social and linguistic—each of which represents one aspect of the young child's experience and development. Thus we are suggesting that the child acquires language through interactions with his environment and that from these interactions he derives the *cognitive* and *social* bases which underlie his mastering of the *linguistic* code of his culture. Further, we are suggesting that this specific linguistic code is acquired through the child's participation in a dynamic partnership with the mature language users in his environment, and that the mutual reciprocity of this process is best characterized by the term "transactional."

Cognitive Bases

We have concluded that language maps a child's existing knowledge and that he therefore must have something to say before he will acquire any language. On the basis of the research reviewed here, it seems that most of the knowledge reflected in the semantics of emerging child language is related to the dynamic properties of objects, events, and relationships with which the child has had direct experience. Thus, it seems that one important component of the young child's environmental interactions must be the perception and motor manipulation of objects which afford action by the child and/or provide dynamic responses which are salient to the child. (For details, see Chapter 2.)

Social Bases

We have also noted that children must have a reason for acquiring and using language and that this reason is most directly related to the function of language as a means of communicating with and effecting responses from the environment. After reviewing the research on early social development and the communicative functions of early language, we concluded (in Chapter 3) that another critical aspect of the child's early interactions with the environment is establishment of ritualized interaction patterns with at least one primary figure, usually the primary caregiver. It was noted that such early interactions provide first a basic level of socialization which is essential if the child is to have any motivation for communication. Second, they secure for the child a repertoire of prelinguistic communicative behaviors and functions which can later be mapped linguistically. (For details, see Chapter 3.)

The Transactional Process of Language Structure Acquisition

In analyzing the process by which the specific linguistic code of a particular culture is transmitted to the prelinguistic infant, we have concluded that the infant enters into a "language-learning partnership with the mature language users in his environment and that, in this partnership, both members have an important role to play. We noted that the mature language user typically facilitates the infant's task by marking the semantically relevant segments of an event or relationship and by providing appropriately modified language models which are reduced in terms of length and complexity and which are frequently repeated or paraphrased. For his part, the infant must bring to this partnership his own mechanisms for establishing joint reference with the mature speaker, selectively listening to the language input which has been modified for his benefit and providing feedback to the speaker concerning the effectiveness of the language modification. (For details, see Chapter 3). We concluded that linguistic structure is thus first acquired receptively as the infant infers the meaning of a heard utterance which co-occurs with a known referent. (Chapter 4 traced the sequential development of linguistic structure in both receptive and expressive performance through the early stages of language development.)

A Visual Model

Figures 1, 2, and 3 present visual models of this transactional process as it underlies both language performance (Figure 1) and language acquisition (Figure 2), and as it directs both research and intervention efforts in this area (Figure 3). As in any attempt to reduce a complex interactive process into a two-dimensional graphic representation, these visual models are necessarily simplistic in that they separate and treat as discrete entities those components of experience and development which, in terms of any psychological reality, are actually nested within or superimposed upon one another. However, such graphic representation serves the purpose of allowing the reader to visualize the model as a gestalt and to see the parallel and interlocking relationship which exists between the different components of the model that we have described separately in the preceding chapters.

Language Performance

Figure 1 is a visual representation of the transactional model as it accounts for the realization process underlying the production or comprehension of a specific utterance. Thus, the model suggests that any given utterance will reflect, at the most basic level, the speaker's *experiential history* in both the social and the cognitive/conceptual domains. Equally important in determining the nature of the utterance are the social and physical aspects of the *immediate context*. Further, our model suggests that the speaker's historical and immediate cognitive reality will determine the *semantic component* of his utterance, while his social/communicative reality (also based on past and immediate experience) will determine the *pragmatic aspect*

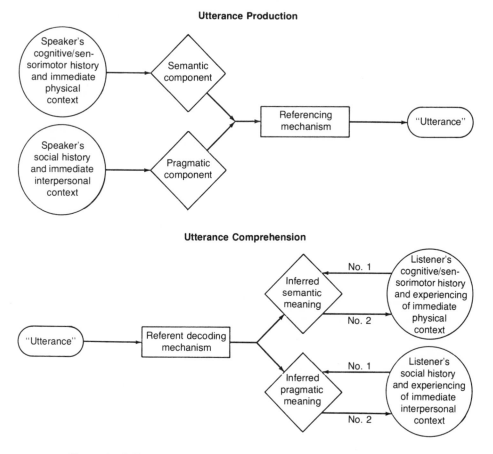

FIGURE 1. A Transactional Realization Model of Language Performance.

of the utterance. Finally, this model suggests that both the semantic and pragmatic components of any particular utterance may have been mapped in a number of ways, and the specific linguistic structure actually uttered will be a function of the speaker's *referencing mechanism*. As discussed in Chapter 2, this referencing process takes into consideration the reality factors of: (a) both the speaker's and the listener's knowledge of the referent, (b) contextual redundancy, and (c) the speaker's linguistic competence and limitations.

Similarly, in presenting the comprehension process, this model suggests that the *listener's cognitive/conceptual* and *social/communicative experience*, in both his past history and in the immediate context, will contribute significantly to his assignment of *semantic* and *pragmatic meaning* to an incoming utterance. (This process is indicated by arrow #1.) Further, a "Referent Decoding Mechanism" is posited as the first step in the comprehension process. It is suggested that this decoding mechanism reflects the listener's linguistic knowledge and experience and will thus also contribute significantly to the listener's ability to interpret a heard utterance correctly—that is, to achieve joint reference with the speaker. Finally, this model suggests that the semantic and pragmatic meanings derived by the listener are ultimately processed and interpreted at the level of the *listener's own past cognitive and social experience* as well as *his experiencing of the immediate physical and social/communicative context*. (This process is indicated by arrow #2.)

Language Acquisition

Figure 2 represents the transactional model as it describes the overall process of language acquisition. We have represented this model in four levels. At the bottom of the figure, the first level represents the critical aspects of the child's interactions with the people and objects in his environment. At the next level are the cognitive, social, and communicative understandings or concepts which the child apparently derives from these environmental interactions and which serve as the bases for the next level of the model. This third level corresponds to the specific aspects of the child's developing language competence—semantic, pragmatic, and structural—which are derived from the two underlying levels. Finally, at the top of the figure is the child's actual language performance, which represents a culmination of all the underlying aspects of development. It should be noted that this language performance may take the form of either a speech act or a response to an incoming linguistic stimulus.

Finally, the reader will note that only the first and fourth levels in this model correspond to behaviors which are actually observable—the child's environmental interactions and his language performance. The two intermediate levels both portray presumed domains of conceptual development which, of course, cannot be directly observed but which are inferred on the basis of the relationships which obtain between a child's environmental interactions and his language performance.

Language Research and Intervention

For purposes of either research or intervention programming, the four levels of this model have fairly direct applications. These are suggested in Figure 3. We are

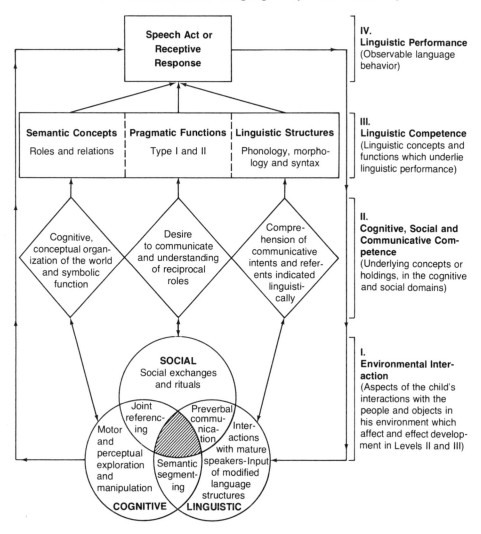

FIGURE 2. A Transactional Model of Language Acquisition.

suggesting that both research and training efforts in the area of early language acquisition must focus not only on observed language behaviors, but on all of the components of the three underlying levels of development. This perspective seems particularly promising for generating research and training with nonverbal children who, because of their failure to exhibit observable linguistic performance might otherwise seem impossible to assess in terms of language development. This model suggests that although a child may not exhibit any language behaviors per se, it is still possible to assess his development in the underlying levels of competence and experience and, from this assessment, to project the areas in which further development must occur before language behavior can be expected to emerge.

The following part of the book will analyze in detail the specific implications of this model for the clinical assessment and treatment of young handicapped children with

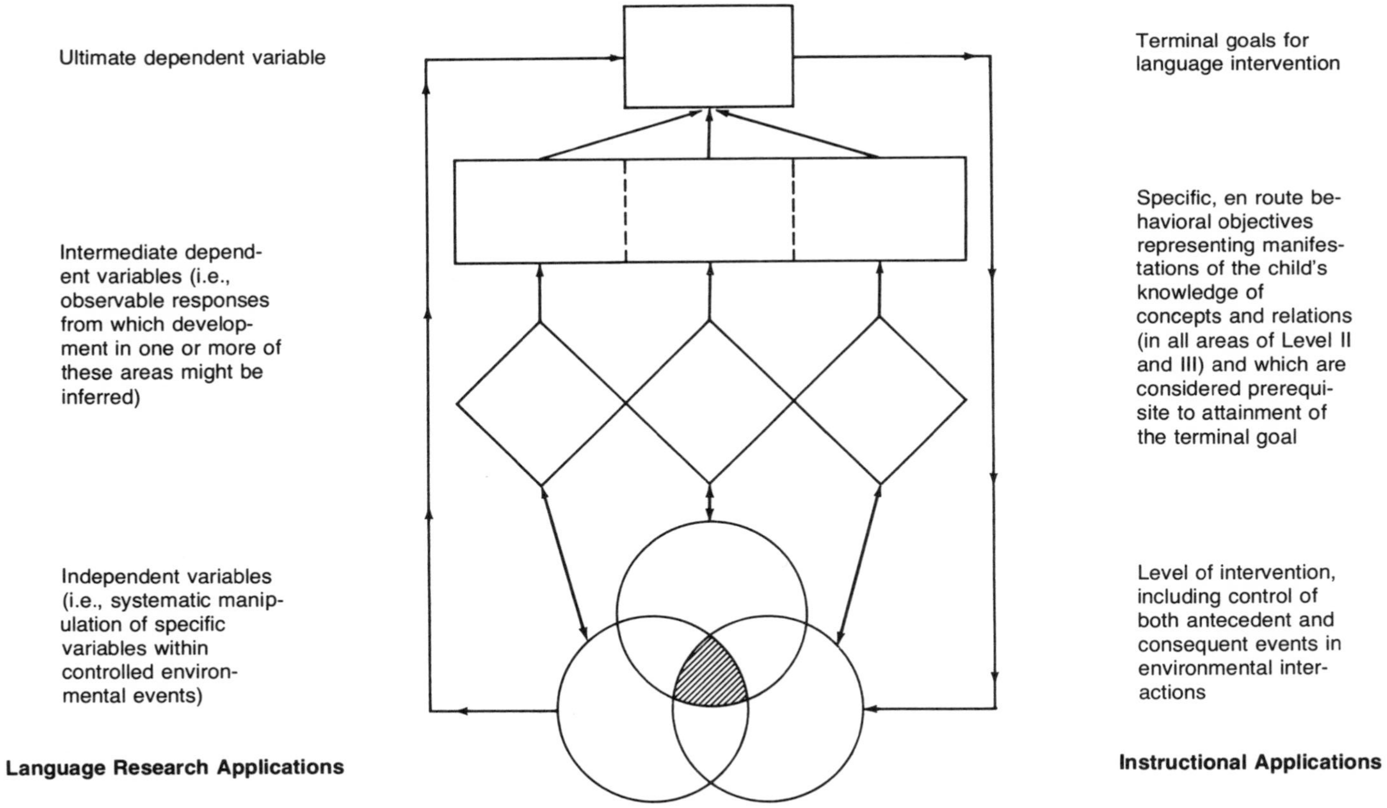

Terminal goals for language intervention

Specific, en route behavioral objectives representing manifestations of the child's knowledge of concepts and relations (in all areas of Level II and III) and which are considered prerequisite to attainment of the terminal goal

Level of intervention, including control of both antecedent and consequent events in environmental interactions

Instructional Applications

Ultimate dependent variable

Intermediate dependent variables (i.e., observable responses from which development in one or more of these areas might be inferred)

Independent variables (i.e., systematic manipulation of specific variables within controlled environmental events)

Language Research Applications

FIGURE 3. Research and Intervention Applications of Transactional Model.

116

severe language delay or deficiency. Finally, we will consider the implications of our findings and conclusions in terms of future directions for research in the area of language acquisition and intervention.

part 3

The Transactional Model and Early Language Intervention

chapter 6

Assessment Implications

In this section, we will discuss the clinical implications of the transactional model of language acquisition developed in the preceding chapters. Recommendations for assessment and treatment which will be offered in this chapter and the next are directly related to the components of this model. In this chapter, we will first examine general implications of the model for assessing language-delayed or language-deficient children. We will then offer specific recommendations for assessment targets and procedures, noting any existing instruments which are consistent with this model.

Two broad qualifications apply to the discussion in this chapter. First, the reader is reminded that the clinical implications presented here are for a very specific population—those handicapped children functioning at or below the three-year-old level in their language behavior for whom such functioning indicates a serious language delay or deficiency. Secondly, the recommendations for assessment and treatment offered here, although highly specific, represent the application of a theoretical model for clinical intervention. As such, they have not yet been validated through implementation in a total-intervention program. Many of the targets and procedures recommended have been used successfully, either through existing programs or through our own pilot work with language-delayed toddlers and pre-schoolers. Nevertheless, the model as a whole has yet to be implemented and validated.

Focus of Assessment

The first decision to be made in planning any assessment is which behaviors to assess. In other words, what are the questions we must ask the child in order to understand the nature of his language disorder and prescribe appropriate treatment? Unfortunately, it seems that all too often this question is answered not in terms of the behavior manifested by the individual child, but rather by the content of the assessment instrument or battery which has been adopted by a particular clinic or school district. As an alternative to this approach, the transactional model suggests several specific targets appropriate for assessment at different levels of development. Further, this model suggests that assessment must target not only language behaviors per se, but also behaviors which are related to the cognitive and social bases for language acquisition. At this point, we will briefly consider the nature of these targets and in a later section will offer a more specific set of guidelines for determining the appropriate targets for a particular child.

Organismic Considerations

Of course, the first question we must ask of the child who exhibits severe language deficiencies is whether or not he is organically capable of the sensation, perception, and production of an aural/oral language system. For production, the child must have appropriate oral musculature and bone structure and, if there is any indication that these components of the speech production system are damaged, the child should first be referred to a speech pathologist for examination. Until recently, the assessment of hearing, particularly in the ranges of sound sensation and perception which are essential for speech processing, has been problematic with very young, developmentally delayed children or children with behavior disorders. In recent years, however, new procedures have been developed (impedance audiometry and operant audiometry) which make this type of assessment not only feasible but quite reliable and therefore clinically functional.

An additional aspect of organismic capability that might be assessed is neurological. For example, we could refer the child for an electroencephalogram to determine whether he showed any "hard signs" of brain damage which might indicate some degree of aphasia as an appropriate diagnosis. However, this type of assessment is not specifically recommended here because, to the best of our knowledge, such a diagnosis would not serve any clinical function—that is, it would not assist us in prescribing appropriate treatment for the child.

If this initial assessment of organismic integrity reveals any significant oral structural damage or hearing loss, the child should be fitted with appropriate prosthetic devices before any further assessment is conducted. In a rare case, it may be that such a device will be sufficient to correct the language deficiency. More likely, however, remedial work will be necessary to compensate for the developmental delay already caused by the uncorrected problem. It is also possible that the problem may be so severe that a prosthesis cannot completely eliminate its effects. Further, the identification of a significant organic handicap may indicate the need for an alternative mode of communication to replace or supplement the aural/oral mode in the child's language program. Such a decision requires the clinician to select a mode which is most appropriate to the child's level of functioning in three domains: motor, cognitive, and social. This point will be discussed more fully in the next chapter. Finally, an oral/aural impairment may, of course, co-occur with a mental or emotional disability which will continue to affect the language development process. Thus, the identification of an organic deficit usually does not eliminate the need for further assessment.

It should be noted that the model outlined in this book is not designed specifically with deaf children in mind, although most of the general principles and procedures described here would be applicable to deaf children. However, if a child is diagnosed as functionally deaf, the clinician should be familiar with procedures and materials which are specifically designed for work with this population. Those interested in such procedures are referred to Berger, 1972; Ling, 1976; and Lloyd, 1976.

Cognitive Bases
for Language

The transactional model of language acquisition suggests that a young child's cognitive development is critical to his language development. Therefore, if a child is identified as having a serious language deficiency, one component of the assessment of that child should focus on his level of cognitive functioning—specifically those aspects of cognitive development identified earlier as being most directly related to language acquisition (see Chapter 2). In assessing the child's cognitive bases for language, there are several major areas to examine. First, we are concerned with the child's *general level of cognitive organization.* This refers to the child's strategies for interacting with the world of things in space and includes such Piagetian constructs as object permanence and symbolic functioning. Second, we need to assess the *specific knowledge/concept base* which the child brings to the language-learning task. This aspect of cognitive assessment focuses on the specific knowledge which the child demonstrates about the objects, events, and relationships in his environment and the extent to which these concepts are related to the dynamic and/or perceptual features of that environment.

A third function of cognitive assessment is to determine if the child is demonstrating, perhaps preverbally, the *semantic relational concepts* which are commonly mapped in early or emergent language (for example, concepts of recurrence, existence, and nonexistence). Of course, these aspects of cognitive functioning are closely interrelated and interdependent. For example, demonstration of one aspect of the child's general level of cognitive organization may also serve as demonstration of a specific semantic concept. Thus, if the child shows surprise at not finding an object where he saw it hidden, he is demonstrating not only a level of object permanence, but also the semantic relationship of nonexistence. Nonetheless, for purposes of clinical profiling and targeting, it is useful to describe each of these aspects of cognitive functioning separately.

Finally, the assessment of cognitive bases for language should also serve to identify the individual child's *unique or idiosyncratic concepts, interactive strategies, and preferences.* This aspect of the assessment will be used for structuring high-probability treatment activities and selecting early language targets which are most probably "maps" of the child's existing knowledge.

Social Bases
for Language

In addition to the cognitive functions and holdings essential for language acquisition, the transactional model suggests that the child who exhibits a serious language disorder or delay may also be lacking some or all of the social bases for language.

These then represent an additional set of recommended targets for the assessment of such a child. The first concern within this component of assessment is the child's *general level of socialization,* as indicated by his interactions with and attachments to the primary figures in his world. A second focus in assessing social development is the child's demonstration of *preverbal communicative behaviors* which reflect a range of communicative functions or intents. Such behaviors may be either vocal (such as crying) or motor (such as tugging or pointing) and may indicate such communicative intents as requesting a desired object, signaling discomfort, indicating a referent of interest, or signaling a desire for proximity or interaction.

Finally, a third focus of this assessment component is the *specific interactive behaviors* which seem to constitute the child's contribution to the "language-learning partnership" described earlier. Thus, for example, we will be interested in the child's establishment of eye contact and following a line of regard toward the establishment of a joint referent. Similarly, it seems important that the child attend to utterances which are directed towards him and that he participate in reciprocal play rituals.

While the analysis of a child's natural environment will be an important aspect of much of the assessment recommended here, this component becomes particularly critical in assessing the aspects of social development which underlie language acquisition and usage. Thus, this phase of the assessment process will include some analysis of the interactions which occur between child and caregiver and will focus not only on the child's contribution, but also on the adult's part in this process. Typically, adults interacting with linguistically immature children manifest what we have referred to as a set of "facilitation strategies," providing the child with modified utterances appropriate to his level of functioning. Further, in such interactions, adults often mark the semantic segments of ongoing events and, by responding to the child's communicative efforts, help him to learn the "communication game."

In the case of severely language-delayed or language-deficient children, there is reason to suspect that these adult contributions to the language-learning process may be only minimal or even nonexistent. This problem may arise for at least two reasons. First, many such children reside in large institutions or even "intermediate-care facilities" in which the caretakers lack either the time, inclination, or authority to interact in these ways with the children. Also, in such settings the often high turnover rate among attendant-level personnel plus the frequent changes in the specific staff members assigned to particular cottages and/or shifts militates against the establishment of one or a few *primary* caregiver(s) with whom the child can establish attachments and rituals of interaction.

A second problem which may affect even children residing in their natural homes is one of extinction. It may well be that the severely delayed child's failure to respond to his parents' natural facilitation behaviors may represent a history of nonreinforcement for the parents which, after some period of time, would lead to the extinction of those behaviors. Thus, in assessing the social bases of language, we will be targeting both child and adult patterns of interaction.

Receptive
Linguistic Skills

In discussing implications for assessment, we will treat receptive and expressive linguistic skills separately. As was explained earlier, these two aspects of linguistic development seem to represent qualitatively different processes, due to the difference in locus of control and the apparently different cognitive demands represented by each. Further, particularly in the early stages of development with which we are concerned, the precedence relationship between these two modes is not yet fully understood or documented. Finally, in cases where there may be some neurological damage associated with the language deficit, it may well be that one of these processes is more significantly impaired than the other and/or that the normal relationship between the two is altered. Therefore, it is recommended that the child's linguistic skills in the receptive and expressive modes be assessed separately.

In accordance with the description of receptive language development presented earlier (see Chapter 4), four major levels of receptive linguistic ability may be targeted in assessment. The first of these is the *ability to discriminate between meaningful units of the language system*. For most children, this means the discrimination between different phonemes, as well as between different supralinguistic or intonational patterns. When an alternative (nonaural) mode of communication is indicated, such discrimination may be between different manual signs or tangible symbols. It should be emphasized here that our focus of concern is on the discrimination of *meaningful* units (as opposed to the discrimination of puretone frequencies, allophones, and so on).

Given this basic ability, the lowest level of comprehension we might expect is that earlier designated "Stage I"—*phonemic and paralinguistic comprehension*. At this stage, the child consistently responds appropriately to familiar, established phonemic and paralinguistic patterns. The next level is *semantic-lexical comprehension*. At this stage, the child appropriately responds to single words, either in isolation or embedded in a longer utterance. At the lowest level, this comprehension is dependent upon contextual cues, while at the highest level the child can identify a referent with no contextual cues and use the semantic properties of the known words to infer the meaning conveyed by a multiword utterance. The third stage of receptive development, and the highest with which we are concerned, is *syntactic-grammatical comprehension*. At this stage, the child responds appropriately to the meaning conveyed by the morphemic and syntactic properties of a heard utterance, as well as to the lexical/semantic components of the utterance. The reader will recall that only the earliest levels of this stage occur within the developmental period of interest here.

Expressive
Linguistic Skills

In Chapter 4, we identified four levels or stages of expressive linguistic structure development and these will serve as the guidelines for assessment in this area. The first stage identified was *single-word utterances*. Assessment of this level of development includes not only the actual number of different words produced but, more importantly, the different semantic relations and cases represented by such utterances (for example, existence, nonexistence, recurrence) and the communicative functions served by these utterances. At this level particularly, then, it is important to analyze not only the structure of the child's utterance, but also the relationship between that utterance and the immediate context in which it was produced.

At the next stage, the child is making the *transition to grammar* and is beginning to chain two or more words together, with the order of the words apparently determined by the temporal order or relative salience of the actual referent event or entities. In the next stage, the child produces *two- and three-word utterances*. These utterances should reflect a variety of different semantic relationships and cases (such as agent-action and entity-location) and, to a lesser extent, some variety of syntactic structures (for example, noun-verb and noun-noun).

The fourth stage of development, for our purposes, is *extension and syntactic refinement of multiword grammatical utterances*. Since this stage extends through the primary school years, our interest is only in the most rudimentary levels of this stage. For our purposes, in addition to longer utterances, this stage is marked by the child's appropriate usage of a few prepositions, function words, and inflectional morphemes. Thus, in assessing expressive linguistic skills, we will be targeting the child's general level of current functioning and the breadth of his functioning at that level—both in terms of the semantic meanings and the communicative functions represented in his expressive language repertoire.

In determining which behaviors to assess, we have suggested that the transactional model offers several general implications. We have identified broad categories of assessment targets in the areas of organismic functioning, cognitive bases for languages, social bases for language, receptive linguistic abilities, and expressive linguistic abilities. Before discussing these targets in more detail, we must consider some implications of this model for the actual procedures and contexts of assessment.

Methods of Assessment

The multidimensional model for language assessment recommended in this book demands a major investment of time and effort by the examiner, particularly in the case of the more severely language-deficient child. If this effort is to produce a clinically valid and prescriptive profile of the child's current functioning, the procedures and contexts of that assessment must be as carefully selected and planned as the actual targets or content. The examiner/clinician must consider such questions as, Where shall the assessment be conducted? By whom? Under what type of conditions? Which standardized instruments, if any, should be used? In the next few pages, we will consider some general implications of our transactional model in terms of these questions. Following this general discussion, we will suggest a set of specific assessment targets and procedures and a guideline for deciding which of these are most appropriate for any particular child.

Contexts for Assessment

Regardless of what specific assessment procedures are to be employed, the clinician should be sensitive to several contextual factors which would seem important in assuring valid results. First, the purpose of assessing a severely language-delayed child is to obtain the most representative picture possible of the child's current level of functioning, in order to prescribe an appropriate treatment program for that child.

Thus, we are interested not so much in how well the child points to or names a preselected set of pictures, but rather in how well he actually functions within his natural environment. That is not to say that assessment procedures which require picture pointing/naming responses are never useful. Rather, our interest in them is in what they tell us about the child's ability to function successfully. We are not interested in test performance as a behavioral end in itself, but only as a means to the end of better understanding one individual child and his unique repertoire of abilities and disabilities.

It is suggested, therefore, that the context for any assessment effort be designed to optimize the child's performance and to evoke the best possible sample of his abilities. Towards this end, we would offer several suggestions (hardly unique to these writers or to this developmental area). First, the assessment setting should be as noninhibiting as possible. Thus, factors of strangeness or "coldness" which may produce anxiety should be minimized, while familiarity and "warmth" or cheerfulness should be maximized. This may be best accomplished by conducting the assessment in the child's own home, in the classroom, or in a comfortably furnished playroom where at least one person familiar to the child is present. The general atmosphere of the assessment situation should be relaxed and "fun." Several procedures and factors may contribute to this atmosphere, not the least of which is the examiner's own attitude. In addition, the examiner should see to it that the session is in fact fun, which may mean alternating periods of not-so-enjoyable testing (as in administering a standardized instrument) with some activity which the child enjoys. Also, the child should be reinforced for cooperative behavior. If the examiner is using a standardized instrument, reinforcement should not be contingent on correctness, of course. However, such contingent reinforcement may be appropriate in more informal procedures, if this serves to provide a better picture of the child's optimal performance. An additional method of optimizing performance is to allow a warm-up period at the beginning of the assessment session before any data are collected. Depending on other variables, this time may be used to allow the child to become comfortable in the assessment setting, to allow the examiner to become sensitive to the child's moods or interests at that particular time, and to allow the child to warm up to the nature of the task.

The question of who should conduct the assessment is also related to the objective of optimal functioning. It has become a truism that in any testing situation the clinician must have developed good rapport with the child before attempting to get a valid profile of the child's abilities. In many cases, this rapport may already exist or may be easily attainable. However, in the cases where this is not so (and with young, handicapped children it often is not), it is recommended that a procedure be selected in which actual contact with the child can be made by a parent, preferred teacher, or even an older sibling. It is possible, for example, to explain to a parent or sibling the types of interactions the clinician would like to observe for the purpose of obtaining a language sample or even the actual procedures for administering some published instruments. Many variables may affect the decision of who will actually interact with the child, including the ease of establishing rapport, willingness and/or ability of parents or others to participate, and the question of who will ultimately conduct the treatment program for the child. In any case, the clinician is, of course, responsible for the selection, planning, and analysis of assessment efforts.

Use of Standardized or
Published Instruments

It is probably true that in a majority of service delivery settings today, the most common procedure employed in the name of assessment is the administration of a standardized instrument or a battery of such instruments. In the case of a child referred for assessment on the basis of a manifest language delay or deficit, the instrument selected is most apt to be one which is specifically identified as a language development scale. Further, the actual selection of the instrument(s) to be administered is probably determined in many cases by one of the following four factors: (1) the instrument/battery has been preselected or adopted by the school district or department responsible for language programming, (2) the instrument/ battery is most readily accessible to the clinician, (3) the clinician is most familiar with the procedures for administering and scoring the particular instrument(s), or (4) the instrument(s) can be administered quickly. Quite obviously, such considerations may be inevitable in applied service delivery settings, but they are not sufficient for the selection of an assessment procedure which will provide the most appropriate and representative profile of an individual child's unique complement of abilities and disabilities. Rather, there are several other variables which need to be taken into consideration in making such a selection.

The nature of the instruments. First, it must be recognized that the plethora of assessment instruments now available vary along several critical dimensions, even though they often have very similar titles. There are five such dimensions which are relevant in determining the appropriateness of any instrument for achieving a specific assessment objective:

1. Instruments may be either *norm-referenced* or *criterion-referenced*. Norm-referenced scales yield age equivalence or age-relative percentile scores and thus primarily describe the child's relative degree of deficit. Criterion-referenced instruments yield data on the child's performance relative to preset criteria of adequate or successful performance on a specific cluster of tasks. Thus such measures tend to be prescriptive as well as descriptive, although the actual usefulness of any instrument for prescriptive purposes depends on several additional variables.
2. Instruments typically reflect a *model of development* adopted by the developers of that instrument, and items are often clustered according to the constructs relevant to that model. If an instrument is based upon a model which is not consonant with the clinician's operating model, the process of translating assessment results into clinical prescriptions is greatly complicated. For example, if a semantic model of language development is the principal focus of a treatment program, then data from a test which is based upon a transformational grammar model of language development will not be directly applicable in prescribing treatment targets for a child.
3. Instruments differ in the *aspects of development* which are assessed or emphasized. This point seems very obvious, but it should be noted that many instruments are titled in very global terms (such as "John Doe's Test of Language Development," or "Susan Jones' Test of Early Cognitive Develop-

ment") which do not provide the clinician with adequate information about the actual focus of the instrument. A test of "language development" may target only expressive use of syntax or may include both verbal and preverbal receptive and expressive behaviors. Similarly, a test of "cognitive functioning" may in fact tap only a specific type of problem-solving ability or may cover a wide range of sensorimotor, perceptual, associative, and conceptual abilities. Thus, in selecting an assessment instrument, the clinician must conduct a careful item analysis and determine if the content of that instrument is actually relevant to the aspect of development which is of concern in a particular case.

4. Another obvious dimension on which instruments will vary is the *level of development* which is targeted. Again, global titles—even those with the qualifying word "early"—do not provide this information. In dealing with handicapped children, the clinician often does not initially know the child's actual level of functioning within a specific developmental domain. He should, however, have a good idea of the *range* within which the child is functioning and be able to select an instrument which provides items appropriate to both the lower and upper ends of that range. If, for example, the clinician believes that a child's level of expressive language is approximately comparable to that of a two-year-old child, then he will want to select a measure appropriate for the age range of, perhaps, one to three years. An instrument normed for children from two to five years would not be selected because of the possibility that the child may well function below the two-year level, at least on several items.

5. Finally, a dimension to some extent related to the dimensions of aspect and level of development is *depth of assessment*. In general, the more global an instrument is in terms of the aspect(s) of development targeted, the more shallow will be the probing in each component or domain represented. Similarly, it is generally true that the wider the age range sampled, the fewer will be the number of items geared to any one particular level of development. Thus, if the examiner wants the results of an instrument administration to yield a more in-depth, fine-grained profile of a student's specific abilities and disabilities, the instrument to select is most probably one which focuses on a rather narrowly defined age range and aspect of development.

Thus, assessment instruments vary along a number of dimensions which are directly related to the nature of the information an instrument will yield. In deciding on an assessment procedure, the clinician planning to use a standardized instrument must consider his purpose in conducting the assessment vis-à-vis the characteristics of available instruments in terms of the five dimensions described above and determine which, if any, are appropriate. Let us briefly consider four questions relevant to this clinical decision: (1) What is the purpose of assessment? (2) When is it appropriate to use standardized assessment instruments? (3) How should these be used? and (4) Which ones are appropriate? We will address these questions as they relate to the clinical applications of our transactional model and thus will focus on the issue of assessing young handicapped children who manifest a serious language delay or deficit.

The purpose of assessment. Assessments may be conducted for several reasons. Perhaps the most common of these, and the one which is the major focus of this chapter, is to provide a *clinical* profile of the child's specific abilities and disabilities. The objective of this type of assessment is to obtain data which are sufficiently detailed and representative to allow the prescription of appropriate treatment targets and procedures, as well as to assess the specific effects of any preceding intervention efforts. A second purpose for conducting an assessment may be to identify those children who exhibit some language delay or deficit but who have not yet been referred for assessment. This type of *screening* effort is most apt to be launched by a school district or other public agency and involves the assessment of a large number of children. A third purpose for assessment may be to *document* the actual number of children served by a particular district or agency who manifest some quantified degree of delay or deficit. This type of assessment is primarily conducted for administrative reasons, such as qualifying for federal or state "excess cost" monies. Finally, assessment may be conducted as part of a *research* project to provide objective and reliable documentation of the subject's pre- and posttreatment levels of functioning. Such assessment data must be not only reliable and valid, but stated in such a form that they allow comparison of the research subject's performance with that of subjects in other studies or treatment settings. Also, it is often desirable for assessment data gathered in a research context to be in a form which will afford statistical treatment.

Using standardized instruments. Standardized assessment instruments offer both advantages and disadvantages and the relative importance of these will vary with the purpose of the assessment. There are two major advantages of such instruments. First, they can usually be administered and analyzed more quickly and efficiently than can nonstandardized, informal assessment procedures. Further, they do not require that the clinician spend time actually designing the assessment and many can be administered by paraprofessionals. Thus we may summarize this first major advantage as one of clinical convenience.

Probably a more significant advantage of the standardized instrument is its very standardization. The detailed specification of procedures, materials, and scoring, if followed by the examiner, results in performance data which can be compared with available norms and with scores of other children and populations on the same instrument. Obviously, there are times when such reliable, objective, and comparable data are highly desirable.

However, standardized instruments are not appropriate in all assessment situations, particularly when administered strictly according to the standardized procedures specified by the developers. Most such instruments, when so administered and scored, are not sensitive to an individual child's unique or idiosyncratic concepts, history of experience, or vocabulary (for example, a child's response of "bow-wow" to a picture of a dog may be scored as incorrect if the designated correct response is "dog"). In addition, there are many cases in which no suitable standardized instrument is available for the level and aspect of development which are of clinical concern.

Further, the generally inflexible administration procedures required for such tests often militate against the possibility of obtaining the most representative sample of a child's optimal abilities, since the child's performance is restricted to a prescribed set of responses and tasks. For example, the response required in a comprehension task may be to point to a particular picture. Any other response offered by the child (such as pantomiming an action related to the picture or making a noise characteristic of the item pictured) will not be scored (or will be scored as an error). Thus, these interesting and potentially useful data will be lost unless noted anecdotally by the examiner. Similarly, there is the danger, particularly with young handicapped children, that the prescribed setting and procedures required for administration of many standardized instruments will "overwhelm" or intimidate the child and inhibit rather than optimize performance.

Finally and most significantly, standardized instruments usually do not provide the type of in-depth probe of a specific skill which is necessary to prescribe treatment. Typically, two or three items will be scored correct or incorrect as an indication that the child does or does not possess a certain skill at a level usually characteristic of children in a particular age range. In many standardized instruments, the actual nature of the error is not even recorded and, where it is, it is usually the examiner's task to conduct an error analysis later and try to derive the significance of that particular error. The prescriptive value of such instruments is often further limited by a relatively small number of items for any one given skill and/or by procedural restraints which prohibit the examiner from probing further to understand better the source of the child's error (as, for example, questioning the child about why he answered as he did, or modifying the item to determine if the child's error reflected lack of ability or failure to understand the particular test item).

These general advantages and disadvantages of standardized assessment procedures help determine when such procedures are appropriate to the purpose of a specific assessment effort. Certainly, the efficiency and convenience advantages would recommend this approach when the major objective is either screening or documentation, in which large numbers of children must be assessed, and fine-grained analysis of individual skills is not necessary. Similarly, for the purpose of research and, again, documentation, the advantages of the comparable and norm-referenced data offered by standardized instruments seem especially important. For clinical prescriptive purposes, however, such procedures are rarely sufficient, particularly in assessing a young child with a serious language delay or deficit. This insufficiency reflects both the specific disadvantages of standardized instruments cited above and the fact that such instruments are not even available for many of the assessment targets which seem critical in the light of our transactional model.

Methods for using standardized instruments. The decision to employ a standardized instrument thus reflects both the purpose of assessment and the specific instrument variables discussed earlier. When the clinician has decided to use such an instrument, he must then decide how the instrument is to be administered. At one level, this decision may seem unnecessary since a standardized instrument is one which, by definition, includes a specifically prescribed set of procedures for administration. Certainly, if a clinician is using such an instrument for the purposes of obtaining normative data which are comparable with those reported by others using the same instrument, it is imperative to adhere strictly to the procedures for administration and scoring as set forth by the instrument's developers.

However, when such normative comparability is less important than clinical validity and utility, the clinician may well consider the possibility of modifying administration procedures and either modifying or disregarding the prescribed scoring procedures. While such modifications must be made specific to a particular instrument and clinical situation, some general suggestions can be offered here. There are three general aspects of instrument usage which are subject to modification: (1) the presentation of stimuli, (2) the consequences of the child's responses, and (3) the scoring of those responses. Let us briefly consider some options for adapting each of these three components for the purpose of increasing clinical validity and utility.

First, the clinician may wish to vary the procedures for *stimulus presentation* in order to optimize the child's performance on a task. There are at least three ways to adapt such procedures for a particular child.

1. The form and content of *instructions* given to the child may be altered through simplification, more repetition than is allowed in the standardized procedure, or additional support provided to clarify the instructions (such as gestures or modeling a correct response).
2. *The topography of the required task response* may be adapted to match the child's abilities better. This is particularly apt to be appropriate when the child manifests physical disabilities which inhibit the standard response, such as pointing to one picture out of four presented on a single page. In such cases, the child may be asked to look at the correct picture or to indicate when the examiner has pointed to the correct item, rather than being required to actually point to the picture.
3. The actual form of the *stimulus material* may be adapted to optimize the child's performance. In the situation described above, the stimulus materials might be adapted by simply cutting the four pictures apart and placing them at greater distances from each other to facilitate the actual motor response requirement. A modification which would be more significant in terms of slightly altering the actual nature of a task might be to use real objects rather than pictures, or photographs rather than line drawings, in cases where it is suspected that the abstraction of diagrammatic pictures is preventing a correct response. Of course, in any case where modifications are made in the prescribed procedures for presenting stimuli, these should be clearly explained in reporting the assessment data.

The second aspect of administration which may be modified is the manner of *consequating the child's responses*. This adaptation may be accomplished in two ways. Although most standardized procedures require the examiner to provide no feedback to the student concerning the correctness of a response, there may be cases in which the clinician chooses to employ some contingent reinforcement for correct responses. This alteration might be indicated where the child's lack of motivation to perform correctly seems to be limiting his performance, or where there is some reason to believe that the child does not adequately understand the task requirement and thus may not realize what constitutes a correct response. The other variation from standard procedures in consequating a child's response is systematic probing to delineate better the parameters of or reasons for a particular response. This may be done either to determine the extent to which a correct response is indicative of the child's general ability or to determine the source of an error response.

Finally, the clinician may deviate from standard procedures in *scoring the child's responses*. In fact, such deviation is mandatory if the administration procedures have been modified in any of the ways described above, since these modifications invalidate the scoring of responses on the basis of standardized norms. Even in cases where the standard procedures have been followed, the clinician may feel that it is either not valid (due to the child's disabilities) or not useful to analyze the child's performance data in terms of the normative scoring standards provided by the instrument's developers.

In such cases, the clinician may prefer to develop an analysis form which clusters items by the nature of the tasks involved and to tally the child's percent of correct and incorrect responses on each type of task. Such a scoring procedure may prove more functional clinically in directing attention to specific areas of deficient performance and affording an error-analysis process not possible with only a norm-referenced score. Further, in scoring specific items, the clinician who is not interested in normatively comparable data may opt to score as correct some responses which indicate that the child has the general ability of interest, but which are technically incorrect because they are not included in the prescribed definition of a correct response for that item.

In the final portion of this chapter, we will present specific implications and recommendations for assessment based upon our transactional model of language acquisition. Where we have identified instruments consistent with this model, these will be indicated. Such instruments may be modified in any of the above ways if modification will increase their clinical, prescriptive, or evaluative utility. We will next discuss *which* standardized instruments are appropriate for the assessment of young children who are language handicapped.

Selecting appropriate instruments. We have repeatedly stressed that the advantages and disadvantages of standardized instruments must be weighed in terms of the specific purpose for conducting any assessment. Given the decision that a standardized instrument is desirable with or without modifications, the clinician must determine which instrument(s) to select in order to achieve that purpose best. Here, the five dimensions of instrument variables noted earlier must be considered vis-à-vis the specific clinical case. The clinician should select an instrument on the basis of these five criteria:

1. The norm-referenced or criterion-referenced nature of the instrument should be consistent with the assessment objective. Where the purpose of assessment is prescriptive, a criterion-referenced instrument is desired.
2. The instrument should be consistent with the treatment model with which performance data must interface.
3. The instrument specifically should target the aspect(s) of development which are of clinical concern in a particular case.
4. The instrument should contain items which reflect that aspect (those aspects) across a range of developmental levels which is most likely to include and adequately represent the child's current level of functioning.
5. The instrument should contain a sufficient number and variety of items to sample adequately that specific aspect of development at that level of functioning.

In reviewing available assessment instruments for this project, we have applied the above criteria. Thus, in identifying instruments which are consistent with our specific model and focus, we have looked for those which (1) are criterion-referenced, (2) yield data which directly indicate a child's performance in terms of the semantic, cognitive, pragmatic, social, or linguistic behaviors represented in the transactional model, (3) target specifically these aspects in such a way that relevant data are easily identifiable (so that the behavior of interest is not sampled by a few items randomly scattered throughout a more general or global instrument), (4) sample behavior associated with the ages between birth and three years, and (5) sample that behavior in sufficient depth to allow the prescription of appropriate treatment or further assessment, or at least provide a more complete profile of the child's abilities than would be readily evident from an initial observation of the child.

Our review process yielded no instrument which would satisfy these criteria for all aspects of our model. Further, of the scores of instruments reviewed, relatively few were found which focused on the indicated early period of development and still satisfied the other criteria. Most of the scales for the infant-toddler level which we did identify were norm-referenced, global, or did not adequately sample the aspects of early development which are implicated as significant assessment targets by our model. Where such instruments have been identified, they have been incorporated within the specific recommended "Assessment Procedures Guidelines" presented later in this chapter. These instruments are described briefly at the conclusion of this chapter.

Certainly, there may be additional instruments which meet these criteria but which have escaped our attention, and in the years to come, more such instruments will appear on the market. For this reason, we have presented here, in somewhat tedious detail, our considerations in identifying those instruments which seem to be most appropriate and consistent with the transactional model of language acquisition. These same criteria may, of course, be used to analyze any additional or future instruments which seem appropriate within this framework.

Nonstandardized Assessment Procedures

We noted early in this chapter that the transactional model of language acquisition suggests a multidimensional model for the assessment of young children with serious language delays or deficits. Such assessment, if it is to be clinically valid and functional, must consider not only the child's language behaviors per se, but also a number of related social and cognitive abilities, environmental variables, and caregiver behaviors. Our review of available assessment instruments has revealed, however, that relatively few instruments are available which probe these behavioral domains at the levels in which we are interested or in a manner which is consistent with our theoretical perspective. Furthermore, the idiosyncratic nature of many of our assessment questions suggests that some of these will never be answerable through the administration of a standardized test or scale. Obviously, then, we must consider some alternatives to the use of standardized measures.

At a very general level, there are two broad types of nonstandardized assessment procedures which are appropriate to our assessment concerns: the observational analysis of nonverbal behaviors and the analysis of language samples. The specific procedures and analysis formats employed in either of these two approaches will vary, of course, with the specific purpose of a particular assessment and the characteristics of the child to be assessed. These more specific considerations will be identified in the "Assessment Procedures Guidelines" offered later in this chapter.

Before going on to a general discussion of these two types of nonstandardized assessment, one point should be stressed which applies to both approaches. Specifically, we would point out that, although these procedures are not standardized, they can be and must be very systematic. Thus, we are not advocating the use of casual observation or clinical intuition as an alternative to the use of formal instruments. To the contrary, we would emphasize that, because these procedures are nonstandardized, it is particularly essential that they be carefully and systematically controlled and analyzed to assure a clinically functional level of reliability and validity. By clinically functional, we mean that the assessment data must accurately reflect a sample of the child's behavior which is truly representative of his actual level of functioning. The following are some general methodological guidelines which should help to assure that this reliability and validity are realized.

Observational analysis of nonverbal behaviors. In conducting an observational analysis, the clinician's specific interest may be in one or several aspect(s) of the child's behavior and/or interactions which are related to language acquisition as this process is represented in our transactional model. For example, the clinician may be interested in the child's social interactions, in his schemata for interacting with objects in space and time, or in his nonverbal communicative repertoire. A further interest may be in assessing specific aspects of the child's natural environment, such as the availability of manipulable objects or opportunities for social interactions. Obviously, the actual context and format of any observational analysis can only be designed in the light of a specific assessment objective. We can, however, offer some general suggestions for conducting this type of assessment.

1. The objectives of the observation should be clearly specified before any other aspect of the observation is planned. Further, these objectives should be stated in observable behavioral terms and should indicate the conditions under which the behavior is to be observed. For example, the statement "I want to observe Billy's social behavior" is too vague to permit appropriate planning or analysis of an observation session. A better statement might be "I want to observe the frequency with which Billy will initiate or maintain a reciprocal game with a familiar adult." Obviously, many such objectives may underlie one observational assessment effort, and greater specificity in defining the behaviors will be required for the actual collection and analysis of data.

2. In planning an observational session, the context should be selected and/or designed in accordance with the objectives for the assessment. Contextual considerations should include variables from both the human and physical environments, as well as the general contextual factors discussed earlier. For example, if one is interested in observing a child's object interaction schemata, it will be important to see that the assessment context contains objects which vary in their familiarity to the child and in their affordance and functional use

properties. Further, in the interest of evoking optimal performance, one would probably wish to avoid the distractions of an overloaded or cluttered playroom.

3. When possible, a parent or someone who is very familiar with the child should be involved in the planning and conducting of the observation. This involvement may take several forms, again depending on the specific objective of assessment. The parent may be asked to suggest objects or toys which would be most likely to evoke optimal performance or even to provide such items from the child's own toybox. In some cases, it will be desirable to observe this person actually interacting with the child. At these times, the clinician should provide some explanation concerning the purpose of the observation and some general guidelines concerning the type of behavior desired from the adult. Finally, after an observation session, the clinician should ask the parent if the behavior observed seemed typical of the child's performance in other settings. A negative response may require probing further or observing the behavior under different conditions.

4. The method to be used for data collection should also reflect the purpose of the assessment. If very fine-grained contextual detail will be important for analysis, then it will probably be desirable to have the session recorded on video tape; while a paper-and-pencil recording procedure may be very adequate if the clinician is looking for a few clearly defined types of behavior and has developed a reliable code for recording these. If verbal behavior of the interacting adult is of interest, it is important to assure before the session that the recording equipment selected is correctly placed and sensitive enough to provide sufficient clarity for transcribing.

5. The type of reinforcement to be used, if any, should be determined before the session, when this is possible. In some cases, the clinician may be specifically interested in the child's performance under natural social consequences, while in other cases it may be determined that more specific, contingently applied social or primary reinforcement should be used. This decision may be made on the basis of discussions with the parents or others who have worked with the child, as well as on the basis of the objectives of assessment. For example, if the focus is the child's level of socialization, it may be most appropriate to observe the child's interaction patterns under conditions of natural social reinforcement. On the other hand, if the objective is to observe the child's action schemata in relation to a number of different objects, it may be decided that the adult should encourage and contingently reinforce this type of behavior.

6. The data collection and analysis system employed should be one which is maximally functional for clinical purposes. Certainly, such a system should be adequate to reflect the critical parameters of the relevant behaviors. However, such procedures should also be consistent with the practical realities of applied clinical settings; the clinician should be realistic about the level of data sophistication which is necessary and feasible. Thus, for example, a very complex coding system which is successful in a research setting may prove to be totally unsatisfactory and unreliable in an applied setting where the training and maintenance of highly reliable observer rating skills are not possible.

7. During the observational session, the adult interacting with the child should attempt to "enter the child's system" and follow the child's lead regarding

preferred toys and activities, to the extent this is possible. This procedure not only promotes adult-child rapport, but also helps to establish a relaxed, "fun" atmosphere and to optimize the child's tendency to emit the behaviors which are of interest. (This assumes, of course, that the context has been appropriately designed to maximize the probability of this type of behavior.) Finally, this procedure will provide the most representative sample of the child's natural behaviors. Of course, the adult may occasionally wish to probe to determine whether the child is capable of producing a specific behavior on request, but this type of adult direction should be minimized and not allowed to interfere with or disrupt the general flow of the session.

8. The assessment should be conducted over a number of days and should consist of at least three observational sessions. This suggestion is offered because (1) a single observation session may yield an atypical sample of the child's behavior, if it happens to be conducted on a "bad day"; (2) repeated sessions will allow both the child and the adult to become familiar with the observational situation and with each other; and (3) it is probable that, with very young children, it will be necessary to keep sessions brief, and thus, a number of sessions will be needed to provide an adequately large sample of behavior for analysis.

In summary, we have suggested that the procedures employed in the observational analysis of nonverbal behavior should be carefully planned in advance and designed in accordance with the specific objectives of a particular assessment effort. Further, observation sessions should be conducted over several days and should incorporate objects, persons, and interactive procedures which are designed to maximize the level and representativeness of the child's behavior. These general recommendations apply to the planning and conducting of all observational assessment activities to be recommended in this chapter, including those designed to evoke language samples. However, the clinician who intends to obtain a language sample for analysis must consider several additional procedural factors.

Analysis of language samples. A language sample is a verbatim, transcribed record of all utterances produced by a child within a given situation over a certain period of time. The collection and systematic analysis of such language samples provide the clinician with a much more complete picture of a child's natural expressive language performance than that obtainable from any standardized instrument. Whereas the standardized language scale indicates only the child's ability to produce a specific, predetermined response to a standardized, predetermined stimulus, the language sample reflects the child's own natural language patterns, lexicon, mapping strategies, and communicative intents.

The procedures for conducting a language-sampling session are very similar to those employed in observing nonverbal aspects of behavior. Most generally, the child is observed in interaction with an adult (with whom rapport is well established) within a partially structured play setting. The adult's primary role in this interaction is to evoke and encourage child language without structuring the form and content of that language. A record is made of both the adult's and child's utterances and all related contextual variables. This record is later transcribed and analyzed in accordance with the specific objective(s) of assessment. In the interest of reliability and validity, the clinician planning this type of analysis might consider the following methodological suggestions.

1. The specific context for the observational session(s) should be selected and structured in the light of the child's general level of functioning, personal style, or preferences and, of course, in accordance with the objective of assessment. If the language sample is to be collected in the child's home, arrangements should be made to reduce the danger of distraction or disruptions which might be caused by other children or activities in the home. The observer may, of course, wish to observe the child in interaction with siblings or even with a family pet, in which case such interactions should be specifically planned in advance with the parent.

2. Toys should be placed in the setting which are most apt to evoke maximum quantity, quality, and variety of the child's utterances, while toys with which the child is known to play in silence or with stereotypic speech routines should be avoided. Here, the advice of a parent or other adult who knows the child well should be sought. The clinician should maintain a collection of toys found to be particularly appropriate for this type of activity (such as a toy telephone, certain picture books, dolls, and puppets) and may also solicit specific toys from the child's own toybox.

3. The data collection procedure used should be adequate to record accurately both the nonverbal and verbal aspects of interactions which occur during the session. Video tape may be used, but it should be noted that the sound quality of such tape is often not of high enough fidelity to allow accurate recording of child utterances, which are frequently poorly articulated or barely audible. It is suggested, therefore, that a high-fidelity audio-tape recorder and microphone be used in place of or in addition to the video tape. Also, the adult who is interacting with the child may be asked to repeat any utterances produced by the child which he is able to understand but which seem particularly inaudible or inarticulate and are thus apt to be difficult to transcribe from the tape. Finally, if video tape is not used, an observer who is not interacting with the child should be used to maintain a written record of the context for each of the child's utterances.

4. The interacting adult should avoid the tendency to structure verbal interactions, thus affecting and limiting the form and content of the child's utterances. Questions such as "What do you call this?" or "What color is the flower?" specify a particular response required from the child and thus yield data which do not represent the child's own mapping strategy, the relative salience of referent features from the child's perspective, or even the child's own volition to comment on that referent at all. Sometimes it will be appropriate to probe in order to determine if the child can qualify or expand upon an utterance which has just been produced, but the general rule here is, again, to follow the child's lead and listen to what he has to say about his immediate environment.

5. The interacting adult should avoid the strong tendency to talk excessively during periods in which the child is not talking. Most adults are quite uncomfortable during long periods of silence (particularly when they know that the purpose of the session is to record language behavior) and research has indicated that adults interacting with low-verbal children tend to fill the void with

their own verbalizations. However, this tendency may further inhibit the child's own tendency to verbalize. This is not to say that the adult should not occasionally attempt to prompt or encourage the child to talk about what he is doing, but only that such prompts should be kept brief and not be allowed to overwhelm the session.

6. The language sample should be transcribed as soon as possible after it is collected. Further, the person who interacted with the child should do the transcribing or assist in this process if possible. These suggestions reflect our experience that, no matter how good the recording equipment is, there are inevitably a number of child utterances which are ambiguous either as to form or meaning. In such cases, the interacting adult is often able to recall the specific utterance, if not much time has elapsed since the session, and can interpret an otherwise untranscribable utterance.

7. The transcription should preserve only that information which is clinically useful. Thus, for example, contextual details which were not relevant to a child's utterance need not be entered and phonetic spelling need not be used unless the clinician is specifically concerned with the child's articulation. Most typically, transcriptions are presented in a two-column format, with contextual and adult-utterance information presented in one column, while child utterances are placed in the other column parallel to the relevant context notes (see Appendix). However, variations on this format may be designed and used for the purpose of specific types of analysis. For example, if the assessment objectives include an analysis of the pragmatics of the child's natural language, it would be desirable to record the context information in terms of antecedents to and consequences of the child's utterances. A recommended format for this type of transcription is also presented in the Appendix.

8. The procedures and formats employed in analyzing the transcription should be consistent with both the objectives of the assessment and the model of treatment with which the assessment data must interface for prescription purposes. There is little value, for example, in an analysis of the number of nouns and verbs contained in a language sample if the clinician's objective is to determine the relative frequency of different semantic relationships mapped by the child.

   Three more specific recommendations concerning the classification of utterances in the analysis of a language sample are: (1) do not try to classify utterances which are unclear or ambiguous; (2) if the utterance occurred as an immediate imitation of a preceding adult utterance, note this by placing an "I" after the utterance; and (3) if the utterance occurred in direct response to an adult question—such as "What is this?"—indicate with an "(R)" after the utterance. Specific procedures for analyzing language samples will be recommended in the "Assessment Procedures Guidelines." The Appendix contains examples of analysis formats which would be appropriate for different assessment objectives and levels of development.

9. If one objective of the assessment is to derive the child's Mean Length of Utterance (MLU), this should be computed on the basis of number of words, not morphemes, unless the child is generally functioning at the level which we have designated as Stage IV of expressive linguistic development. A general procedure for computing MLU in clinical contexts is provided in the Appendix.

General Implications for Assessment: Summary

In considering the implications of our transactional model for the assessment of young children with serious language delays or deficits, we have noted several very general implications. Regarding the issue of *appropriate targets* for assessment, the model suggests the importance of assessing not only receptive and expressive linguistic abilities, but also the aspects of social and cognitive development which review has indicated are critical to language acquisition. In looking at the issue of *appropriate procedures* for assessment, we have considered the advantages and disadvantages of standardized instruments and the criteria for determining when these are appropriate to the assessment objectives implied by our model. Noting that few such standardized measures are available and that much of the assessment suggested by this model is by nature idiosyncratic to each child, we have also discussed the use of nonstandardized procedures. Specifically, we have suggested some general procedures for the observational analysis of nonverbal behavior and the analysis of language samples.

In the following sections, we will consider the more specific implications for assessment derived from the transactional model of language acquisition. We will also present an assessment model based on this acquisition model and will offer a set of specific "Assessment Procedures Guidelines" for each of the broad target areas identified as important for the assessment of young children with serious language delays or deficits.

Assessment Model

Introduction

The assessment model to be presented and discussed in the remainder of this chapter reflects, at a more specific level than our preceding discussion, the implications of a transactional model of language acquisition in terms of the clinical assessment of children with significant language delays or deficiencies. Most basically, this model suggests that an observed language deficit be viewed as a manifestation of a breakdown somewhere in the complex transactional system which supports normal language development. The goal of assessment in such a case is to identify the specific source(s) of this breakdown so that appropriate intervention efforts can be brought to bear on the system.

Obviously, the children referred to a language teacher or clinician vary greatly in both the nature and the degree of their language disorder or delay. Further, it is obvious that these factors will be directly related to the relative emphasis given to each component of the transactional language system in the assessment process for any child. For this reason, our transactional assessment model includes guidelines for the initial identification of appropriate assessment targets. The model also includes assessment procedures guidelines for each of the major target areas identified, as well as guidelines for the interpretation and application of assessment data. On the following pages, each component of this model will be presented and explained briefly. Again, it should be emphasized that this model is based upon (and assumes the reader's familiarity with) the perspectives on language acquisition and development discussed in Chapters 2 through 5 of this book. Also, the more general assessment considerations and procedural suggestions offered in the first portion of this chapter will not be reiterated, but are assumed in the following specific guidelines.

A Transactional Assessment Model: Overview

The schematic presented in Figure 1 represents an overview of the transactional language assessment model derived from the findings of this project. The model is presented in a decision-map format, and the critical decision points and processes suggested by this model which are not self-explanatory are explained briefly below.

"Screening: apparent problem?"   Screening is used here to refer to the process by which children who are potential candidates for some form of language intervention are first identified. Such screening may be conducted in two general ways. First, professionals and parents may be educated on a mass basis regarding the symptoms of early language disorder or delay and asked to refer any children in their care who manifest such symptoms for further language assessment. In addition to this referral process, a state or local agency may conduct direct screening through the administration of a screening instrument or battery to a large population of children. The review activities of this project revealed a number of language tests which would be appropriate for such screening purposes, although they do not meet the criteria set forth earlier in this chapter for truly prescriptive clinical usage. These instruments are identified and briefly described at the end of this chapter.

"See child in informal session."   If screening activities suggest that a child may be significantly delayed or deviant in language development, the child should first be seen by the language therapist or teacher in an informal session. If possible, this session should be conducted in an environment familiar to the child and should involve a parent or familiar adult who has already established rapport with the child. In addition, time should be allowed for the therapist to obtain the parent's or referring adult's specific perceptions and concerns regarding the child's language ability. From this brief informal session, the teacher or therapist should be able to make some very general clinical judgments concerning the child's need for further assessment.

"Language delay or deficit?"   The most basic judgment to be made after the initial observation is whether or not the child actually exhibits a significant language problem. In some cases, it may be that the screening results reflected an unrepresentative performance and that, when carefully observed in a natural setting, the child actually does not display any serious functional language disorder. In such cases, the decision map in Figure 1 indicates that the child is not a candidate for language intervention and no further assessment is required. However, if the clini-

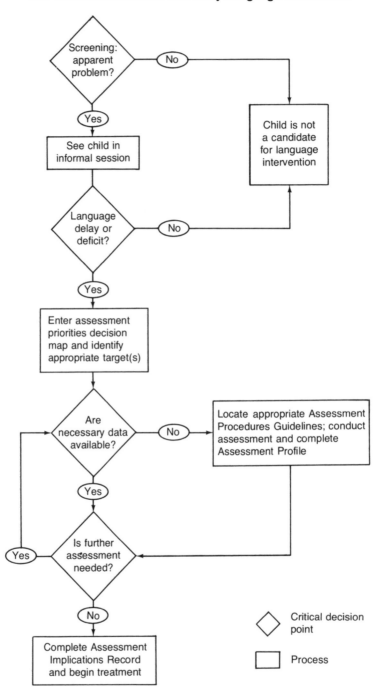

FIGURE 1. A Transactional Model for the Assessment of Children with Severe Language Deficits.

cian and the parent or referring adult agree that the child is a candidate for such intervention, then the clinician's general judgments regarding the child's apparent level of functioning will serve as the basis for identifying the appropriate targets for more specific assessment.

"Enter Assessment Priorities decision map." If further assessment is indicated, the clinician must determine which specific components of the child's transactional language system should be the first priorities for such assessment and at what levels those components should first be assessed. A decision map for identifying these priority targets is presented in Figure 2. This map assumes that the clinician has completed an informal observation of the child and has formed some judgments concerning the child's general level of functioning.

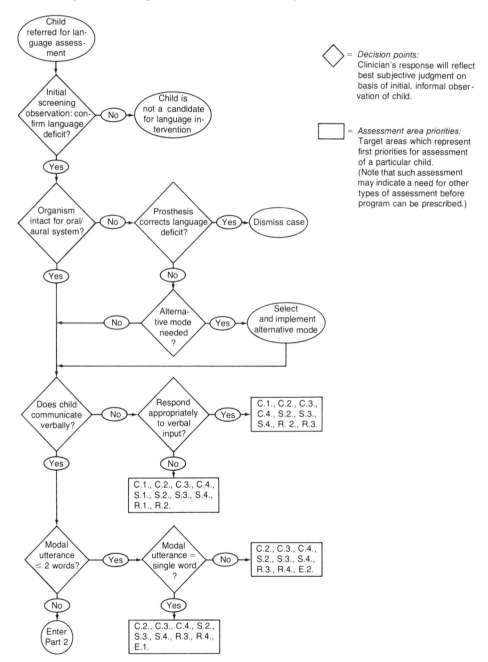

FIGURE 2. Guidelines for Determining Assessment Priorities. *(cont. on p. 144)*

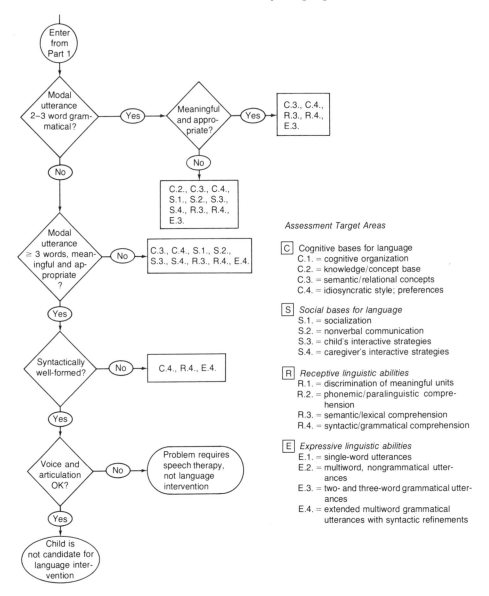

FIGURE 2. Guidelines for Determining Assessment Priorities. (*cont.*)

"*Locate appropriate Assessment Procedures Guidelines; conduct assessment and complete Assessment Profile.*" On the assessment priorities decision map (Figure 2), 16 general target areas or levels have been identified—four in each of four major categories (cognitive bases for language, social bases for language, receptive linguistic abilities, and expressive linguistic abilities). The decision map indicates which of these target areas would probably be most appropriate and important for the assessment of a child manifesting a particular general level of functioning. Following this decision map is a set of Assessment Procedures Guidelines for each of the 16 target areas. These guidelines include general sugges-

COMMUNICATION ASSESSMENT PROFILE

Child's name _____

+ Ability demonstrated/mastered
– Ability not demonstrated
+/– Ability minimally demonstrated
o Ability not tested

Examiner _____ (1st)
_____ (2nd)
_____ (3rd)

Date _____ (1st)
Date _____ (2nd)
Date _____ (3rd)

Cognitive Bases

C.1. Cognitive Organization	1st	2nd	3rd
Object permanence			
Means/ends causality			
Symbolic/representation			
Short-term memory			

C.2. Knowledge/Concepts	1st	2nd	3rd
Novel object manipulatory exploration			
Functional attributes			
Perceptual attributes			

C.3. Semantic Relational	1st	2nd	3rd
Existence			
Nonexistence			
Rejection			
Recurrence			
Location			
Possession			
Agency			
Objective			

C.4. Style/Preference	1st	2nd	3rd
Indicate if completed and attach summary			

Social Bases

S.1. Socialization	1st	2nd	3rd
Cooperative responses			
Maintain interaction			
Initiates interactions			
Differential preferences			

S.2. Nonverbal Communication	1st	2nd	3rd
Mode (indicate)			
Functions:			
Relief			
Assistance			
Rejection			
Proximity			
Notice			
Information			

S.3. Child's Strategies	1st	2nd	3rd
Joint reference			
Selective listening			
Imitation:			
Spontaneous			
Prompted			
Questions/hypothesis test			
Verbal imitation			

S.4. Caregiver Strategies	1st	2nd	3rd
Responds			
Joint reference			
Segments			
Object use opportunities			
Modifies utterances			

Receptive Linguistic Abilities

R.1. Discrimination	1st	2nd	3rd
Intonation patterns			
Common words			
Phoneme contrasts			
Visual symbols			

R.2. Phonemic/Paralinguistic	1st	2nd	3rd
"Tone of voice"			
Intonation + context			
Phoneme class			
Specific phonemes + intonation			
Phoneme only			

R.3. Semantic/Lexical	1st	2nd	3rd
Words + cues			
Words alone			
Semantic relationships			
Semantic and syntactic meaning			

R.4. Syntactical	1st	2nd	3rd
S-V-O word order			
Tense			
Plurality			
Pronouns			
Attributes			
Negative			

Expressive Linguistic Abilities

E.1. (One Word)	1st	2nd	3rd
Number of semantic relationships expressed			
Number of pragmatic functions			
Number of different words			

E.2. Nongrammatical	1st	2nd	3rd
Percent of nongrammatical utterances			
Percent of grammatical utterances			
Evidence of transition to grammar			

E.3. 2-3 Word	1st	2nd	3rd
Number of semantic relations expressed			
Number of pragmatic functions			
Number of structured forms			

E.4. Multiword	1st	2nd	3rd
Present progressive			
Prepositions			
Plural (reg.)			
Past (irreg.)			
Possessive			
Copula			
Articles			
Past (reg.)			
3rd person (reg.)			
3rd person (irreg.)			
Auxiliary			

FIGURE 3. Communication Assessment Profile: A Suggested Format.

145

tions for assessment in each particular area and identify any available instruments reviewed during this project which would be appropriate for assessment in that area. A brief profile of the assessment activities should be completed as a summary record for later reference. A sample profile sheet is presented in Figure 3.

"Complete assessment implications record and begin treatment." After all necessary assessment data have been collected, it is recommended that a summary sheet, reflecting the implications of that assessment in terms of treatment targets for the child be completed. An example of how such a record might be organized is presented in Figure 4. In the following chapter, recommendations for actual treatment procedures appropriate to such targets will be presented.

Summary of Assessment Implications: Communication Intervention Targets

Child's Name _____ Date _____ Completed by _____

General area development	Specific targets/objectives	Objective achieved	
		Date	Initials
Cognitive/ Motor-sensori	1. _____		
	2. _____		
	3. _____		
Social communication	1. _____		
	2. _____		
	3. _____		
Receptive linguistic	1. _____		
	2. _____		
	3. _____		
Expressive linguistic	1. _____		
	2. _____		
	3. _____		

FIGURE 4. Suggested Format for Assessment Implications Summary.

Assessment Priorities: A Suggested Decision Map

The multidimensional nature of the transactional model presented in this text increases the complexity of the language assessment task by increasing the number of developmental domains which may be of concern to the language therapist. Further, within each of these domains, several levels or aspects of development may be selected for assessment. Thus, this model requires that the therapist have some guidelines for determining, on the basis of only brief, informal observation, the specific target areas which would appear to be most relevant to the language delay or disorder manifested by any one child. That is, he must have some guidelines for establishing *assessment priorities* in accordance with each child's general level of observable language functioning. In Figure 2 we presented a decision map for determining such priorities, reflecting the developmental data and perspectives reviewed in the first part of this book. Those components of the decision map which are not self-explanatory are briefly explained below.

"Organism intact for oral/aural system?" As noted at the outset of this chapter, any child who manifests a language deficiency should be examined to determine whether there is an organic etiology or confounding factor associated with the deficit. This may include not only audiological examination, but also examination by a speech pathologist to determine whether the child is handicapped by neuro-muscular or skeletal defects which would impair his ability to produce oral speech.

"Prosthesis corrects language deficit?" In those cases where some organic source has been identified, it may well be that the child can be fitted with a prosthetic device to compensate for the organic impairment. Once the child has become accustomed to such a device, the therapist should observe the child again to determine if the prosthesis has been sufficient to correct the original language deficit. In many cases, it is probable that remedial or further compensatory therapy will be needed.

"Alternative mode needed?" For the organically impaired child, it may be appropriate to use an alternative mode as a support for, or even in place of, oral/aural language. The use of such modes is currently the subject of much debate and controversy, thus we can only state our own bias on this issue. We believe that if a child has attained a level of cognitive and social skill development sufficient to support a functional communication or language system, and if that child has failed to develop such a system in the oral/aural mode, then an alternative mode should be provided so that the child can begin learning the "rules of the communication game," as well as the rules of linguistic structure. If the child is capable of acquiring an aural/oral mode, the data suggest that it will be easier to teach the child to use that mode to express a language system which he has already developed than to wait until he has learned to use the oral/aural mode and then try to teach him a communicative language system. (In our discussion of treatment implications in the next chapter, this issue will be addressed again in relation to the nonverbal child who does not manifest any oral/aural impairment but who, due to severe mental retardation or autism, has failed to develop any functional oral/aural language.) Considerations involved in the selection of an appropriate alternative mode will be discussed in Chapter 7.

"Does child communicate verbally?" Does the child produce expressive language in some mode? The word "language" refers here to a conventionalized system of signs or symbols which connote different meanings. Thus a child who produces meaningless sounds or jargon is not considered to be communicating verbally.

"Modal utterance ≤ 2 words?" Note that here, as in the next several decision points in the diagram, the term "modal" is used rather than "mean." The clinician's

interest here is in whether *most* of the child's utterances are two words or less in length. As was noted in Chapter 4, long strings of words apparently learned in rote association (such as "Pat-the-Bunny-book") are best treated as single words.

"Meaningful and appropriate?" The phrase "meaningful and appropriate" appears at two decision points and refers to the semantic and pragmatic aspects of the child's language. If the child is producing multiword, grammatical utterances, the clinician should ask, Are these appropriate to the context in which they are uttered and do they seem to convey some meaning intended by the child? Examples of nonmeaningful or inappropriate speech are provided by children who produce only echolalic speech ("echoing" words they hear) or who repetitively produce one or a few utterances regardless of the immediate context. The remaining cells in Figure 2 are self-explanatory and will not be discussed here.

Assessment Procedures: Some Guidelines

Having identified the priority target areas for an assessment, the therapist must next select the appropriate procedures and instruments to achieve that assessment. In the remainder of this chapter, we will offer some general guidelines for such procedures. These guidelines are offered for each of the 16 target areas identified in Figure 2 and include any published instruments which were found (through the review activities of our project) to be consistent with the perspectives of this model and designed in such a way as to yield clinically useful prescriptive information. Each set of guidelines includes a code in its title that corresponds to the decision map codes in Figure 2. A general description of each of the instruments listed here is provided at the conclusion of this chapter.

C. I.

Assessment Procedures Guidelines

Assessment area: Cognitive bases—cognitive organization

General procedures: Use procedures for *Observational analysis of nonverbal behaviors* (this chapter). Context should include objects which will afford the manipulations and activities described below and should include at least one object known to be of high appeal to the child.

Specific behaviors/abilities of interest: Does the child exhibit—

Cognitive schemata	Examples of indicative behaviors
1. *Object permanence* Object exists in time and space independently of child's immediate perception.	Child seeks a desired object which has fallen out of visual range or has been hidden by adult; child goes to seek familiar object where it is usually kept (e.g., in a closed toybox).
2. *Means-ends and causality*	Child repeats an action which was effective in obtaining interesting/desired results; child manipulates a toy to achieve desired effect (e.g., turns crank on jack-in-the-box); uses 2 objects together to achieve effect (e.g., uses mallet to pound pegs in a toy work bench).

C.1. (cont.)

3. *Symbolic function* Representation; short-term memory.	Child uses one object to represent another in play; can match an object to its picture; if picture is shown and then covered, child can recall and identify object pictured; identifies objects and animals by characteristic sounds; deferred imitation of observed motor act.

Relevant published instruments:
1. *Ordinal Scales of Psychological Development* (Uzgiris & Hunt)
2. *Albert Einstein Scales of Sensori-Motor Development* (Corman & Escalona)
3. *Infant Cognitive Development Scale* (Mehrebian & Williams)

Assessment implications:
1. If child fails to demonstrate these three general types of cognitive organization, treatment target = *Sensorimotor Development*.
2. If child successfully demonstrates awareness of object permanence and causality, but shows deficits in short-term memory and/or representational function, see discussion of *Alternative Modes* (Chapter 7).
3. If child demonstrates all three levels of cognitive organization, proceed to next assessment area.

C.2.

Assessment Procedures Guidelines

Assessment area: Cognitive bases—knowledge/concept base

General procedures: Use basic procedures for observing nonverbal behavior. Equip setting with both familiar and unfamiliar toys and common household objects. To assess knowledge of perceptual attributes, ask the child to match items which differ in one perceptual feature (color, size, shape, etc.). Assess the child's performance in the following three general areas.

Specific behaviors/abilities of interest: Does the child exhibit—

Knowledge/strategy	Examples of indicative behaviors
1. Demonstrates productive manipulation and exploration strategies when confronted with unfamiliar objects.	(a) Manipulates the object so that its visual and auditory properties can be perceived (e.g., turns over, shakes, etc.); (b) tests affordance properties (tries to fit inside a container; tries to roll, etc.); (c) integrates in play activities with other objects.
2. Demonstrates knowledge of the functional attributes of common objects.	(a) Exhibits appropriate use of toys and household objects (e.g., spins top, runs brush through hair, stirs with spoon); (b) groups objects together which are functionally related (e.g., spoon and fork, sock and shoe); (c) recognizes the affordance properties of objects (rolls an orange, bounces a rubber eraser)
3. Demonstrates knowledge of the perceptual attributes of common objects.	(a) Can match an object to its picture; (b) can match objects which have the same color, size, or shape; (c) can identify the object associated with a sound produced by that object (e.g., a phone with a ringing sound, toy dog with a barking sound).

C.2. (cont.)

Relevant published instruments:
1. *Environmental Pre-Language Battery* (EPB) Test #1 (Play with Objects)
2. *Parent-Child Communication Inventory*

Assessment implications:
If the child demonstrates none of these abilities, treatment should initially target object manipulation and use. If functional attribute knowledge and object exploration are demonstrated, but perceptual attribute knowledge is not demonstrated, proceed to C.3. assessment and include perceptual attribute matching as a treatment target. If target behaviors are demonstrated with only one or a few objects, plan to incorporate these in initial training, while targeting expansion of the child's object manipulation/use repertoire. If all abilities are demonstrated, proceed to the next area of assessment.

C.3.

Assessment Procedures Guidelines

Assessment area: Cognitive bases for language—semantic/relational concepts

General procedures: Use basic procedures for observing nonverbal behavior. To maximize the probability of observing demonstrations of these relations, the environment should contain: objects which belong to the child (his own cup, coat, etc.); objects which can be filled and emptied; and objects which are associated with particular locations. In some cases, a parent may be asked to observe the child at home and to record occurrences of each type of behavior.

Specific behaviors/abilities of interest: Does the child exhibit—

Target relations	Examples of indicative behaviors
Existence	Child directs attention to object which is moved or makes a sudden sound; seeks out desired objects when they are out of sight.
Nonexistence	Shows surprise or disappointment if object is not found where expected; indicates that cup is empty.
Rejection	Gesturally or physically rejects a toy, food, or activity not desired.
Recurrence	Enjoys repeating actions; indicates desire for more of an object or activity when stopped; enjoys collecting multiple examples of a type of object.
Location	When an object is handed to the child, he looks to the place where it was previously; goes to seek a desired object in the place where it is usually kept; returns object to place from which it was taken, etc.
Possession	Selects his own cup, coat, shoes, etc., when several are available. Hands an object which belongs to another to that person.
Agency	Attempts to perform an action performed by another; participates in alternating, role-exchange reciprocal play (e.g., ball rolling).
Objective	Given an object, demonstrates an action typically carried out upon that object (e.g., kicks a ball, pushes a truck, opens a book).

Relevant published instruments:
None

C.3. (cont.)

Assessment implications:
If none of the relations are demonstrated, treatment should initially target just a few basic relations and C.2. target areas should be assessed if not already completed. If a few of the relations are demonstrated, these should serve as the initial targets for language training, while treatment is directed at expanding the child's relational concept base. If all concepts are demonstrated, proceed to next assessment area.

C.4.

Assessment Procedures Guidelines

Assessment area: Cognitive bases for language—idiosyncratic
style/preferences

General procedures: These data can be obtained concurrently with other assessment data collected through observation of nonverbal behavior and/or the collection of a language sample. Also, interview data from a parent or familiar adult may be obtained. Depending on the child's current level of functioning, some or all of the following types of information should be collected:

1. Specific objects, people, actions, and relationships which are particularly significant or salient to the child.
2. Relational or semantic concepts which are manifested with highest frequencies in the child's current nonverbal and/or verbal repertoire.
3. The relative salience of perceptual vs. functional attributes of objects as demonstrated by the child's performance on C.2. assessment tasks and/or as indicated by the semantic content of his existing language.
4. The relative frequency of object-oriented (referential) vs. social-interaction-oriented (expressive) language and/or behavior produced by the child.

Relevant published instruments:
None
Assessment implications:
These data will allow the teacher/therapist to maximize the probability of successful intervention by selecting initial language-training targets which are consistent with the child's own interests, preferences, and style of cognitive organization and thus are most apt to "map" the child's existing knowledge.

S.1.

Assessment Procedures Guidelines

Assessment area: Social bases for language—socialization

General procedures: (1) Use procedures for observation of nonverbal behavior to observe child in interaction with family members, peer group, and teacher(s); (2) collect interview data from parents or other adults who know the child well.

Specific behaviors/abilities of interest: Does the child exhibit—
1. Cooperative or compliant responses to initiations by others.
   a. Complies with specific requests or commands?
   b. Joins in a game or other joint activity initiated by another?
2. Attempts to maintain an interaction when stopped.
   a. Indicates distress, frustration when interaction is interrupted?
   b. Actively attempts to maintain interaction?

S.1. (cont.)

3. Attempts to initiate interactions with caregivers? other adults? peers?
   a. For no apparent specific purpose; "just to get attention"?
   b. For purpose of obtaining needed assistance?
   c. For purpose of engaging in reciprocal or cooperative play activity?
4. Differential preference for a few persons (e.g., primary caregivers, etc.)?
   a. Responds cooperatively more often to preferred persons?
   b. Directs more initiations toward preferred persons?

Relevant published instruments:
1. *Balthazar Scales of Adaptive Behavior II. Scales of Social Adaptation* (selected items)
2. *Infant Behavior Record* (component of the Bayley Scales of Infant Development) (selected items)

Assessment implications:
If child shows none of these indications of socialization, this should be a priority target area for treatment. Also, complete assessment for area S.2. If child demonstrates some of these behaviors, treatment should target communication behavior corresponding to the child's demonstrated social development, while also targeting further development in this area. If differential preference is exhibited, the preferred person(s) should be involved in treatment to the extent possible.

S.2.

Assessment Procedures Guidelines

Assessment area: Social bases for language—nonverbal
                 communication

General procedures: See general procedures for observation of nonverbal behavior. Preferably, child should be observed in natural contexts. Observational data may be supplemented with interview data from parents and/or adults who work closely with the child.

Specific behaviors/abilities of interest: Does the child—
1. Communicate through one or more nonverbal modes?
   a. Physical contact?
   b. Gesture?
   c. Vocalization?
2. Communicate to achieve one or more of the following functions?
   a. To obtain relief from discomfort or fearful situations?
   b. To get assistance in obtaining desired object or activity?
   c. To indicate rejection or displeasure?
   d. To bring adult into proximity or contact?
   e. To indicate notice of object or event in immediate context?
   f. To obtain information about a novel object or event?
3. Communicate only in specific settings or situations?

Relevant published instruments:
Balthazar Scales of Adaptive Behavior II. Scales of Social Adaptation (selected items; does not specify functions of communication)

Assessment implications:
If child exhibits no communicative behavior, assess area S.1. (socialization) and target the development of basic communication in treatment. If only a few functions are exhibited, these should be targeted as initial language targets while concurrent treatment is aimed at expand-

S.2. (cont.)

ing the child's communicative repertoire. If only physical contact is used, treatment should target the child's movement to more symbolic modes (gestures, vocalizations). If the child demonstrates a wide repertoire of communicative modes and functions, treatment should target the child's acquisition of conventionalized language forms to express those functions.

S.3.

Assessment Procedures Guidelines

Assessment area: Social bases for language—child's interactive
strategies

General procedures: See the general discussion titled *Observational analysis of nonverbal behaviors* (this chapter).

Specific behaviors/abilities of interest: Does the child—
1. Demonstrate joint reference mechanism?
   a. Attend to a referent indicated gesturally by an adult?
   b. Follow the adult's line of regard to a referent?
2. Show selective listening?
   a. Attend to an adult who is speaking directly to him?
   b. Orient to an adult or cease ongoing activity when spoken to by an adult in another part of the room?
3. Imitate behavior?
   a. Imitate observed behavior spontaneously?
   b. Imitate when prompted?
4. (if verbal) Ask questions or test hypotheses concerning names for objects, attributes, etc.?
5. (if verbal) Imitate words he is just beginning to produce when he hears these spoken?
   a. Spontaneously?
   b. With prompting?

Relevant published instruments:
None identified

Assessment implications:
If these behaviors are not demonstrated, they should probably be targeted in treatment. It would seem that joint referencing to a gesturally indicated referent, selective listening and attending, and imitation on a prompt are the most appropriate targets for early intervention. Further research will be needed to determine the full implications of the presence or absence of these behaviors.

S.4.

Assessment Procedures Guidelines

Assessment area: Social bases for language—caregivers'
interactive strategies

General procedures: Observation of verbal and nonverbal caregiver behavior in interaction with the child—preferably in the home or other familiar context.

Specific behaviors/abilities of interest: Does the caregiver—
1. Respond to and encourage the child's communication, if any?

S.4. (cont.)

2. Assure joint reference by either:
   a. Directing the child's attention to a referent?
   b. Following the child's visual or gestural indication of a referent?
3. Verbally "mark" segments of dynamic activities?
4. Demonstrate, encourage, and provide opportunities for object manipulation, exploration, and appropriate use?
5. Modify utterances directed to the child in accordance with the child's level of functioning by:
   a. Reducing length?
   b. Reducing complexity?
   c. Paraphrasing and repeating?
   d. Exaggerating intonation and stress to highlight key words and segments?
   e. Using words which are appropriate to the child's level of lexical/semantic development?

Relevant published instruments:
None

Assessment implications:
If the caregiver does not exhibit most of these behaviors, the teacher/therapist should consider initiating a parent-training program as part of the child's treatment. This may also be extended to include siblings or other caregivers. Factors such as overall family stability and resources, as well as existing vehicles for home-school liaison, will affect the actions taken on the basis of these data.

R.1.

Assessment Procedures Guidelines

Assessment area: Receptive linguistic abilities—discrimination
                  of meaningful units

General procedures: To assess discrimination abilities, it will be necessary to structure a task in which the child behaviorally indicates that he discriminates between two perceived stimuli. If the child can be assessed using one of the instruments below, this would be the most efficient procedure. Two alternatives for auditory discrimination would be: (1) through operant procedures, train the child to produce a specific response when he hears a change in a repetitive string of sounds or words (e.g., ball, ball, ball, fall, ball); (2) use a habituation paradigm in which the examiner observes to see if the child responds to a change in a repetitive stimulus to which he had become habituated. Auditory discriminations to be tested will depend on the child's level of functioning. At the most basic levels, the child should be able to discriminate between rising and falling intonations and between a number of words which are commonly spoken to the child ("milk" and "mommy," "shoe" and "juice," "cookie" and "coke," etc.). More sophisticated contrasts between words which differ only in one sound are appropriate at higher levels and are reflected in the instruments listed below. For a complete analysis of the child's auditory discrimination, the child should be referred to a professional with specialized training in auditory processing (e.g., an audiologist, speech pathologist, or learning disabilities specialist). If an alternative mode is to be used, the child's ability to visually discriminate the meaningful forms should be assessed using a "match-to-sample" or "same-different" task format.

R.1. (cont.)

Relevant published instruments:
1. (Goldman-Fristoe) *Woodcock Test of Auditory Discrimination*
2. (Goldman-Fristoe) *Woodcock Auditory Skills Test Battery: Tests #2 & 3* (Diagnostic Auditory Discriminations Tests)
3. *Preference Procedure for Testing Phonological Discrimination*
(All the above tests require that the child have a basic receptive vocabulary.)

Assessment implications:
Most basically, receptive input should be appropriate to the child's current discrimination abilities. If these abilities are limiting his language development, discrimination training should be initiated or an alternative mode considered.

R.2.

Assessment Procedures Guidelines

Assessment area: Receptive linguistic abilities—Phonemic and paralinguistic comprehension

General procedures: Ask the parent or other primary caregiver if the child seems to know when the parent is angry or pleased from the "tone of voice" and whether the child seems to recognize different voices. Also, ask if the child ever seems to understand what is being said to him, and if so, specifically what phrases he seems to understand. After this information is obtained, observe the parent/caregiver in interaction with the child under partially structured conditions in which the parent is asked to produce the phrases to which the child is thought to respond appropriately. Observe and record the child's responses to these. Also, look for the following:

1. Does the child show distress or otherwise respond differentially if the parent uses an "angry" tone of voice? Does the child laugh or smile when the parent uses a very pleased or happy tone of voice?
2. If the child responds correctly to a phrase as spoken normally, how does he respond when:
   a. The phrase is spoken in a monotone (with and without gestural cues).
   b. Dissimilar consonant phonemes are substituted while maintaining the same extra- and paralinguistic characteristics (e.g., for "Show me your *nose*," substitute "kow tee soor *gose*")?
   c. Similar consonant phonemes are substituted (e.g., "Fow nee oor *mose*" for "Show me your nose")?

Relevant published instruments:
1. *Sequenced Inventory of Communication Development* (SICD)—*Receptive Scale* (selected items could be modified to obtain this type of information)
2. *REEL* (several receptive items for ages 0–12 months are relevant—this is an informant scale and does not allow control of factors of intonation, etc.)
3. *Parent-Child Communication Inventory, Receptive Language Tasks* (with modifications to control for intonation, etc.)

Assessment implications:
After analyzing the child's responses, determine whether he: (1) shows no differential responding to incoming linguistic stimuli; (2) responds only to gross differences in "tone of voice"; (3) responds to the overall intonation pattern and extralinguistic cues; (4) responds to the general phoneme sound-class as well as to intonation and extralinguistic cues;

R.2. (cont.)

(5) responds to the combination of a specific intonation contour and the specific phonemic elements of a phrase; or (6) responds to the segmental/phonemic elements of a phrase, regardless of intonation. If statement 5 or 6 best describes the child, complete assessment for target area R.3. If statement 1 best describes the child, assess target areas R.1., S.1., and C.1. If statements 2, 3, or 4 best describe the child, receptive training should begin at the child's current level. (The clinician is urged to review the discussion of receptive language development in Chapter 4 for a better understanding of this assessment area.)

R.3.

Assessment Procedures Guidelines

Assessment Area: Receptive linguistic abilities—lexical/semantic comprehension

General procedures: Ask the parent/caregiver what words and phrases the child seems to understand. Set up a context in which the referents for these words and phrases can be manipulated. The stimulus utterances should be produced by an adult who already has good rapport with the child. In a semistructured play context, observe and record the child's responses to the words and phrases suggested by the parent under the following conditions:

1. Produced in normal manner and context (i.e., do not attempt to restrict the gestural, contextual, and paralinguistic cues which normally accompany the word or phrase).
2. Single words produced without supporting cues. Arrange context so that several responses are equally probable (e.g., place three objects in front of the child). In a monotone and avoiding any gestural or gaze-direction cues, ask the child to "show me _____ ," substituting a word which refers to an observable object or action.
3. Modify the word order of the utterance by:
   a. Just scrambling the key words (e.g., "baby the kiss" for "kiss the baby").
   b. Reversing the subject and object ("show me—the wagon pushes the boy").

Relevant published instruments:
1. *SICD* (Receptive Scale)—selected items
2. *Vocabulary Comprehension Scale*
3. *Assessment of Children's Language Comprehension* (ACLC)

Assessment implications:
After analyzing the data, determine whether the child: (1) does not respond consistently and appropriately under any of these conditions: (2) responds to the "gestalt" of a familiar phrase; (3) comprehends single lexical items; (4) responds on the basis of expected semantic relationships between key words in an utterance, regardless of word order; or (5) responds to the syntactic relationship between key sentence elements as suggested by the word order of the sentence. If statement 1 best describes the child, assess target area R.2. If statement 5 best describes the child, assess target area R.4. If statements 3 and/or 4 describe the child, a further analysis should be made of the child's receptive vocabulary. List words understood within major categories (name of family member or pet, label for game or social ritual, manipulable object/toy, body parts, food-related, others). Using pictures and/or objects, assess the child's knowledge of other common words. Treatment should target expansion of the child's receptive vocabulary, increasing comprehension of semantic and syntactic relationships in accordance with the natural developmental sequence (see Chapter 4) and beginning expressive use of receptively known words. If statement 2 best describes the child, treatment should focus on the development of lexical comprehension of single words from known phrases.

R.4.

Assessment Procedures Guidelines

Assessment area: Receptive linguistic abilities—syntactic/
grammatical comprehension

General procedures: In assessing this level of purely linguistic/syntactic comprehension, it will be important to control contextual and semantic cues which may confound assessment results (see Chapter 4 for a discussion of this problem). Therefore, a relatively structured situation will be required for this type of assessment and it is recommended that standardized instruments, which have been carefully designed to control for such factors and to reflect the normal sequence of syntactic/grammatical comprehension development, be used when this is feasible. Of course, some modifications in the procedures for administration may be required, as discussed earlier in this chapter. The specific receptive linguistic abilities of interest at this level are:

1. Meaning associated with S-V-O word order.
2. Differences in tense and plurality signaled by inflectional suffixes and verb agreement.
3. Meanings associated with the different pronouns and attributes.
4. Differences in meaning of the negative and affirmative form of a sentence.

Relevant published instruments:
1. *Northwest Syntax Screening Test-Receptive* (provides a quick screening which may be followed up with one of the scales below)
2. *Test for Auditory Comprehension of Language* (Carrow)
3. *Comprehension Tests for Syntactic Constructions*
4. *The Miller-Yoder Test of Grammatical Comprehension*
5. *Assessment of Children's Language Comprehension* (ACLC)

Assessment implications:
If all of these abilities are displayed by the child, he is functioning receptively at a level beyond the scope of this project. If the child shows none of these abilities, target area R.3. should be assessed. If the child demonstrates some of these abilities, but not all, specific deficits should be targeted in receptive training and/or current repertoires expanded. A child functioning at this level of receptive development should be using multiword grammatical constructions in his expressive language. If the child is not functioning at this level expressively, treatment efforts should focus on expressive development.

E.1.

Assessment Procedures Guidelines

Assessment area: Expressive linguistic abilities—single-word
utterances

General procedures: See general discussion of procedures for collecting language samples (this chapter) and the Appendix for sample transcription and analysis formats. At this level, language sample data collected in the home will provide the most useful data for clinical purposes. This sample should be analyzed to determine:

1. What general semantic classes are expressed in the child's utterances?
2. What are the pragmatic functions/intents expressed by the child's utterances?
3. Specifically, what words does the child produce spontaneously?

E.1. (cont.)

If very few words (25 or less) are produced by the child spontaneously, an effort should be made to evoke words by asking the child to label objects or pictures. If no words are evoked, an imitation task may be used to see if the child is stimulable for word production training. Also, the parent may be asked to keep a record of words produced by the child.

Relevant published instruments:
None identified

Assessment implications:
If the child produces only a few words, treatment should first focus on expanding his basic lexicon. If the child is producing approximately 10 words or more, treatment should focus on expanding the semantic classes and/or pragmatic functions of the child's utterances as necessary, so that the child is capable of expressing several different semantic relationships and pragmatic intents/functions. If each word is used to express just one semantic case or pragmatic function, treatment should target the child's ability to use the same word in multiple cases and/or functions. At this level, all treatment should include as a target the expansion of the child's expressive lexicon.

E.2.

Assessment Procedures Guidelines

Assessment area: Expressive linguistic abilities—multiword,
nongrammatical utterances

General procedures: See general procedures for collecting language samples (this chapter) and the Appendix for examples of transcription and analysis formats. At this stage, it is important that transcriptions accurately reflect any pauses which occur between two words or utterances and relevant context cues. In analyzing the sample, determine:

1. What semantic relationships and pragmatic functions are expressed by the child as these are inferred from context information?
2. Are there any relationships or functions which are consistently expressed in correct word order?
3. Are there instances in which the child corrects or expands his own utterances after he has produced them (e.g., "juice want—want juice—I want juice")? If so, is the second more correct than the first? Does this happen more for one specific relationship or function?
4. Are any consistent, incorrect patterns apparent in the child's utterances (e.g., always produces action before agent)?
5. Does the child pause more between words which are produced in incorrect order than between those which are produced grammatically?

When the child produces an incorrect word order, the adult should occasionally model the correct form and ask the child to imitate. (This procedure should be used only a few times as it may be perceived as annoying or punishing by the child.) Note whether the child repeats the correct form or the original form.

Relevant published instruments:
Environmental Language Inventory (ELI) for semantic analysis

Assessment implications:
Affirmative answers to questions 2, 3, and 5 would suggest that the child is in a transition stage and has a functional strategy for mastering the rules of word order. Correct imitation of a corrective model would also support this conclusion. In this case, treatment should target those relationships and functions expressed most often by the child and for which he is not yet

E.2. (cont.)

consistently using correct word order. If the data suggest that the child's incorrect word-order patterns are not transitory, then it will be necessary for treatment to target specifically the acquisition of word-order rules, most probably following the sequence of normal development as discussed in Chapter 4. Again, specific referents reflected most often in the child's natural speech will serve as high-probability words for use in training.

E.3.

Assessment Procedures Guidelines

Assessment area: Expressive linguistic abilities—two-, three-
word grammatical utterances

General procedures: See procedures for collecting language samples (this chapter) and the Appendix for examples of transcription and analysis formats. Collect at least 50 utterances. For later intervention evaluation purposes, it may be desirable to compute an MLU which can be compared with the child's MLU at subsequent points during and after the treatment program. For prescriptive purposes, analyze the language sample to identify:

1. Semantic relations expressed.
2. Pragmatic functions/intents expressed.
3. Structural forms used.

Relevant published instruments:
ELI (for semantic analysis)

Assessment implications:
Treatment should target any specific gaps or imbalances noted when comparing the child's language sample data with those reflecting the major communication and semantic utterance types found in normal development (see Chapter 4). General expansion of the child's utterance repertoire may also be indicated. If the child demonstrates a relatively large repertoire of utterance types, forms and functions, treatment should target the child's development or more refined syntactic/grammatical structures, and target area E.4. should be assessed.

E.4.

Assessment Procedures Guidelines

Assessment area: Expressive linguistic abilities—extended
multiword grammatical utterances with syntactic
refinements

General procedures: See general procedures for collecting language samples (this chapter) and the Appendix for examples of transcription and analysis formats. At this level, the primary clinical concern is with the syntactic and grammatical aspects of the child's language. While semantic and pragmatic factors continue to be important to the form and content of that language, the clinician will probably want to focus on structures in the assessment. A language sample will provide the most complete profile of the child's language usage, although a few structured instruments (see list below) are available which may be used for analyzing and identifying specific syntax or grammar deficits. In analyzing a language sample, utterances may be classified according to the 14 early grammatical morphemes identified by Brown (see Chapter 4) or using a published procedure, such as Lee's "DSA" (listed below).

E.4. (cont.)

Relevant published instruments:
1. *Berko's Test of the Child's Learning of English Morphology*
2. *Berry-Talbott Language Tests: I, Comprehension of Grammar*
3. *Developmental Sentence Analysis*
4. *Northwest Syntax Screening Test*—expressive (to screen for general deficit area)

Assessment implications:
Specific deficits identified should be targeted for treatment. If many deficits are found, these may be prioritized in accordance with the sequence of normal development of syntactic/ grammatical structures (see Chapter 4).

Assessment Implications: Summary

In this chapter, we have considered both general and specific implications of the transactional model of language acquisition for the assessment of young children who manifest significant language deficits. We noted that the model has implications for the targets, contexts, and procedures of such assessment. Specifically, we have suggested that assessment of a language-deficient child must include consideration of not only the child's expressive and receptive linguistic abilities, but also his cognitive and social bases for language. Further, it was argued that assessment contexts and procedures should be designed to provide the most representative profile possible of the child's actual ability to function in his natural environment, as well as on structured tasks. Recommended procedures included observational analysis of both verbal and nonverbal behavior, as well as the use of standardized instruments, where these were found to meet the criteria of content relevance and clinical, prescriptive utility. In the following chapter, we will examine the implications of the transactional model for the design and implementation of treatment procedures appropriate to the needs of young handicapped children who are seriously delayed or deviant in their language development. We now turn to a discussion of assessment instruments listed in the Assessment Procedures Guidelines.

Selected Assessment Instruments

On the following pages, we have provided brief descriptions of those instruments identified, through the review processes of this project, as relevant to the overall assessment needs implicated by our transactional model. Two types of instruments are distinguished, on the basis of our own criteria: those suitable for *screening* purposes and those useful for *clinical/prescriptive* purposes.

The most basic criterion for including clinical/prescriptive instruments in this chapter is that they were found to be consistent with at least one component of the assessment model described in this chapter and were specifically indicated as relevant to one or more of the assessment target areas for which Assessment Procedures Guidelines were suggested. In addition, we have attempted to include those instruments which may already be available to the clinician/teacher or which may already have been administered to children seen by the therapist. Thus, several instruments which are very similar in scope and procedures may be listed for one assessment area, allowing the clinician to select the one which is most readily available. In some cases, procedures which seem especially appropriate are not available through a commercial publisher. In these cases, relevant publication reference information is provided.

We wish to emphasize that (1) many instruments listed here are cited only for specific components which we found to be related to the assessment implications of the transactional model (see Assessment Procedures Guidelines in this chapter); (2) many items or entire scales must be supplemented or modified in administration to obtain the type of assessment data desired; and (3) this list is not exhaustive, but only reflects the instruments we have identified during the course of our review. It is hoped that clinicians and teachers in the field will augment this list with the instruments and procedures which they find to be useful in implementing the implications of our transactional model, as discussed in this chapter.

The assessment instruments are divided into two sections: screening instruments and clinical/prescriptive instruments. Within each section, instruments are listed in alphabetical order according to title. The reader should refer back to the Assessment Procedures Guidelines provided in this chapter to identify specific target areas for which each instrument was recommended.

Additional information concerning published language-assessment instruments is provided in the following sources:

Cicciarelli, A., Broen, P. A., & Siegel, G. M., Language assessment procedures. In L. L. Lloyd (Ed.), *Communication assessment and intervention strategies*. Baltimore: University Park Press, 1976.

Miller, J. F. (Ed.) *Procedures for assessing children's language: A developmental process approach* (second draft). Madison, Wisconsin: University of Wisconsin, Waisman Center on Mental Retardation and Human Development, 1976.

Section 1

Screening Instruments

TITLE: *Communication Evaluation Chart* (1963)

AUTHOR(S): R. M. Anderson, M. Miles, & P. A. Matheny

SOURCE: Educator's Publishing Service, Cambridge, Mass.

BEHAVIORS/ABILITIES ASSESSED: Perceptual, motor, and language development

AGE RANGE: Birth–5 years

GENERAL DESCRIPTION: The *Communicative Evaluation Chart* is a three-page summary of language and physical development. Items are arranged by levels—at three-month intervals for year one, six-month intervals for year two, and yearly intervals above two years. The items are drawn from standard infant early childhood scales and assess general development of speech musculature, auditory acuity and discrimination, and receptive and expressive language. Scoring of items is simply plus (+), minus (−), or fluctuating (±). Minus or fluctuation markings should serve as a warning that further, more extensive evaluations are needed.

TITLE: *Houston Test of Language Development: Part I* (1958, 1963)
AUTHOR(S): M. Crabtree
SOURCE: Houston Test Company, P. O. Box 35152, Houston, Tex. 77035
BEHAVIORS/ABILITIES ASSESSED: Receptive and expressive language (including basic vocabulary and articulation lists)
AGE RANGE: 6 months–36 months
GENERAL DESCRIPTION: This scale includes tests of vocabulary (receptive and expressive), articulation (commonly misarticulated phonemes in initial, medial, and final positions), and functional use of language. Items are assigned a point value and summed to become the Language Age. Administration time is approximately 30 minutes.

TITLE: *Preschool Attainment Record* (PAR) Experimental Education (1966)
AUTHOR(S): E. Doll
SOURCE: American Guidance Service, Circle Pines, Minn.
BEHAVIORS/ABILITIES ASSESSED: Motor, cognitive, social, and communication development
AGE RANGE: 6 months–7 years
GENERAL DESCRIPTION: The *Preschool Attainment Record* (PAR), Research Edition, is a downward extension of the Vineland Social Maturity Scale and follows the general format of the original scale. As with the Vineland, the PAR is an informant scale and does not require the presence of the child being assessed, although direct observation may be used. The items are scored on the basis of what the child usually does rather than on what he *can* do. Thus, the profile is meant to portray the child's usual performances. The author of the PAR recommends that the profile be used as a baseline for educational planning in a preschool curriculum. General divisions of the PAR are: Physical skills (subdivided into Ambulation and Manipulation), Social skills (Rapport, Communication, and Responsibility). There are two general items per year under each of the above categories. Two examples will suffice to demonstrate the generality of the items: "Nurses" covers the period from birth to six months under the heading "Responsibility"; "Regards" summarizes the same period under the heading "Rapport." The reported administration time is 20–30 minutes.

TITLE: *Preschool Language Scale* (1969)
AUTHOR(S): I. L. Zimmerman, V. G. Steiner, & R. L. Evatt
SOURCE: Charles E. Merrill, 1300 Alum Creek Drive, Columbus, Ohio 43216
BEHAVIORS/ABILITIES ASSESSED: Receptive and expressive language
AGE RANGE: 18 months–6 years
GENERAL DESCRIPTION: This scale attempts to assess both auditory comprehension and verbal ability, using an equal number of items at each age level (six-month intervals). Items are drawn from several standard early developmental

scales and schedules. The authors emphasize that the scale is an evaluation instrument, not a test. A total of 40 Auditory Comprehension and 40 Verbal Ability items are listed and administration time is less than 30 minutes. The manual provides the examiner with the procedures and rationale for each item along with appropriate references from the child-development literature.

TITLE: *Utah Test of Language Development* (1967)
AUTHOR(S): M. J. Mechan, J. L. Jex, & J. D. Jones
SOURCE: Communication Research Associates, Salt Lake City, Utah
BEHAVIORS/ABILITIES ASSESSED: Receptive and expressive language
AGE RANGE: 1 year–15 years
GENERAL DESCRIPTION: The *Utah Test of Language Development* is a screening instrument designed to assess major developmental milestones of receptive and expressive language. Emphasis is on the function of language, and test items are drawn from standardized developmental tests. For each year from one through eight, five to eight items are listed. The UTLD takes approximately a half hour to administer. An informant-interview version is available.

TITLE: *Verbal Language Development Scale* (1959)
AUTHOR(S): M. Mechan
SOURCE: American Guidance Service, Circle Pines, Minn.
BEHAVIORS/ABILITIES ASSESSED: Receptive and expressive language
AGE RANGE: Birth–15 years
GENERAL DESCRIPTION: Since the Vineland Social Maturity Scale and its downward extension, the Preschool Attainment Record, have few references to milestones in language development, the *Verbal Language Development Scale* was designed to serve as the language assessment test which may be used in conjunction with these scales. The scale consists of 50 items, with approximately seven to ten items for each year period, from birth through year 15. Items are general and follow development schedules. The items are arranged in order of occurrence and are to be scored on the basis of routine performances as either "passed," "failed," or "transitional." A manual of definitions is available.

Section 2

Clinical/Prescriptive
Instruments

TITLE: *Albert Einstein Scales of Sensori-motor Development* (1969)
AUTHOR(S): H. H. Corman & S. K. Escalona
SOURCE: Albert Einstein College of Medicine, Child Development Project, 1165 Morris Park Avenue, Bronx, New York 10461 (described in *Merrill Palmer Quarterly,* 1969, *15*, 351–361)
BEHAVIORS/ABILITIES ASSESSED: Cognitive/sensorimotor development

AGE RANGE: 1 month–2 years

GENERAL DESCRIPTION: The *Albert Einstein Scales of Sensorimotor Development* is a Piagetian-based assessment instrument. The method Corman and Escalona used in constructing their scales was to survey the published works of Piaget in order to arrive at definitions of the stages of sensorimotor development. Correlated behaviors demonstrating the presence of each stage were noted along with techniques used to induce these behaviors. Transitional items were discarded in favor of items assessing behaviors that were representative of each stage. These items were then arranged in the sequence suggested by Piaget and observer reliability was assessed (94% for Object Permanence Scale and 95% for Spatial Relationships Scale). The Scales are presently available from the authors on request and measure stages of sensorimotor development in three areas: prehension, object permanence, and spatial relationships.

The Prehension Scale begins at the level of primary circular reactions (Stage II) and progresses through the various behaviors characteristic of this stage, to the stage at which secondary circular reactions and coordinations of differing modalities are demonstrated.

The Object Permanence Scale begins with Stage III in which the infant makes no attempt to retrieve a hidden object. Subsequent items catalogue through Stage VI, and are essentially a series of progressively more difficult situations in which the infant is expected to locate hidden objects. Success at the upper end of this scale assumes an internalized "mental representation" and demonstrates displacement.

The Spatial Relationships Scale begins with Stage III and reflects changes in the schemas of physical space through Stage VI, again requiring "mental representation."

TITLE: *Assessment of Children's Language Comprehension* (ACLC) (1969, 1973)

AUTHOR(S): R. Foster, J. Giddan, & J. Stark

SOURCE: Consulting Psychologists Press, Inc., Palo Alto, Calif. 94306

BEHAVIORS/ABILITIES ASSESSED: Receptive language: Lexical-semantic and syntactic

AGE RANGE: 3 years–7 years

GENERAL DESCRIPTION: This scale consists of four subtests and requires that the child point to a correct picture in response to a linguistic stimulus. The first subtest assesses the child's comprehension of 50 words (count nouns, adjectives, present progressive verb forms, and prepositions) which are used in the remaining subtests. The next three subtests assess the child's comprehension of utterances with two "critical elements" (i.e., semantic-lexical items), three critical elements, and four critical elements. Responding would seem indicative of purely semantic-lexical comprehension on many items. This test can be administered in approximately 15 minutes.

TITLE: *Balthazar Scales of Adaptive Behavior—II. Scales of Social Behavior* (1973)

AUTHOR(S): E. E. Balthazar

SOURCE: Consulting Psychologists Press, Inc., 577 College Avenue, Palo Alto, Calif. 94306

BEHAVIORS/ABILITIES ASSESSED: Social and adaptive behavior

AGE RANGE: Institutionalized, ambulatory mentally retarded children and adults (chronogical age 5 through adult)

GENERAL DESCRIPTION: This scale is administered through direct observation of the subject in his natural environment. The subject is rated on several items within each of eight social scale categories:

1. Unadaptive self-directed behaviors
2. Unadaptive interpersonal behaviors
3. Adaptive self-directed behaviors
4. Adaptive interpersonal behaviors
5. Verbal communication
6. Play activities
7. Response to instructions
8. Checklist items (e.g., personal care, health, toileting, etc.)

Subjects are to be observed approximately six times and data consist of tallies of the occurrences of different types of behavior during these observation sessions.

TITLE: *Berko's Test of the Child's Learning of English Morphology* (1958)

AUTHOR(S): J. Berko Gleason

SOURCE: Reprinted in Bar-Adon & Leopold (Eds.), *Child language: A book of readings*. Englewood Cliffs, N.J.: Prentice-Hall, Inc., 1971, 153–67.

BEHAVIORS/ABILITIES ASSESSED: Expressive knowledge of English morphology

AGE RANGE: 4 years–7 years

GENERAL DESCRIPTION: This test was developed by Berko for use in an experimental study. It has not been published in the form of a test kit, but is described with sufficient detail in her article that the clinician can prepare a set of test materials and duplicate the test. The test materials consist of 27 stimulus-picture cards and a list of statements to be read with each card. The cards contain colored, cartoon-like pictures of objects and creatures in varying states and activities. The statements are read to the child who is asked to supply a missing word. Nonsense words are introduced as labels for the objects, states, and/or actions depicted on the cards and the child must apply the rules of English morphology to generate the correct form of the nonsense word to complete the sentence. Berko reports that it took from 10 to 15 minutes to administer the test and that the task was easily understood by all children tested. Relative performance data for each item are presented, comparing the percentage of correct responses by the study's preschool and first-grade subjects. The morphological rules tested include those of: plurality, tense (past and present), derived adjectives, comparative and superlative adjectival forms, third-person singular verb form, possession, and compound words.

TITLE: *Berry-Talbott Language Tests: 1. Comprehension of Grammar* (1966)

AUTHOR(S): M. F. Berry & R. Talbott

SOURCE: M. F. Berry, 4332 Pinecrest Road, Rockford, Ill. 61107

BEHAVIORS/ABILITIES ASSESSED: Expressive language: morphology

AGE RANGE: 5 years–8 years

GENERAL DESCRIPTION: This test is very similar to Berko's test, described above. The Berry-Talbott test includes a booklet with 30 picture-stimulus plates, and a set of response record sheets is provided. The test booklet includes general instructions for the administration and analysis of this instrument. The morphological rules tested are those concerning: plurality, possession, third-person singular verb form, tense (past and progressive), and comparative and superlative adjectival forms. The test can be administered in approximately 15 minutes.

TITLE: *Comprehension Tests for Syntactic Constructions* (1971)

AUTHOR(S): U. Bellugi-Klima

SOURCE: Bellugi-Klima, U. Some language comprehension tests. In C. Lovateli (Ed.), *Language training in early childhood education.* Urbana-Champaign: University of Illinois Press, 1971.

BEHAVIORS/ABILITIES ASSESSED: Syntactic comprehension

AGE RANGE: Not specified

GENERAL DESCRIPTION: This chapter describes a general procedure for assessing children's comprehension of meaning conveyed by the syntax of a heard sentence (see Chapter 4 for a discussion of Bellugi-Klima's research with this procedure). The child is given objects (e.g., a boy and girl doll, a toy truck, etc.) and asked to act out a sentence read by the examiner. The author provides sentences to assess the child's knowledge of these syntactic/grammatical rules:

1. Active sentence (S-V-O)
2. Singular vs. plural nouns
3. Possession
4. Negative vs. affirmative
5. Singular vs. plural with noun and verb inflections
6. Adjectival questions
7. Negative affix
8. Relativization
9. Comparatives
10. Passives
11. Self-embedded sentences

The general procedure is one which can be adapted by the examiner to assess specific grammatical rules of interest.

TITLE: *Developmental Sentence Analysis (DSA)* (1974)

AUTHOR(S): L. Lee

SOURCE: Lee, L. *Developmental sentence analysis.* Evanston, Ill.: Northwestern University Press, 1974.

BEHAVIORS/ABILITIES ASSESSED: Expressive language: syntax and grammar

AGE RANGE: Not specified—verbal child

GENERAL DESCRIPTION: Laura Lee's *Developmental Sentence Analysis: A Grammatical Assessment Procedure for Speech and Language Clinicians* provides a section on normal grammatical development and discusses atypical development of each grammatical level. A Developmental Sentences Type Chart (DSTC) is included by which the clinician can classify fragmentary utterances obtained in a language sample into quantifiable syntactic/grammatical categories. For complete utterances, Lee outlines procedures for Developmental Sentence Scoring (DSS). The DSS procedure analyzes the child's use of eight syntactic categories: indefinite pronoun or noun modifier, personal pronoun, main verb, secondary verb, negative, conjunction, interrogative reversal, and wh–question. (The use of this instrument is restricted to those children learning standard American-English grammar.) Lee also includes suggestions concerning the construction of language and teaching goals from the analysis of the language samples. The use of this assessment procedure would be of more value with the child who is using sentences than the child producing only one- or two-word utterances.

TITLE: *Environmental Language Inventory (ELI)* (Component of *Environmental Language Intervention Program*) (1978)

AUTHOR(S): J. D. MacDonald & D. S. Horstmeier

SOURCE: Charles E. Merrill, 1300 Alum Creek Drive, Columbus, Ohio 43216

BEHAVIORS/ABILITIES ASSESSED: Semantic cases in two- and three-word expressive language

AGE RANGE: None specified—verbal child

GENERAL DESCRIPTION: The assessment is based on developmental data drawn from Schlesinger's study of the work of a number of researchers concerned with the period of two-word constructions in the normally developing child (see Chapter 2 for a discussion of this research). From Schlesinger's study, operationally defined semantic-grammatical rules were incorporated into the *Environmental Language Inventory,* an observational language coding system. The child's language is sampled in situations requiring *imitative* speech, prompted "conversational" speech, and spontaneous speech in *play* situations. The semantic-grammatical categories included in this instrument are:

1. Agent + Action
2. Action + Object
3. Agent + Object
4. Modifier + Head (possession, recurrence, and attribution)
5. Negation + *X*
6. Location (agent or object and action)
7. Introducer + *X*

In addition, mean length of utterance is computed for the free-play language sample of 50 utterances.

TITLE: *Environmental Prelanguage Battery (EPB)* (Component of *Environmental Language Intervention Program*) (1978)

AUTHOR(S): D. S. Horstmeier & J. D. MacDonald

SOURCE: Charles E. Merrill, 1300 Alum Creek Drive, Columbus, Ohio 43216

BEHAVIORS/ABILITIES ASSESSED: Spontaneous and imitative motor and verbal behavior; receptive skills

AGE RANGE: Not specified—language-delayed children functioning at or below single-word production level

GENERAL DESCRIPTION: The *Oliver* (see separate description) serves as the basis for the *Environmental Prelanguage Battery* (the *EPB*), to be completed by the diagnostician/interventionist. To establish a basal on the *EPB*, the diagnostician uses the information from the *Oliver* and begins the *EPB* assessment at a level "slightly below" the child's estimated ability. The *EPB* is a unique assessment instrument in that it is semantically based and can be used with the language-delayed child functioning at or below a single-word level. The purpose of this assessment is to determine the child's present skills vis-a-vis the Nisonger Center's prescriptive training procedures (contained in a prescriptive language-teaching handbook, *Ready, Set, Go: Talk to Me*). Entry-level skills are assessed beginning with attending and following simple commands. Areas to be tested were determined on the assumption that certain behaviors are necessary before communication training can begin. Thus, the *EPB* assesses not only the child's entry communication skills, but also his manner of interaction with the adults in his environment through the use of "meaningful play," imitation (verbal and motor), and demonstrated understanding of adult speech. The results of the *EPB* are used in determining a match between the child's entry skills and the Center's existing program. There is, therefore, no developmental quotient or language-age score. The only score obtainable from the *EPB* is a percentage of change (i.e., the effects of the intervention). Of additional value in the *EPB* is the built-in analysis of the ways in which the child learns. The diagnostician establishes, through a graded series of probes, the procedures necessary to produce responses from a particular child.

TITLE: *Goldman-Fristoe-Woodcock Auditory Skills Test Battery: Scales No. 2 & 3—Diagnostic Auditory Discrimination Test—Parts I & II* (1976)
AUTHOR(S): R. Goldman, M. Fristoe, & R. W. Woodcock
SOURCE: American Guidance Service, Circle Pines, Minn.
BEHAVIORS/ABILITIES ASSESSED: Discrimination of speech sounds
AGE RANGE: 3 years through adult
GENERAL DESCRIPTION: These two scales can be administered in approximately 30 minutes and are designed to provide a diagnostic profile of specific speech sounds which are not discriminated by the subject. The child's task is to select the correct picture (from a two-picture stimulus plate) named by a prerecorded stimulus word. Thus, this test can only be administered to subjects who have a basic receptive vocabulary.

TITLE: *Goldman-Fristoe-Woodcock Test of Auditory Discrimination* (1970)
AUTHOR(S): R. Goldman, M. Fristoe, & R. W. Woodcock
SOURCE: American Guidance Service, Circle Pines, Minn.
BEHAVIORS/ABILITIES ASSESSED: Discrimination of speech sounds
AGE RANGE: 4 to adult
GENERAL DESCRIPTION: This is a screening test in which the child is asked to point to the correct picture from a plate of four pictures upon hearing a stimulus word pronounced on a prerecorded audio tape. This is intended as a *screening* instrument and can be administered in approximately 10 to 15 minutes.

TITLE: *Infant Behavior Record* (Component of *Bayley Scales of Infant Development*) (1969)

AUTHOR(S): N. Bayley

SOURCE: The Psychological Corporation, 304 East 45th Street, New York, N.Y. 10017

BEHAVIORS/ABILITIES ASSESSED: Social behavior

AGE RANGE: Birth–30 months

GENERAL DESCRIPTION: Bayley's *Infant Behavior Profile* is based on a series of rating scales to be used after administration of the Bayley Scales of Infant Development. (It would seem that this profile could also be completed after other types of interaction with the child.) No age norms are given for the observationally determined items in the following areas:

1. Responsiveness to persons (no differentiation between objects and persons; behavior is affected by awareness of persons present)
2. Responsiveness to examiner (Avoiding–Inviting)
3. Responsiveness to mother (Withdrawn–Inviting)
4. Cooperativeness (Resists–Enthusiastic)
5. Fearfulness (Does not respond–Accepting)
6. Tension (Flaccid–Taut)
7. Happiness (Unhappy–Animated)
8. Object orientation (No interest in objects–Reluctantly relinquishes test materials)
9. Object orientation (Responsiveness, Attachment, Imaginative play)
10. Goal directedness (No direction–Absorption in task)
11. Attention span (Fleeting–Absorption)
12. Endurance (Tires easily–Continues to respond)
13. Activity level (Quiet–Hyperactive)

For each item, the examiner indicates the statement (on a one to nine rating) that best describes the child's behavior. It should be emphasized that these ratings are summations of the examiner's *impressions*, not verbatim recordings of actual behaviors.

TITLE: *Infant Cognitive Development Scale* (1971)

AUTHOR(S): A Mehrabian & M. Williams

SOURCE: *Journal of Psycholinguistic Research*, 1971, *1*, 113–26.

BEHAVIORS/ABILITIES ASSESSED: Representational ability

AGE RANGE: 4 months–20 months

GENERAL DESCRIPTION: This scale consists of 28 items which measure the following general types of responding:

1. Denotation and representation (six items)
2. Observing (three items)
3. Reciprocal assimilation: Visual and tactual (one item)
4. Reciprocal assimilation: Auditory and visual (one item)
5. Reciprocal assimilation: Visual and prehensive (one item)
6. Causality (six items)
7. Object stability (six items)

8. Imitation (four items)

The scale can be administered in 15 to 30 minutes and uses common objects (provided by the examiner). The scale was standardized on a sample of 196 middle socioeconomic class children and test-retest reliability (for a four-month interval) was found to be .72.

TITLE: *Miller-Yoder Test of Grammatical Comprehension, Experimental Edition* (1972)

AUTHOR(S): J. Miller & D. Yoder

SOURCE: University of Wisconsin Bookstore, Madison, Wis.

BEHAVIORS/ABILITIES ASSESSED: Comprehension of morphemic and syntactic contrasts

AGE RANGE: 3 years–6 years

GENERAL DESCRIPTION: The test consists of a set of picture-stimulus plates (four pictures on each) and 42 stimulus sentence pairs. The child must select the correct picture for a heard sentence. The sentence pairs provide contrasts along the following grammatical dimensions:
1. Active (e.g., "The girl washes the boy" vs. "The boy washes the girl")
2. Prepositions
3. Possessive
4. Negative/affirmative
5. Pronouns
6. Singular/plural, noun and verb
7. Verbal inflections
8. Adjective modifiers
9. Passive reversible (e.g., "John is pushed by Sally" vs. "Sally is pushed by John")
10. Reflexivizations (e.g., "The girl is feeding *her*" vs. "The girl is feeding *herself*").

At this time, this test is still available only in the experimental edition.

TITLE: *Northwest Syntax Screening Test (NSST)* (1971)

AUTHOR(S): L. Lee

SOURCE: Northwestern University Press, Evanston, Ill.

BEHAVIORS/ABILITIES ASSESSED: Receptive and expressive grammar and syntax

AGE RANGE: 3 years–8 years

GENERAL DESCRIPTION: This is a screening instrument designed to assess the child's mastery of syntax rules and consists of two subtests—Receptive and Expressive—with 20 items in each. The receptive tasks require the child to select the correct picture (from a plate of four black-and-white line drawings) which corresponds to a sentence read by the examiner. The expressive tasks require the child to listen while the examiner reads two sentences about a picture and then to repeat the correct sentence. Sentences for both tests are arranged in contrast-pairs to assess the following grammatical forms and rules: prepositions, personal pronouns, negation, tense, plurality (noun and verb inflections), possession, reflexive, active and passive constructions, indirect object, and interrogative constructions. The test can be administered in approximately 15 minutes.

TITLE: *Oliver: Parent-Administered Communication Inventory* (Component of *Environmental Language Intervention Program*) (1978)
AUTHOR(S): J. D. MacDonald
SOURCE: Charles E. Merrill, 1300 Alum Creek Drive, Columbus, Ohio 43216
BEHAVIORS/ABILITIES ASSESSED: Receptive and expressive communication; motor and verbal imitation; play behavior
AGE RANGE: Not specified
GENERAL DESCRIPTION: The *Oliver: Parent-Administered Communication Inventory* assesses the child's communication skills within the natural environment. This inventory is to be completed by the child's parents or teachers and includes a brief family history section, asks for descriptions of child's method of communication, and suggests interactions which require that the child respond. From this single "preprofessional assessment," the diagnostician can surmise the child's usual means of communicating, typical language utterances, receptive abilities, cognitive stage, ability to attend, ability to imitate, ability to retain information, and knowledge of the function of objects. For each of these behaviors, the parent is asked first to record any remembered instances of that behavior and second to carry out (utilizing test instructions) an activity designed to produce that behavior. For example, "Take some objects your child regularly uses, sees, or plays with. Have him show you if he understands certain words by asking him to point, touch, or in some other way indicate that certain words mean certain things. Give him chances for each object until he shows he understands." The format of the inventory is clear, and the manner of presentation reinforcing, encouraging parents to assist the professional in helping the child.

TITLE: *Ordinal Scales of Psychological Development* (1975)
AUTHOR(S): I. C. Uzgiris & J. McV. Hunt
SOURCE: Urbana, University of Illinois Press (1975)
BEHAVIORS/ABILITIES ASSESSED: Cognitive/sensorimotor development
AGE RANGE: 1 month–2 years
GENERAL DESCRIPTION: The *Uzgiris-Hunt Ordinal Scales of Psychological Development*, a Piagetian-based instrument, contains six scales which seriate behavioral reactions representative of sequential cognitive schemata. Methods of presenting the assessment materials are delineated along with suggestions for establishing rapport. The areas tested are:

Scale I: The Development of Visual Pursuits and the Permanence of Objects. The first item on this scale assesses the infant's ability in tracking an object through a 180° arc. The second step in this series is visual fixation of the place at which an object disappears. The latter part of this scale assesses the infant's ability to locate hidden objects.

Scale II: The Development of Means for Obtaining Desired Environmental Events. This scale begins with the appearance of the infant's hand-watching behavior and progresses through grasping to the use of an object as a tool with which to obtain another object. The upper end of the scale measures the element of foresight in problem solving.

Scale III: a) The Development of Vocal Imitation, and b) The Development of Gestural Imitation. The first item on the Vocal Imitation Scale determines if vocalizations other than crying are present. Response to familiar auditory stimuli is assesed, culminating in vocal imitation of words within the infant's vocabulary. The first item on the Gestural Imitation Scale section assesses imitation of familiar gestures (already present in the infant's behavioral repertoire). Progression on this subscale continues through imitation of familiar gestures to imitation of unfamiliar gestures which the infant is able to observe (raising his leg) in his own performance, and finally, imitation of unfamiliar gestures which he cannot see himself perform (blinking his eyes, opening his mouth).

Scale IV: The Development of Operation Causality. This scale is related to Scale II, The Development of Means for Obtaining Desired Environmental Events, in that this scale also begins with hand-watching behavior. The difference between the two scales involves a recognition by the infant that he can cause the repetition of an occurrence either by "requesting" another person to reactivate the object (demonstrating his recognition of the individual as a causal agent) or by activating the object himself after witnessing a demonstration (the object used is a wind-up toy).

Scale V: The Construction of Object Relations in Space. Item one consists of determining if the infant can observe two objects alternately, then testing the infant's ability to follow the trajectory of a falling object. The ability to localize sound reveals the coordinating of information from differing sensory modalities. Stacking objects (renamed by Uzgiris-Hunt: placing objects in equilibrium one upon another), dropping objects (and observing their landing), and retrieving objects tied to a string are some of the items in this scale which ends with the infant's ability to indicate the physical absence of a family member.

Scale VI: The Development of Schemes for Relating to Objects. The beginning item in this scale involves the presentation of simple objects. Options involve varying hand-eye coordinated responses such as placing in mouth, placing in front of eyes (to observe objects), hitting, shaking, and finally, showing objects to persons (suggesting joint reference). The upper limits of this scale require naming of recognized objects.

TITLE: *Preference Procedure for Testing Phonological Discrimination* (1975)

AUTHOR(S): P. Waryas & C. Waryas

SOURCE: Waryas, P. A., & Waryas, C. L. Phonological discrimination of normal-hearing and hearing-impaired retarded children. *Acta Symbolica*, 1975, *6*, 27–40.

BEHAVIORS/ABILITIES ASSESSED: Speech-sound discrimination

AGE RANGE: Not specified

GENERAL DESCRIPTION: This procedure is designed to assess the child's ability to discriminate phonemes arranged in three different sets of phoneme contrasts, which vary in the probability of discrimination error. For each phoneme contrast pair, the child is given two Language Master cards which produce words that differ only in the critical phoneme. The child's task is to select the card which names a picture stimulus. Thus, the child must have a basic receptive vocabulary to complete the task as described by the investigators. However, by having the child match the card to an auditory rather than to a visual stimulus, this procedure may be adapted for use with children who show no receptive language.

TITLE: *Receptive/Expressive Emergent Language Scale (REEL)* (1970)
AUTHOR(S): K. R. Bzoch & R. League
SOURCE: Anhinga Press, Assorted Publications, Inc., 420 Boulevard, P. O. Box 13501, Gainesville, Fla. 32604
BEHAVIORS/ABILITIES ASSESSED: Receptive and expressive aural/oral language skills
AGE RANGE: Birth–36 months
GENERAL DESCRIPTION: A test of infant language skills, the *Receptive-Expressive Emergent Language Scale* (the *REEL*), begins with assessing the startle response (0–1 month). Six items (three expressive, three receptive) are listed for each one-month interval through the first year. The second year, items span two-month intervals, the third year, three-month intervals. The value of this scale lies in its applicability to neonatal language as well as that of older infants. The functional use of language is tested; the items are heavily socio-affective. Scoring is based on an interview with a knowledgeable informant.

TITLE: *Sequenced Inventory of Communication Development (SICD)* (1975)
AUTHOR(S): D. L. Hedrick, E. M. Prather, & A. R. Tobin
SOURCE: University of Washington Press, Seattle, Wash.
BEHAVIORS/ABILITIES ASSESSED: Receptive and expressive language abilities
AGE RANGE: 4 months–48+ months
GENERAL DESCRIPTION: This test consists of two scales: Receptive and Expressive. Information is obtained both through parent reporting and through direct observation of the child in partially structured and structured tasks. Most materials needed for the assessment are provided in the test kit. The Receptive Scale consists of 35 items which assess the child's abilities in six areas: environmental sound awareness, speech sound awareness, environmental sound discrimination, speech sound discrimination, understanding of words with supporting cues, and understanding of words alone. The Expressive Scale consists of 67 items which assess the child's expressive ability in terms of eight different types of expressive behavior: motor imitation, vocal imitation, verbal imitation, motor initiating, vocal initiating, verbal initiating, vocal responsive, and verbal responsive. In addition, the scale includes an analysis of a language sample to be collected during the examination. Age norms are provided for both scales.

TITLE: *Test for Auditory Comprehension of Language: English* (1969)
AUTHOR(S): E. Carrow
SOURCE: S. W. Educational Development Corp., Austin, Tex.
BEHAVIORS/ABILITIES ASSESSED: Receptive language
AGE RANGE: 3 years–7+ years
GENERAL DESCRIPTION: This test consists of 101 items. For each item, the examiner reads a phrase or sentence to the child and the child's task is to select the

correct picture from a plate of three pictures. The test assesses lexical-semantic and grammatical comprehension of the following types: common nouns, quantitative and ordinal nouns and adjectives (pair, some, second), perceptual attributes, spatial prepositional relationships, verbs, adverbs, comparative adjectives, derivative nouns, personal pronouns, tense, plurality, passive vs. active construction, direct vs. indirect object, conjunction, conditional relationships (if . . . then), imperative, negation, and wh– questions. Age norms are provided in terms of ages at which 75% and 90% of the standardization sample passed each item. Administration time is approximately 20 minutes.

TITLE: *Vocabulary Comprehension Scale* (1976)
AUTHOR(S): T. E. Bangs
SOURCE: Learning Concepts, Austin, Tex.
BEHAVIORS/ABILITIES ASSESSED: Receptive vocabulary
AGE RANGE: 2 years–6 years
GENERAL DESCRIPTION: The *Vocabulary Comprehension Scale* assesses the child's understanding of pronouns, prepositions, attributes (size, weight, etc.) and quantitative concepts such as all, more, and less. Within each general category, items are arranged in order of difficulty. Actual objects are used in assessment and a nonverbal response is required. The test employs a game-like format and the child's task is to manipulate the test items in accordance with a verbal/oral stimulus provided by the examiner within the context of four game-like activities. Developmental norms are provided for each item. The test kit includes all objects to be used, as well as the response-record forms and manual.

chapter 7

Implications of the Transactional Model for Treatment Programs

Overall Treatment Program Needs

Earlier in this book, we noted that current treatment programs in language for severely developmentally delayed children necessarily reflect their specific theoretical view of language. For example, if a teacher or clinician views language as a set of syntactic rules, he would design treatment procedures which seek to attain these syntactic rules. On the other hand, with a view of language as a collection of expressed semantic relationships or as a collection of utterances designed to evoke certain reinforcing consequences from the environment, a therapist or teacher will target semantic relationships such as agent-action or specific reinforcement-seeking utterances such as "want drink."

The empirical and theoretical discussions in the previous chapters have shown that each of these various individual target categories described above are appropriate to some aspect of language. It is also true that each of these language dimensions is related to each of the others in basic and mutually affecting ways. Because they are so basically related, it is literally impossible to seek one of them without involving the other two. Yet, most current programs do not explicitly consider all three of these dimensions. In fact, it is rare if a program is definitive in its concern with two of the three dimensions. Most often, a language-intervention program's underlying theory will be directed toward structure, semantics, or function, and that element is the one which is targeted. The other two elements will thus often not be treated in any but an incidental or uncontrolled way.

When such unidimensional perspectives undergird a treatment program, it seems questionable whether the program can attain optimal results. Since these three dimensions are interrelated, the attainment of a single target would appear to be seriously inhibited by ignoring either of the other dimensions involved. Thus, the targeting of syntactic structures in isolation from adequate consideration of the cognitive and pragmatic elements which undergird such structures seems both ill-advised and potentially costly in terms of attaining the goals of such treatment. Most language programs miss representing this concern because they concentrate on the *language system* and not on the fullest and richest interpretation of the overall *communicative system*. In view of the biases engendered by various theoretical views of language, this unidimensionality in current programs is understandable, if not acceptable.

It appears appropriate, however, for such delimiting biases to be modified by attempts to approach language in terms of not only its specific structure, but also its underlying cognitive prerequisites. It seems appropriate, too, to attempt to consider language more in terms of its critical place in the social repertoires of people and to apply these considerations to the targets and the consequences which are sought in language programs for handicapped children. If we remember Olson's (1970) admonition that people cannot talk about what they do not know and DeLaguna's (1963) statement that people talk in order to influence the attitudes and actions of other people, then we will have the basis for a three-dimensional targeting matrix for language rather than our current, one-dimensional approaches. In the three-way matrix, language programming identifies targets for each dimension of the communicative act: (1) functions of communicative acts, (2) content of communicative acts, and (3) structure of communicative acts.

Figure 1 illustrates the matrix for targeting, and provides some additional details about those things which are involved in each dimension. In this matrix, we see each of the nested elements of a language utterance, and, thus, we see the various target dimensions which must be considered within each response set forth for language-deficient children. Regardless of the exclusiveness of our theoretical perspectives, each of these elements is there whether we recognize it programmatically or not. As a consequence, if we target a syntactic *structure* without giving attention to the *content* and the *function* of that structure, we most probably will not attain that targeted structure in any truly productive form. Conversely, if we were to target a certain communicative function without appropriate consideration of possible constraints in both the content and the structure possible for a child, we would in all probability not attain that function in any productive form.

The question becomes, then, how do we develop a *model* for language intervention with young handicapped children which adequately reflects these multiple elements? The first step, obviously, is to understand more thoroughly each of these three elements and their relationship to one another. When this is accomplished, we can begin to consider how best to include each of them in the targets of an intervention program. In the preceding discussions on the cognitive, social, and linguistic bases of language, we have discussed the function, content, and structure of language rather thoroughly as it has been identified within the normative data of language development. In the immediately preceding chapter on assessment, we provided the fine-grain data relating to these areas as comprehensively as we could, given current constructs and available instrumentation for such quantification. In many ways, we would like for clinicians and teachers in the field to take these constructs and quantifications and go on from here. Nevertheless, we will continue and attempt to relate the information introduced in previous chapters to treatment programs for young handicapped children who manifest severe language delay.

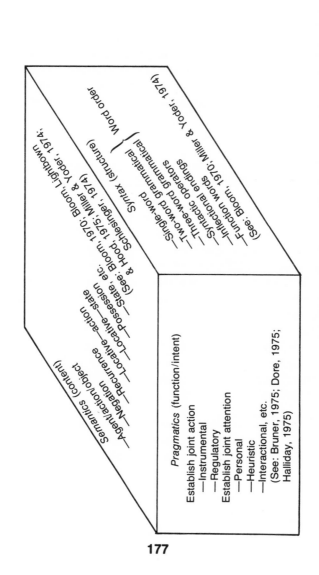

Note:
Any utterance, of necessity,
includes all three elements:
1. It has function
2. It has content
3. It has structure
Target selection and procedures
must consider each element in
covariance with each
other element.

FIGURE 1. Selected Examples of the Possible Elements of a Three-way Matrix for Selection of Language Intervention Targets.

Because there is so much information which suggests so much for treatment applications, it is also tempting to develop a specific treatment program as we would interpret its form from the perspectives we have been discussing. This, however, would be most unfortunate, for it appears to us that there are enough specific treatment programs. What we would seem to need at this time are more general treatment strategies and treatment styles, for these are the levels which will allow us truly to treat each child or group of children. Specific programs return us to the adult perspectives which appear insensitive to the individual child's needs. More specific programs should emerge from these perspectives and these data in the future. Hopefully they will emerge only as a result of empirical data regarding the effect of various treatment strategies directed by these perspectives on specific kinds and levels of individual children's problems. In other words, children, first individually and then collectively, should "write" the *specific* programs emerging from these perspectives.

The remaining chapters in this book will not be as finely detailed as preceding chapters. Therefore, while we hope it will be relatively comprehensive, our discussion on treatment implications will put forth general implications and strategies in each of the major dimensions of language treatment. We will be discussing, then, the clinical implications of (1) the function of communicative acts, (2) the content of communicative acts, (3) the structure of communicative acts, (4) the context for language intervention, (5) alternative mode consideration, and, (6) a summary of treatment applications.

The Function of Communicative Acts: Pragmatics*

As detailed in Chapter 4, communicative acts appear to be produced in order to attain certain consequences. Because language is what it is, these consequences are deliverable only by other organisms who can "understand" the language being used. Thus, we wish to reestablish the reality that language and its intended communication function are broadly social in nature. This fact can be made more operational in language programming—particularly for young, severely handicapped children.

Making the communicative function more operational in language-intervention programming begins with targeting specific pragmatic classes in such programming. It is further operationalized by assuring the delivery of the appropriate social consequences for these classes and by assuring that the semantic forms and syntactic structures necessary to carry such pragmatic messages are available to the child. Thus, while we will be concentrating on the pragmatic aspects of language intervention in the next few pages, we will be projecting their implications for both the semantic content and syntactic structure targets which will be discussed in detail in later sections of this chapter. We hope to provide rather specific examples of our contention that language-intervention programming for early language users must

---

*The reader is reminded that our use of the term *pragmatic* can be translated *performative* in light of the more extensive treatment afforded it in the recent linguistic literature (Bates, 1976).

be representative of all three covarying dimensions of language systems and communication.

While we can be both definitive and highly illustrative in the area of targeting pragmatic classes, it is possible at this time to be neither exhaustive nor totally specific about all that might be undertaken in this area of pragmatic programming. Empirical data exist which identify pragmatic classes present in human language and which indicate some general developmental hierarchy for certain of these broad classes. What is *not* available at this time are clinical and research experience in these areas as they might be applied with populations of handicapped children. Thus, we are in the position now of suggesting broad *guidelines* for modified language-intervention programs which have extremely high logical and empirical validity but which need rigorous experimental evaluation and directed modification.

Targeting
Pragmatic Classes

In Chapter 3 of this volume, we discussed several levels and units for identifying pragmatic classes in human language. A table from that chapter is presented again here to review that discussion. As Table 1 shows, Halliday (1975) has identified seven general classes of pragmatic function and Dore (1975) has provided nine specific exemplars of the various types of utterances in these classes. While the two systems are not completely parallel, they are related enough to allow a programmer

TABLE 1

Communicative Functions of Children's Language

Bruner	DeLaguna	Halliday Stage I	Halliday Stage II	Dore
I Regulating joint actions	Influence a listener's acts	Instrumental	Pragmatic	Requesting action
		Regulatory		Calling
				Protesting
II		Interactional		Greeting
		Personal		Labeling
Regulating joint attention	Influence a listener's attitudes	Heuristic	Mathetic	Requesting answer
		Imaginative		Repeating
		(Informative)		Answering
				Practicing

to get a good and rather refined start on providing important classes of language function for language-delayed children. By following the suggestions of these data, language interventionists can set up programs which might allow a child to discover the various ways language can function for him. Most importantly, they can set these programs up with systematic procedures and with optimal procedural power. This latter point is critical, for we know that these various functions are eventually discovered by normal-learning language users. We do not know, however, that they can be so discovered by severely delayed language learners, even when opportunities to discover them are rather carefully designed and maximized.

Further, one can see that two of the general functions identified by Halliday (1975) (Instrumental and Regulatory) might be considered both more primitive in their basic functions and earlier in their developmental emergence than some of the other classes. If we look to Dore (1975) to provide more specific examples of these two classes, we see such functions as requesting action, calling, and protesting. Thus, the details of such classes of communicative functions tend to confirm the conclusion that they are most basic human communication exchanges. In fact, these most basic communicative functions are universally sought by the human infant long before formal language and speech forms are possible. Before speech, infants accomplish these functions through the use of various cries, noises, and nonvocal motor movements, like armwaving, cup banging, and active squirming. Given such basic and primitive needs, and thus motivation for expressing these needs, are there any better indications for where to start with a particularly difficult, nonverbal child? Similarly, is it not compelling to see that the studies which identify the content and form of child language all report the early emergence of such one-word utterances as "no," "more," "fix," "want," and the many-splendored variations on "mama" which mean "come-here," "don't do that," "help me do this," "get me the toy I dropped out of my crib," and so on?

The lack of attention in current language programs to these pragmatic functions in language seems obvious and is demonstrated by the fact that so many current programs begin with the almost exclusive targeting of the ability to "name" things. Obviously, naming functions are eventually important to all of the various pragmatic functions, but it also makes rather basic sense to concentrate on some basic reasons why we learn to name things. Thus, for example, the labeling of milk might be better taught to a child within another established functional context, such as "more milk," "want milk," "no (want) milk." While these latter examples go beyond our specific point, they help to illustrate our bias that the various individual classes of language function are not only important in and of themselves but seem also important to the attainment of all other functions and forms of language. In the milk example, the labeling function might be sought initially within the context of other basic functions like instrumental or protesting (or rejection).

In designing for targets in pragmatic or functional classes of language behavior, the language interventionist might literally train a child in ways that would allow the discovery of these various classes of language use. Thus, requesting action, calling, and protesting would be early targets for young, severely language-delayed children. These classes are generally well represented in most language programs, and likewise are well represented in adult language present in the child's normal verbal environment. Similarly, greeting, labeling, requesting answers, and answering are also well represented in both child-directed programming and in adult speech directed toward children in everyday environments. What seems not to be present, however, is careful attention to the specific and systematic assurance that these functions are presented again and again in optimal training fashion. Normal children learning language seem to acquire awareness of these functions from rather uncontrolled and, thus, haphazard exposure to them. Severely language-delayed children may well not be able to acquire them without much more concentration on them. We propose, as do other authors, specific research on the verbal and nonverbal representation of these various pragmatic functions within the behavior of severely and profoundly retarded children.

Until more data is available, however, individual language teachers and clinicians must analyze their current caseloads to see how well these targets are now represented in their children's repertoires. No known program for language currently incorporates these classes into their targets in the form discussed here. Naturally, behaviorally based programs (such as Guess, Sailor, & Baer, 1974) contain so-called "functionally useful" classes of language responses. Usually, however, these are approached in rather specific forms directed toward the attainment of primary needs related to food, drink, and toileting. While such targets do relate most favorably to the suggested functions, they do not represent an adequate representation of any one or all of the classes of language functions. One might consider, for example, that so-called wh- questions are often early targets in language programs for moderately to mildly retarded children. Such targets occur early in programs because they are extremely functional types of behavior for children. Thus, existing programs do reflect the basic validity of language function as an indicator of appropriate language targets. Unfortunately, at this point in time, wh- questions occur primarily as a syntactically based target and not a functional one. If, instead of viewing these as only syntactic forms, we could consider the types of heuristic functions children require to operate in their environment and teach the appropriate structures required to satisfy them, we might arrive at much more efficacious acquisition of many forms of question structures.

As an aside on this topic, children request much information (heuristic function) in forms other than the appropriate syntactic forms of wh- forms or the front-shifted verb grammatical structure. Consider, for example, the functional effect of a child's uttering of a single word with an upward pitch inflection. Most generally, such an utterance form will be reacted to as though it were a heuristic: milk↑ will often evoke such responses as "Yes, that's milk"; "No, that's orange juice"; "No, you've had enough milk for now"; "Yes, you may have some more milk." Similarly, a child's stating "Me go outside" as a simple declarative statement might function as though it were a request for permission to go outside. These examples simply indicate that many functions of language (for example, heuristic), although they have a preferred adult syntactic form, may be easily attainable through structural forms which are markedly different from the preferred adult form. Thus, while there is an important concordance between syntactic structures and language functions, many such functions can be attained with language forms which differ from the standard one. As a consequence, function of several types can be treated quite independently of complex, standard syntactic forms. Young children learning language, for example, seem well able to ask questions about location, cause, and labels of entities long before they have acquired the wh- forms "where," "why," and "what." Most importantly, however, children seem to need to carry out this function prior to their acquistion of the standard forms through which to do so. Such functions, then, would appear to be well considered as targets in language programs for young, severely delayed language cases. They should, therefore, be specifically targeted in their own right rather than occurring as a "bonus" because a structural target like a wh-question happens to be selected.

In summary, language programs for young or severely language-delayed children should specifically consider the pragmatic functions identified for human language as specific and carefully sought targets for such programming. Further, such functions may well include a concordance with the targeting of a specific syntactic or semantic target. However, if such structural or content targets are not possible for a particular child, the function might be taught through other, less formal linguistic realization forms, such as the use of upward inflections, gestures, or tag-forms. Such less formal forms are commonly used by children in their developmental progressions toward the standard linguistic forms of the adult culture. From such apparent approximations in less mature developmental forms, one might conclude that all language users should be allowed (aided/helped) to attain the ability to carry out the several functions of language even though they cannot attain the standard structural forms of the culture for these functions. In other words, since we respond functionally appropriately to a normal child's utterance of "milk↑," why not attend to the assurance of such a heuristic function by a retarded child before he has arrived at the level of interrogative or wh- form syntactic targets? Obviously, unless such functions are specifically considered target classes within language-intervention targets, an enforced delay or denial of the function might well occur.

Contingent Reinforcement and Pragmatic Functions

If the functions of language are to be targeted as distinct and specific classes of behavior, a primary variable in effecting such learning will be that concerned with the consequences of language utterances (or appropriate receptive responses) by clinical subjects. It would appear that we have become relatively constrained in our applications of consequences in language programs, and these constraints need to be radically altered. The further considerations of the pragmatic function classes of language would seem to be highly directive in guiding these alterations in target identification.

Current applications of reinforcement in language training. As in all behaviorally oriented training programs, the contingent use of reinforcing stimuli is routine in language-training programs. The application of reinforcement is somewhat narrow in such programs, however. Our observations indicate that the use of reinforcement is limited to that which primarily reinforces the structure or the linguistic content of children's utterances. Where this is true, the relative function of an utterance might well be ignored in that it may evoke differential consequences.

For example, much language training is carried out in the area of naming objects in the environment. In such training, reinforcement for the appropriate lexical response which matches the antecedent stimulus consisting of a picture or an object is appropriate. Thus, if a child is shown a picture of the sun and utters "sun," reinforcement is applied—perhaps in the form of a tangible reinforcer such as a token or an edible. If, however, a child is being trained to carry out the regulatory function of language by acquiring the structure and content for calling someone ("mama come"), it would not seem adequate to deliver the standard consequence of a verbal reinforcer "good talking" accompanied by a token or a piece of candy. Rather, the consequences for an utterance of that particular *function* should serve to *identify* that function for the child. Thus, a regulatory utterance should be followed by a compliance *response to the regulatory message* (mama comes). While many such "in-kind" reinforcements do occur in most language programs, they are not often systematically anticipated or planned as part of the reinforcement contingencies. If pragmatic function classes are to be efficaciously attained, the function of the reinforcing consequence must be carefully analyzed and applied in differential form for the different classes.

Perspectives for the use of reinforcement in language intervention. There are factors which indicate the need for careful consideration of the reinforcer, and these are quite basic in terms of their rationale. One can see, for example, that the very construct of functional intent for language utterances is based on the assumption that the person has some reason for producing the utterance. For example, the speaker wishes to regulate someone's actions or evoke someone else's actions in ways that are instrumental to the speaker. Thus, the consequences of such utter- ances are specified by the message being uttered. If someone says, "come here," the only truly effective reinforcement of that form would be the fact that the object of the utterance allowed such regulation of his behavior and, indeed, went "there." Such a relationship between an utterance and its natural reinforcer is that which defines Skinner's class of verbal behavior labeled "manding." In his definition of a manding response, Skinner (1957) describes this class of response as one which specifies its own reinforcer. Thus, responses which regulate other's behaviors ("come here," "look at me," "do that," "help me open this," etc.) are "mands." Interestingly, if we accept the overall construct that all human language behaviors have some specific function to affect the behaviors or the attitudes of other people, we could easily state that *all* language behavior is, in some sense, "manding" in nature. Thus, even when a child names or labels an entity (for example, "that doggie"), he expects some response of affirmation or correction from the listener. So, in this broad sense, even labeling is a form of "mand" in its full social function.

In normal language-learning environments, the consequences of most language utterances are determined by the listener's assumed function of that utterance for the speaker. The classic study by Brown and Hanlon (1970) which indicated that parents react to children's language utterances in terms of their truth value is a case in point. In this study, Brown and Hanlon reported that parents rarely reacted to the grammar of a child. Rather, they reacted to the semantic content of the child's utterance in terms of its appropriateness—presumably, then, to the *functional intent* of the child. Thus, if a child uttered "there a doggie" and the parent assumed it was intended to label the kitty which was passing by, the parent would correct the utterance. By the same token, a child who uttered "there a kitty" under identical circumstances would evoke the consequence of affirmation from a parent—"yes, honey, that's a kitty." The irony is that many (such as Ervin-Tripp, 1971) have interpreted Brown and Hanlon's data as prima facie evidence that parents do not reinforce their children's utterances. On the contrary, these data simply indicate that parents reinforce the semantic and pragmatic aspects of children's utterances as opposed to the grammatical. Yet, if we review our intervention programming objectively, it would seem that most professionals do not follow the examples set by parents. Generally, the biases which have caused us to target grammar rather than communication have led us to reinforcement contingencies based on the wrong response units. So, we most frequently reward the grammatical structure of a child's utterance while we often totally ignore its functional intent. We suggest that clinicians sensitize themselves to this point and listen to language interventionists in many programs. They would often hear, as we have heard—Clinician: "Say 'Is this an orange?'" Child: "Is this an orange?" Clinician: "Yes; is this an orange? Good talking" (delivers a token/edible).

The clinical implications of the recent data on pragmatic functions of language are great, having impact on such basic elements of clinical procedure as reinforcement contingency. Current determination of appropriate reinforcement forms and targets should be totally reviewed and modified in the light of these new dimensions of language targets. Certainly, much of our reinforcement for the structure of responses should be maintained. Just as certainly, however, reinforcement contingencies will need to be supplemented by inclusion of consequences which are appropriate to the functional intent of language as well as its grammatical form.

These changes are not easy to design or to apply. For one thing, the pragmatic function of an utterance is essentially determined by a need which takes form inside the speaker. For example, if a child utters an instrumental response, such as "help fix car," the need basis for that pragmatic class of response has been determined by the child. It is relatively easy to get language teachers to reinforce utterances of this class in appropriate ways—for example, "Fix it? OK. Let me see what's wrong. Oh, there, the wheel needs to be put back on. There, it's fixed," while accompanying this verbal response with the motor responses of taking the car and acting as the instrument of its repair. It is much more difficult to set the occasions in which such instrumental requests will occur so that their function can be demonstrated. This problem of creating intervention settings in which various pragmatic functions will be sought by children and appropriately reinforced by teachers signals the need to develop modified *contexts* for language intervention. The need for modified language-teaching contexts has other dimensions, too. We will, therefore, discuss context designs in some additional detail in the following section.

Contexts for Pragmatic Training Goals

There are two keys to the development of contexts which function to evoke and reinforce pragmatic targets for young, severely language-delayed children. The first is that such a context include people to talk to. Secondly, the *people must respond* to the specific intent and content of children's communication attempts. The combination of these key demands suggests that the targeting and attainment of pragmatic classes of communication can only be attained in a situation where there is a truly interactive relationship between the subject child and the teaching adult. Further, the nature of the target classes suggest that the context of this relationship should increase the probability that various of the language functions which make up these pragmatic classes can and do occur. In other words, contexts should be developed which enhance the probability that children will request *instrumentality* from the adult, *regulate* the adult's behavior, indicate and *name* items, *request* information, and so forth. Ideally, from a teaching efficiency standpoint, a context should evoke just a few of these functions several times during any one training period. If this proves to be an impossible goal, the context should at least be consistent in evoking various of these functional classes; so that, over an extended period of training time, a child would have been exposed to appropriate reinforcement of these classes many times.

What kind of context can be developed which meets these demands? Actually, at this point in our clinical experience with targets such as we are discussing here, we can better state what a context should not include if it would hope to meet these needs. First, a language-training context for young, severely handicapped children who require systematic exposure to the pragmatic classes of communication should not place the child in a static, passive role in the context. In other words, the child should probably not be seated at a table with all of his activities for language development being presented *to* him by the teacher. Similarly, the context should probably not be concentrated exclusively on pictures. Rather, it should more probably be concentrated on an activity of actions with real objects and other people. Thirdly, such contexts, if they are to be effective in this area, should not concentrate solely on evoking specific language forms from children. Rather, such contexts should, initially, be seeking communication attempts on the part of the child regardless of the specific form of the request (see, for example, Longhurst & Reichle, 1975). Language structures which are most appropriate for the request can be provided later. Often, this type of child's need or desire to communicate is extremely difficult to evoke.

If we were to attempt to project such evoking elements into specific contexts, we would visualize conditions such as:

1. A transparent box of desirable objects or edibles which is "childproof"—that is, required adult instrumentality to open.
2. A construction of simple assembly task in which each successive element is under the control/possession of the adult and, thus, must be requested.
3. The ubiquitous "pig-in-a-poke" grab-bag games in which children reach in and get objects and, in variation, contexts in which children select and request objects which are put into the bag for other children to find.
4. Situations in which various of the above contexts are set up and other children are offered/requested to take their turn.
5. Contexts rich with various toys and which *must* be passed to another child or adult at regular intervals—with opportunities to communicate preferences.
6. "Where is it?" games.
7. "Find another" games.

Experienced child workers can, of course, extend such interactive contexts ad infinitum. Those who lack such experience or training might observe mother-child interactions in home contexts where such needs for instrumentality, regulation naming, requesting information, and so on need not be artificially constructed. In fact, in many group situations in preschools, such contexts for pragmatic communication classes occur in the natural event of things. Too often, however, when they do occur, they might not be meeting the predetermined goals of an activity or an activity period and, therefore, might not be utilized to attain desirable language function targets. The language teacher should be sure he is properly sensitive to occasions where functions are requested by children and mark them for utility in later targeting or pragmatic language targets.

Nevertheless, it is true that many severely to profoundly handicapped children will not have the basic behavioral repertoires necessary to develop such ideal and facilitative interactive contexts. With these children, desirable and necessary interactions must be targeted at much lower levels. For example, the clinician might target dressing help with buttons, zippers, and shoe strings; toileting and other caretaking interactions; or feeding activities in which children are prompted to express preferences for the next bite. Again, if we observe natural mother-child interactions, we see that many of the interactive behaviors and, thus, the functional uses of language and communication occur in routine caretaking activities. Similarly, in all instructional settings, much communication of functional importance occurs in the context of caretaking and instruction giving. Certainly, the *requests for action, calling, labeling, protesting,* and *greeting* functions are highly prominent in such activities.

In manipulating these contexts for intervention, we are trying to set up conditions in which:

1. Children will form specific desires or needs through their own internal processes.
2. Children will seek to communicate to other human beings those actions, compliances or aids which would satisfy internally developed needs or desires.
3. Those people in the environmental context will react so as to demonstrate to the communicating child the nature and the effectiveness of his communicative act.

Within such contexts the specific nature of the functional communicative response could be changed to become successively more complete or developmentally sophisticated. The teacher or clinician might start with only a child's "line of visual regard" as an effective communication of a specific desire for an object, for example. Later, a gesture might be required. An "uh" plus pointing might be accepted as communicative for a while, and then a word approximation might be required. Finally, the language-oriented intervener can attempt to attain the higher forms of semantic and syntactic orthodoxy in stating such needs or desires.

Whatever the level of target being attempted, the differential demonstration of the several classes of language function seems to be a critical and basic discovery for children. Naturally, many children with delayed-language problems may indicate that such functions are already known to them. But those professionals who have had experience with severely and profoundly handicapped know too that many such children have not made these discoveries. If the context of language intervention continues to be directed solely at syntactic targets and reinforcement continues to be simplistically and one-dimensionally applied only to response topography, ignoring response function, many of our severely handicapped children may never discover many of the functions to which their language may be directed. Thus, contexts in which to demonstrate these functions must become vital dimensions of clinical language intervention.

It is apparent in this task of context design that we could benefit greatly from additional research in this area. There is much activity in this area of investigation (e.g., Broen, 1972; Greenfield & Smith, 1976; Huttenlocher, 1974; Mahoney, 1975; Nelson, 1973a) and more is being undertaken. From such research we might expect to be able to identify hierarchies within the development of specific functions along with the nature of the contexts in which certain functions have the highest probability of being expressed. With such data, language-intervention contexts can be designed which have high levels of reliability for evoking and reinforcing certain functional communication classes. Particularly helpful would be research that facilitates derivation of such classes and their evoking contexts from actual children's language instead of from an adult's synthesis about what is important to children.

Even without highly illustrative data, however, we can now recognize where the contexts for language intervention can be made to depart from the static "clinical" atmospheres now used to develop tightly controlled utterance structures. We can begin to develop dynamic, social interaction milieus which will bring language training into contact with the functional contexts of people and purpose from which language emerges naturally and for which contexts it is designed to function.

Social Prerequisites of Communication

All of the above discussion, whether it is concerned with types of communication functions or conditions designed to evoke or reinforce such functions is predicated on a most basic construct, namely, that human beings are imbued with (or quickly acquire) a drive state directed toward interactions with other members of their species. Considering the helplessness and the needs of young human infants, such a drive state is clearly related to survival. In fact, it is generally accepted that the most basic motivations of so-called human social orders are based on survival needs. As one of the slowest, weakest, and physically most defenseless groups in the animal kingdom, humans have been forced to establish mutually serving social orders in order to survive. The attainment of such complex group structures literally requires a complex communication system. That these social orders also serve to provide human diversions in the form of entertainment, humor, and mutual affection does not alter the more primitive and life-sustaining basis of their existence.

If we keep in mind, then, that social functions among humans include the most basic, survival-oriented functions, we can perhaps better appreciate the depth of human deficiencies sufficient to disrupt a keystone of these functions such as language. Viewing social function in this larger perspective, perhaps we can also comprehend better how crucial is a child's understanding of the nature and functions of a communication system. Also, in this larger perspective, we come to see components of content and structure more as the means to certain ends—not just as ends in and of themselves.

Once the concept of language as a means to a larger end is accepted, one must analyze the various elements involved in the larger ends sought in language as in the preceding discussion sections. In addition, we must analyze the basic state of the individual according to level of understanding or perception of these ends. At what level, for example, does a child currently manifest the need, understanding, or desire to attain broad social ends? Are these ends limited to primary life-sustaining needs like food and drink? Do such needs or desires as need for help, need for interaction, or need for pleasure manifest themselves in the child's language or nonlanguage behavioral repertoire? If such needs, desires, or understandings do not exist in a child, intervention aimed at developing the complex communication forms which serve as means to these ends cannot be very successful. Or, in more usual cases, language forms which aim at needs, desires, or understandings which are not those of children similarly cannot be attained either easily or efficaciously. There is an old educational maxim which applies here: Start where the child is. In too many language programs we seem, rather, to start where our theories of grammar are or where we think the child should be.

In preceding discussions in this chapter, in Chapter 3, and in Chapter 6 on assessment, we have emphasized the social function of language. All of these discussions recognize that such functions are related to perceived and desired needs which must be determined by the language user. Particularly in Chapter 6's discussions on assessment of these needs and desires within children we have indicated our belief that children must bring social needs into language-learning situations if such situations are to be successful. Certainly, most children will do so. There are children, however, who are seriously and basically deficient in this area of social awareness and functions. The autistic child, for example, shows this deficiency as part of the basic syndrome of the disorder. The severely and profoundly retarded child may also show serious deviances in this area, both because of his basic deficiencies in various cognitive areas and because the environments in which he may have resided were not those which provided any reinforcing responses to such needs or desires. Obviously, communicative needs which are not responded to are not maintained in a child's repertoire. Further, if the most basic needs are not responded to, there is little motivation or reason to attempt to attain social needs of a less basic nature. Thus, if children cannot attain consistent responses to such basic needs as requests for help with food or clothing, they would have little basis for developing requests for joint play or requests for information about something.

Such considerations of children's existing repertoires and perhaps their history of social reinforcement indicate that language programs should approach intervention at appropriate target levels in regard to language function. Thus, children who manifest absent or seriously deficient repertoires of verbal or nonverbal communicative acts will require intensive programs aimed not at language so much as at the development of social and nonverbal communicative interactions which precede formal language usage. As we have noted previously, Mahoney (1975) has emphasized that communication (and thus social interaction) begins long before language. Consequently, with the severely language-delayed child, attention to social interaction and communication should begin before specific language targets are sought.

Where preassessments indicate, then, language programs for seriously deficient children may have to seek nonlanguage levels of interaction and functional communication classes specifically. In the design of such procedures, the pragmatic classes of language will still serve to identify the types of interactions which are appropriate. Therefore, nonverbal interactions directed toward requests for action responses, protesting responses, calling responses, and so on will be necessary and productive. In addition, when such classes of nonlanguage interaction are identified or trained for children, they become the basis for the selection of certain language targets at content and structure levels.

Even though these considerations have been in the context of severely deficient children, the same considerations can be extended to less severely involved children, too. It would appear most productive to identify desirable communicative functions which are problematic for any level of child as a target for language instruction. In fact, such a perspective is obvious at even the more refined levels of our culture's language instruction—for example, "Say 'please,'" "Ask for the butter to be passed."

The preceding discussion stresses the nonlanguage aspects of communication behavior. The desire or need to communicate to other members of the social order is basic to human existence. If such a desire is missing or severely deficient, attention must be directed toward its development in people for whom language learning is expected or desired. For humans already possessing such a desire, there exist natural motivations for certain forms of language structure and content. To ignore these relative levels of motivation and need in language-intervention programs seems, at the least, ill-advised and extremely costly to the overall process of teaching and learning.

Summary:
Communicative Function

The implications of the function of communicative acts for clinical or intervention procedures are concentrated in each of the elements of such intervention programs for severely language-delayed young children:

1. The antecedent event element must offer *contexts* which evoke the need for communication between the subject and persons in his environment.
2. The response event element must offer language targets which represent the various communication *function classes* of human interaction.
3. The consequent event element must offer *reinforcement* which consists of in-kind, human responses to the function inherent in the communicative act being targeted.

Table 2 offers a graphic summary of language-intervention procedures and their various elements from the point of view of the function of language. These dimensions do not replace content and structure targets in language intervention, rather supplementing these other targets. The complementary relationships among the various elements of language-intervention programming will also be important as we continue our discussion of the content and structural targets which are generated by a transactional model of language. At this point, we offer only these implications related to pragmatic functions as they are manifested clinically.

TABLE 2

Clinical Representation of Language Functions
in Intervention Procedures

Antecedent events	Response events	Consequent events
Social context for intervention	Functional target classes for intervention	Reinforcement for functional targets
-Makes available a social milieu of people and joint activities	Targets: -Requesting of action -Calling -Protesting	-Provides in-kind human consequences to the specific class(es) of response event by child
-Makes available a social milieu of people and joint attention	-Greeting -Labeling -Requesting of answer -Answering, etc.	
-Evokes functional needs for communication on part of child		

Content of Communicative Acts: Semantics

Introduction

Previous chapters in this book have provided much discussion and analysis of recent perspectives regarding the cognitive bases for language. The implications of these perspectives are already beginning to revolutionize language-intervention strategies and procedures and promise to provide the basis for even more changes as they are further interpreted and experimentally applied. While this rich lode of empirical and theoretical information is nearly overwhelming in its volume of information and in the scope of its implications, there are two major dimensions of it which appear to require immediate experimental translation into treatment perspectives. The first of these compelling dimensions is that concerned with the construct of "reference" in communication between members of the human species. The second dimension is the cognitive-base construct which views language as "mapping onto" the existing knowledge holdings of a language learner. Both of these dimensions were discussed in some depth in Chapter 2 and, along with constructs related to the social bases of language, represent the source of major change in the strategies, targets, and procedures for language-intervention programs for young, severely language-delayed children. Each of these major sources of change will be discussed here in terms of their specific treatment implications.

The Function of
Semantic Content

Language-intervention programs have been greatly affected by the development of semantically based approaches (e.g., McDonald, 1976; Miller & Yoder, 1972, 1974). We have chosen here to discuss the referencing[1] and the mapping constructs because they are, in the most basic sense, the sources of the semantic content of language forms. In the same way that syntax is an after-the-fact description of the structure of language—but not an adequate explanation of it—semantic categories and relationships are after-the-fact descriptions of the content of language but not explanations of it. It is, for example, explicit in the work of Bloom (1970, 1973), Bowerman (1973a, 1974), and Slobin (1973) that they believed that the semantic elements of the children's language that they observed were as they were because they represented both the facilitating and constraining elements of children's "knowledge" about the elements of their environment.

In a different, but complementary way, Olson's (1970) summary of the construct of referencing in communicative utterances also becomes quite explicit in its indications that a language user's cognitive holdings are the best basis for explaining the content of language utterances. Thus, this construct also functions as a source of the semantic categories and relationships which have been identified in children's language. As such, the referencing function is, like the mapping function, dependent on the cognitive holdings of the speaker.

Thus, it would seem to us, any productive clinical applications of the plethora of semantic data which have been provided by the several excellent contributors in this area will depend on our ability to interpret these data in rich and insightful ways. It will not be enough, in our opinion, simply to teach semantics just as it has not been enough (again in our opinion) to teach syntax. For, if we do attempt just to teach semantics, we will again be running the risk of adopting teaching targets which might have little or no reality to our child subjects. Rather, our targets would be (as they were in syntactic approaches) adult perceptions of what child semantic structures should be. Bowerman (1974) has made this point specifically. She noted that currently identified semantic relationships like agent, action, location, and recurrence "may or may not actually correspond to constructs in the normal child's own rule system" (p. 204).

We do not suggest that semantic targets are not appropriate sources for language-programming targets. Rather, we hold that semantic data should be interpreted and applied with the awareness of their reasons for being in the language of children. If we can apply the constructs of reference and knowledge mapping as our best current indications of these reasons for being, then we are better equipped to interpret, select, and apply various of the semantic content categories in programs for young handicapped children.

Referencing construct reviewed. Referencing was discussed in Chapter 2 and refers to Olson's (1970) characterization of communication between two persons as an interaction in which a speaker attempts to provide a listener with information

---

[1]Again, the reader must be aware that our construct of *referencing* and *referencing strategies* was drawn from Olson (1970). In recent linguistic literature our referencing construct is subsumed in the more extensive and definitive constructs of *presupposition* and *topicalization* (Bates, 1976).

which is definitive enough to allow the listener to understand or share the speaker's *referent*. Thus, the content of language utterances in communicative acts is for the purpose of providing information about that which the speaker is talking. As we have seen in previous discussions (Chapter 2), speaker's referents include all kinds of entities and relationships among and between entities. Thus, speakers' (or communicators') utterances are attempts to provide information about all kinds of entities and relationships among and between entities so that their listeners will be able to identify these intended referents. So, Olson (1970) suggests that there are several variables involved in the determination of the content of a speaker's utterance. All of the variables are essentially "cognitive," according to Olson, and include (1) the speaker's own knowledge about the intended referent, (2) the speaker's assumptions about the listener's knowledge of the referent, and (3) the alternatives to the intended referent which the speaker must rule out by the information he provides to the listener.

Thus, we have the reference construct which states that the content of an utterance is determined by at least three variables, each of which is designed to specify what information must be included in an utterance if it is to be successful as a communication to a listener.

Treatment implications of the reference construct. There are three primary treatment implications of this construct. The first is simply that, at one level at least, people talk about things that are real to them—they don't just utter grammatical structures. Secondly, in order to talk about things that are real to them, people necessarily must have knowledge about the things about which they talk. Thirdly, people may talk about things in widely varying ways, both because of their varying knowledge about them and because of their assumptions about what their listener knows about their topic.

The summary effect of these three implications seem to us enormous in their impact on the selection of *content* targets for children's language. The effect of these three perspectives forces the language worker to supplement previous perspectives of language targets which, as we have noted previously, have been recently determined either in terms of syntactic structures or in terms of adult-determined "functionally" productive utterance forms. This is not to say that targets should not have *structure* or that they should not have *function*. On the contrary, these perspectives simply state that such structure and functions as are targeted should be developed in complementary relationships with the content of the targeted utterances. If, in turn, the content of targeted utterances is selected with full consideration of the several referencing-oriented bases for it, we should finally be targeting language responses among severely handicapped young children which are real to them, useful to them, and highly possible for them to attain efficaciously and productively.

Muma's (1975) insightful observations suggest that children do not apply referencing strategies at highly effective levels in their early communicative acts. Quite the contrary, it is well reported that children's attempts at referencing in early years most often send an adult madly searching the immediate context of the child's utterance to discover the referent of the communicative act. Even though we must recognize, then, that the young children's referencing strategies are primitive, we still should realize that referencing is, necessarily, the basis unit of the communication process. Thus, a child's representation of it must concern us clinically.

The same observations which identify the problems inherent in children's deficiencies in referencing strategies are also the source of suggestions for the adaptation of the overall referencing construct which might be made in order to accommodate children's deficiencies in this area. Muma (1975) points out that children's referencing strategies tend to be egocentric. This would mean, essentially, that the utterances of young children probably show major deficiencies in manifesting their considerations of listener knowledge about intended referents. Instead, children's attempts to communicate would most probably concentrate on their own knowledge or perceptions about the referent they intend.

If we translate the foregoing into slightly more specific intervention targets, we would then state the referencing constructs as suggesting that we:

1. Teach children to talk *about* entities, events, and relationships between and among such entities and events.
2. Teach children to talk about such topics in terms of *their knowledge* about them.
3. Teach children to talk about such topics in as many *different ways* as their knowledge allows.
4. In sum, teach children *to provide information about referents in their world* about which they will be communicating to others.

Interface of reference construct with semantics. Obviously, the goals listed above lack the specificity and the total definitiveness required for the design of language-intervention programs. What these general targets do provide, however, are perspectives which allow us to be more specific and definitive in our interpretation of the available semantic data in intervention programming. One might consider that the semantic data that have been gathered are the empirically identified manifestations of children's representations of the referencing targets identified above. In other words, the data of the developmental semanticists actually document the entities and the relationships which are manifested in children's language. If, further, we can adopt Muma's (1975) observations regarding the egocentric nature of children's referencing strategies, we can further assume, then, that current semantic data reflect primarily the knowledge that children have about their communication topics. The semantic data would appear, therefore, to indicate to us the most important and salient aspects of the entities and the relationships which children perceive in their environment. In sum, the current developmental semantic data reflect both the referents which are prevalent in the language of normally developing children and, further, the information children have about these referents. Since current semantic data quantify the content of child utterances, they are our best source of information about *what* is "real" to children and, additionally, *why* and *how* such things are real.

Language as Mapping Knowledge

One can see that the preceding analysis of referencing has brought us to a point which coincides with the construct that language maps onto the child's existing knowledge. This has been stated in various ways by all of the researchers and theorists who have emerged in the so-called semantic school, such as Bloom (1970), Bowerman (1973b), and Slobin (1973). That these perspectives on the knowledge base of language coincide, even though they come from slightly different perspectives, is confirming rather than negative. If we realize that the available semantic data have been gathered within the contexts of children's communicative acts with adults, we can quite readily accept these data as representative of children's referencing strategies and styles.

What the mapping construct adds to the referencing construct is the awareness that the most basic source for the particular semantic categories and relationships that are used for referencing information lies in the nature of human intelligence itself. Thus, we have those professionals who are identifying the semantic categories and relationships which exist in child language stating their hypotheses that semantic categories are, broadly, isomorphic with the overall and specific categories in which human intelligence is organized. Nelson (1974) is particularly representative of this assumption and Slobin (1973), Bruner (1975), and Schlesinger (1971, 1974) reflect positions near that of Nelson. Bloom's (1970) views would also appear very close to these in that she finds Piagetian sensorimotor schemas highly related to the categories and relationships reflected in her data. Although Bowerman (1974) has understandable questions about how well current semantic quantification units match the cognitive reality of children, she generally would also seem to be near the basic cognitivist position.

Treatment implications of the "mapping" construct. What these cognitive-semantic views suggest for treatment applications is both profound and simple. First, as we have noted previously, these views hold that the basis for language units is quite real to children. In other words, children "know" about that which they talk and they talk about that which they "know." What is profound about that observation is that it goes counter to our often demonstrated adult assumption that language learning teaches children about things. Certainly, in older, language-using children and adults this latter assumption is true. It is, however, seemingly not an assumption which can be used to undergird early language-intervention programs. Quite the contrary, the mapping construct, in concert with the referencing construct, would direct us to teach at least severely language-delayed children to talk about things, relationships, and events about which they already demonstrate some awareness and knowledge. This is obviously a direct application of the mapping construct, and while it might be *implicit* in many current language programs, it has been made *explicit* in only a few programs—most notably Premack's (1971) programming with a chimpanzee, Bereiter and Engelmann's (1966) program for disadvantaged children, and Bricker and Bricker's (1974) work with retarded children.

While such a demand might seem to be constraining to language-intervention designs, it appears to us to be a particularly facilitating one for many reasons. Because of the need to assure a child's knowledge for a particular language target, language teachers must become more sensitive to children's cognitive styles and content and, thus, their psychological reality. This reality factor seems, to us at least, one of the major problems facing language teachers for young, severely language-delayed children. What words? What structures? What contexts for language teaching? All of these questions begin to find at least some tentative answers as those teachers begin to observe the behavioral manifestations of children's cognitive holdings. Do children use a hammer, a toy car, or a baby blanket appropriately? Then, target "hammer hit," "car go," and "cover baby." Does a child search for a ball that has rolled under a shelf unit? Then, target "ball allgone," "no ball," "more ball," "get ball," and so on. Do children exhibit the pragmatic construct of requesting help by walking to the teacher for help with a particularly bulky coat? Then, target "help me (please)."

Obviously, however, language programs cannot become systematic and comprehensive by simply following children around, seizing on demonstrated knowledge for "mapping." Programs can, however, develop observation/assessment systems and categorize the child's knowledge that is shown to be available and set up group teaching contexts in which this demonstrated knowledge has a high probability of appropriateness. Further, using these contexts, teachers and clinicians can target certain "maps" with systematic procedures.

Certainly, many current language programs already do this. Just as certainly, however, there are many which bring into their intervention programs targets which are based on a language lexicon or structures which have no demonstrated reality for the children in the program.

Mapping construct and semantic data. If the mapping relationship between children's utterances and children's cognitive holdings is a valid one, current semantic data should reflect at least some of the cognitive holdings of normally developing children. While such data might not serve for direct projection to children with severe handicaps, they are at least "child-sized" perspectives which seem logically closer to potential reality for handicapped children than are adult perspectives.

If then, we can view the semantic data available to us from the broad perspective that it represents children's knowledge about the world, we should have at least a reasonable basis for attempting to structure the targets, contexts, and procedures for language-intervention attempts aimed at the most basic levels. Such basic levels of targeting should suggest appropriate targets even for children who show severe developmental deficiencies. The type and levels of analysis of semantic data needed to attain these perspectives, however, appear to be beyond those currently applied in intervention programs for severely delayed children.

Analyzing Semantic Data for Structuring Intervention Targets

The foregoing discussions on the referencing and mapping constructs have their strongest impact on intervention design in their insistence that language content has a quite direct relationship to a child's psychological world. In other words, children's language utterances appear to be based on their perspectives of the elements of their environment and the knowledge they, as children, have about these elements. Thus, rather than a very young child's knowledge being organized by language, the reverse is true: a child's early language is organized by his knowledge. The ultimate deduction from such a perspective is represented by both Bruner's (1974/75) and Nelson's (1974) suggestions that a child's language makes explicit inner cognitive strategies and their resulting schema.

If this latter perspective is true—and it would appear to be most difficult to refute it at this point in our knowledge—it would appear quite fruitless to continue to impose purely linguistic targets on young developmentally delayed children. Since semantics is essentially still a linguistic construct, such prohibition would extend even to these structures. If, however, we were to consider semantic categories as indicators of the nature of children's knowledge and psychological perspectives, we can see that current semantic perspectives provide most useful guides to broader language targets. These latter perspectives lead us to view semantic categories not as linguistic targets, but rather as indicators of the potential referents and the information about these referents that children, even young handicapped ones, might know about and therefore be able to talk about. Viewing them in this way suggests some rather subtle modifications in our perspectives about semantics. These modifications can be represented by the comparisons inherent in a semantic linguistic target like agent-object and a semantic psychological target like talking about the actions that various entities afford. Both targets are essentially the same to an adult who has already learned and forgotten the relationship between the psychological event and the semantic linguistic representation of it. We would submit, however, that the distinction between these targets has important and, in our opinion, productive clinical implications for language intervention with young handicapped children.

The implications of these perspectives for the utilization of currently available semantic targets are straightforward. In essence, they suggest that the various demonstrated semantic categories and relationships of children's language should not be targeted as linguistic structures which "label" or "represent" demonstrated physical entities or events. On the contrary, the current semantic data should be more broadly interpreted to suggest to clinicians the types of physical entities, relationships, and events which children have knowledge about and therefore should be able to talk about. That this latter perspective yields response forms as targets which are highly similar to those yielded by the former view might confuse the issue somewhat, but the differences in the underlying basis of the two perspectives should be clear to clinicians and teachers. Most basically, the *cognitive/semantic* view is specifically child-centered while the *linguistic/semantic* view represents child-data which seem to have been distilled through the perspective of mature language users who use language in many ways which are beyond the ability of young children and who have, therefore, gone far beyond those perspectives and realities under which children operate.

With this prologue, we are now ready to suggest how current semantic data might be operationalized in language-intervention programs for young severely language-handicapped children.

Language targets suggested by semantic constructs and data. Obviously, no amount of analysis or philosophizing about the real nature of semantic data can alter those data. Such activity can, however, alter our perspectives about what such data mean and therefore how they can be parsed and ordered for utilization in applied intervention tasks. Semantic relationship data currently available were discussed in Chapter 2. For convenience in reading this section, however, we will present again a table from Chapter 2 (Table 3 in this chapter). This table summarizes semantic data as quantified by Bloom (1970). It shows the semantic relationships identifiable in the language of Bloom's three subjects and is well corroborated both by subsequent studies (such as Bowerman, 1973a) and previous studies which have been reanalyzed for semantic content (such as Brown, 1973).

TABLE 3

Bloom's Meaning Categories
from Children's Utterances

Meaning	Grammatical structures	Examples
Nomination	that +Noun (N)	that book
	it +N	it car
Notice	hi +N	hi belt
Recurrence	more +N	more milk
	Verb (V) +'gin	fall 'gin
Nonexistence	no+N	no doggie
	all gone +N	all gone milk
Attributive	Adjective +N	big train
Possessive	N +N	mommy lipstick
Locative	N +N	sweater chair
Locative	V +N	sit chair
Agent-action	N +V	Eve read
Agent-object	N +N	mommy sock
Action-object	V +N	read book
Conjunction	N +N	umbrella boot

NOTE. Adapted from *Language Development: Structure and Function* by P. S. Dale. Copyright 1972 by Dryden Press. Reprinted by permission.

In addition to reviewing those semantic categories identified by Bloom (1970) in her observations and interpretations, we would also like to look again at the so-called "case-grammar" relationships which Fillmore (1968) identified (Table 4 in this chapter). The reader will remember from Chapter 2 that Fillmore's "cases" represented his effort to show that language structure reflected certain semantic intents, and thus grammatical structure might as well be described by indicating the semantic role which was played by the noun phrase in any sentence. In other words, Fillmore's "cases" were used to analyze language utterances from the point of view of what they were intended to talk about. Even further, his work suggested that the ordering rules of language structure might be controlled by these semantic relationships rather than by a set of rules specific only to syntactic forms of a language.

After reviewing these categories briefly (remembering that "case-grammar" refers to grammar structures generated on the basis of *semantic* relationships), reading the following excerpts from Bruner (1975) about the appropriate analysis of existing semantic data should clarify the relationships in this discussion. Bruner states:

"The PRIMITIVE categories of grammar refer rather to ACTIONS as carried out by AGENTS and having EFFECTS of particular KINDS in particular PLACES, etc. And these categories, as we shall see, are of particular importance in the early acquisition of

TABLE 4

Fillmore's Case Grammar Relationships

Case name	Definition	Example (italicized noun as in designated case)
Agentive (A)	The typically animate, perceived instigator of action	*John* opened the door. The door was opened by *John*.
Instrumental (I)	The inanimate force or object causally involved in the state or action named by the verb	The *key* opened the door. John opened the door with the *key*.
Dative (D)	The animate being affected by the state or action named by the verb	*Adam* sees Eve. John murdered *Bill*. John gave the book to *Bill*. *Daddy* has a study.
Factitive (F)	The object or being resulting from the state or action named by the verb	God created *woman*. John built a *table*.
Locative (L)	The location or spatial orientation of the state or action named by the verb	The sweater is on the *chair*. *Chicago* is windy.
Objective (O)	The semantically most neutral case: anything representable by a noun whose role in the state or action named by the verb depends on the meaning of the verb itself	Adam sees *Eve*. The *sweater* is on the chair. John opened the *door*.

NOTE. Adapted from *A First Language: The Early Stages* by R. Brown. Copyright 1973 by Harvard University Press.

language. It is quite beside the point here that linguists have raised serious doubts about Fillmore's (1968) effort to give such case grammar the status of a generative base structure for adult speech. From the psychologist's point of view, the seeming isomorphism of action categories and case-grammatical ones requires close scrutiny for what it suggests about how language is first used, and therefore how it is acquired.

We shall try to illustrate later some examples of how this correspondence between case-grammar and the structure of joint action carried out by the infant and caretaker aids the former in acquiring a starting grammar. For the infant first learns prelinguistically to make the conceptual distinctions embodied in case grammar and, having mastered privileges of occurrence in action sequences in which these distinctions are present, begins to insert nonstandard signals that mark the distinctions. Initially, of course, the context is sufficient for the mother to interpret the child's intentions—to supply the grammar, so to speak. In time, and by substitution, the signaling becomes more conventional and can be comprehended with less contextual support. It is, as we shall see, much closer to the picture set forth long ago by DeLaguna (1927) than to the structural descriptions of how syntactic knowledge differentiates out of innate knowledge of linguistic universals. What is universal is the structure of human action in human infancy which corresponds to the structure of universal case categories. It is the infant's success in achieving joint action (or the mother's success, for that matter) that virtually leads him into language. In this sense, mastery of the "utterer's meaning"—effectiveness or felicity in achieving ends—provides the child with the conceptual structure that is also embodied in the language he is to learn. (pp. 5–6)

This extensive quotation suggests the base for the consideration of both the pragmatic and the cognitive bases of language. Since here we are concerned primarily with the conceptual bases, we shall refrain from comment on the functional aspects. (That topic was discussed in both Chapter 3 and the initial sections of this chapter as well as being well represented in Chapter 6 on assessment.) In this quotation, it seems quite clear that Bruner equates demonstrated semantic structure of relationships (case grammar) with existing conceptual action schemas which are "universal" with human infants. Thus, he considers that, since beginning language learners tend to view the world in terms of its action sequences, any semantic system of language must necessarily accommodate such knowledge by providing the means to encode it.

If, in addition to Fillmore's "cases" and Bruner's "action sequence" concepts as contributors to the specification of semantic forms and classes, we also consider Nelson's (1974) empirically generated view that an early language learner's cognitive knowledge about entities and relationships in his world is also shaped, as Piagetian views had suggested, through his sensory and motor experiences with these entities and relationships, we can begin to identify other types of semantic categories: those required to encode knowledge of sensory and sensorimotor properties of entities or referents.

If, even further, we realize that the semantic content of a child's language also represents his communicative strategies—that is, his *selections* of semantic categories for use in referencing the topic of a particular utterance—we can see that explaining semantic content is not a simple, one-dimensional task. In fact, children's semantic systems accommodate knowledge of many different types and sources. They also allow that knowledge to be used in many different referencing strategies.

Table 5 demonstrates the various factors which might determine a specific child's referencing-utterance. It shows possible sources of knowledge which might be available to a child, the resulting referencing strategy, and the form of this strategy's realization in an utterance. Table 5 also shows the semantic relationship which might be assigned to such an utterance according to categories in available taxonomies.

Table 5 indicates the problems inherent in viewing children's utterances in terms of a single-dimensional semantic construct in isolation from attempts to understand the nature of the information chosen for use in the referencing task. Just as Bloom's "mommy sock" demonstrated that syntactic structural analysis can be misapplied, so can an utterance like "car go" demonstrate that semantic relationships can be misapplied if the referencing mechanism and its underlying informational base is not fully included in the analysis. The utterance "car go" would be most routinely described as a semantic (case) relationship of "instrument + action." However, it might actually be "entity + attribute" to its utterer. Even though the same basic knowledge underlies both relationships, the semantic intent and form of the identical utterance structures are quite different. It is possible even to consider that a young child wishing to reference the *nonexistence* of a car he was playing with might also

TABLE 5

Comparisons of Possible Knowledge, Referencing Reality, and
Adult-Perceived Semantics of Sample Child Utterances

Possible sources of knowledge and resulting schemata of referent knowledge	Speaker's possible referencing strategies (child's semantic content)	Exemplary utterances	Adult-perceived semantic category
A. Referenceable properties experienced through direct manipulation of an entity			
—Tactual properties	Mark tactual properties	soft (bunny)	Attribute
—Actions afforded by entity	Mark afforded action(s)	(make) go car	Action-instrument
—Constraints to manipulation (too big to manipulate)	Mark size factors	big (ball)	Attribute (perceptual)
B. Referenceable properties experienced through nonmanipulatory sensory perceptions with entity			
—Auditory experience	Mark action properties	tic-toc (clock)	Action-instrument
—Auditory experience	Mark action properties	bow-wow	Action-instrument
—Visual experience	Mark action properties	car go	Instrument-action
—Visual experience	Mark size properties	big (ball)	Attribute
—Visual experience	Mark color properties	red (ball)	Attribute
—Visual experience	Mark action properties	roll (ball)	Action
C. Relational properties experienced sensorily or socially			
—Social experience (e.g., hears "no, that's mommy's lipstick")	Mark taboo attribute	mommy lipstick	Possession
—Sensory/manipulable experience	Mark association attribute	bunny hat	Possession
—Sensory/manipulable experience with assembly task	Mark part/whole relationship as attribute	car wheel	Possession
D. Relational properties experienced or perceived in action sequence			
—Receiver of agent effect	Mark receiver	car	Nomination
—Instigator of effect	Mark source of effect	mommy car	Agent
—Effect	Mark effect	go	Action
—All components of action sequence	Mark effect's source and receiver and effect	mommy car go	Agent-object-action

choose to express this as "car go" (in such case, we must confess, we do not know exactly what semantic relationship might be applied to describe such a semantic intent; our best guess would be the standard "X + nonexistence").

Thus, semantic relationships are, like any single analysis unit applied to language, highly relative when applied in isolation from other possible analytical units. Consequently, we cannot just outline Bloom's categories or Fillmore's (1968) cases and suggest these as specific targets for children's utterances. Rather, we would suggest that Bloom's categories and relationships, Fillmore's cases, Bruner's action states, Nelson's dynamic attributes, and Olson's referencing information constructs and data *all* be used to conceptualize and structure the targets in children's language which are related to its content. In other words, it is our view that interveners in child language must take *all* of our information and attempt to teach children contentive forms and substance which reflect realizations of the following nature:

1. The contentive forms and substance targeted should enable children to provide information about various referents.
2. These referents might include entities, events, and/or states which might be talked about in many different ways.
3. The various ways in which various referents might be talked about would require the ability to provide information about any potential attribute of that referent which is known by the language user.
4. Such attributes as are indicated to be useful in providing information about a referent might include any part or whole of its: (a) static perceptual features, (b) dynamic perceptual features, (c) functional-use features, (d) affordance features, (e) action-sequence features, (f) relational features, or (g) status as an occupant of the environment's space and time.

If we would apply such realizations, our semantic targets for child language might appear more in the nature of those categories shown in Table 6.

From these proposed categories which might be targeted, there are many commonalities among the entities represented in the examples. Most of the examples may be referenced in many ways—it is simply a matter of perspective or choices of referencing strategies. It is this fact that causes us to think more about teaching children *ways to talk about things* or ways to *mean* than to think about teaching the possible structures of utterances apart from meaning. Bloom, Lightbown, and Hood (1975) state that semantics and structure are, in actuality, inseparable. We would agree: there must be structure, and within this structure, there are requirements in order to allow intended meaning to be clear. Obviously, however, it is our view that structure does not have much reality when it is separated from meaning.

From all of this, then, come our suggested strategies for applying the various "meaning" perspectives outlined in Table 5:

1. *Target several attributes of the same referent in sequence*—e.g., talk about baby doll in many ways: "baby cry," "kiss baby," "rock baby," "hug baby," "baby sleep," "see baby's eyes."
2. *Target action attributes and action schemas early and consistently*—e.g., "car go—rrrrr," "push car," "Bill push car," "make car go," "push car," "oh car goes—rrrrr," "car goes fast."
3. *Always evaluate/select attributes to mark from child's perspective and possible knowledge.*

TABLE 6
Proposed Categorizations of Various Meaning Categories
Which Might be Targeted in Early Language

I. Attributes of referent's perceptual properties
   A. Dynamic attributes
      1. Action *provided* by referent (ball bounce, light on, [carousel] go-round, etc.)
      2. Action *afforded* by referent (shakey [rattle], push [button], wind [clock], etc.)
      3. Auditory attribute provided by referent (tick-tock [clock], bow-wow [doggie], moo [cow], etc.)
   B. Static attributes
      1. Tactual attributes (soft, cold/hot, sticky, etc.)
      2. Size attributes (big, little)
      3. Form properties (long, pointed)
      4. Color properties (primary colors only)
II. Attributes by way of referent's relational properties
   A. Dynamic attributes
      1. Functional uses (hammer hit, drink cup, candy eat, etc.)
   B. Static (or less dynamic) properties
      1. Possession (my kitty, mommy lipstick, bunny hat, policeman hat, etc.)
      2. Part/whole (baby eyes, car wheel, house chimney, etc.)
      3. Entity location (ball there, ball in, baby bed, etc.)
      4. Action location (sleep bed, bye-bye car, play room, etc.)
III. Attributes of referents as elements in dynamic event
   A. Object or receiver of action (hit ball, kiss baby, eat candy)
   B. Agent or instrument of action (mommy kiss, stick hit)
   C. Agent/instrument and object/receiver of action (mommy [read] book, knife [cut] finger, etc.)
   D. Agent/instrument, action/state, object/receiver (mommy push car, knife cut meat, baby smiling me, etc.)
IV. Attributes of referents as occupants of time and space
   A. Existence (here ball; there baby; choo-choo train [pointing])
   B. Nonexistence (ball allgone, no choo-choo)
   C. Recurrence (more ball, ball agin)

NOTE. No order is implied in this organization of categories.

Structure of Communicative Acts: Syntax

We agree with Bloom, Lightbown, and Hood (1975) that semantics and syntax are inseparable. They are nested in one another. This view necessarily implies that we cannot accept syntactic structure as a totally independent dimension of language which is generated in isolation or independence from the speaker's intention to mean something. Rather, we view the syntax of a language as inexplicably intertwined with semantic intent and referencing strategies on the part of the speaker. Thus, syntax is not targeted separately and in isolation. Rather, it is imbedded within the targeting of semantic and referencing intents and strategies. In clinical programs, we are beginning to develop from the "transactional" language model: syntactic targets are indeed being sought, but they are being sought within the context and content of referencing or talking about things (events, relationships, and so on) in various ways and from varying viewpoints. Such meaning targets will eventually generate all forms of syntactic structure. Indeed, we believe that syntactic structures acquired within the various semantic and referencing targets will come to have rules that are real and functional for their users.

Thus, our only real disagreement with the structuralists lies in our inability to accept their premise that syntactic rules have any internal reality among young children separate from their meaning and their reflection of referencing strategies and styles. Obviously, if we do not accept the reality suggested by structuralists like Chomsky (1957) and McNeill (1970), we must have an alternative source of reality by which to explain a child's ability to acquire and generalize structural topographies to "novel" utterances. From all of the theories and hypotheses that we have reviewed, we think that there are two possible and related sources of such reality for utterance structure. Both of these sources necessarily lie within the cognitive bases of language, and we have discussed them both at some length in several places in this book. To be specific, it would appear to us that *reality* for the *structure* of any utterance must lie in both its *semantic content* and the *referencing strategy* selected by the language user.

Within this reality, we would suggest that a speaker would select the desired or possible referent(s), select from personal knowledge about such referent(s), and then select the structures necessary to communicate the information called for by all of these selections. In greatly simplified terms, a child would select what he wanted to talk about, see how his available knowledge could be applied to this topic, and construct the utterance in the form dictated by these previous selections.

The operational hypothesis reflected in this view suggests that an utterance has two levels of structure. The first would be dictated roughly by the referent of the utterance. The second level would be dictated by the specific content of the information about that reference that was utilized. In our current view, the first level would simply be an overall communication strategy and the second an execution of that strategy. Obviously, this two-level hypothesis requires additional discussion. The next section centers on this topic and its clinical implications.

Communication Strategy

For us, Olson's (1970) hypothesis that a speaker provides information about a selected communication referent is the basis for one level of communication strategy. This hypothesis insists that there is a psychological base for an utterance in which a speaker chooses to talk about something. This topic is the referent of a speaker's utterance. Within a speaker's choice of what referents to talk about, there are also decisions regarding how to talk about the chosen topic. As Olson (1970) has shown rather powerfully (see Chapter 2), how to talk about something requires consideration of several areas including (1) what is known about the referent by the speaker and (2) what is known about the referent by the listener. In other words, a speaker must consider what information about a referent will allow it to be communicated. Then, he must set about to provide that information.

The possible strategies for communicating a referent are, of course, somewhat constrained; but, even with these constraints, possible strategies are considerable in number. Given Muma's (1975) observations noted in the section on semantics in this chapter, we can conclude that children will not have as many choices as would an adult. But, even with children's limitations in knowledge and their egocentric view of their referent(s), they still might have several ways to attack the communication problem. They could, as we have seen demonstrated in the discussion on semantics just completed, choose to provide information about some attribute of their referent. Perhaps instead of this, however, a child might choose to talk about a referent in terms of its relationship to some other entity or person. In some cases, a child's referent might be an entire event and he might have to discuss this event in terms of all of its elements. It can happen that a child might actually wish to reference only one of those elements in an event. In doing so, however, he must include all other elements in order to talk about the one he is most interested in. Thus, there are things that a child might wish to reference, and there are many possible ways to communicate these referents. It is the particular way that a speaker chooses to attempt communication that we consider an overall communication strategy.

The research literature on children's language is filled with examples of possible referencing strategies. A small sampling of them was offered in Table 5 of this chapter. Let us here construct a few specific examples. Table 7 shows some possible referents and the possible strategies which a child might use to communicate these.

Table 7 is, of course, a contrived set of referents, strategies, and utterances. They seem, however, quite reasonable in view of the types of utterances which have been shown in the language samples of children. In addition, if these examples do bear the relationship to children's communicative attempts that we think they do, they show the overall communication strategy level at which structure is to some degree determined. We think Olson's (1970) hypothesis would support this example, and further, we think other work by Bruner (1975) also offers support to the potential of this level of structural determination as a reasonable hypothesis.

The work of Bruner to which we alluded above reports his observation that children's utterances seem to reflect a basic structuring of "topic-comment" structure (Bruner, 1975). This topic-comment structure is a psychological structure and it is the structure reflected in the utterances constructed for Table 7. The psychological structure's realization, however, can be described at other levels. It can be described grammatically as "subject-predicate." In fact, it would seem that the topic-comment structure is not totally antithetical to Chomsky's (1957) most basic perspectives. Interestingly, according to Bruner (1975, p. 4), Chomsky (1965) considered topic-comment to be a surface structure which corresponds roughly to a deep structure of subject-predicate. In essence, Chomsky casts the most basic psychological representation of this relationship in subject-predicate terms (which is consonant with his hypothesis that grammar is the most basic cognitive representation of language), while Bruner casts the most basic psychological representation of the same relationship in terms of topic-comment (which is consonant with his hypothesis that grammar realizations are a product of certain cognitive bases).

Consonant with our view that applied language-intervention programs would benefit from targets which have high potential psychological reality for children, we would suggest that the topic-comment construct for overall utterance structure might

TABLE 7

Possible Referencing Strategies by Which a Child Might Structure an Utterance

Nature and context of specific referent	Context of communication attempt	Communication strategy chosen	Example of resulting utterance form
Toy cow—desired for play	Roomful of toys with mother present and attending	Mark attribute of desired object	"Moo" plus reaching response
Finger, hurting and needing attention	Dog has bitten finger—mother present	Mark specific referent and source of state of hurt	Ouch finger, Buffy!
Favorite ball—desired	Ball has been thrown away by brother	Mark desired object and source of problem	My ball, Billy throw
Interesting event on television	Tell mother about Superman event	Mark elements of event	Man fly in sky
Car-trip with father—desired	Tell father about desired event	Mark event, mark desired outcome	Daddy go bye-bye, me go too
Favorite ball—lost under bed	Mother in other room	Mark event—mark needs—mark location	Ball allgone, Mommy come, allgone, bed
Picture in book	Mother, sharing book, asks, "What's kitty doing?"	Mark elements of shared referent, start with topic	Kitty, sleeping in her bed

be a most productive perspective from which to target structural forms for treatment programs. Such an overall structural form does not generate utterances which preclude the use of grammar structures as they have been described. Rather, this perspective simply sets a psychological base from which the various grammatical structures might be realized.

We would emphasize here, also, that we are concentrating on *early* child structures and not mature forms of utterances. There are points in linguistic and psychological development when many of the utterances shown in Table 7 would be undesirable. In later stages of development, when knowledge, communication conventions, and full language systems are available to speakers, more grammar-based targeting might be desirable. It might be interesting, however, to observe how often even normal adult conversations are marked by topic-comment structuring rather than by a strong control to utter complete and comprehensive grammatical forms—for example, "Hurt something? Yeah, my finger. Damn dog bit it!"

In summary, our perspectives for selecting structural targets for early language forms are based in part on the psychological process level at which a speaker selects a communication strategy for structuring the specific content of an information-bearing utterance.

Execution of
Communication Strategy

We have presented a rationale for suggesting that one level of language structure targeted in language-intervention programs should reflect the awareness that utterances result from some selection of an overall communicative strategy. Now, we will provide a brief rationale which considers the other major contributor to a final utterance form—namely, execution of the details of the communication strategy chosen. At this specific level, the commonage and inseparability of syntactical structure and semantic structure seem to be demonstrated to their highest degree. In other words, it appears clear to us that the various semantic relationships and many of the various syntactic structures are only different perspectives on the same basic event. The cognitive-semantic bases for explaining the content and structure of children's utterances do have the greater level of empirical and logical support at this point in time. Even further, it would also appear that these bases offer the most potential for generating a psychologically real context and structure for intervention experimentation with handicapped subjects. While this latter statement does not necessarily follow from the first one, the test of intervention potential and reality seems no small matter in this area. We seem to have spent an inordinate amount of time, effort, and money on the application of constructs whose reality lay primarily in the minds of a few linguistic theorists. It seems eminently justifiable to proceed now with the perspectives of persons who are most basically concerned with understanding people and all of their behavior, not just understanding language.

For these reasons, the structural targets which we will be suggesting on the more detailed level are based on semantic relationship rules as opposed to grammatical relationship rules. In this view, we would even suggest that we may even be reaching for the reality of the very "deep structures" which Chomsky posits, but in a form different from that which he visualized.

If we sum all of the various positions used to support the hypothesis of semantic bases for utterance structural rules, we have a compendium of notions which appear extremely compatible and integratable. What we will be structuring in the next few paragraphs are structural targets suggested by the summed cognitive-semantic views.

We indicated at the beginning of this section that it is in the execution of a selected communication strategy that the final level of structure is determined. At this execution level, the specific knowledge of the topic and the comment on that topic is encoded. It is right here, then, that we must face up to the reality of communication and, thus, language structure. For example, there is no assurance that the topic of a child's utterance is (or can be mapped by) a *noun* or even a *noun phrase*. A child's topic may be a desired action which itself cannot even be "mapped" by a verb—for instance, "up" might be the topic of a child who wants to be picked up and given a "horsie-ride" on Daddy's foot. In other such examples, "moo-moo" might be the topic of the child who is attempting to "establish a joint reference" of a visible cow with Mother; "draw" might be the topic for a child who desires to get Mother to give him a crayon; and "allgone" might be the most salient aspect of a topic of a desire for more milk in his cup. All of the semantic data show such "holophrastic" structures (Bloom, 1970; Bowerman, 1973; and others). Somehow, though, when language interventionists start programs, they most often begin by teaching referencing nouns. This basic point regarding the mapping of a topic referent leads to the first general structure selection for young developmentally delayed children:

1. *Target single-word utterances to "map" topic attributes of all types and forms.* Bruner's (1974/75, 1975) ideas relating to both the contexts and functions of early utterances stressed the child's knowledge of the action sequence and his desire to establish joint-action schemas with the primary caretaker through the use of early language utterances. This view of Bruner's combines well with Nelson's (1974) observations about a child's early semantic bases being strongly reflective of action and dynamic attributes of his topics. These observations, then, give rise to the second and third propositions regarding structural targets in early language programs for handicapped children. At this point, word order becomes the primary source of structural topography.
2. *Target two-word utterances which map the elements of an action sequence,* such as agent-action, action-object, and agent-object.
3. *Target the sequencing of two, two-word utterances which map an action sequence,* such as agent-action plus action-object ("Daddy go-bye-bye, go-bye-bye car").

These same basic constructs about action posited by Bruner and Nelson give rise to the next rules. In addition, however, these following rules also add other relationship attributes to the referent-mapping structure. At this point, such utterances begin to reflect and move closer to the full representation of a topic-comment intent and thus a subject-predicate structure.

4. *Target two-word utterances which mark various attributes and relationships among and between referents*—for example, perceptual attributes ("red

ball," "big ball"); functional relationships ("knife cut," "drink cup," etc.); possession ("mommy lipstick"); part-whole ("baby's nose," "mommy's nose"); nonexistence ("no ball," "juice allgone"); recurrence ("more juice," "ball back again"); location ("in cup," "under bed").

From this point, the combining of several acquired two-word phrases will lead to both expanded topic-comment forms consisting of two words each and will also begin to provide more standard three-element utterances of agent-action-object form as well as others, such as "clock tic-toc," "go tic-toc," "clock go tic-toc." These latter suggested guidelines have been derived from observations of both Bloom (1970) and Slobin (1971, 1973).

5. *Target three-word and/or multiword utterances containing action elements, attributes, and relationships attained at two-word levels.*

At this point, the word-order rudiments and the *systems morphemes* or *function words*[2] needed to allow action on an entire utterance proposition (such as interrogative or negation) must be specifically targeted. Although much of this can be done in two-word utterance forms, often such functions require propositions of greater length before their appropriate structural realization rules can be appropriately acquired. Thus, structural target six can be specified.

6. *Target word order and function words used to operate on an overall proposition,* for instance, interrogative forms (wh- words, front-shift-of-verb, tags), negation of all forms (rejection and denial are added to nonexistence).

At about this point, also, another type of structural target must be assured. This one is not strictly at the syntactic level, although it is important to syntax in the sense that these structures also indicate relationships and attributes. We are talking about so-called "inflectional" or "bound" *systems morphemes* which mark plurality, possessives, comparatives, and various quantifiers. Thus the seventh general structural target-guide:

7. *Target multiword utterances of appropriate word order with inflectional morphemes carrying information relating to number, tense, possession, comparatives, quantifiers, and so on.*

Sequencing of structural targets. The structural guidelines presented above are for the purpose of enabling a child to execute whatever basic communication-strategy he chose. The structural targets indicated in these general propositions are required to allow a child (or any speaker for that matter) to accurately "map" whatever knowledge or perspectives he is bringing to the communicative act. Thus, we have specified the basic structures that allow certain semantic elements and relationships to be encoded in language form.

---

[2]For the reader who desires review on *systems morphemes* and related constructs (e.g., *function words, inflectional endings*), we might suggest that N. Stageberg (1971) provides an extremely comprehensive and lucid exposition of these constructs.

Since the knowledge, perspectives, and strategies of children will vary considerably, it is apparent that certain messages will have higher probabilities for occurring than will others. Thus, there are certain messages which may reach structural levels of considerable complexity before some other messages do. It is, then, inappropriate for the language interventionist to consider that the sequence of the stated structure-guidelines should be rigidly maintained for all utterances. Quite the contrary: some messages may be targeted at all seven levels before certain other messages are attained at the third or fourth level. Obviously, though, a child cannot progress to the fifth level on *any* message unit unless the previous four levels have been attained in *some* message contexts. In this sense, the sequence of targets is thought to be generally appropriate. The possible exception is proposition number six which, as is stated within the text, may be applied at any level, including the one-word level, for example, "no" (rejection); "what?" "huh?" This target must simply be generally assured and its structure formalized at level six.

Summary of Structure Targets

The transactional model of language acquisition suggests that the structures of a language form are related to and controlled by the psychological elements of a language utterance. Thus, we believe the structural targets for intervention with young severely handicapped children should be generated from semantic and communicative perspectives. By training word-order targets which are required by certain selected communication strategies and their detailed execution, the syntactic structures of a language are targeted in the context of their semantic or meaning-bearing function. By adding structural targets which are formed at the morphological levels and then inserted appropriately in word-order slots, additional syntactic forms are attained.

This view considers structure vital to language and communication. It reflects the need to model and condition appropriate syntactic forms. It also considers syntactic structure inseparable from semantics, however, in that *both* dimensions of language form function to increase the probability that a listener will respond to the message of a speaker.

Within Chomsky's transformational model, syntax has come to be viewed as extremely complex. Certainly it is when considered in only abstract forms and extracted from contrived models of possible adult utterances. If, however, it is considered at the level of a child and within forms which have psychological and thus meaning-carrying functions, syntax becomes simply some word-ordering rules which make the meaning and communicative function of the various morphemes uttered in one particular message less ambiguous.

If the language-intervention specialist targets the word-order slots which are necessary to mean certain things, syntax becomes "real." If, further, the interventionist targets the other structural units at the morphological level which pattern with word-order rules to "mean" (such as negative particles, wh- words, inflectional endings), the rules of language form can be sought both systematically and within contexts which enhance their acquisition and stable use. Such rules should be targeted with appropriate sensitivity to the *developmental constraints* which inhibit the full development of this rule system. By this we mean that *all* word-order rules cannot be expected from *all* children at any one time. Rather, there appears to be some necessary sequence of development within the system itself—for example, three-word agent-action-object structures seem to require previous experience at two-word representations of these relationships. This developmental factor is reflected in our previous sequencing of structure rules. As we state there, such sequencing is not to be considered rigidly, but we do hold that some *successive approximations* of the final forms of multiword structures are appropriate. In this sense, we break from the behaviorist's view that such structure does not necessarily require developmental considerations.

In sum, we have cast our structural targets from the context of the cognitive-semantic data. We have analyzed those data in order to identify what children's knowledge and communicative styles produce in the way of language content and structure. From these data, then, we have attempted to develop appropriate language structure targets for intervention programs with young handicapped children.

Context for
Language Intervention

All of the foregoing bases for the generation of treatment targets in language have some extremely important implications for the contexts in which such treatments should be implemented. These implications are both straightforward and rather simple in their overall substance. They are, however, extremely demanding in terms of their requirements for actual implementation. Each of the three dimensions of language (function, content, and structure) makes its demands on the context and procedures in which intervention is offered. The first two dimensions (function and content), however, make the most specific and critical ones.

Context for Intervention
with Function and
Content Targets

In the section on communicative functions (pragmatics), we indicated the need for an intervention context to include the potential for differential reinforcement of utterances in terms of their pragmatic intent. This requirement suggests the need for a context in which language-intervention targets are sought within the dynamics of "communication nets." Such nets require *responders* to the pragmatic element imbedded in an utterance. As we have indicated previously, setting the occasion for appropriate responses to pragmatic content-forms of a certain targeted class requires some careful designs.

Similarly, contexts for intervention in language must assure that the *content base* for children's utterances is known and available in the treatment setting. If children both talk about what they know and must know about whatever they talk, treatment contexts must be set up both to evoke existing knowledge and to provide the basis for acquiring new knowledge.

While we do not have adequate knowledge at this point in our attempts to implement treatments according to the model of language, we have begun to implement some of these contextual requirements. At this point, we are finding two productive conceptual bases for these attempts.

The first base focuses on developing *instrumental physical contexts*. This means simply that we must assure a setting which provides a high probability of children's actions *upon* and *within* it. Naturally, this brings to mind immediately a setting where there are toys and materials which can be manipulated in many ways: acted upon, assembled, disassembled, allowing shared action, and so on. Such a setting would include both large and small items, both familiar and unfamiliar items, along with items which provide a variety of attributes for the setting, such as items that make noise, items that have distinctive tactual properties, and items which have clear functional uses.

The second base combines with the first in providing an *instrumental communication context*. Within the physical context, there must be discriminative elements which mark this as a context where things are talked about and where such talking evokes good consequences. Naturally, this requires people who function as communicators, both modeling and reinforcing all aspects of the communicative utterances of children, particularly the pragmatic functions. One way to enhance and focus such contexts is to set up conditions in which certain actions and communicative forms have high probability. For example, we have set up physical settings of toy kitchens and role-played meal preparation and eating. Most children can at least begin to adopt various action roles in such a setting, and specific pragmatic acts can be assured occurrences. Foods can be marked according to their existence, nonexistence, need for recurrence, and so on; requests can be made; and actions can be described at many levels. Bedroom settings offer similar physically rich environments which have the potential to structure action routines and, therefore, communication routines: bathing "baby," preparing baby for bed, feeding and cuddling baby, and so on. Such physical settings and action routines are, in fact, very near to those in which much "natural" language learning occurs for the normally developing child. With some experience and concentration on the part of the language teacher, such environments can be developed so that the communicative functions and content can become highly controlled and predictable. In this way, training can become rather systematic in its targets and procedures.

We have found too that such settings accommodate small groups of children who are at different levels of language work. Such settings will, for example, allow a nonverbal child to gain manipulative experience with the entities and the actions in the setting, while also providing for receptive language modeling with a second child and expressive training with yet another child. The primary benefit, however, is that language training seems to be best approached in a context in which both the content and the function of language exchanges are readily apparent and associatable with their respective referents and consequences. Many language programs are often carried out in contexts in which the referents and/or the functions of particular utterances are not very evident to children in ways that match their perspectives.

As we noted at the outset of this short section, the context demands of a transactional approach to language are simple and straightforward but highly demanding on the part of the program implementer. It would seem, however, that such facilitating contexts can be designed and made to have highly predictive functions for both content and function of language utterances. If this can be done, language-intervention programs will represent better the variables which normal developmental data indicate are highly functional in the language-acquisition process. Such targets must be rigorously pursued and designed.

The Transactional Model and Alternative Modes of Training

Most people who are concerned with the language problems of severely handicapped children are well aware of the strong trends toward the use of nonspeech, alternative modes in the language training of certain such children. Children with severe motor deficiencies which interfere with adequate speech production are prime candidates for training in language systems which use structural modes like Bliss Symbols (Bliss, 1965) or electronic communication boards in which to encode their language content and functions. Similarly, there are many applications of manual sign systems and plastic-symbol systems as alternative modes for use with mentally retarded children. (For information on variants of these approaches, see chapters by Vanderheiden and Harris-Vanderheiden; Wilbur; and Carrier, in Lloyd, 1976.) The rationale for these systems is both obvious and solid. Such alternatives to speech are considered to be prosthetic devices which duplicate the function of the natural language mode.

There is nothing in the transactional model which would at all contradict the appropriateness and the functionality of finding alternatives to the speech mode for language when this primary mode appears to be highly problematic as a target. In fact, there is nothing in the transactional view of language which would dispute even a temporary use of an alternative mode with a shift to speech at a point when its attainment had better potential. Indeed, the transactional model considers the communicative function to be most basic to the human condition and would, therefore, seem to encourage some representation of such function in whatever way(s) this could be attained. The perspectives we have gained in this study encourage the consideration of alternative modes at any of several levels.

The transactional model does, however, seem to preclude the consideration of alternative modes as if these were simply a "structure" which could be trained with superficial considerations. Rather, the transactional model places on *any* communication mode the same basic demands for pragmatic and cognitive bases. Communication still "means" and "functions" regardless of the mode in which it is transmitted or received. Thus, its bases are the same whatever the mode. The referential functions, the structural forms, and the various communicative functions must still undergird a string of Bliss symbols, a string of manual signs, or a line of plastic forms placed on a response tray.

One of our concerns is that the so-called alternative modes are being treated somewhat superficially with some populations, most often the mentally retarded. Some clinicians seem to assume that alternative modes solve all of the problems of a nonverbal retarded child. Certainly, this is not true. A sign or a plastic form is not a "symbol" until it marks a referent. Similarly, these forms are not communicative until they are "intended" to mean something by a "speaker." Thus, these alternative modes, just as other language modes, can only map existing knowledge or signal communicative functions which have been determined by their users. It would appear to us, then, that alternative-mode users should approach such utterance forms in the same way we would approach standard speech modes—that is, firmly associated with referent attributes of many kinds, strongly consequated in terms of the function of the utterance being targeted, and well-considered as a *communication form,* not as an assembly task of putting various forms together on a board.

Summary: Treatment Implications and Existing Language Programs

In this chapter, we have sketched out a strategy for a language-intervention program based on a view of language acquisition as a transactional process. We have suggested that a treatment program should make special efforts to help children *discover* the various functions that language could carry out in their environment arranged as it were to allow a group of human beings to coexist productively and cooperatively. We also suggested how one interested in enhancing language acquisition might concentrate on talking about things that children interacted with and knew something about. Further, we even suggested that the specific form or structure of children's language might be considered not a separate grammar system to be learned, but rather a process in which certain word-order sequences and relationships are learned in order to say the things a person wants to say.

As we outlined these suggestions, we were aware at some level that programs which fleshed out these overall strategies and guidelines did actually exist. Unfortunately, however, these existing programs are not those which are published and available for teachers, speech pathologists, or parents to apply to populations of young handicapped children. Rather, these strategies are actualized in language-learning programs transacted between "good" mothers and normal-learning children throughout the world. In other words, what we think we have outlined are the principles, procedures, and strategies which result in normal language acquisition.

As we outlined these procedures, we had the concomitant awareness that no currently developed and reported language program for enhancing the language acquisition of handicapped children provided full representation of the principles, procedures, and strategies which were presented in this outline. Thus, we have the makings of a paradox: the best representations of the outlined process are probably provided by those least knowledgeable and trained to do it. The reasons underlying this paradox are not as pessimistic and condemning as they might be expected to be. They are, however, highly instructive.

First of all, the concordance between our basic intervention strategy and so-called "natural" mother-child transactions is the result of the circularity of our process for designing the transactional intervention program outline. The data which provided most of the direction and guidance to our derivation of program strategies came from empirical study of the normative language-development process. Those ideas which were not direct observations of that process were, at least, theoretical constructs derived from the observations and considerations of the "natural" process of language learning. Using such data and theory, it would be both surprising and distressing to come up with a model of an intervention process that looked much different from the process which had been the source of its design. Thus, it is not surprising that our program suggestions seem highly represented in the activities of mothers who are involved with their children in language-learning transactions.

That available compensatory language-intervention programs for handicapped children do not reflect all of these dimensions has two primary causes. The first is that handicapped children are not "normal," and thus the opinion is strong that normal language-teaching methods would not be powerful enough to provide the compensatory help needed by handicapped children. While, of course, such a view is essentially valid, it does not seem reason enough to conclude that nothing in the normal process would be productive or helpful in the design of clinical programs for nonnormal children. Thus, this one reason or attitude does not seem sufficient to explain the lack of "normative" dimensions within clinical language programs. What seems more to explain this deficit in current programs is that, until very recently, very little was actually known about the process of normal language learning. In fact, many psycholinguists, particularly, overtly despaired that such a complex and apparently disorganized process could be found to demonstrate any quantifiable systematic or functional dimensions.

Because of this wide belief that natural language acquisition could not be explained in sufficiently rigorous ways, such positions as Chomsky's (1957) "innateness" hypothesis and Skinner's (1957) postulations explaining "verbal behavior" came into being. These explanations of language by Chomsky and Skinner were, essentially, theoretically consistent models from which the products of language acquisition could be accounted for in the absence of any real knowledge about the normal acquisition process. In a way, then, Chomsky and Skinner created their own best ideas about what language systems were and created logical processes to account for these systems and their units. The only problem was that both of these skillful theoreticians and empirical observers naturally looked to construct processes which would result in language products only of the type which fitted their ideas about what such products were. Chomsky, therefore, looked for processes that would produce *syntactic products* and Skinner looked for processes that would produce *discriminative verbal operants*. The results of these two dominant deductive efforts were two widely different "explanations" of the processes by which language products could be attained by human subjects.

Since in order to develop a program of goals and procedures, one must have a theory of what language is and how it gets to be what it is, those who would intervene in language-acquisition enhancement programs with handicapped children were essentially provided with two possible theoretical bases from which they could generate their program goals and procedures. Many, therefore, designed programs which sought Chomsky's *structure* and others designed programs which would attain Skinner's *functions*.

The recent spate of compelling and productive perspectives about the contents (semantics) and the social functions (pragmatics) of language has caused professionals everywhere to begin to revise and update their concepts about what language is. Thus, it follows that revised constructs about the nature and the dimensions of the products of language learning will require modifications in the perspectives about what the process of language learning entails. This is exactly what has happened. The more analysis that children's language samples and exemplars were subjected to, the more dimensions these products were seen to have. When Bloom added the semantic dimension to her standard syntactic analysis protocols, she identified aspects of their products which required that the explanation of the process of language acquisition be revised. Her work alone was sufficient to suggest that Chomsky's perspectives were not adequate to explain the language-acquisition process. As soon as the existing explanation was identified as inadequate to explain the dimensions of the product as Bloom was now viewing it, new dimensions of the explanatory process had to be identified. Now, this process had to include cognitive factors related to semantic meaning.

Similarly, when Bruner (1975) and Luria (1974/75) began to suggest that language *function* was a critical dimension of the product of children's language, the variables related to the acquisition of differential function-forms of language had to be accounted for in the process being proposed for language-learning. Thus, once Bruner's work began to suggest that the ability to establish "joint action routines" and the ability to regulate "joint attention" were specific functions of the language products acquired by children, language programmers now had to begin to consider what aspects of the overall learning process in language might result in this dimension of the product.

From these examples, we can see that, as perspectives about the language *products* of children have expanded, so the perspectives about the *process* which produces them have had to expand. Today, then, our design of language-intervention processes must account for products which include (1) the semantic content of children's language, (2) the structural forms of children's language, and (3) the functions of children's language within a social environment. Since no *one* of our previous theoretical bases for language-intervention programs can account for all of these dimensions, no *one* of our various theoretical perspectives can serve as an adequate base for the generation of language-intervention programming. At the same time, however, it also becomes obvious that no one of our theoretical bases has been totally unrelated to the task. Language does need structure; thus, some basis for determining structural rules must be incorporated in programming. Language does need to mean things important to a child; thus, semantic content must be targeted in such programming. Language utterances do evoke differential consequences from the environment; thus, some broad functional-analysis perspectives must be represented in programming design. The need is, however, to integrate these various theoretical bases into compatible and summing perspectives, and this requires modifications in each of them in their current singular or isolated forms.

Analysis of Current Programs from Transactional Model Perspectives

A review of currently available programs reveals that many of these programs went through their initial developmental phases before the semantic data were well known, and all of them predated the most recent pragmatic data. The degree to which these current programs might reflect the variables which are represented in the transactional model are determined by (1) the most basic theoretical bases from which they emanate, (2) their relative time of development in terms of the availability of certain of the more recent theories and data, and (3) their relative receptivity to evolutionary change.

These three factors have had such highly differential effects on various programs that it is impossible to discuss them in any collective way. Instead, each program must be considered within its own specific history if it is to be considered in any fair and productive way. Before initiating these considerations of currently available programs, we will specify the perspectives directing our discussion of them.

1. We will only be discussing major *published* programs.
2. We will only be discussing programs which have been directed by their authors to young severely communicatively deficient children.
3. We will *not be judging* such programs; rather, we will be discussing them in terms of the perspectives reflected in the transactional model we have derived from current literature.
4. Within this discussion, we will indicate those areas in which we think there is deviance from what the transactional model indicates; thus, we will be identifying what we see in these programs as contraindications of the perspectives explicit in the transactional model.

It is possible for our discussion of such contraindications to the transactional model to be considered as criticisms of these programs and, in a broad sense, perhaps they are. We would prefer to view our discussions of existing programs as objective evaluations of their deviance from our admittedly biased view of a model for such programs. Thus, for those who can subscribe to the transactional view as a viable base for generating intervention programs, our evaluation of current programs will be constructive criticism. For those who reject the transactional model, our evaluation of other programs in comparison to such a model can be dismissed as unwarranted and biased. Ultimately, the reader must make a decision about his own orientation.

MacDonald's current program. The work of MacDonald and his colleagues (MacDonald, 1976; MacDonald & Blott, 1974; MacDonald, Blott, Gordan, Spiegel, & Hartmann, 1974; MacDonald & Nickols, 1974) culminates in a semantically based program directed specifically to young, severely delayed children. As the most recently developed of such programs, MacDonald's work manifests the most consistent reflection of the semantic perspectives. This program, for example, reflects not only *semantic content* targets, but also targets such content in consistently *semantic realization* rules, at least as they are suggested by Schlesinger's (1971, 1974) work. Thus, MacDonald and his associates target action sequences as agent-action-object word-order structures. They also target such semantic relationships as attribution, possession, location, and negation.

MacDonald provides two assessment inventories which are exemplary. The first, the *Environmental Prelanguage Battery* (EPB), assesses various elements which are believed to be important to the child's becoming a language learner. As such, it attends to both the social and cognitive underpinnings of the language acquisition process, as well as the more traditional behavioral targets of imitative responsiveness in both the motor and speech domains. The second assessment instrument is prescriptive for the more formal language targets of the program. Thus, the *Environmental Language Inventory* (ELI) is a semantically based instrument. It samples language across several evoking contexts, and MacDonald (1976) reports high correlations between the ELI-evoked findings and the semantic rules expressed in free-speech samples of both normally developing and delayed children.

Both of these assessment inventories (EPB and ELI) are complemented by training programs developed by MacDonald and his associates. The prelanguage targets are covered in a training manual designed for use by parents or professionals (Horstmeier, MacDonald & Gillette, 1975). Entitled *Ready, Set Go—Talk to Me!*, this program seeks behaviors deemed important for successful language acquisition such as attention, motor and speech imitation, and appropriate functional play with objects. The program which complements the ELI is MacDonald's semantically based program described above.

The MacDonald program is so strongly reflective of the cognitive bases of language that it anticipated Bruner's (1975) suggestions about the action-sequence and its role in language learning. As a consequence, this program stresses a context of social-play interaction between mother/teachers and children as the context for language learning. To accomplish and support this interactive context, MacDonald and his colleagues have designed what appear to be most excellent examples of the "instrumental teaching contexts" we have referred to previously. MacDonald has developed a multistationed classroom in which language-realization targets are targeted in an interactive milieu. In this arrangement, targeted structures are made to occur at high rates and within contexts in which their communicative function(s) are salient and appropriate. In this sense, even though MacDonald's work predated the most recent pragmatic perspectives, his attention to the cognitive and social bases of language have led to the development of highly relevant and dynamic interactive events in which children can talk about things and events for some purpose. It would seem that such a context would have a high probability of evoking most pragmatic functions. It will be helpful, however, when and if such formal pragmatic categories are made explicit as specific targets in this program.

Above all, MacDonald's programming innovations in both content and context reflect the tremendous facilitation of a move to look at language from the standpoint of the child as opposed to looking at it from an adult-centered theoretical base.

All in all, it appears that MacDonald's program reflects more of the transactional elements than any of the other programs, except perhaps that of Miller and Yoder which we will be discussing next. This program does, however, need considerably more extension into areas of more detailed pragmatic classes and, thus, more attention to structures other than the simple action relationships. In addition, we think that MacDonald's program does not offer the needed formal attention to the effects of the *referencing* strategy on structures produced *in situ*. Based, as it is, on a strong commitment to semantics and psychological reality, we would expect this program to continue to accommodate new perspectives and, thus, to show considerable evolution in its form over the next few years. This program, in other words, appears to be highly viable.

Miller and Yoder's program.   The work of Miller and Yoder (1972, 1974) has produced a rich, developmental exposition of semantic-based intervention programming. This program's entry requirements specify a child who is on the language continuum at least at the level of using a few single words. From this point, Miller and Yoder's program carries him through a program modeled after Bloom's (1970) semantic Relational Functions, Substantive Functions, Functional Relationships, and Semantic Relationships. This program culminates, structurally, in three- and four-word relational structures based on the agent-action-object sequence and the expansion of the noun phrases within these sequences.

Miller and Yoder's was the first major semantically directed training program. Because of its relatively early date of initial development (1972), it reflects a combination of perspectives in its selection of terminology to describe its structural targets. Since it has maintained its basic representation of Bloom's perspectives, it often specifies its targets in terms of grammatical structures rather than semantic case-structure. It is frankly difficult to assess the overall effects of this inconsistency of perspective. This program communicates well to the teacher but does seem to lack an internal consistency in this domain.

Like MacDonald's program, Miller and Yoder's also omits any consideration of the referencing stragegies we have found so compelling. Affecting realization structure as much as they do, this omission in current programs seems an important deviance from the transactional model directives. We note that the referencing perspectives (Olson, 1970) were available at the time both Miller and Yoder's and MacDonald's programs were developed. These perspectives were not processed within the programs' respective program-development activities, however.

Miller and Yoder's program also predated the full thrust of the so-called pragmatic perspectives and, therefore, does not reflect them in the same form as does the transformational model. Nevertheless, like MacDonald, Miller and Yoder are so sensitive to the basic social and cognitive functions that there is much attention to various types of "mapping" functions within language and the interactive learning of language. Thus, there are good representations of these issues. In addition, this program's overall sensitivity to the communication function of language brings it to pragmatic functions of some sophistication, even in the absence of the more compelling suggestions of Halliday (1975) and others which have appeared on this topic.

All in all, then, Miller and Yoder's program comes very close to the demands of a transactional model. It does not provide a full representation of the effect of referencing strategies on structure nor, as we have indicated, a full representation of specific pragmatic categories. It is also slightly disconcerting in that it is not consistent in its strategy for specifying realization forms. This problem and MacDonald's failure to expand the repertoire of his semantic structures fully are really the products of both programs' void in their consideration of the role of referencing in determining structure.

Like MacDonald's work, Miller and Yoder's program appears to be highly viable at this point. Both are still working along complementary lines of research and clinical perspectives and we would expect these to be reflected in further updates of their views in program form.

Stremel-Waryas' program. The detailed program offered by Stremel and Waryas (1974) is somewhat enigmatic from our perspectives. At face value, this program is most basically a syntax-teaching program. Obviously, from the views we have expressed in sections previously, we do not accept syntactic structure as a good representation of a child's reality in language and, thus, do not view this as a good form from which to structure response targets for young handicapped children.

From both personal experience and from the published materials, however, we know Stremel-Campbell to be an excellent and experienced clinician whose procedures reflect a strong predisposition to teach children to "talk about" things. As a consequence, her procedures demonstrate that a semantic and referencing perspective undergirds this program.

Stremel and Waryas (1974) state that they use syntactic structure only to be able to describe the linguistic forms necessary to express semantic relationships, and indeed, examination of their content and control sequences shows them to be stated in essentially semantic terms. In a sense, Stremel and Waryas are similar to Miller and Yoder in that they specify their targets in syntactic form but seem to generate them from semantic bases.

Even with this expressed semantic base for these structures, however, the syntactic target forms evoke that problem of internal consistency that we also see to a lesser degree in Miller and Yoder's program. The specific effects of this inconsistency are visible in Stremel and Waryas' program in that the sequence of training seems very much dominanted by expansion along a syntactic line rather than a semantic line per se. Just as an example, inflectional endings (such as "-ing") and wh- questions forms occur extremely early in this program. While we appreciate the possible pragmatic value of such forms as wh- questions, our previously stated preference is not to target these necessarily in their most refined syntactic form. Similarly, a structural grammar view seems also to lead Stremel and Waryas to an early attention to pronoun forms and even articles. Perhaps our perspectives about the population of young severely communicatively delayed children and Stremel and Waryas' perspectives about their target population are at odds here; but it would appear to us that there are many semantic targets which are more highly desirable (functional) than those involving systems morphemes like articles and case-controlled pronoun forms of extreme complexity (see Waryas, 1973). Even though this program is stated to be dominated by semantic realizations through syntax, the syntactic developmental sequence applied seems to negate this posture. Clearly, the transformational grammar system leads this program, even though its procedures and general training contexts have strong reflections of semantic instincts on the part of the programmers.

In their most recent publication (Waryas & Stremel-Campbell, in press), these program developers confirm their grammatical bias while also accepting the need to accomodate the recent semantic and pragmatic perspectives. They point out that language must have structure and that any final accountability regarding language training must be judged in terms of appropriate structure being available in the child's language repertoire. Perhaps it is good that Waryas and Stremel-Campbell counter the move away from grammar to some extent—we do need to become integrative rather than exclusionary in our consideration of all of these variables. We would, however, also maintain our point that transformational grammar is a descriptive system and an adult perspective. As such, it cannot be used singularly to structure children's language-acquisition programs without considerable risk of missing a child's reality rather completely.

Overall, the Stremel and Waryas program has much to commend it. It is highly systematic and its teaching contexts seem excellent. (We recommend the film "Perspectives on Language" by Ruder and Stremel which demonstrates this program. It is available through the Bureau of Child Research, University of Kansas, Lawrence.) At this time, however, this program does not offer a full exploitation of the semantic perspectives as they are now perceived. Naturally, because of its time of development, it also lacks adequate representation of the pragmatic perspectives basic to the transactional model. Like the other programs reviewed to this point, the Stremel and Waryas program also lacks any explicit reflection of referencing strategies in determining structure. The dynamic contexts offered within Stremel's training do, however, evoke and allow referencing strategies informally.

Like the other programs reviewed to this point, Stremel and Waryas' program still appears to be viable. In fact, their new chapter (in press) adds considerations of both semantic realization forms and pragmatic functions.

Guess, Sailor, and Baer's program. This program represents the "purest" application of the functional analysis of behavior approaches to severely communicatively deficient persons (Guess, Sailor, & Baer, 1974; Guess, Sailor, Keogh, & Baer, 1975). In its analysis of the functions of language, the program identifies *reference* and *control* (of environment) as primary and generates its targets in this perspective. In this sense, these program ideas represent the best current representation of strictly pragmatic analysis. Approaching these functions from the behavioral point of view, however, results in perspectives which show some subtle but highly significant deviations from the pragmatic functions which have been identified by those who have been processing language per se (Dore, 1975; Halliday, 1975). Since such formal pragmatic views were not available during the development of Guess, Sailor, and Baer's program, it cannot be ascertained whether or not these recently emphasized views would have been incorporated in the program. Interestingly, however, the basis of the later work in pragmatics has long been available (DeLaguna's work was first published in 1927) but has never been formally considered in any behavioral approaches that we are familiar with.

The primary differences between the current behavioral representations of function and those identified by the pragmatic-linguistic views lie in the generalization we have made previously—namely, that behavioral views continue to differentiate only one class of language responses as "mands" (Skinner, 1957) which act upon the environment to evoke or specify reinforcing consequences. In behavioral perspectives, these manded reinforcing consequences are most likely to be identified from among so-called primary reinforcers (food, water, and so on) and high-probability conditioned reinforcers (toys, preferred activities, and so on). In the more recently emphasized views of pragmatic functions, the reinforcers for communicative utterances are considered in much broader social perspectives (including secure help, secure interaction, attaining joint reference, attaining interpersonal response, and so on). Thus, current pragmatic perceptions extend the basic "mand" function to *all* human communicative efforts. These say, in effect, human communication attempts are all mands for human response in the broadest sense, and further, the reinforcers for language must be viewed within these broader views of language as a regulator of *social interaction* and *cooperation*.

Thus, while there is nothing in the current behavioral perspectives about language functions that we would deny, there are, we think, serious deficiencies in the *scope* of functions specifically identified in current behavioral programs. In a very real way, the transactional model provides an *extension* of functional analysis views, not a refutation of them.

In another philosophical area, the current behavioral construct of *reference* manifest in Guess, Sailor, and Baer's (1974) work is also somewhat constrained when compared to this construct as it is represented in the transactional model. Again, the difference seems to be one only of degree and scope, not one of basic contradiction.

It is axiomatic that the behaviorist cannot consider "inside events" when developing constructs. In other words, the behaviorist considers processes within the mind or a person's covert psychological processes to be unquantifiable and, thus, unusable in developing behavioral approaches. Consistent with this constraint, current behavioral language programs do not consider the structure or the basic content of a child's cognitive processes in language. As a result, Guess, Sailor, and Baer's programming for referencing (labeling) considers only the quantifiable aspects of the controlling antecedent events, the differential responses, and the consequential events in developing referential skill responses. It ignores any consideration of developmental cognitive factors in its structural targets. Similarly, it does not consider possible cognitive prerequisites to the content of its targeted response forms. This program, then, reflects no consideration of a psychological reality for language which is beyond specific manipulations of functional variables. Such a view essentially precludes any representation of a cognitive-semantic perspective in programming. With such a priori exclusions incumbent on their programming approaches, behaviorists must necessarily ignore the overall cognitive-based referencing construct as outlined by Olson (1970), the mapping construct, the presuppositions which appear to underlie pragmatic functions, and the semantic-based structural forms which appear to be products of all of these psychological processes.

In the face of such theoretical preemptions, we cannot consider language programs produced only from behavioral perspectives complete in any sense. It is particularly paradoxical that the radical behaviorist has, to this point at least, seemed to reject so many possible "functional" variables. As in the case of many programs, however, we must again note that many of these theoretical and empirical perspectives were not available to people like Guess, Sailor, and Baer at the time their current programs took form. It will be most interesting to observe modifications that may be forthcoming. The pragmatic perspectives, particularly, would appear most productive for their further behavioral analysis. As in the previous programs discussed to this point, it would appear that the authors of this program will continue to be productive in this area for some time to come, and we would fully expect some program evolution in the future.

As we have stated previously, there is much credit due the behaviorists, in general, and researchers like Guess, Sailor, and Baer in particular. Without their constant efforts, there would probably have been very little programming for the severely deficient populations that they have been working with. It is further important to note that the behavioral programs have been the only language programs which have been committed to attempts to understand and insure communicative functions. It is, therefore, particularly ironic that behaviorists are somewhat at odds now with the rather compelling positions related to the function of communication. The problem of an appropriate consideration of the psychological dimensions of language and language usage which happens "inside the head" obviously have made for this irony. It will be most interesting (and, we're sure, instructional) to see how the first-line behaviorists deal with this basic confrontation on communication function.

Kent's program. The *Language Acquisition Program for the Severely Retarded* (Kent, 1974; Kent with Klein, Falk, & Guenther, 1972) is a behavioral program in that its procedures are all systematic and drawn from functional analysis of behavior principles (Holland & Skinner, 1961; Skinner, 1953). This program is different from Guess, Sailor, and Baer's, however, in that it seems to draw its targets and procedures more from a clinical view than a strictly theoretical one. In doing so, Kent and her colleagues have produced targets which compare somewhat favorable with the types of targets generated on the basis of the cognitive-semantic data which came along some time after the basic elements of this program had already been developed. In this sense, Kent's program, based as it is on some intensive experimental experience with retarded children, seems to offer some *pro forma* validation of some of the suggestions which have been generated from the application of the semantic data.

For example, Kent's targets reflect a strong representation of both the action sequence which Bruner's (1975) work suggests to be most important and the action-attributes as semantic features underlying early lexicon as Nelson's (1974) work would suggest. That Kent's program also targets the labeling of commonly experienced objects and actions from the environment of her subjects also reflects trends suggested by current cognitive views. It seems clear that Kent, like other clinicians, had clear intuitive appreciation that language requires some reality to children in the form of existing knowledge and referential characteristics.

Kent's program is also notable for its procedural commitment to a *Receptive Phase* in which she seeks accurate behavioral indicators of language comprehension. We have not discussed the basic expressive-receptive dichotomy in this section because it is discussed in such depth in Chapter 3. Restating our positions in a clinical perspective, however, we basically agree with MacNamara's (1972) position that children come to language learning through the process of matching up receptive language patterns with their already present knowledge about entities and relationships in their environment. As indicated in previous discussion, we do not think that there is necessarily a one-to-one relationship between receptive acquisition and expressive usage. Rather, although we accept a receptive primacy, we view eventual expressive productions as coming from another set of variables—including pragmatic intent and referencing strategies. Much as Guess and Baer's (1973) demonstration of the independent relationship between receptive and expressive responses, the two processes are under quite different controls but are highly related. If you will recall, Figure 1 in Chapter 4, which presents our overall model(s), schematizes the way we perceive the realization processes in these two modalities.

At any rate, Kent's program contains a highly systematic receptive phase which precedes her move toward attaining expressive realization of targets. We find this approach appealing, particularly because it is made to occur in dynamic contexts. Although Kent's program is not guided by the systematized consideration of the cognitive-semantic categories that are found in later-developed programs, like those of Miller and Yoder (1972, 1974), MacDonald (1976), and MacDonald et al. (1974), her overall targets offer a fairly good representation of the semantic categories which are related to actions and referential attributes, including some relational attributes.

As we have stated previously, we also appreciate the contexts Kent structures for the playing of many language games. Her missing objects, part/whole, and contextually controlled presentation of target-objects seem highly productive. That she structures these for receptive language games makes them highly useful, because often such contexts and procedures are difficult to design.

All in all, Kent's program seems to us useful and well-designed, particularly considering the relative time of its development. We would suggest, however, that Kent's basic program can be significantly enhanced by careful integration of many of the missing semantic relations and certainly by consideration of new pragmatic intent constructs. We also think that Kent's realization structures might be modified somewhat by more sensitivity to the referencing strategy construct. Most of her structures are, to our way of thinking, perhaps too structurally generated for a young population.

If the clinician approaches Kent's program armed with supplemental perspectives in semantics, cognition, and social functions of communication, we would think it will prove highly productive. Interestingly, this is one of the programs for which we have no firm expectations for revision in the near future. Kent has left her institutional research setting and, although we are sure she will remain productive in the field of language for the handicapped, we cannot be sure that she will ever return to it at the levels necessary to produce significant evolutionary changes in her programs. We certainly can hope!

Brickers' programs. The Brickers' (W. Bricker, 1972; Bricker & Bricker, 1970, 1974; D. Bricker, Dennison, & W. Bricker, 1976; Bricker, Dennison, Watson, & Vincent-Smith, 1973) overall approach to language is an interesting one. It differs from all others in that it does not appear to us to be a program for generating a specific language repertoire so much as it is a program for generating a class of behavior called "language." Brickers' work seems classifiable as a truly "psychological approach" to language behavior. As such, it covers more ground and involves more process variables than any other language program directed to young handicapped children.

The Brickers were the first to incorporate considerations of the child's sensorimotor intelligence and schemata into a language program. They were, therefore, the first researchers actually to apply the "mapping construct" which has come to dominate the more recent language programs. As a result of their conviction that language had to have a cognitive base, the Brickers taught children the functional use of objects (such as "drink cup") prior to mapping that event. They also worked diligently on discrimination programs in which children differentiated among various objects on the basis of any of their several attributes or properties. All of this was directed by their conviction that children had to know something before they talked about it, a position which is now widely accepted.

The Brickers' work has also reflected a basically developmental perspective in which prerequisites are well considered. In this developmental perspective, they have attended to all aspects of the child's system, from his basic hearing sense through babbling, cognitive discriminations, receptive language, and on to expressive language. They suggest work on gross motor imitation with children and provide elaborate programs for imitative shaping of phonological approximations of the target words in their program.

In their latest program (D. Bricker, Dennison, & W. Bricker, 1976), they target the basic semantic structure associated with the action-sequence (that is, agent-action-object) and, in so doing, have generally moved with the so-called semantic revolution. They also reflect a good awareness of semantic intent as it is related to cognitive bases, as might be expected given their previous strong Piagetian applications in language. Similarly, their representation of the action-sequence reflects their early awareness of "functional use" categories between verbs and object nouns.

The Brickers' programs have also manifested a strong assessment dimension which reflects their developmental view. Although well-identified as overall "behaviorists" in their procedures, they have consistently remained eclectic in their ability to accept other theoretical input into the substance of their programming efforts. Consequently, their programs move from nonverbal, sensorimotor levels to receptive levels and from there to speech realizations. Further, they suggest assessments at these various levels as prerequisites for moving to other levels.

The Brickers' programs have also always reflected at least a gross interactional approach in that they have been carried within an overall preschool classroom environment where all of the developmental activities have been represented. They do carry out a lot of one-one-one sessions (or small-group sessions) within the overall classroom context, particularly on imitation and discrimination activities.

As we list the various activities of the Brickers' programs, it is obvious that they well represent most of the elements offered in the basic cognitive-semantic perspectives. As a whole, however, the Brickers' programs do not approach the overall sharp focus attained by other language programs. Perhaps this should tell us something important. First, the Brickers have also worked directly with developmentally delayed children in developing their programs. As a result, they have had to be sensitive to all of the dimensions involved in the process of language-learning by many handicapped children. This sensitivity has led to a program which some (for example, Guess, Sailor, & Baer, 1974) have considered to be so complex that it is unapplicable. There is some truth in this. Perhaps the fault lies not in Brickers' program, however, so much as in the problems inherent in a population of young children who require special attention to their overall severe developmental deficiencies. This population of children is not homogenous, even though it is often considered to be so. Brickers' programs have attempted to span the full scope of the heterogeneity involved in this population. Consequently their programs present the myriad of details which might be required at any level within this population.

As a result of their attention to all of the possible needs which might be required for this overall population, the Brickers have actually concentrated on the many process variables involved in such attention. In addition, they have perceived these process variables as separate and sequenced in hierarchal fashion. Indeed, some children may require that each and every process variable be programmed as it is outlined in the Brickers' lattice. Other children, of course, might be exempted from some process variable as a result of assessment results. Thus, while we share some of the "overwhelmed" reaction to the processing details in the Brickers' programs, we still cannot consider these inappropriate. It may well be that the Brickers are much closer to full-range programming reality for such children as we are talking about than are many other programs.

At the same time, however, we would like to suggest that perhaps some of the Brickers' processing details might be programmed simultaneously rather than sequentially. In addition, we concur with MacDonald's (1976) observation that much of their attention to phonological imitation might not be needed. If, for example, the motivation (social) and the semantic (cognitive) bases for communication are well developed, speech realization might be possible by children without all of the attention to speech imitation given in the Brickers' programs very early in their sequence.

In other areas of concern, the Brickers' programs do not yet reflect the formal pragmatic function categories which antedate their development. Nor do they show much sensitivity to overall referencing constructs except as that construct is inherent, to some degree, in a cognitive-semantic approach. As to the final criticism concerning whether the Brickers' work is so sequenced and task-analyzed in terms of the process that it lacks an overall perspective, that seems unanswerable at this point.

We have said in other contexts (McLean, 1977) that language programming for young handicapped and severely developmentally delayed children will never be "elegant." Perhaps the Brickers' programs demonstrate that fact more than some other ones do. The Brickers' programs do seem highly "adult" in their perspectives of the language-learning process as a whole. Perhaps some movement toward a child's perspectives on the same process elements might alter their programming perspectives somewhat. As an example, we might consider that a more communication-oriented view might obviate some of the heavily programmed elements of Brickers' current program efforts. If, for example, more intent and motivation came from the child as a result of social interaction, perhaps some of the elements of their current program would become unnecessary. This, of course, is unanswerable at this point in our empirical experience.

From an overall view, then, we find the Brickers' program rather enigmatic—yet provocative and stimulating. Certainly no one interested in the overall problems of language intervention with young children can overlook the immense contributions and the perspectives offered in the work of the Brickers and their colleagues.

Carrier's program. Because this program is specifically directed toward mentally retarded children and, thus, may find wide application with young communicatively deficient children for whom some alternative, nonspeech mode seems desirable, we feel we should discuss this program in the context of the transactional model. It should be obvious from all of our discussions to this point that we cannot be very positive in our view of Carrier's (Carrier, 1974; Carrier & Peak, 1975) program as it now stands.

Our negative reaction to this program is *not* related to its use of an alternative-mode approach. Indeed, as we commented earlier in this chapter, there are many children for whom communication must be the first and foremost concern, and if an alternative (nonspeech) mode serves this goal, we are most positive about it. Our concern with Carrier's program lies in the language form which he targets in the alternative mode. He has moved to a totally structural grammar in his realization forms, and this, we think, is an unfortunate decision.

In moving to a grammar-based repertoire, Carrier ignores all of the psychological "reality" of language with a population for whom this reality is perhaps most important. The targeting of a seven-element syntactic string complete with articles, inflectional endings, and function words as a "tact" (Skinner, 1957) for a static picture-stimulus does not reflect what we consider to be appropriate in an initial language-learning process. Such an approach ignores all of the interactive variables in language learning suggested by Bruner (1974/75, 1975). It goes counter to Nelson's (1974) call for dynamic variables. It rejects any consideration of developmental factors in both semantics and syntax.

Interestingly, the work that this approach is based on reflected one of the earliest realizations that language "maps onto existing knowledge." Premack's initial work (1970) with his chimpanzee was carefully programmed to teach language encoding of only knowledge which the chimp had demonstrated in nonlanguage ways (such as match-to-sample responses). Carrier instead makes the age-old assumption that children acquire knowledge about their world through learning language rather than assuming the cognitive-mapping view that is now prevalent.

We have little doubt that there are some children for whom Carrier's program might be most helpful. A child with adequate cognitive holdings about the entities and relationships in his "world" might do well in learning to map these concepts in Carrier's nonspeech language structures. Severely motor-impaired children, deaf children, and children with severe auditory-processing problems might do extremely well in learning complex syntactic forms and using them. In fact, we have no doubt that Carrier's retarded children learned the "stringing rules" of Carrier's program through the careful sequencing of color-coded-elements training which he provides. What we doubt is that this learning was actually syntax rule-learning for many of these children. In this sense, then, we find great problems in accepting that such stringing-rules had the reality of language-rules, at least for most children involved.

What we would see from the transactional model would suggest that Carrier's nonspeech program could be easily adapted to a developmental communicative perspective and could be modified to mark the semantic and pragmatic aspects of language most productively. As it stands now, it is a syntax-teaching program of considerable elegance but limited scope currently directed toward a population for whom its value is greatly in doubt.

The Strengths of Current Programs

We have stated our opinion that no program available today manifests explicit attention to all of the targeting and procedural concerns which are indicated within a transactional model for language. Since each of these current programs was developed before many of the perspectives covered in this book were widely known or available, such deficits in current programs are totally understandable.

Even though current programs do not yet reflect *all* of the perspectives in the transactional model, some of them are relatively close to doing so. The latest available programs (Miller & Yoder, 1974; MacDonald, 1976) strongly reflect the semantic bases which we have discussed. Even programs which were developed prior to the availability of semantic and pragmatic data but which were developed with strong empirical bases in direct clinical research with retarded children reflect sensitivity to several of the "new" issues. For example, Kent's (1972, 1974) program reflects a strong bias toward action sequences and action attributes even though Bruner's (1975) work was not available to her. Similarly, both Kent and Brickers' (1976) programs reflect high awareness about the need for children's knowledge to undergird targeted language forms. The Brickers, in fact, were pioneers in the application of Piagetian cognitive constructs to language programming, and Kent's long experience with retarded children led her to assure that program language targets were entities which were well known and experienced by the child.

In parallel areas, the most recent representations of behavioral approaches to severely retarded children by Guess, Sailor, and Baer (1974) reflect the awareness of language functions as critical to acquisition. Although, as we have stated in earlier sections, the behaviorists had not analyzed language functions to the degree that now appears possible in the light of the work by Bruner (1975) and the taxonomies offered by Dore (1975) and Halliday (1975), their programs nevertheless reflect this dimension rather strongly. We would certainly expect future work by the behaviorist group to move even more strongly in this direction.

As indicated above, there are several excellent programs in language intervention for young severely communicatively delayed children available today (see Graham's chapter and Fristoe's Inventory in Lloyd's 1976 volume for an up-to-date analysis of all available programs). Since most of these programs have emerged from ongoing clinical programs, most of them reflect at least intuitive sensitivity to the dimensions of language and the language-acquisition process that has been outlined in this book. In fact, many of today's programs have excellent intuitive representations of some of the newer perspectives we have discussed, if one would analyze them carefully. Except for the most recent semantic programs, however, none of the available programs is organized along the specific dimensions presented in this book. Thus, in order to find representations of these newer perspectives, the clinician will need to approach current programs inductively. He will need to make the perspectives suggested in the transactional model and look for targets and activities in existing programs which are pertinent to these perspectives. As we have indicated, there are many such possibilities in the various programs.

At this point, we shall briefly recapitulate some of the evaluative discussions of the preceding section so that the reader may identify the various strengths which we could identify in current programs—strengths which need to be fully analyzed in developing strategies which are more inclusive of all of the most recent perspectives provided by the transactional view of language. We have stated that both MacDonald and Miller and Yoder have developed programs which offer excellent representations of the semantic content of children's language. We have also judged that Kent's program offers good procedures and targets for the action sequence and dynamic attributes, even though her work preceded the emergence of these constructs in the literature. We have also noted that the Brickers' work reflects much insight into the overall process of language acquisition and that Guess, Sailor, and Baer's program, along with that of Kent, offers us many perspectives related to the view of the functions of language which prevailed prior to the fuller exposition of this area in current pragmatic perspectives. Finally, we have noted that the Stremel-Waryas program seems to reflect a slightly broader functional approach to attaining syntax structure.

The Weaknesses of Current Programs

Even though the model from which we are operating stems from a relatively un-proven theoretical base, it still seems appropriate to indicate the areas in which current programs appear weak from the perspectives offered by this base. For even if all of our current perspectives would prove not to be totally accurate, there is little possibility that they will all prove to be totally unfounded either. In pointing out these perceived weaknesses, we will stay only within the areas which appear to have the very highest levels of face validity and logical probability.

We see two major weaknesses in today's available programs: a lack of *internal consistency* in terms of current theoretical positions and a serious lack of *prescriptive properties* which specify the populations of children for which they are appropriate. In order to understand these weaknesses and what we consider to be their important implications, we shall need to discuss them each briefly.

Internal consistency. As shown in our analyses of current programs, most of them are based on one of three currently dominant theories about the nature of language: transformational grammar, behaviorism, or semantic realization. We can see that each of these theories is directed at different aspects of the language system. The grammar approaches concentrate on the structural realizations of a language system. The behavioral theories concentrate on the controlling variables involved in language acquisition and usage. The semantic theories are generally directed toward a fuller implementation of the overall psychological aspects of language realization forms from the point of view of their content. As we have noted, a fourth theoretical base is now available in the area of the pragmatic functions of language. This base is not yet fully represented in an available language program, however.

Of the programs which are available and are representative of each of the theoretical bases identified above, each concentrates on the aspects of programming which are best covered by the particular theoretical base it represents. Thus, grammarians concentrate on generating a full repertoire of base syntactic structures and their transformations. Behaviorists concentrate on bringing a repertoire of verbal responses under antecedent and consequential stimulus control. Semanticist programmers concentrate on attaining realization forms which encode the various properties and relationships functional in making reference.

Weaknesses in each of these program bases arise when it must deal with a dimension of language which is not adequately considered and treated from that particular base. Therefore, transformationalist-based programs do not treat the psychological aspects of language content at all, and as a result, these grammatical approaches offer little in the way of directing the appropriate content of language forms. Similarly, behaviorists have no base for determining the absolute forms or structure of the responses which they bring under stimulus control, so they most often move to the products of the grammarians in order to describe language realization forms for their paradigms. Except for MacDonald, even semantic programs still manifest no coherent view when describing the structure of their targeted responses. Miller and Yoder, for example, describe some of their structural targets in grammatical forms (such as subject-verb), some in form-class terms (for example, noun plus noun), and some in semantic terms (agent-action-object). Stremel and Waryas claim a semantic base and then target grammatical form "rules."

The final result of such cross-theory movement seems best described as a problem of *internal consistency*. Since no one of these theories adequately treats all dimensions of the language system, each is almost bound to manifest such inconsistencies.

Such problems of internal consistency cannot possibly be solved until we adopt perspectives on language which are cognizant of all of the dimensions of language. There is structure, there is meaning, and there is function in language. The key to proper consistency in dealing with each of these dimensions is to deal with each of them in interaction and relationship with the other. Thus, the response topographies in language must be considered in terms of all of their determining properties. A language utterance's structure seems affected by its selected semantic content and its user's referential strategy. An utterance's function seems determined by internal events controlling the user's needs for social effects. An utterance's content seems determined by the interactive relationship between a speaker's communicative strategy and his knowledge about various referents which are possible within that strategy. With these perspectives, such mismatches as those identified above should be minimized. So long as language program developers work from single-pole theoretical approaches, however, such inconsistencies will continue to manifest themselves and plague both the language teacher and the language learner.

Prescriptive properties. The second major weakness in many current programs for language intervention lies in their inadequate prescriptive properties. If there is one thing that our model-building process should have made clear, it is that language is exceedingly complex in terms of its interdependence on all aspects of the human condition and its different behavioral domains.

Current programs appear to fall far short of offering targets and procedures which differentiate their clinical consumers in terms which are appropriately discrete. The detail we have presented in Chapter 6 on assessment indicates the sources of much potential variation among members of populations which are considered relatively homogeneous for other purposes. The so-called severely retarded population, for example, can reflect vast differences among its individual children along cognitive, social, and linguistic continua. Current programs are inadequate in their provision for differential programming for individual or collective differences among the various populations included in early education programs.

It is this general lack of prescriptiveness which makes the fair evaluation of today's programs problematic. As an example, all of our criticism of the behavioral programs which target syntactic structure are predicated on the assumption that the children to whom such programs are applied will need some careful attention to the semantic and pragmatic elements of the language system. Indeed, however, there are child populations for whom this assumption might not be proper. Many so-called learning disabled children may have perfectly adequate cognitive and social structures for language and merely manifest the problems inherent in auditory-processing and motor-sequencing skills which make syntactic form alone a clinical problem. If such cases exist, programs such as Gray and Ryan's (1973), Stremel and Waryas' (1974), and even Carrier's (1974) nonspeech alternative mode programs might be highly appropriate in targeting the slot-class correlations, inflectional endings, and syntactic operator usage that these programs target. If, however, we maintain our focus on severely delayed children, we must assume that this population will present the language interventionist with broader systemic deficits which will affect both the cognitive-semantic and social-pragmatic domains.

Such specific population issues do indicate the problems which are most apparent in judging current programs. They also point up an overall problem of perspective that has existed throughout the book. We stated at the outset of this project that we would maintain our focus on young severely communicatively deficient children. In doing so, we drastically lowered the scope of our perspectives on language. We have attempted to keep our perspectives firmly fixed on the earliest forms of language as they might be targeted in programs which were dealing with nonverbal children and children who were extremely developmentally delayed in their representational skills with language. Thus, throughout this project we have maintained our perceptions that the programs that we were creating a model for would allow programming to start from zero language repertoires and terminate with language levels roughly equivalent to Stage II levels (Brown, 1973). With this limited scope firmly in mind, our assessments of current programs can be interpreted within their appropriate context. When we are forced to react critically to the work of many gifted and sincere colleagues, our biases and their resultant contexts for judgment should be clear.

Thus, our evaluations of the programs in the preceding pages are biased by our perception of their appropriateness for young severely deficient clinical subjects. It does seem clear that none of the programs mentioned above is really intended to be limited to children with only syntactic problems. In fact, Carrier's program was specifically developed for severely mentally retarded children and Stremel and Waryas' program is also directed to moderately to severely retarded populations.

There are some provisions in this dimension, however, and these should be recognized. MacDonald's program includes excellent assessment instruments calibrated to his treatment programs. Other programs are highly developmental in their structure and specify entry behaviors (Miller & Yoder; Stremel & Waryas). Still other programs, like the Brickers', are multidimensional and include some assessment procedures. Thus, their program offers some appropriate accommodation of individual differences in several domains. Most other programs, however—some by philosophical constraints and others by omissions—do not offer adequate or specific accommodation to individual or population differences. Even those programs which do offer some basis for selective use do not do so in a fashion sufficient to meet the demands of the overall problem.

In a sense, this lack of prescriptive properties among current programs is a reflection of the knowledge constraints under which they have been developed. Most of these programs have been developed without the current pervasive and productive perspectives about language and language-acquisition dynamics. Given the knowledge bases clinicians have had to work from over the past decade, it is not surprising that current programs do not reflect adequate or appropriate prescriptive dimensions in their targeting selection or their sequencing patterns. This is an area of relative weakness that we must be aware of and work to strengthen; for, unless we attend to some very careful work in developing differential programming for various types of specific deficits among children, we cannot hope to become truly effective in our language-intervention services to the highly diverse group of children under the label of young, severely communicatively handicapped.

When we suggest becoming more prescriptive, we mean that programs must be designed to offer appropriate targets and procedures for a complex of subject deficits and, most likely, combinations of deficits. For example, a program should be designed to meet a subject's (or a group's) cognitive level in interaction with his social level in interaction with the linguistic level. Current programs offer too little in the way of integrated specifics to provide such prescriptive offerings. Hopefully, more theoretically integrated future programs will offer more potential along these lines.

Designing Intervention Strategies for Educational Settings

It seems obvious from the discussion above that the only real solution to the language-intervention needs of our various handicapped populations lies in a realization that we cannot develop a language program for severely communicatively delayed young children. What we can and must develop is an overall language-intervention strategy from which any necessary language-intervention component program could be generated. Until we can truly start with every child (or homogeneous population) where he is, we will not be effective enough to meet the needs of our severely communicatively deficient children.

If we realize the need for task analysis and individualized programming in all other areas of special education and clinical speech pathology, it is obvious that we also realize these needs in cases of severe language deficiency. The problem has been, it would appear, that we have not had detailed and discrete enough knowledge of the broadest elements and parameters of language and language acquisition to initiate such a strategy approach. In the light of the high face validity of the recent theory and data in the areas of semantics, case grammar, and pragmatic functions, it would appear that there is now the basis for attempting to become more prescriptive in our approaches and to get away finally from the idea that there is a universally definitive language program just ready to roll off the presses.

In fact, we would be most heartened if higher level professionals in the language areas would, essentially, stop writing "programs" and, instead, outline strategies and report on their effect in clinical programs run in conjunction with interested and competent professional teachers or clinicians. All clinicians and teachers should eventually be talking and reporting on their strategies and their results in specific and definitive terms. This would mean clear models and precise terminology to describe the applied components of these models. It would also mean good clinical research data for communicating with one another.

Naturally, the above ideal is not within reach. Yet, even if the ideal is not readily attainable, all of us can at least attempt to reach toward the ideal. At the risk of sounding self-serving, we believe this book can begin to provide the bases for forming a strategy of language intervention. We have given extensive discussions to specific components of our strategy. We have translated our strategy into its various language dimensions of semantics, structure, and function. We have attempted to provide an analysis of the most appropriate starting places for assessment and subsequent treatment targets. Overall, we have simply outlined what we think is a greatly expanded perspective on language and its dimensions.

In addition, we have indicated that the model we have sketched is not a demonstrated fact at this point. It is simply the best derivation we could make of a model which could be supported by current theory and data in the area of the psychological aspects of language as we have read and interpreted them.

part 4

Conclusions and Summary

chapter 8

Implications for Research

Where We Are: Nature of Current Knowledge

The model of language presented in this book represents a relatively complete exposition of the major areas of knowledge about children's language as we have found them to be pertinent and productive in finding better bases for generating applied language-intervention programs for young handicapped children. However, by the time this book is published, much of the information included will have been modified or extended by new data. Nonetheless, it is doubtful that the general areas of research in language identified here will be significantly altered for a few years to come. The general topics and targets now being investigated appear to be extremely pertinent and productive areas of investigation, and it appears to us that these areas will be considerably extended but not radically altered in the research trends of the near future. Additionally, and very importantly, today's research is surprisingly multidoctrinaire. By this we mean that the several bases of today's major research thrusts in language create a research posture which is more open-ended and heuristic in nature than those have been in the immediate past. These bases are less inductively designed to demonstrate a particular theory of language. Rather, they seem to us to be directed toward gaining basic knowledge about language and language acquisition in children from which theories may be developed in more deductive fashion. After more than a decade of polarized postures on the linguistic or behavioral dichotomy, this is both a more productive and more stable state than most of us have known.

As a result of this more heuristic posture in language research, it appears to us that we now have a developing and most promising body of knowledge about language in terms of both theoretical and applied potential. Certainly the current knowledge is extremely rich in terms of providing direction for educational research. The relationships of language to other important areas of development, like the cognitive and social domains, bring language in from its previous position isolated from other educational efforts. Similarly, the strongly demonstrated functional relationships between language acquisition and the child's interactions within both the physical and social environment will be most productive of pedagogical variables and the manipulative treatment of such variables.

Finally, in overall, general terms, today's research in language offers a strong trend toward individual and child-oriented perspectives which should be considered most appropriate and productive by special educators. If, for example, the language of children can be understood in terms of the child's reality, perhaps we can forsake the frustration and limited productivity of having to view it in terms of either Chomsky's or Skinner's reality. While this may seem to be a somewhat facetious, or worse, and anti-intellectual posture, we don't mean it as either of these. Rather, we mean to repeat our earlier stated position that highly reductionistic descriptive systems are not the most productive bases from which to investigate or treat the severe problems manifested in individual (or homogeneous groups of) handicapped children.

Instead of bare-boned abstractions about language, then, today's research is giving us some beginning perspectives, at least, about the specific nature of children's language in its early forms. Certainly, information on *what* children talk about, *how* they talk about it, and the reasons *why* they talk about it, is the stuff of which effective language-facilitating environments are or should be made.

How We Got Here:
Prevalent Research
Strategies and Styles

If we are, as we think, in a particularly productive period in terms of the developing of more useful knowledge about language and language acquistion, it is of real importance to examine the basis of our being here. By analyzing the research philosophy and styles which produced today's relatively rich state of "reality" in language, perhaps we can derive some perspectives which will serve to maintain this productive state.

One of the more interesting elements revealed by an analysis of today's research is that we find ourselves on the threshold of what we think will be most productive applied programs in language as a direct result of research which has been predominantly nonmanipulative and relatively on the "basic" side of the research continuum. For example, if we examine what we have found to be the most productive and provocative pieces of the current literature, we find that many of them were based on retrospective analysis of observational data—for example, Bowerman (1973), Brown (1973), Halliday (1975), Huttenlocher (1974), and Nelson (1973a, 1974). Further, some of the most productive pieces of literature were empirically derived theoretical constructs—such as Bruner (1974/75, 1975), Luria (1974/75), Olson (1970), Dore (1975), Fillmore (1968), and MacNamara (1972). All in all it appears that we owe our current, optimistic intervention attitudes to the basic heuristic psychological research into relationships between language and cognition and into the ethology of language acquisition within mother-child assemblies.

It should be noted that this conclusion does not assume that basic psychological research is the only way that such knowledge could have been attained. It is important to note, however, that this is the reality of the situation. While we shall have more to say later about the voids which are evident because of this pattern, for now we wish to make some additional comments regarding the positive aspects of this growth.

First, attention should be called to the specific virtues of observational and ethological research which, in its inception, eschews directionality in its expected dependent measures. We do not reject directionally manipulative research, rather we support *initial*, expository observations as a constructive prelude to manipulative endeavors. The variables identified in the observational research mentioned above are unbelievably productive for generating applied experiments. Yet, many of them might never have been identified except through nondirectional observational research efforts.

Secondly, regarding the productivity of open-ended, heuristic research, we wish to reemphasize an earlier statement regarding the implications of the nature of recent psychological data on early language development. Specifically, in the chapter on the cognitive bases of language, we observed that any reductionistic theory of language requires that only the units of that system be used to describe language. In subsequent discussions of cognitive bases, it became rather clear that the units prescribed by either of the two universal accounts of language systems (the transformational and the radical behavioral) did not quantify all of the observable dimensions of the language utterances of children. Specifically, for example, the widely applied reductionistic systems have specified data units which ignore semantic relationships, as well as communicative intent in its fullest dimensions. Further, such reductionistic data units have imposed severe constraints on the perspectives directed toward any analysis of environmental facilitation of language behaviors by children.

The move from the inductive research postures generated by the reductionistic systems into the more open-ended, observational data approaches allowed the quantification units to be dictated by the behaviors and the relationships being charted. In the prevailing research up to this point, the imposition of predetermined units on children's language data had been so constraining that truly open inquiry in language was almost nonexistent. Instead, there occurred a closed system of inductive research which was, in many ways, stultifyingly narrow. It appears to us that we owe a great debt to those psychologists who ignored the momentum of both radical transformationalism and radical behaviorism and remained open in their inquiry methods and viable in their determination of appropriate quantification units.

The overall conclusion here must be a somewhat cautious one. A certain amount of selective enthusiasm seems both inevitable and, in many ways, productive, in that it will beget a heavy density of research in specific areas. What should be learned from the recent history of language research is that the scope of inquiry into important areas of human behavior should not be allowed to become constrained by theoretical cabals. While the inductive pursuit of promising theories must necessarily be encouraged, this must not be allowed to stifle or narrow the total body of ongoing inquiry in an area.

How we guarantee such scope is, of course, problematic. It requires conscientious and dedicated effort among funding sources, researchers, and research review groups to do so. However, we cannot afford repetition of the more than a decade which we have spent moving language research back into its current open state.

In summary, after analyzing how we got to today's rather optimistic state in our knowledge about language, we would simply conclude that we got here because the nature of both scientific inquiry and the professionals charged with carrying it out once again manifested the resiliency and iconoclasm which is expected of them. In a sense, they followed their inductive theories to a dead end from which they broke out into basic and eclectic strategies of inquiry which are producing new and rich bases for further pursuit.

Where We Are Not: Voids in the Research

One important aspect of the current state of knowledge about language is that an overwhelming portion of it has been generated in the past three to four years. A large portion of this new knowledge has been generated from the basic study of normal language development among young children. The opening of correlative and substantive relationships between cognition and language came from both old and new empirical observations of the language-learning products of the children of several cultures. The recognition of the important relationships between physical and social environments and the content and structure of children's language came about through empirical observations of normal, language-learning children *in situ*. Even the highly productive theoretical constructs regarding case-grammar systems, communication theory, and pragmatics are the result of the analysis of normal language systems. These latter perspectives are still somewhat suspect, because they are, at this point, primarily from an adult point of view. A review of the most recent literature, however, indicates that these adult views are being reviewed at children's levels (Bates, 1976).

Where we are not, then, is unfortunately obvious when we turn our attention to handicapped children. We have almost no data regarding any of the newer perspectives as they relate to handicapped children in general. We do not know, for example, the relationship between deficient cognitive products and language except at the grossest levels. We do not know the status of handicapped children's social ecology and how that might both reflect and affect their language-acquisition patterns. We do not know what the language acquisition of handicapped children who are learning to communicate might tell us about both language and the various types and levels of various handicapping conditions. Most certainly, we do not know what the current developmental theories about language might produce if they were to be incorporated into new, broader treatment milieus for language intervention with handicapped children. With all too few exceptions, notably MacDonald (1976), MacDonald et al. (1974), and Miller and Yoder (1972, 1974), most language programming for the handicapped is still being directed by either the polarized radical behavioral positions or the structurally directed transformational theories. While many of these programs reflect some extremely worthwhile aspects, they are still too theoretically constrained, that is, too limited in the nature and scope of both their independent and dependent variables to be considered truly adequate. In addition, existing knowledge and programming for the handicapped is still too homogenized in that they do not yet represent the qualitative differences which exist even on a normal developmental continuum.

The voids in language research among the handicapped, then, appear clear. We need additional open-ended research which will tell us more about the handicapped child's cognitive and social bases for language and communication. Then we need the application of those data in applied programs designed to provide the instrumental and responsive environments which will extend those existing cognitive and social holdings into language and communicative repertoires. It appears to us that we simply will not make it on the basis of continued product-oriented, technologically implemented attacks which are guided by the "task-analysis" of adult perceptions of the language-performance task. Rather, we must attain resonance with children's knowledge and motivation and help them construct a communicative repertoire of both appropriate content and function.

How We Got Here: Prevalent Strategies in Research

Researchers whose efforts are directed toward attaining improved and integrable behavioral repertoires among handicapped children and adults are truly on the horns of a dilemma. While the highest priorities are being placed on efforts toward implementation in the clinical field, it must be recognized that our currently available programs fail significant elements of our various targeted populations. Specifically, we seem inadequate to the task of attaining appropriate language repertoires among our population of severely language-deficient persons, be they young, preschool handicapped children or severely to profoundly retarded older persons.

Since the project on which this book is based was directed toward problems at emerging language levels, we cannot attend appropriately to the adequacy of programs and research being directed toward the populations whose language is beyond these levels—for example, the moderately retarded, learning disabled, or the sensorially deficient. In terms of the population of severely language-deficient children on which we have focused, however, we find that a continuation of product-oriented research based on old, narrow theoretical models is most certainly inadequate to the overall task. At the same time, however, we realize that the further development of the more recent knowledge bases will require a broad and sustained commitment to research at both *basic* and *applied* levels by those who are specifically charged to develop appropriate programs for the handicapped child.

We assign this dual-level responsibility to those concerned with the handicapped, because our data indicated that very little of the research which has been carried out in the most productive areas of language investigation has been with language-handicapped children. Further, it seems unlikely that many of the current trends will be extended to the handicapped at adequate levels by professionals who are not directly involved with this population. This means that individual professionals in all disciplines who are involved with the handicapped must make a concerted effort to extend the normal data regarding the sociopsycholinguistic process into its appropriate relationship with varying groups of handicapped children.

In light of the current programs available, it would appear to us that language deficiencies require a radically new classification system. This system must integrate language status with the quantitative and qualitative aspects of the cognitive and social domains and, additionally, bring it into a more specific, fine-grained relationship with so-called adaptive behavior levels. Such reorganization of our constructs can only be made possible and productive for handicapped children by the extensive analysis of the language variations among such children. In short, we must become more definitive in our considerations of language problems among the handicapped population, and such definitiveness cannot be attained unless we supplement our current knowledge base significantly. Inherent in this supplementation is some real expansion of our scope of research to include more attention to the broad process of language behavior and acquisition among both normal and handicapped children.

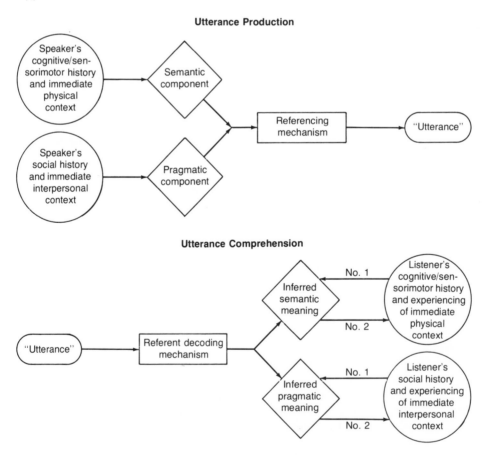

FIGURE 1. A Transactional Realization Model of Language Performance.

Recommendations for Language Research

The Psychological Dimensions of Children's Language

Obviously we cannot presume here to outline anything approaching a comprehensive program of research necessary in language. What we can do, however, is to identify the areas of research voids which are suggested by the nature of the language model which we have derived from our analysis of existing theory and research. Perhaps too, we can provide some exemplar of specific research needed in each of the various areas we identify.

The model of language acquisition we have derived suggests a language realization model as represented in Figure 1. If we consider that this schematic represents several critical areas of psychological reality which contribute to the overall realization basis of children's language, we can see that each of these areas demands full and definitive detailing and validation. It is these areas, then, from which a set of basic research needs can be most readily identified at this point. These areas include (1) the pragmatic functions of children's language, (2) the semantic bases of children's language, and (3) the referencing mechanisms of children's language. If we can extend and validate the general trends and variations in these areas, we will have made important progress in identifying the most critical dimensions of the elements which underlie a linguistic system. If, in addition, we can identify differences between the qualitative relationships among these elements which occur in the development of normal and handicapped children, we will have made important progress in identifying both the dependent and independent variables critical to language-intervention programming for severely language-deficient, handicapped children.

Pragmatic bases. As discussed in Chapter 3, the pragmatic aspects of language refer to those psychological realities that give rise to the overall purpose of any child's utterance(s) (for example, an *instrumental* function, a *regulatory* function, a *heuristic* function). The bases for the pragmatic realities of children's utterances lie in the social contexts of communicative attempts and in the social history of the individual child. The current knowledge about the pragmatics of children's language is still relatively speculative in that it is based on the categories developed from adult language (Dore, 1975) or deduced from small samples of children's language (as in Halliday, 1975). Thus there is still much research necessary to attain the definitive state required in this area. Some examples of these research needs are:

1. *The pragmatic functions of early, natural children's language.* There is a need for research which will (a) identify these functions on a more rigorous empirical basis and define them in terms of constructs which are more psychologically "real" for children's perspectives, (b) document and compare the relative frequencies of these functions among normal and deviant populations of children, (c) identify any interpopulation or intrapopulation differences in the

frequency of occurrence of various pragmatic functions, and (d) identify the possible population-specific variables which might predict or account for any observed differences.

2. *The environmental and ecological variables in differential pragmatic functioning.* There is a need for research which will identify human and physical variables which are associated or correlated with specific types of pragmatic functions in children's language—for example, what immediate or longitudinal environmental conditions might be needed to assure the instrumental function?

3. *The prelinguistic representation of pragmatic functions.* There is a need for research which will develop reliable and valid definitions of prelinguistic representations of pragmatic functions and relate these to later linguistic patterns.

Semantic bases. As we have discussed previously (Chapter 2), the identification of relatively consistent semantic relationships in the language utterances of children brought about a radical modification of our perspectives on language and language acquisition. It was the analysis of semantic content which brought us first to the point where children's language utterances could again be considered in terms more real than the abstractions of a transformational system. It was also the semantic analysis of children's language which began to reveal at least one of the possible sources of a child's language reality—namely, his cognitive holdings.

While there are considerably more data in this area than in the other areas that we are considering, there are still important research needs in this area. Some examples are:

1. *Further analysis of semantic content as it relates to cognitive styles, strategies, and developmental stages.* There is a need for research which will determine if children's semantic categories are relational, abstractional, or both. Are various semantic categories and relationships related to quantifiable cognitive dimensions or stages?

2. *Environmental and/or ecological variables reflected in semantic content.* There is a need for research which will identify both physical and human variables which are associated or correlated with specific semantic relationships—such as what manipulative or socially reciprocal experiences might be needed to assure the agentive semantic relationship.

3. *Cognitive prerequisites to semanticity.* There is a need for research which will identify those dimensions of the cognitive functions of children which are correlated with the ability to represent entities and relationships by various levels of signs.

Reinforcing mechanisms. As discussed in Chapter 2, the mechanics of communication appear to exert considerable influence on the form and structure of children's utterances. Specifically, such mechanisms involve the selection of lexical and word-order structures which will provide information about the referent to the degree necessary for its understanding by the listener. As covered in the previous discussion, the nature and form of the referencing information is determined by (1) the speaker's knowledge about the referent, (2) the speaker's assumptions about the listener's knowledge about the referent, and (3) the alternatives to the desired referent which are available to the listener.

Thus, the mechanics and cognitive bases of referencing seem to be important effectors of the specific semantic aspects of children's utterances. Yet, most of the currently available semantic categorization research generates its semantic judgments in isolation from any consideration of the referencing functions of the utterance. Just as semantic considerations proved most productive in analyzing the syntactic structures of children's utterances, it would appear that referencing considerations would be productive in analyzing the semantic structure and content of children's utterances. This is simply one other important area in which the psychological reality of children rather than adults must be pursued. Thus, there is still much research needed to attain the necessary definitive state in this overall area of communicative referencing styles and strategies among children. An example of research of this *genre* follows.

Referencing styles of normal and handicapped children. There is a need to identify the interpopulation and intrapopulation variations in referencing strategies and styles. Such work is highly correlated with the needed research in semantics and cognitive styles previously identified. In the work on referencing, however, the communication mechanics of an utterance could be utilized to analyze better the cognitive aspects of the semantic relationships expressed in children's utterances. As indicated, this work would strongly indicate the language researchers' recognition of the need to become more sensitive to and knowledgeable about children's perspectives in language and communication.

The Ethological Dimensions of Language Acquisition

The recent empirical identification and analysis of many environmental interactions which operate in natural language acquisition have radically altered and improved our knowledge of the functional variables involved in such development. In turn, these natural variables provide important information regarding potential variables (both dependent and independent) for clinical/educational intervention programs with language-deficient handicapped children.

The research needs in these areas, then, offer high potential for contributing to applied programs for the handicapped. Specifically, we identify two aspects of the child's environmental interactions which seem to offer such potential productivity and which will require further ecological and ethological research efforts: (1) the child's interactions with and within the physical environment and (2) the child's interactions with the primary figures in the environment.

Interactions with/within the physical environment. In our earlier discussion of the cognitive bases for language acquisition, we suggested that many of these bases are derived from the child's sensori-motor exploration, manipulation, and experiencing of the world of physical entities as these exist in time and space. As such, much of this model reflects strongly the constructs and theory of early cognitive development suggested by Piaget. While this theory is widely accepted in many circles, there remains much to document and quantify empirically in these constructs as they are applied to a model of language acquisition in normal and deviant populations. Further, there is a need to identify empirically the specific nature and parameters of the functional relationships which do obtain between specific environmental variables and specific behaviors of children—both verbal and nonverbal. Some examples of these needs are:

1. *Analysis of environmental variables vis-à-vis language behavior.* There is a need for research which will systematically analyze specific aspects of a child's physical environment as these are functionally related to production of specific utterance forms and to a general referencing style (for example, what is the relationship between experience in playing with manipulable vs. stable play objects and the content, structure, and pragmatics of a child's utterance?).
2. *Analysis of interpopulation environmental differences.* There is a need for research which will identify any significant differences between the nonhandicapped child and the seriously language-deficient child in terms of their physical environments and their strategies for acting upon/within those environments. Specifically, such research should focus upon those environmental variables identified as functionally related to language development and usage.

Interaction with primary figures. In Chapter 3, we concluded that the literature on early social interactions indicated that the young child's interactions with the primary figures in his social environment—specifically the primary caregiver(s)—were critical to language acquisition. We noted three broad functions of such interactions: (1) the child becomes "socialized" and learns to play the communication game through established patterns of mutual responsiveness, (2) the child learns to mark the semantic segments of the dynamic events and relationships in his world, and (3) the child masters the linguistic code through facilitating interactions with mature language users. Here again, the dynamics and parameters of these posited processes will require much additional research directed specifically at these issues. Some examples of the research needed in this area are:

1. *Preverbal communication.* There is a need for research which will (a) identify the characteristics of child-caregiver interaction patterns which are associated with the development of effective communication exchange at the preverbal level, (b) develop reliable and valid definitions of the functions and forms of preverbal communication, (c) identify any intra- and interpopulation variations and the functional relationships which may account for these, and (d) document and analyze the relationship between preverbal communication behaviors and styles and later verbal linguistic/pragmatic patterns.
2. *Behaviors of caregivers as language facilitators in natural development.* There is a need for research which will (a) empirically document the supportive function of adult action-segmenting and utterance-modification in terms of the child's language acquisition and development, (b) identify more specifically the nature of such modifications and segmenting in such a way that these could be duplicated under controlled conditions, and (c) reanalyze and examine adult consequating behaviors (such as expanding and responding to truth value) in terms of how these relate functionally to the semantics and pragmatics of preceding children's utterances and how these affect the child's subsequent behavior.

3. *Behaviors of caregivers of children with serious language delay.* There is a need for research which will compare the interactive behaviors or strategies of caregivers whose children manifest serious language delay with those whose children are nonhandicapped. Specifically, such research should focus on those variables or behaviors which have been demonstrated to be functionally related to the language-acquisition process. If such comparative research reveals that apparently critical behaviors of caregivers are absent or minimally represented in the repertoire of the handicapped child's caregiver(s), further research will be required to determine the source of this variation.

4. *Children's acquisition strategies or behaviors.* There is a need for research which will (a) document, quantify, and define the parameters of such posited children's "strategies" as selective listening, visual attending (that is, eye contact, tracking, following a line of regard) and providing feedback to a speaker, (b) identify the antecedent and/or consequent variables which control these behaviors, (c) describe the relationship between the manifestation of these behaviors and the subsequent acquisition of development of language skills, and (d) determine which, if any, of these strategic behaviors are lacking or deficient in the young language-delayed child.

Application of New Perspectives to Handicapped Populations

The relatively richer knowledge base about language and language acquisition derived from the empirical analysis of normal language development already offers many new perspectives for applied programs for severely language-delayed handicapped children. Obviously, the intervention products of these new perspectives offer important directions for modifying current intervention targets and procedures. In fact, most of the recent knowledge demands modification of current procedures. The applied research needs in this area are far too extensive to be detailed here. It must suffice to list the general characteristics we think should exemplify such experimental applied research efforts. These characteristics should include:

1. Targets/dependent variables for such research should include criterion behavioral repertoires in the other basic developmental domains demonstrated prerequisite, interactive and/or isomorphic with language acquisition. In other words, when the acquisition of language forms and functions is attained, the status of related cognitive and social behaviors should be carefully quantified.

2. Language targets for such research should include all dimensions of language utterances—not just the linguistic structures per se. For example, (a) certain pragmatic functions might be targeted in simple linguistic form and (b) communicative referencing functions might be targeted by evoking several different rudimentary referencing responses for the same entity.

3. The overall dependent variables of such experimental programming should actually represent a functional class of communicative behaviors which is understood by a child and is functional for him. This overall target is in contrast to programs for young, severely handicapped children which seek

either an abstract syntactic structure or a particular utterance which is tightly controlled by specific antecendent or consequential stimuli.

4. The independent variables of such experimental programs should better represent the ethological variables observed in natural language acquisition. Thus, such programming should manipulate variables of far greater scope than are now in general use. For example:

    a. Referents being "mapped" by targeted language structures should be represented dynamically in the intervention contexts—for example, do not just "name pictures," "talk" about something that's happening.

    b. Language targets should only be sought for referents or referent relationships which a child has indicated that he "knows" by virtue of some nonlinguistic response, such as match-to-sample, gestures, or functional use of an object.

    c. The language-intervention context should be designed to be instrumental in that it evokes and affords a high probability that children will interact with things in ways that can be "talked" about. In other words, reduce the isolated clinic room context for severely language-deficient children and create, instead, a naturally facilitating action milieu for intervention.

    d. The language-intervention context should be designed to be appropriately responsive to the language of children. In other words, wherever possible, children's utterances (both targeted and incidental) should be responded to "in kind" rather than *only* by an arbitrary, nonrelated reinforcing stimulus.

Obviously, the list of contextual variables could be extended considerably. The variables listed above and others have already been identified in our Chapter 7 on treatment implications of the transactional model.

Applied language research programs with young, seriously language-deficient children should reflect important changes from current programming. Program targets should be significantly expanded and modified. In addition, the ecology or contexts of intervention should show considerable expansion. We might even begin to entertain the possibility of finally attaining that hackneyed construct of teaching "communication."

Summary of Research Needs

The magnitude of the research needs in the area of the handicapped defy parsimony and logical constraints. In short, we need it *all*. We must have extension and validation of current basic findings relating to natural language-acquisition products and processes. In addition, we must extend these natural developmental data and constructs into comparative investigations with several types and levels of handicapped children. Then, too, we must translate the wealth of new knowledge and perspectives about language and language acquisition into experimental programs designed to enhance the language performance of handicapped children.

The latter two needs are both inherently and practically the responsibility of agencies and researchers who are charged with or who have pursued the problems of the handicapped. Even the first need is sufficiently contributive to the needs of the handicapped that it too is a legitimate concern of agencies and professionals concerned with the handicapped.

Priorities will be most difficult to establish.

chapter 9
Summary

In the preceding eight chapters of this book, we have examined both theoretical and empirical perspectives; we have considered both normal and deviant development; we have perused the literature of many fields, including linguistics, developmental psychology, psycholinguistics, speech pathology, audiology, and special education; and we have discussed the implications of all this in terms of both a model of normal language acquisition and a model for intervention aimed at the young handicapped child who manifests a significant language delay or deficit. At this point, then, to bring these many topics together, we will recapitulate the major findings and conclusions of the two-year project which preceded the writing of this book.

Normal Language Acquisition and Development

Cognitive Bases for Language Acquisition

1. Language content has its primary bases in the child's knowledge about the entities and the relationships among and between these entities in his environment. As such, then, language content represents the products of a child's processing of the sensory and social information gained through interactions within the environment. A child's language seems appropriately considered to reflect the psychological reality of the environment which he has constructed.
2. A child's language thus "maps" his existing knowledge about the objects, events, and relationships in his world.
3. The universality of many aspects of language development reflects the relative universality of experiences and, therefore, cognitive holdings of almost all very young children.

4. As a general rule, objects and activities which involve the young child in dynamic interactions or afford his manipulation are the most probable referents for early language.

5. Language development is based on two broad aspects of cognitive development (a) the achievement of such general cognitive constructs as object-permanence and symbolic functioning and (b) the attainment of specific concepts which can be "mapped" linguistically.

6. While the categories of semantic relationships (such as nonexistence) or cases (for instance, agentive) have proven much more productive than the syntactic categories such as noun-phrase and verb-phrase in our studies of children's language, we still must not assume that these adult-defined categories actually match the child's psychological reality.

7. The function of an utterance is a reflection of a child's knowledge that (a) other humans are instrumental and otherwise reinforcing and that (b) communicative acts influence and evoke such instrumental and reinforcing conditions with other humans.

8. Thus the *content*, the *function*, and the *form* of child language all reflect a child's psychological/cognitive "reality"—that is, the language utterances of children "map onto" their existing knowledge about (a) the relationships inherent in their physical world, (b) the nature and function of human, social environments, and (c) the nature and function of communication in human environments.

Social Bases for Language Acquisition

1. A critical issue in any attempt to understand the language system and its acquisition is that raised by the question *Why* do people use language? The often overlooked answer to this question is that humans communicate through language in order to regulate the actions of other humans—most often toward the attainment of cooperative or joint activities of many and various types.

2. In analyzing this social function of children's language, the language worker must avoid simplistic preconceptions regarding the nature of reinforcing consequences to language. This modified view of reinforcers does not reject current behavioral paradigms; it simply expands them in broader social terms.

3. Language function seems to have been underestimated or inadequately considered in the analysis of children's language. While it is generally accepted that children's language is communicative in function, the details and the mechanics of communication have not been sufficiently represented in current theory and application. In this regard, the functions of language to (a) establish joint or common referents and referential relationships and (b) establish joint or cooperative social routines have not been adequately treated as to their influence on both the content and the structure of children's language.

4. Language is acquired because (and only if) the child has a reason to talk. This, in turn, assumes that the child has become socialized (very possibly through

some attachment process) and has learned that he can affect the environment through the process of communication.

5. Language is first acquired as a means of achieving already existing communicative functions, and these preverbal communicative functions seem to be directly related to the functional or pragmatic aspect of later language.

6. The recent interest in the pragmatic aspect of language has resulted in productive schemata for categorizing communicative functions (for example, Halliday has suggested four functions characteristic of the earliest stage of language use—instrumental, regulatory, interactional, and personal).

7. Child language form must be viewed in terms of its function. Further, this relationship between form and function must be viewed from the child's, rather than the adult's perspective.

Language Acquisition Process

1. We cannot fully understand the products of language development if we do not understand the dynamics of the acquisition process itself.

2. Early language forms are learned as children *seek* to understand them when they are produced by mature language users in co-occurrence with referents and functions which are already within the child's cognitive and social schemata.

3. Linguistic structure is thus initially acquired through the process of decoding and comprehending incoming linguistic stimuli. At later stages of development, the processes of imitation and expansion may serve to help the child refine an emerging language system.

4. Language is learned in dynamic social interactions involving the child and the mature language users in the immediate environment. The mature language users facilitate this process through their tendency to respond appropriately to the pragmatic function of child communication, to segment and mark the components of an ongoing interaction, and to provide appropriate linguistic models.

5. The child is an active participant in this transactional process and must contribute to it a set of behaviors which allow him to benefit from the adult's facilitating behaviors.

6. The adult's linguistic contributions, which we term "facilitation strategies," include such unconscious tendencies as reduction of utterance length, reduction of utterance complexity, and frequent repetition or paraphrasing.

7. The child's participation in this process, which we term "acquisition strategies," must include both a set of interactive behaviors which enable the child to gather information about the language code (such as selective attending, establishing joint reference, and later, selective imitation) and a set of cognitive schemata for processing that information.

8. Language acquisition and development seem clearly to require a child's interactions with the environment and with the mature language users within that environment.

Linguistic Structure or
Form of Early Child Language

1. Early language seems not an innately preprogrammed system of grammar rules, but rather a complex and useful behavioral system which is the constructed product of the interactions between and among the child's cognitive, social, and communicative systems.
2. It seems that most early linguistic forms are learned first receptively as they are heard in co-occurrence with a referent which is already within the child's cognitive organizational schemata.
3. The actual roles of reception and expression in the process of language acquisition are not yet fully understood. We do know that the relationship between these modes is not simply one-to-one—that is, the first words comprehended are not necessarily the first words spoken.
4. The form/structure of an utterance reflects a child's knowledge about (a) the relationships of entities and actions in the world, (b) the functions of communicative acts in attaining joint actions among humans, and (c) the requirements of a communicative act—namely, attaining joint reference between speaker and listener (that is, a child's language utterance reflects, at once, psychological reality regarding its semantic content and its pragmatic intent and its referencing requirements).
5. The grammar of early "child language" is quite directly related to the child's meaning or semantic intent.
6. The structure of a child's utterance is determined, in part, by the nature of the relationships contained in the content of the utterance—that is, the structure of an utterance "maps" the relational attributes of its referent(s). Thus, the structure of an utterance is not independent of meaning.
7. The structure of a child's utterance seems to reflect its speaker's psychological perception of the relative values of the utterance's elements—that is, the psychological topic and the predication (or commenting) on the topic.
8. The structure of a child's utterance seems to depend primarily on word-ordering "rules" which serve to represent both the referential relationships and the psychological reality identified above.
9. The younger the child, the more idiosyncratic his language will be. As the child's language skills develop, they more closely approximate the structural norms and standards of the linguistic community.

Language Intervention for Young Handicapped Children

Implications for Assessment

1. In determining the targets for assessment of a young handicapped child who manifests significant language delay or deficit, the teacher/therapist must consider not only receptive and expressive linguistic abilities, but also the child's cognitive and social bases for language development.

2. The relative emphasis and specific targets to be assessed within each of these four areas (cognitive, social, receptive, and expressive) will vary in accordance with the nature and degree of language delay or deficit exhibited by the child.

3. The procedures and contexts for assessment should be designed to provide clinically useful (prescriptive) data and to assess the child's true ability to perform the targeted task(s) in a functional or natural situation.

4. A review of existing instruments revealed that many popular language tests would be appropriate for initial screening or identification of children with significant language delays or deficits, but that relatively few yield prescriptive data—particularly for the very early stages of development which have been the focus of this book.

5. Because of the number of assessment targets for which no appropriate published instrument could be identified, as well as the number of targets which, by their very nature, require individually designed assessment procedures and contexts, an observational approach to assessment was recommended for many target areas.

6. Two general types of observational or informal assessment were recommended and described: (a) observation of nonverbal behaviors, including observation of the child's natural environment and interactions within that environment and (b) the collection and analysis of language sample data.

Implications for Treatment

1. Language-intervention programs for young, significantly language-deficient children which apply only the dependent and independent variables suggested by either transformational grammar systems or radical behavioral modification systems appear inadequate to the task of attaining productive language repertoires for such children.

2. Language-intervention programs which would attain adequacy with such children must, instead, apply variables derived from theoretical language models which include consideration of a child's cognitive functions and holdings, social functions, and both the physical and human elements and functions in the intervention environment.

3. Language-intervention programs for such children must target the development of expanded cognitive bases for language and specific language targets which represent semantic/linguistic "maps" of the child's demonstrated existing cognitive holdings.

4. Similarly, the treatment program for many severely language-delayed or deficient young children will need to target the expansion of social-interaction repertoires and the development of preverbal communication exchange rituals which can later be mapped linguistically.

5. In designing treatment programs for verbal children, the clinician/teacher must target not only a broad and generative repertoire of linguistic structures, but also—and primarily—a full and functional repertoire of semantic relationships or meanings and pragmatic functions or intents.

6. In the light of the multidimensional and pervasive nature of the language-intervention model suggested here, it is unrealistic to expect such treatment to

be implemented effectively through short, infrequent, and isolated language-training sessions. Rather, such treatment must be generated and implemented in all contexts in which the child has natural opportunities for interaction and communication.

7. A review of existing treatment programs revealed a few which are consonant with some of the implication of this model—particularly for verbal children whose deficits are primarily in the area of linguistic structure or even semantic mapping. However, for the nonverbal child with deficient social and cognitive bases for language, no existing programs were identified which would be consistent with the intervention model described in this book.

8. Language-intervention programs for handicapped children must be designed to reflect the ethological and transactional variables of normal language development and the child-perspective orientation inherent in that process.

A Final Note: The Need for Further Research

We would like to conclude this book on a note of cautious optimism. We are optimistic because we believe that the new perspectives set forth in this book and made possible by recent theoretical and empirical advances in several fields of study offer real promise for greatly improving the effectiveness of programs available to young handicapped children with significant language deficits. We have just glimpsed the potential productivity of these perspectives through our own pilot work with a handful of young developmentally delayed and autistic children during the past two years. We are further encouraged by the enthusiastic reception these perspectives have received each time we have presented them to clinicians and teachers in the field who work with this population and who have been frustrated by the inadequacy of existing programs and procedures to effect change in many of these children.

Finally, however, we must emphasize that we are also cautious in our enthusiasm. Much research is still needed to better our understanding of the dynamics of the transactional processes which lead to the successful acquisition of a functional language system. As such research is completed, we are certain that many of the perspectives and conclusions presented will need to be revised, as well as refined and extended. At the time of this writing, the relationship of semantics to cognitive development is only beginning to be understood; while the relationship of pragmatics to a child's overall pattern of social development and interaction has yet to be subjected to any direct empirical study. How all of these interlocking aspects of early development interface with each other and how they are realized in the form and function of one child's emergent language is a question which will demand the most creative and rigorous research efforts which can be mustered. Similarly, the actual translation, refinement, and validation of the intervention model suggested in this book will demand a major investment of clinical expertise and direct experience coupled with an intellectual commitment to the developmental perspectives reflected in this model and an adherence to the strictest principles of rigorous and reliable research design.

This, then, is our final note of caution: to the extent that these challenges for future research are met, and *only to that extent*, can we expect that the full potential of these new perspectives will be ultimately realized in the form of improved language-intervention programs for young handicapped children.

appendix

Language Sample Data

Suggested Forms and Procedures for Transcription and Analysis

Suggested Format for Two-column Transcription of Language Sample

Child's name:_____ Adult with child:_____ Page __ of __ pages

Date:_____ Setting:_____ Analyzed by:_____

Utt. No.	Context	Child's Utterance

Suggested Format for Three-column Transcription of Language-sample Data

Child's Name:_____ Adult with child:_____ Page___ of___ pages

Date:_____ Setting:_____ Analyzed by:_____

Utt. No.	Antedecent context (*=see consequence of preceding utterance)	Child's utterance	Consequent event(s) (occurring within 5 sec. after child's utterance)

Suggested Format for Semantic Analysis of Language-sample Data: Primarily Single-word Utterances

Child's name: _____   Date collected: _____   Analyzed by: _____   Page ___ of ___ pages

Total number of utterances: ___   (I): Produced in imitation   (R): Produced in response to adult prompt or question

Existence (e.g., "there" or "label")	Recurrence (e.g., "more")	Disappearance (e.g., "away," "all gone")	Nonexistence (e.g., "no")	Cessation (e.g., "stop")	Rejection (e.g., "no")	Action (e.g., "up")	Location (e.g., "up," "chair")

Suggested Format for Semantic Analysis of Language-sample Data: Multi-word Utterances (Section 1)

Child's name: _____ Date collected: _____ Analyzed by: _____ Page ___ of ___ pages

Total number of utterances: ___ (I): Produced in imitation of adult; (R): Produced in direct response to adult prompt or question

Relationship components	Action			Location				
	Agent	Action	Object	Agent	Action	Entity/object	Location	
Two-word grammatical								
Three+ word grammatical								
Nongrammatical and one-word utterances								

Suggested Format for Semantic Analysis of Language-sample Data: Multi-word Utterances (Section II)

Page___ of ___ Pages

Relationship components	Demonstrative		Attribute			Possession (Possesses + possession)	Conjunction (noun + noun)
	Nomination ("that," etc. + n)	*Notice* ("hi," etc. + n)	*Recurrence* (verb + "more"; "more" + noun)	*Nonexistent* ("allgone," etc. + noun)	*Attribute* (adjective + noun)		
Two-word grammatical							
Three ⁺ word grammatical							
Nongrammatical and one-word utterances							

261

Suggested Format for Pragmatic Analysis of Language-sample Data

Child's name: _____ Date collected: _____ Analyzed by: _____ Page ___ of ___ pages

Person interacted with: _____ Total number of utterances: _____

"Utterance"	Type I Functions							Type II Functions						
	Regulatory			Acquire infor- mation	Metalin- guistic	Give infor- mation to listener	Labeling	Imitation	Answering	Initiate/ terminate social	Entertainment	Other		
	Instru- mental	Protest	Request											
TOTAL														
% of all utterances														

Suggested Format for Linguistic Structure Analysis*

Child's name: _____ Date collected: _____ Analyzed by: _____ Page ___ of ___ Pages

⊞ form is obligatory or optional and present ⊡ form is obligatory and not present ⊠ form is incorrectly used
(*Categories derived from Brown's [1973] list of 14 grammatical morphemes)

Utterance	Present progressive -ing	Preposition in	Preposition on	Plural (regular) -s	Past-irregular (came, ran, etc.)	Possessive -'s	Uncontractible copula is, am, are	Articles a, the	Past regular -d, -ed, -/t/	3rd person—irregular (e.g. does, has)	3rd person—regular -s /-/z/ (e.g. runs)	Uncontractible auxiliary (e.g. are running)	Contractible copula 's, 'm, 're (she's pretty)	Contractible auxiliary 's, 'm, 're (she's running)

(Continue on additional pages)

% correct $\left(\dfrac{\Sigma \; \boxplus}{\Sigma \boxplus + \boxdot + \boxtimes} \right)$ (compute on last page for total sample)

263

Suggested Guidelines for Clinical Computation of
Mean Length of Utterance (MLU) in *Words*

1. Transcribe language sample and count total number of utterances.
2. For MLU computation, you should have between 50 and 100 utterances.
3. If enough utterances were collected, approximately the first 10 utterances should be discounted.
4. Count the total number of single words in the sample. In counting words:
    a. Do not count fillers such as "ummm," "uh," and so on.
    b. Count as single words any compound, inflected, or contracted words.
    c. Count as single words any connected words pronounced by the child with a single-word inflectional pattern (e.g., "Winnie-the-Pooh"), unless the child also produces the single components of the phrase separately.
5. Compute the MLU as: $\dfrac{\text{Total no. of single words}}{\text{Total no. of utterances}}$
6. If the language sample included a large percentage of utterances which contained nonintelligible words or direct imitations of adult utterances, compute a separate MLU for the language sample with and without these utterances.

References

Ainsworth, M. D. S., & Bell, S. M. Attachment, exploration and separation: Illustrated by the behavior of one-year-olds in a strange situation. *Child Development,* 1970, *41,* 49–67.

Ainsworth, M. D. S., Bell, S. M., & Stayton, D. J. Infant-mother attachment and social development: "Socialisation" as a product of reciprocal responsiveness to signals. In M. P. M. Richards (Ed.), *The integration of a child into a social world.* London: Cambridge University Press, 1974.

Anglin, J. The child's first terms of reference. In S. Erlich & E. Tulving (Eds.), Special issue of the *Bulletin de Psychologie on Semantic Memory,* 1975.

Austin, J. L. *How to do things with words.* London: Oxford University Press, 1962.

Baldwin, C. P. Comparison of mother-child interactions at different ages, and in families of different educational levels and ethnic backgrounds. Paper presented at the biennial meeting of the Society for Research in Child Development, Philadelphia, 1973.

Bandura, A. Modeling theory: Some traditions, trends and disputes. In R. D. Parke (Ed.), *Recent trends in social learning theory.* New York: Academic Press, 1972.

Bangs, T. E. *Language and learning disorders of the pre-academic child.* New York: Appleton-Century-Crofts, 1968.

Bates, E. *Language and context.* New York: Academic Press, 1976.

Bateson, M. C. The interpersonal context of infant vocalizations. Quarterly Progress Report, Research Laboratory of Electronics, Massachusetts Institute of Technology, January 15, 1971, No. 100, 170–76.

Bayley, N. *Bayley Scales of Infant Development.* New York: The Psychological Corporation, 1969.

Bell, S. M., & Ainsworth, M. D. S. Infant crying and maternal responsiveness. *Child Development,* 1972, *43,* 1171–90.

Bellugi, U. The development of interrogative structures in children's speech. In K. Riegel (Ed.), *The development of language functions.* University of Michigan Language Development Program, Report No. 8, 1965, 103–38.

Bereiter, C., & Englemann, S. (Eds.). *Teaching disadvantaged children in the preschool.* Englewood Cliffs, N.J.: Prentice-Hall, Inc., 1966.

Berger, S. L. A clinical program for developing multimodal language responses with atypical deaf children. In J. E. McLean, D. E. Yoder, & R. L. Schiefelbusch (Eds.), *Language intervention with the retarded: Developing strategies.* Baltimore: University Park Press, 1972.

Bing, E. Effect of childrearing practices on development of differential cognitive abilities. *Child Development,* 1963, *34,* 631–48.

Blank, M. Cognitive functions of language in the preschool years. *Developmental Psychology,* 1974, *10,* 229–45.

Bliss, C. K. *Semantography.* Sydney, Australia: Semantography Publications, 1965.

Bloom, B. S. *Compensatory education for cultural deprivation.* New York: Holt, Rinehart & Winston, 1964.

Bloom, L. *Language development: Form and function in emerging grammars.* Cambridge: M.I.T. Press, 1970.

Bloom, L. *One word at a time: The use of single word utterances before syntax.* The Hague: Mouton, 1973.

Bloom, L. Talking, understanding, and thinking. In. R. L. Schiefelbusch & L. L. Lloyd (Eds.), *Language perspectives: Acquisition, retardation and intervention.* Baltimore: University Park Press, 1974.

Bloom, L., Hood, L., & Lightbown, P. Imitation in language development: If, when and why. *Cognitive Psychology,* 1974, *6,* 380–420.

Bloom, L., Lightbown, P., & Hood, L. Structure and variation in child language. *Monographs of the Society for Research in Child Development,* 1975, *40,* No. 2.

Bowerman, M. F. *Learning to talk: A cross-linguistic comparison of early syntactic development, with special reference to Finnish.* London: Cambridge University Press, 1973a.

Bowerman, M. F. Structural relationships in children's utterances: Syntactic or semantic? In T. E. Moore (Ed.), *Cognitive development and the acquisition of language.* New York: Academic Press, 1973b.

Bowerman, M. F. Discussion summary: Development of concepts underlying language. In R. L. Schiefelbusch & L. L. Lloyd (Eds.), *Language perspectives: Acquisition, retardation and intervention.* Baltimore: University Park Press, 1974.

Bowlby, J. The nature of the child's tie to his mother. *International Journal of Psychoanalysis,* 1958, *39,* 350–73.

Bowlby, J. *Attachment and loss: Volume I. Attachment.* London: Hogarth Press, 1969.

Braine, M. On learning the grammatical order of words. *Psychological Review,* 1963, *70,* 323–48.

Braine, M. D. S. Children's first word combinations. *Monographs of the Society for Research in Child Development,* 1976, No. 164.

Bricker, W. A systematic approach to language training. In R. L. Schiefelbusch (Ed.), *Language of the Mentally Retarded.* Baltimore: University Park Press, 1972.

Bricker, W., & Bricker, D. A program of language training for the severely handicapped child. *Exceptional Children,* 1970, *37,* 101–11.

Bricker, W., & Bricker, D. An early language training strategy. In R. L. Schiefelbusch & L. L. Lloyd (Eds.), *Language perspectives: Acquisition, retardation and intervention.* Baltimore: University Park Press, 1974.

Bricker, D., Dennison, L., & Bricker, W. A language intervention program for developmentally young children. *MCCD Monograph Series,* No. 1, Mailman Center for Child Development, University of Miami, 1976.

Bricker, D., Dennison, L., Watson, L., & Vincent-Smith, L. Language training program for young developmentally delayed children: Vol. 2. Training in the basic actor-action-object proposition. *IMRID Behavioral Science Monograph No. 22,* Institute on Mental Retardation and Intellectual Development, George Peabody College, Nashville, 1973.

Broen, P. A. The verbal environment of the language learning child. *Monographs of the American Speech and Hearing Association,* 1972, *17.*

Brown, L. Personal communication, October 1976.

Brown, R. *Words and things.* New York: Academic Press, 1958.

Brown, R. *Social psychology.* New York: The Free Press, 1965.

Brown, R. *A first language: The early stages.* Cambridge: Harvard University Press, 1973.

Brown, R., & Bellugi, U. Three processes in the child's acquisition of syntax. *Harvard Educational Review,* 1964, *34,* 133–51.

Brown, R., Cazden, C., & Bellugi-Klima, U. The child's grammar from I-II. In J. P. Hill (Ed.), *The Minnesota Symposium on Child Psychology,* Vol. 2. Minneapolis: University of Minnesota Press, 1969.

Brown, R., & Fraser, C. The acquisition of syntax. *Monographs of the Society for Research in Child Development,* 1964, *29,* 43–78.

Brown, R., & Hanlon, C. Derivational complexity and order of acquisition in child speech. In J. R. Hayes (Ed.), *Cognition and the development of language.* New York: John Wiley, 1970.

Bruner, J. S. The growth and structure of skill. In K. J. Connally (Ed.), *Mechanisms of motor skill development.* New York: Academic Press, 1970.

Bruner, J. S. Volition, skill and tools. In L. J. Stone, H. T. Smith, & L. B. Murphy (Eds.), *The competent infant: Research and commentary.* New York: Basic Books, 1973.

Bruner, J. S. From communication to language—A psychological perspective. *Cognition,* 1974/75, *3,* 255–87.

Bruner, J. S. The ontogenesis of speech acts. *Journal of Child Language,* 1975, *2,* 1–19.

Buddenhagen, R. G. *Establishing vocal verbalizations in mute mongoloid children.* Champaign, Ill. Research Press, 1971.

Carrier, J. Application of functional analysis and a nonspeech response mode to teaching language. *American Speech and Hearing Monograph No. 18,* Washington, D.C., 1974.

Carrier, J. Application of a nonspeech language system with the severely handicapped. In L. Lloyd (Ed.), *Communication assessment and intervention strategies.* Baltimore: University Park Press, 1976.

Carrier, J. K., Jr., & Peak, T. J. *Non-Speech Language Initiation Program (Non-SLIP).* Lawrence, Kans.: H & H Enterprises, 1975.

Carrow, Sister M. A. The development of auditory comprehension of language structure in children. *Journal of Speech and Hearing Disorders,* 1968, *33,* 99–112.

Cassirer, E. *Structure and function and Einstein's theory of relativity.* (trans. by W. C. Swaby and M. C. Swaby). New York: Dover Publications, 1953. (Originally published, Chicago: Open Court Publication, 1923.)

Cazden, C. Environmental assistance to the child's acquisition of grammar. Unpublished doctoral dissertation, Graduate School of Education, Harvard University, 1965.

Chafe, W. L. *Meaning and the structure of language.* Chicago: University of Chicago Press, 1970.

Chapman, R. S., & Miller, J. F. Word order in early two and three word utterances: Does production precede comprehension? *Journal of Speech and Hearing Research,* 1975, *18,* 355–71.

Chomsky, N. *Syntactic structures.* The Hague: Mouton, 1957.

Chomsky, N. *Aspects of the theory of syntax.* Cambridge: M.I.T. Press, 1965.

Clark, E. V. What's in a word? On the child's acquisition of semantics in his first language. In T. E. Moore (Ed.), *Cognitive development and the acquisition of language.* New York: Academic Press, 1973.

Clarke-Stewart, K. A. Interactions between mothers and their young children: Characteristics and consequences. *Monographs of the Society for Research in Child Development,* 1973, *38.*

Collis, G. M., & Schaffer, H. R. Synchronization of visual attention in mother-infant pairs. *Journal of Child Psychology and Psychiatry,* 1975, *16,* 315–320.

Dale, P. S. *Language development: Structure and function.* Hinsdale, Ill.: Dryden Press, 1972.

DeLaguna, G. A. *Speech: Its function and development.* Bloomington, Ind.: University Press (first published 1927), 1963.

Dore, J. Holophrases, speech acts and language universals. *Journal of Child Language,* 1975, *2,* 21–40.

Eimas, P. D. Linguistic processing of speech by young infants. In R. L. Schiefelbusch & L. L. Lloyd (Eds), *Language perspectives: Acquisition, retardation and intervention.* Baltimore: University Park Press, 1974.

Eimas, P. D., Siqueland, E. R., Jusczyk, P., & Vigorito, J. Speech perception in infants. *Science,* 1971, *171,* 303–306.

Ervin-Tripp, S. An overview of theories of grammatical development. In D. Slobin (Ed.), *The ontogenesis of grammar: A theoretical symposium.* New York: Academic Press, 1971.

Escalona, S. K. Basic modes of social interaction: Their emergence and patterning during the first two years of life. *Merrill-Palmer Quarterly of Behavior and Development,* 1973, *19,* No. 3.

Fernald, C. Control of grammar in imitation, comprehension and production: Problems of replication. *Journal of Verbal Learning and Verbal Behavior,* 1972, *11,* 606–13.

Fillmore, C. The case for case. In E. Bach & R. T. Harms (Eds.), *Universals in linguistic theory.* New York: Holt, Rinehart & Winston, 1968.

Fisichelli, V. R., & Karelitz, S. The cry latencies of normal infants and those with brain damage. *Journal of Pediatrics,* 1963, *62,* 724–34.

Flavell, J. H. *The developmental psychology of Jean Piaget.* Princeton: D. Van Nostrand, 1963.

Fraser, C., Bellugi, U., & Brown, R. Control of grammar in imitation, comprehension and production. *Journal of Verbal Learning and Verbal Behavior,* 1963, *2,* 121–35.

Friedlander, B. The effect of speaker identity, inflection, vocabulary and message redundancy on infants' selection of vocal reinforcers. Paper presented at meeting of the Society for Research in Child Development, New York, March 1967.

Friedlander, B. Z. The effect of speaker identity, voice inflection, vocabulary and message redundancy on infants' selection of vocal reinforcement. *Journal of Experimental Child Psychology,* 1968, *6.* 443–59.

Friedlander, B. Z., Jacobs, A. C., Davis, B. B., & Wetstone, H. S. Time-sampling analysis of infants' natural language environments in the home. *Child Development,* 1972, *43,* 730–40.

Goldberg, S., & Lewis, M. Play behavior in the year-old infant: Early sex differences. *Child Development,* 1969, *40,* 21–32.

Gordon, T. J. Early child stimulation through parent education. A final report to the Children's Bureau, U.S. Department of Health, Education & Welfare, June 1969.

Gray, B., & Ryan, B. *A language program for the nonlanguage child.* Champaign, Ill.: Research Press, 1973.

Greenberg, J. H. Some universals of grammar with particular reference to the order of meaningful elements. In J. H. Greenberg (Ed.), *Universals of language.* Cambridge: M.I.T. Press, 1963.

Greenfield, P., & Smith, J. *The structure of communication in early language development.* New York: Academic Press, 1976.

Greenman, G. W. Visual behavior of newborn infants. In A. J. Solnit & S. A. Provence (Eds.), *Modern perspectives in child development.* New York: Hallmark, 1963.

Guess, D. A functional analysis of receptive language and productive speech: Acquisition of the plural morpheme. *Journal of Applied Behavior Analysis,* 1969, *2,* 55–64.

Guess, D., & Baer, D. M. An analysis of individual differences in generalization between receptive and productive language in retarded children. *Journal of Applied Behavior Analysis,* 1973, *6,* 311–29.

Guess, D., Sailor, W., & Baer, D. To teach language to retarded chidlren. In R. L. Schiefel-busch & L. L. Lloyd (Eds.), *Language perspectives: Acquisition, retardation and inter-vention.* Baltimore: University Park Press, 1974.

Guess, D., Sailor, W., Keogh, W. J., & Baer, D. M. Language development programs for severely handicapped children. In N. Haring, E. Sontag, & L. Brown (Eds.), *Teaching severely and profoundly multihandicapped children.* New York: Grune & Stratton, 1975.

Guillaume, P. Les debuts de la phrase dans le language de l'enfant. *Journal of Psychology,* 1927, *24,* 1–25.

Halliday, M. Learning how to mean. In E. Lenneberg & E. Lenneberg (Eds.), *Foundations of language development: A multi-disciplinary approach, Vol. I.* New York: Academic Press, 1975.

Holland, J., & Skinner, B. F. *Analysis of behavior.* New York: McGraw-Hill, 1961.

Horstmeier, D., MacDonald, J. D. and Gillette, Y. *Ready, Set, Go — Talk to Me!* Columbus: Nisonger Center, The Ohio State University, 1975.

Hunt, J. McV. *Intelligence and experience.* New York: Ronald Press, 1961.

Hunt, J. McV. Intrinsic motivation and its role in psychological development. In D. Levine (Ed.), *Nebraska Symposium on Motivation.* Lincoln: University of Nebraska Press, 1965.

Huttenlocher, J. The origins of language comprehension. In R. Solso (Ed.), *Theories in cognitive psychology.* New York: Halsted Press, 1974.

Ingram, D. Transitivity in child language. *Language,* 1971, *47,* 888–910.

Irwin, O. C. Infant speech: Effects of systematic reading of stories. *Journal of Speech and Hearing Research,* 1960, *3,* 187–90.

Jacklin, C. N., Maccoby, E. E., & Dick, A. E. Barrier behavior and toy preference: Sex differences (and their absence) in the year-old child. *Child Development,* 1973, *44,* 196–200.

Kagan, J. *Change and continuity in infancy.* New York: Wiley, 1971.

Kagan, J., & Lewis, M. Studies of attention. *Merrill-Palmer Quarterly of Behavior Development,* 1965, *4,* 95–127.

Kaplan, E. L. The role of intonation in the acquisition of language. Unpublished Ph.D. thesis, Cornell University, 1969.

Kaplan, E. L., & Kaplan, G. A. The prelinguistic child. In J. Elliot (Ed.), *Human development and cognitive processes*. New York: Holt, Rinehart & Winston, 1970.

Kendon, A. Some functions of gaze-direction in social interaction. *Acta Psychologica*, 1967, *26*, 22–63.

Kent, L. *Language acquisition program for the severely retarded*. Champaign, Ill.: Research Press, 1974.

Kent, L. (with Klein, D., Falk, A., & Guenther, H.) A language acquisition program for the retarded. In J. McLean, D. Yoder, & R. Schiefelbusch (Eds.), *Language intervention with the retarded*. Baltimore: University Park Press, 1972.

Leonard, L. B. The role of nonlinguistic stimuli and semantic relations in children's acquisition of grammatical utterances. *Journal of Experimental Child Psychology*, 1975, *19*, 346–57.

Leopold, W. *Speech development of a bilingual child*. Evanston, Ill.: Northwestern University Press, 1939.

Leopold, W. Semantic learning in infant language. *Word*, 1948, *4*, 173–80.

Leopold, W. *Speech development of a bilingual child: A linguist's record. Volume III*. Evanston, Ill.: Northwestern University Press, 1949.

Lewis, M. *Infant speech, a study of the beginnings of language*. New York: Harcourt Brace Jovanovich, 1936 (republished, New York: Humanities Press, 1951).

Lewis, M., & Freedle, R. Mother-infant dyad: The cradle of meaning. Paper presented at a symposium on "Language and Thought: Communication and Affect." Erindale College, University of Toronto, March, 1972.

Ling, D. *Speech and the hearing-impaired child: Theory and practice*. Washington, D.C.: Alexander Graham Bell Association for the Deaf, 1976.

Ling, D., & Ling, A. H. Communication development in the first three years of life. *Journal of Speech and Hearing Disorders*, 1974, *17*, 146–59.

Lloyd, L. L. (Ed.) *Communication assessment and intervention strategies*. Baltimore: University Park Press, 1976.

Longhurst, T., & Reichle, J. The applied communication game: A comment on Muma's "Communication game: Dump and play." *Journal of Speech and Hearing Disorders*, 1975, *40*, 315–19.

Lovell, K., & Dixon, E. The growth of the control of grammar in imitation, comprehension, and production. *Journal of Child Psychology and Psychiatry*, 1967, *8*, 31–39.

Luria, A. Scientific perspectives and philosophical dead ends in modern linguistics. *Cognition*, 1974/75, *3*, 377–85.

MacDonald, J. D. Environmental language intervention: Programs for establishing initial communication in handicapped children. In F. Withrow & C. Nygren (Eds.), *Language and the handicapped learner: Curricula, programs and media*. Columbus: Merrill, 1976.

MacDonald, J. D., & Blott, J. P. Environmental language intervention: A rationale for diagnostic and training strategy through rules, context and generalization. *Journal of Speech and Hearing Disorders*, 1974, *39*, 244–56.

MacDonald, J. D., Blott, J. P., Gordon, K., Spiegel, B., & Hartmann, M. C. An experimental parent-assisted treatment program for preschool language delayed children. *Journal of Speech and Hearing Disorders*, 1974, *39*, 395–415.

MacDonald, J. D., & Nickols, M. *Environmental language inventory manual*. Columbus: The Ohio State University, 1974.

MacNamara, J. Cognitive basis of language learning in infants. *Psychological Review*, 1972, *79*, 1–13.

Mahoney, G. An ethological approach to delayed language acquisition. *American Journal of Mental Deficiency,* 1975, *80,* 139–48.

Marshall, M. R., & Hegrenes, J. R. A communication therapy model for cognitively disorganized children. In J. E. McLean, D. E. Yoder, & R. L. Schiefelbusch (Eds.), *Language intervention with the retarded: Developing strategies.* Baltimore: University Park Press, 1972.

Mason, W. A. Environmental models and mental modes: Representational processes in the Great Apes and man. *American Psychologist,* April, 1976, 284–94.

Mason, W. A., Davenport, R. K., & Menzel, E. W. Early experience and social development of rhesus monkeys and chimpanzees. In G. Newton & S. Levine (Eds.), *Early experience and behavior.* New York: Thomas, 1968.

Matheny, A. P., Dolan, A. B., & Wilson, R. S. Bayley's infant behavior record: Relations between behaviors and mental test scores. *Developmental Psychology,* 1974, *10,* 696.

McCall, R. B. Exploratory manipulation and play in the human infant. *Monographs of the Society for Research in Child Development,* 1974, *39.*

McLean, J. E. Introduction: Developing clinical strategies for language intervention with mentally retarded children. In J. E. McLean, D. E. Yoder, & R. L. Schiefelbusch (Eds.), *Language intervention with the retarded: Developing strategies.* Baltimore: University Park Press, 1972.

McLean, J. E. Articulation. In L. L. Lloyd (Ed.), *Communication assessment and intervention strategies.* Baltimore: University Park Press, 1976.

McLean, J. E. Implications of language research for changing perspectives in special education. In R. D. Kneedler & S. G. Tarver (Eds.), *Changing perspectives in special education.* Columbus: Merrill, 1977.

McNeill, D. *The acquisition of language: The study of developmental psycholinguistics.* New York: Harper & Row, 1970.

McNeill, D. The capacity for the ontogenesis of grammar. In D. I. Slobin (Ed.), *The ontogenesis of grammar.* New York: Academic Press, 1971.

Meadow (Goldin-Meadow); S., Seligman, M. E. P., & Gelman, R. Language in the two-year-old. *Cognition,* 1976, *4,* 189–202.

Menyuk, P. *Sentences children use.* Cambridge: M.I.T. Press, 1969.

Menyuk, P. Early development of receptive language: From babbling to words. In R. L. Schiefelbusch & L. L. Lloyd (Eds.), *Language perspectives: Acquisition, retardation and intervention.* Baltimore: University Park Press, 1974.

Miller, J., & Yoder, D. A syntax teaching program. In J. McLean, D. Yoder, & R. Schiefelbusch (Eds.), *Language intervention with the retarded.* Baltimore: University Park Press, 1972.

Miller, J. & Yoder, D. An ontogenetic language teaching strategy for retarded children. In R. L. Schiefelbusch & L. L. Lloyd (eds.), *Language perspectives: Acquisition, retardation and intervention.* Baltimore: University Park Press, 1974.

Milner, E. A study of the relationship between reading readiness in grade one children and patterns of parent-child interaction. *Child Development,* 1951, *22,* 95–112.

Moffitt, A. R. Consonant cue perception by twenty to twenty-four week old infants. *Child Development,* 1971, *42,* 717–31.

Morehead, D. M., & Morehead, A. A Piagetian view of thought and language during the first two years. In R. L. Schiefelbusch & L. L. Lloyd (Eds.), *Language perspectives: Acquisition, retardation and intervention.* Baltimore: University Park Press, 1974.

Morse, P. A. The discrimination of speech and non-speech stimuli in early infancy. *Journal of Experimental Child Psychology,* 1972, *14,* 477–92.

Muma, J. The communication game: Dump and play. *Journal of Speech and Hearing Disorders,* 1975, *40,* 296–309.

Murphy, L. B. Development in the first year of life: Ego and drive development in relation to the mother-infant tie. In L. J. Stone, H. T. Smith, & L. B. Murphy (Eds.), *The competent infant: Research and commentary.* New York: Basic Books, 1973.

Nakazima, S. A. A comparative study of the speech developments of Japanese and American English in childhood. *Studies in Phonology,* 1962, *2,* 27–39.

Nelson, K. Structure and strategy in learning to talk. *Monographs of the Society for Research in Child Development,* 1973a, *38,* No. 149.

Nelson, K. Some evidence for the cognitive primacy of categorization and its functional basis. *Merrill-Palmer Quarterly of Behavior and Development,* 1973b, *19,* 21–39.

Nelson, K. Concept, word and sentence: Interrelations in acquisition and development. *Psychological Review,* 1974, *81,* 267–85.

Nelson, K. E., & Bonvillian, J. D. Concepts and words in the 18-month old: Acquiring concept names under controlled conditions. *Cognition,* 1974, *2,* 435–50.

Olson, D. Language and thought: Aspects of a cognitive theory of semantics. *Psychological Review,* 1970, *77,* 257–73.

Phillips, J. R. Syntax and vocabulary of mothers' speech to young children: Age and sex comparisons. *Child Development,* 1973, *44,* 182–85.

Piaget, J. *The origins of intelligence in children.* New York: Norton, 1952.

Piaget, J. *The construction of reality in the child.* New York: Basic Books, 1954.

Piaget, J. *Play, dreams, and imitation.* (trans. by C. Gattegno and F. M. Hodgson) New York: Norton, 1962.

Piaget, J. *The language and thought of the child.* New York: World Publishing Co. 1971.

Premack, D. A functional analysis of language. *Journal of the Experimental Analysis of Behavior,* 1970, *14,* 107–125.

Premack, D. *On the assessment of language competence in the chimpanzee: Behavior of non-human primates.* New York: Academic Press, 1971.

Richards, M. P. M. First steps in becoming social. In M. P. M. Richards (Ed.), *The integration of a child into a social world.* London: Cambridge University Press, 1974.

Ruder, K. F., & Smith, M. D. Issues in language training. In R. L. Schiefelbusch & L. L. Lloyd (Eds.), *Language perspectives: Acquisition, retardation and intervention.* Baltimore: University Park Press, 1974.

Ryan, J. Early language development: Towards a communicational analysis. In M. P. M. Richards (Ed.), *The integration of a child into a social world.* London: Cambridge University Press, 1974.

Sackett, G. P. Manipulatory behavior in monkeys reared under different levels of early stimulus variation. *Perceptual and Motor Skills,* 1965, *20,* 985–88.

Schaefer, E. S., Furley, P. H., & Harte, T. J. Infant education research projects, Washington, D.C. In *Preschool Programs in Compensatory Education* (No. 1). Washington, D.C.: Government Printing Office, 1968.

Schaffer, H. R. *The growth of sociability.* Baltimore: Penguin Press, 1971.

Schlesinger, I. M. Production of utterances and language acquisition. In D. Slobin (Ed.), *The ontogenesis of grammar.* New York: Academic Press, 1971.

Schlesinger, I. M. Relational concepts underlying language. In R. L. Schiefelbusch & L. L. Lloyd (Eds.), *Language perspectives: Acquisition, retardation and intervention.* Baltimore: University Park Press, 1974.

Schmidt, R., & Erikson, M. T. Early predictors of mental retardation. *Mental Retardation,* 1973, *11,* 27–29.

Shatz, M., & Gelman, R. The development of communication skills: Modifications in the speech of young children as a function of listener. *Monographs of the Society for Research in Child Development,* 1973, *38* (No. 152).

Shipley, E. F., Smith, C. S., & Gleitman, L. R. A study in the acquisition of language: Free responses to commands. *Language,* 1969, *45,* 322–42.

Siegel, G. M., & Harkins, J. P. Verbal behavior of adults in two conditions with institutionalized retarded children. *Journal of Speech and Hearing Disorders, Monograph Supplement,* 1963, *10,* 39–46.

Sinclair-deZwart, H. Developmental psycholinguistics. In D. Elkind & J. Flavell (Eds.), *Studies in cognitive development: Essays in honor of Jean Piaget.* New York: Oxford University Press, 1969.

Sinclair-deZwart, H. Sensori-motor action patterns as a condition for the acquisition of syntax. In R. Huxley & E. Ingram (Eds.), *Language acquisition: Models and methods.* New York: Academic Press, 1971.

Sinclair-deZwart, H. Language acquisition and cognitive development. In T. E. Moore (Ed.), *Cognitive development and the acquisition of language.* New York: Academic Press, 1973.

Skinner, B. F. *Science and human behavior.* New York: Macmillan, 1953.

Skinner, B. F. *Verbal behavior.* New York: Appleton-Century-Crofts, 1957.

Slobin, D. I. (Ed.) *A field manual for cross-cultural study of the acquisition of communicative competence.* Berkeley: University of California ASVC Bookstore, 1967.

Slobin, D. I. Imitation and grammatical development in children. In N. S. Endler, L. R. Boulter, & H. Osser (Eds.), *Contemporary issues in developmental psychology.* New York: Holt, Rinehart & Winston, 1968.

Slobin, D. *Psycholinguistics.* Glenview, Ill.: Scott, Foresman & Co., 1971.

Slobin, D. I. Cognitive prerequisites for the development of grammar. In D. I. Slobin & C. Ferguson (Eds.), *Studies of child language development.* New York: Holt, Rinehart & Winston, 1973.

Smith, M., Ruder, K., & Stremel, K. Independent vs. interdependent linguistic behaviors: A componential analysis. Bureau of Child Research Working Paper, University of Kansas, Lawrence, 1973.

Snow, C. E. Mothers' speech to children learning language. *Child Development,* 1972, *43,* 549–65.

Spitz, R. *No and yes.* New York: International Universities Press, 1957.

Stageberg, N. C. *An introductory English grammar* (2nd ed.). New York: Holt, Rinehart & Winston, 1971.

Stern, D. N. Mother and infant at play: The dyadic interaction involving facial, vocal and gaze behaviors. In M. Lewis & L. A. Rosenblum (Eds.), *The effect of the infant on its caregiver.* New York: Wiley, 1974.

Stone, L. J., Smith, H. T., & Murphy, L. B. (Eds.) *The competent infant: Research and commentary.* New York: Basic Books, 1973.

Strain, B. A. Early dialogues: A naturalistic study of vocal behavior in mothers and three-month-old infants. Unpublished doctoral dissertation, George Peabody College, Nashville, May, 1974.

Stremel, K., & Waryas, C. A behavioral-psycholinguistic approach to language training. In L. McReynolds (Ed.), *Developing systematic procedures for training children's language. ASHA Monographs No. 18,* 1974.

Tizard, J., & Tizard B. The institution as an environment for development. In M. P. M. Richards (Ed.), *The integration of a child into a social world*. London: Cambridge University Press, 1974.

Trehub, S. E. Infant's sensitivity to vowel and tonal contrasts. *Developmental Psychology, 1973, 9,* 91–96.

Trehub, S. E., & Rabinovitch, M.S. Auditory-linguistic sensitivity in early infancy. *Developmental Psychology, 1972, 6,* 74–77.

Turnure, C. Response to voice of mother and stranger by babies in the first year. *Developmental Psychology, 1971, 4,* 182–90.

Uzgiris, I. C. Organization of sensori-motor intelligence. In M. Lewis (Ed.), *Origins of intelligence*. New York: Plenum Press, 1976.

Vanderheiden, G., & Harris-Vanderheiden, D. Communication techniques and aids for the nonvocal severely handicapped. In L. L. Lloyd (Ed.), *Communication and assessment: Intervention strategies*. Baltimore: University Park Press, 1976.

Vietze, P., & Strain, B. Contingent responsiveness between mother and infant: Who's reinforcing whom? Paper presented at SEPA, Atlanta, March 1975.

Vygotsky, L. S. *Thought and language*. Cambridge: M.I.T. Press, 1962 (1st edition 1934).

Waryas, C. Psycholinguistic research in language intervention programming: The pronoun system. *Journal of Psycholinguistic Research, 1973, 2,* 221–37.

Waryas, C., & Stremel, K. On the preferred form of the double object construction. Unpublished manuscript. Parsons Research Center, Parsons, Kans., 1973.

Waryas, C., & Stremel-Campbell, K. Grammatical training for the language delayed child. In R. L. Schiefelbusch (Ed.), *Language intervention strategies*. Baltimore: University Park Press, in press.

Welker, W. I. An analysis of exploratory and play behavior in animals. In B. W. Fiske & S. R. Maddi (Eds.), *Functions of varied experience*. Homewood, Ill.: Dorsey, 1961.

Wells, G. Learning to code experience through language. *Journal of Child Language, 1974, 1,* 243–69.

Werner, H., & Kaplan, B. *Symbol formation*. New York: Wiley, 1963.

Wetstone, H. S., & Friedlander, B. Z. The effect of word order on young children's responses to simple questions and commands. Paper presented at the Meeting of the Society for Research in Child Development, Philadelphia, 1973.

Wilbur, R. B. The linguistics of manual languages and manual systems. In L. L. Lloyd (Ed.), *Communication assessment and intervention strategies*. Baltimore: University Park Press, 1976.

Wittgenstein, L. *Philosophical investigations*. Oxford: Basil, Blackwell & Mott, 1958.

Wolff, P. H. Observations on the early development of smiling. In B. M. Foss (Ed.), *Determinants of infant behavior, II*. New York: Wiley, 1963.

Wolff, P. H. The natural history of crying and other vocalizations in early infancy. In B. Foss (Ed.), *Determinants of infant behavior, IV*. London: Methuen, 1969.

Yarrow, L. J., & Peterson, F. A. The interplay between cognition and motivation in infancy. In M. Lewis (Ed.), *Origins of intelligence*. New York: Plenum Press, 1976.

name index

Ainsworth, M. D. S., 58, 62
Anderson, R. M., 161
Anglin, J., 71
Austin, J. L., 62

Baer, D. M., 4, 86, 181, 220, 221, 223, 224, 227, 228
Baldwin, C. P., 71, 72
Balthazar, E. E., 164
Bandura, A., 57
Bangs, T. E., 4, 174
Bar-Adon, A., 165
Bateman, M. C., 70
Bates, E., 48, 178, 191, 238
Bateson, M. C., 62
Bayley, N., 95, 152, 169
Bell, S. M., 58, 62
Bellugi-Klima, U., 7, 64, 65, 68, 76, 85, 166
Bereiter, C., 4, 194
Berger, S. L., 122
Berko Gleason, J., 160, 165, 166
Berry, M. F., 160, 165, 166
Bing, E., 70
Blank, M., 8
Bliss, C. K., 212
Bloom, L., 4, 6, 8, 17, 18, 19, 20, 21, 23, 29, 30, 33, 36, 42, 67, 82, 85, 87, 98, 100, 101, 102, 103, 104, 106, 107, 191, 194, 196, 197, 199, 201, 202, 207, 208, 215, 218
Blott, J. P., 8, 216, 223, 238
Bonvillian, J. D., 27
Bowerman, M. F., 4, 6, 20, 21, 22, 23, 24, 33, 34, 35, 36, 191, 194, 196, 207, 236
Bowlby, J., 57, 58
Braine, M., 17, 18, 82, 103, 104, 105
Bricker, D. D., 4, 194, 223, 224, 225, 227, 228, 230
Bricker, W. A., 4, 194, 223, 224, 225, 227, 228, 230
Broen, P. A., 71, 161, 187
Brown, L., 34
Brown, R., 17, 20, 24, 36, 64, 65, 68, 70, 71, 76, 82, 85, 105, 106, 107, 108, 109, 159, 183, 196, 198, 230, 236
Bruner, J. S., 24, 25, 26, 27, 37, 38, 39, 42, 43, 48, 49, 52, 55, 56, 59, 60, 61, 62, 69, 70, 72, 74, 75, 179, 194, 195, 197, 199, 201, 204, 207, 215, 217, 222, 226, 227, 236
Buddenhagen, R. G., 4
Bzoch, K. R., 173

Carrier, J. K., 33, 40, 212, 225, 226, 230
Carrow, E., 157, 173
Carrow, M. A., 91, 94, 95, 96
Cassirer, E., 29

Cazden, C., 17, 64, 65, 70
Chafe, W. L., 20, 23, 34, 37, 39
Chapman, R. S., 86, 93, 95
Chomsky, N. A., 6, 13, 14, 16, 17, 19, 20, 21, 35, 39, 40, 81, 82, 203, 204, 206, 214, 215, 236
Cicciarelli, A., 161
Clark, C. R., 33
Clark, E. V., 29
Clarke-Stewart, K. A., 70
Collis, G. M., 69
Corman, H. H., 149, 164
Crabtree, M., 162

Dale, P. S., 64, 65, 67, 81
Davis, B. B., 65, 72
DeLaguna, G. A., 47, 48, 49, 52, 55, 98, 176, 179, 198, 220
Dennison, L., 223, 224
Dick, A. E., 27
Dixon, E., 68, 85
Dolan, A. B., 24
Doll, E., 162
Dore, J., 50, 52, 53, 54, 55, 61, 66, 77, 179, 180, 220, 227, 236, 241

Einstein, A., 149, 163, 164
Elmas, P. D., 74, 89
Engelmann, S., 4, 194
Ervin-Tripp, S., 183
Escalona, S. K., 62, 63, 68, 85, 149, 163, 164
Evatt, R. L., 162

Falk, A., 222
Fernald, C., 85
Fillmore, C., 20, 23, 34, 37, 39, 82, 197, 198, 199, 201, 236
Fisichelli, V. R., 75
Flavell, J. H., 32
Foster, R., 164
Fraser, C., 17, 68, 85
Freedle, R., 56, 70, 73
Friedlander, B. Z., 65, 72, 74, 90, 92, 95
Fristoe, M., 155, 168, 227
Furley, P. H., 70

Gelman, R., 71, 86, 91
Giddan, J., 164
Gleitman, L. R., 67, 73
Goldberg, S., 27, 70
Goldman, R., 155, 168
Gordan, K., 216, 223, 238
Gordon, T. J., 70
Graham, L. W., 227
Gray, B., 4, 40, 230
Greenberg, J. H., 37

Greenfield, P., 20, 21, 24, 100, 102, 103, 104, 187
Greenman, G. W., 74
Guenther, H., 222
Guess, D., 4, 86, 181, 220, 221, 222, 223, 224, 227, 228
Guillaume, P., 89

Halliday, M., 50, 51, 52, 55, 59, 60, 179, 180, 218, 220, 227, 236, 241, 251
Hanlon, C., 64, 183
Harkins, J. P., 71
Harris-Vanderheiden, D., 33, 212
Harte, T. J., 70
Hartmann, M. C., 216, 223, 238
Hedrick, D. L., 173
Hegrenes, J. R., 4
Holland, J., 222
Hood, L., 67, 201, 202
Horstmeier, D. S., 167
Hunt, J. McV., 24, 72, 149, 171
Huttenlocher, J., 73, 86, 91, 92, 97, 187, 236

Ingram, D., 98
Irwin, O. C., 70

Jacklin, C. N., 27
Jacobs, A. C., 65, 72
Jex, J. L., 163
Jones, J. D., 163
Jusczyk, P., 89

Kagan, J., 70, 90
Kaplan, B., 29, 74, 102
Kaplan, E. L., 89
Kaplan, G. A., 89
Karelitz, S., 75
Kendon, A., 62
Kent, L. R., 222, 223, 227, 228
Keogh, W. J., 220
Klein, D., 222
Kopchick, G. A., 33

League, R., 173
Lee, L., 159, 166, 167, 170
Leonard, L. B., 34
Leopold, W. F., 28, 29, 90, 165
Lewis, M., 27, 28, 56, 61, 70, 73, 89, 90
Lightbown, P., 67, 201, 202
Ling, A. H., 65, 71
Ling, D., 65, 71, 123
Lloyd, L. L., 33, 123, 161, 212, 227
Longhurst, T., 185
Lovateli, C., 166
Lovell, K., 68, 85
Luria, A., 43, 215, 236

Maccoby, E. E., 27
MacDonald, J. D., 4, 8, 106, 107, 167, 171, 191, 216, 217, 218, 223, 225, 227, 229, 230, 238
MacNamara, J., 6, 43, 68, 222, 236
Mahoney, G., 56, 59, 72, 75, 187, 188
Marshall, M. R., 40
Mason, W. A., 43

Matheny, A. P., 24
Matheny, P. A., 161
McCall, R. B., 27
McLean, J. E., 4, 225
McNeill, D., 6, 17, 98, 203
Meadow, S. G., 86, 91
Mechan, M. J., 163
Mehrabian, A., 149, 169
Menyuk, P., 61, 91, 98
Miles, M., 161
Miller, J. E., 4, 6, 8, 48, 157, 170, 191, 218, 219, 223, 227, 229, 230, 238
Miller, J. F., 86, 93, 95, 161
Milner, E., 70
Moffitt, A. R., 74
Morehead, A., 32
Morehead, D. M., 32
Morse, P. A., 89
Muma, J., 192, 193, 204
Murphy, L. B., 74, 75

Nakazima, S. A., 89
Nelson, K. E., 8, 24, 27, 28, 29, 30, 36, 39, 42, 43, 56, 65, 66, 71, 73, 75, 76, 77, 99, 100, 102, 187, 194, 195, 199, 201, 207, 222, 226, 236
Nichols, M., 106, 107, 216

Olson, D., 8, 35, 38, 39, 42, 43, 176, 191, 192, 201, 203, 204, 218, 221, 236

Peak, T. J., 40, 226
Peterson, F. A., 24
Phillips, J. R., 71, 72
Piaget, J., 6, 23, 24, 25, 27, 29, 30, 31, 32, 42, 164, 199, 243
Prather, E. M., 173
Premack, D., 6, 33, 55, 194, 226

Rabinovitch, M. S., 89
Reichle, J., 185
Richards, M. F. M., 61
Ruder, K. F., 6, 8, 220
Ryan, B., 230
Ryan, J., 4, 40, 62

Sackett, G. P., 27
Sailor, W., 4, 181, 220, 221, 222, 224, 227, 228
Schaefer, E. S., 70
Schaffer, H. R., 69, 76, 89
Schlesinger, I. M., 4, 6, 20, 21, 34, 42, 82, 106, 167, 194, 216
Seligman, M. E. P., 86, 91
Shatz, M., 71
Shipley, E. F., 67, 73
Siegel, G. M., 71, 161
Sinclair-deZwart, H., 6, 23, 32
Siqueland, E. R., 89
Skinner, B. F., 13, 14, 40, 54, 183, 214, 220, 222, 226, 236
Slobin, D. I., 4, 6, 8, 22, 23, 28, 33, 42, 43, 65, 102, 106, 191, 194, 208
Smith, C. S., 67, 73
Smith, H. T., 74
Smith, J., 20, 21, 24, 100, 102, 103, 104, 187

Smith, M. D., 6, 8
Snow, C. E., 72, 73, 75
Spiegel, B., 216, 223, 238
Spitz, R., 90
Stageberg, N. C., 80, 208
Stark, J., 164
Stayton, D. J., 58, 62
Steiner, V. G., 162
Stern, D. N., 62
Stone, L. J., 74
Strain, B. A., 62
Stremel, K., 4, 8, 219, 220, 228, 229, 230

Talbott, R., 160, 165, 166
Tizard, B., 58
Tizard, J., 58
Tobin, A. R., 172
Trehub, S. E., 89
Turnure, C., 74

Uzgiris, I. C., 25, 26, 27, 149, 171

Vanderheiden, G. C., 33, 212
Vietze, P., 62

Vigorito, J., 89
Vincent-Smith, L., 223
Vygotsky, L. S., 56

Waryas, C. L., 4, 172, 219, 220, 228, 229, 230
Waryas, P. A., 172
Watson, L., 223
Welker, W. I., 27
Wells, G., 70
Werner, H., 29, 102
Wetstone, H. S., 65, 72, 92, 95
Wilbur, R. B., 212
Williams, M., 149, 169
Wilson, R. S., 24
Wittengenstein, L., 36
Wolff, P. H., 61, 74
Woodcock, R. W., 33, 168

Yarrow, L. J., 24
Yoder, D. E., 4, 6, 8, 48, 157, 170, 191, 218, 219, 223, 227, 229, 230, 238

Zimmerman, I. L., 162

subject index

Acquisition of linguistic structures, 63–77
  child's role in the process, 72–77
  and comprehension, 68
  facilitating adult behaviors, 69–72
  role of adult expansions, 64–65
  role of imitation, 65–67
  role of reinforcement, 64
  transactional model of, 68–69
Adult speech to language learning children,
  69–72
Assessment, 121–173. See also Assessment
  instruments
  of cognitive bases, 123, 148–51
  contexts for, 126–27
  of expressive linguistic skills, 125–26, 157–60
  language samples, 137–39, 257–63
  nonstandardized procedures for, 134–39
  observational procedures for assessing non-
    verbal behavior, 135–37
  of organismic factors, 122
  priorities, suggested decision map for deter-
    mining, 143–48
  profile, suggested format, 145
  purposes of, 129–30
  of receptive linguistic skills, 124–25, 154–57
  of social bases, 123–24, 151–54
  summary, suggested format, 146
  transactional model of, 140–46
Assessment instruments, standardized or published
  advantages and disadvantages, 130–31
  general characteristics of, 128–29
  modifications in administering, 131–33
  selection of appropriate, 133–34
  specific instruments, descriptions of, 160–73
  use of, 128–34
Attachment theory, 57–59

Behavioral theory
  of infant socialization, 57
  mand and tact as language functions, 54
  role of reinforcement in language acquisition,
    64
  as treatment basis in language intervention,
    13, 14

Case grammar, 20, 82
  examples, 21
  and intervention targets, 197–99
Cognitive bases of language acquisition. See
  also Cognitive development
  issues and perspectives, 15–16
  summary, 44–45
  summary statements, 249–50
  synthesis of, 39–45

Cognitive bases, continued
  universal knowledge base for language,
    22–31
Cognitive development. See also Cognitive
  bases of language acquisition
  assessment of, 123, 148–51
  child as constructor of knowledge, 27
  early, prelinguistic, 23–28
  dynamic events, and focus on, 28–30
  sensorimotor development and language ac-
    quisition, 28–31, 42–43
  sensorimotor stage, 24–28
  skill action development, 26–27
Communication function of language. See Functions of language; Functions of child language; Pragmatic functions
Communication, preverbal. See Preverbal
  communication
Communication strategy, 203–9
  as determiner of structure, 203–5
  influence on treatment targets, 206–9
Comprehension. See also Receptive language;
  Receptive language development
  and "receptive language", terms, 83
  role in language acquisition, 68
Concept formation
  relational vs. abstractional theory, 29–31
Context for language treatment, 210–12
  as related to pragmatic functions, 184–87

Expressive language. See also Expressive language development vs. receptive, 83
Expressive language development, 96–109
  assessment of, 125–26, 157–60
  and Brown's stages, 105–6
  first words produced, 99–100
  four major stages of development, 97–98
  grammatical morphemes, 108–9
  one-word utterances, 97–103
  and prelinguistic vocal development, 97
  semantic relations and functions expressed,
    100–2, 106–7
  Stage I: "One word utterance production,"
    97–103
  Stage II: "The transition to grammar," 103–5
  Stage III: "Two- and three-word grammatical
    utterances," 105–7
  Stage IV: "Extension and syntactic refinement
    of multiword grammatical utterances,"
    107–9
  successive single-word utterances, 103–5
Feedback to more mature speakers, 75–76
Functions of child language, 50–56. See also
  Pragmatic functions; Functions of language
  to acquire and organize knowledge, 54–55

Functions of child language, continued
to entertain, 56
and illocutionary force, 52
to indicate willingness to cooperate, 55
to regulate listener's overt response, 54–55
to signal initiation or termination of social interaction, 55
two major types, 54
and use of term *intent,* 59–60
Functions of language, 47–56. *See also* Functions of child language; Pragmatic functions
global accounts, 49–50
mand and tact, 54
as means for achieving social ends, 47–49
traditional accounts, 47

Grammars
child, 82
descriptive, 81–82
phrase structure, 81
transformational, 81–82

Imitation, role in language acquisition, 65–67
Interrogatives, production of grammatical, 109. *See also* Questions

Joint reference, establishment of
child's strategies for, 74–75
as function of preverbal communication, 60

Language, as mapping knowledge, 193–95. *See also* Mapping construct
Language acquisition process. *See also* Expressive language development; Receptive language development; Linguistic development; Acquisition of linguistic structures
summary statements, 251
Language samples
procedures for collecting, 137–39
transcription and analysis, suggested formats, 257–63
Language structure. *See also* Linguistic structures
summary statements, 252–53
summary of treatment targets, 209–10
targeting bases, 202–09
Linguistic development, sequence of, 79–109. *See also* Expressive language development; Receptive language development
Linguistic structure, acquisition of. See Acquisition of linguistic structures
Linguistic structure, nature of, 79–82
descriptive grammars, 81–82
morphology defined, 80
phonology defined, 80
syntax defined, 81

Mapping construct
and semantic data, 195
treatment implications, 194
Meaning in child language, 16–22. *See also* Semantic relationships; Reference
Bloom's categories, 197
categorizations for treatment targeting, 202

Meaning in child language, continued
"language game" as determiner of, 36. *See also* Reference; Semantic content
in one-word utterances, 100–2
Mean Length of Utterance (MLU), 105–6, 139, 264
Morphology, defined, 80
Mother-child interactions
and acquisition of linguistic structures, 63–77
and development of preverbal communication, 61–63
and infant socialization, 57–59

One-word utterances
early production of, 97–103
as holophrases, 98
meanings of, 100–2
"rich interpretation" of, 100
successive single-word utterances, 103–5

Paralinguistic features
infant's discriminative responding to, 89–90
as marking of illocutionary force in Primitive Speech Acts, 52
Perception of sounds
as initial stage in receptive language development, 89–90
vs. receptive language, 83
Phonology, defined, 80
Pragmatic functions. *See also* Functions of language; Functions of child language
implications for reinforcement contingencies, 182–84
implications for treatment contexts, 184–87
summary of treatment implications, 189–90
as treatment targets, 179–82
Pragmatics, 48–56
defined, 48–49
of emerging language, 50–52. *See also* Functions of child language
Preverbal communication, 56–63
development of, 61–63
form of, 61
functions of, 59–61
and infant socialization, 56–59
Primitive Speech Act (PSA), 52–53
Psychological aspects of communication, 34–39, 40–42. *See also* Reference
adult vs. child perspectives, 15, 34

Questions
asking, by adult, in collection of language samples, 138
asking, as metalinguistic device, 76–77
one-word forms, in first 10 and 50 words, 99
production of grammatical, 109

Receptive language, 83–87. *See also* Receptive language development
defined, 83–84
precedence of in normal development, 85–87
unique demands on organism, 83–84
vs. expressive language, 83
vs. sensation and perception, 83

Receptive language development, 85–96. *See also* Receptive language
assessment of, 124–25, 154–57
comprehension of function words, 95
first words comprehended, 91–92
as initial stage in noun and verb class acquisition, 86
responding to syntactic meanings of S-V-O word order, 92–93, 95–96
Stage I: "Responding to phonemic and paralinguistic features," 89–90
Stage II: "Responding to lexical-semantic features," 90–93
Stage III: "Responding to syntactic-grammatical features," 93–96
three major stages in, 88
Reference, 33–39
construct reviewed, 191–93
implications of, 38–39
and influence on structure, 203–6
as mechanism for communication realization, 35–38
possible strategies by children, 199–202, 204–6
Reference, joint. *See* Joint reference
Representational or symbolic behavior, 31–33
Research in language
current voids, 238–39
new perspectives for, with handicapped, 245–46
prevalent strategies and styles, 236–38, 239–40
recommendations for, 241–47

Selective listening, 73–74
Semantic content
analyzing for intervention targets, 195–202
function of semantic content, 191–95
implications for treatment, 190–202
Semantic relationships
in developing language, 16–19
expressed in two- and three-word utterances, 106–7
as grammar, 20, 34, 82. *See also* Case grammar

Semantic "revolution" in theory, 17–22
contributors to, 20–21
summary of views emanating from, 31–32
Social bases of language acquisition, 47–48
assessment of, 123–24, 151–54
summary statements, 250–51
Socialization of infants
attachment theory of, 57–59
learning theory account, 57
Subject-predication. *See* Topic–comment
Syntax
defined, 81
as structure for communication acts, 202–3

Topic-comment
defined, 37
and early word order, 104
as structure for treatment targeting, 204–5
Transactional model of language acquisition
general implications for research and intervention, 114–17
implications for research, 235–47
implications for treatment, 175–232
and language performance, 113–14
summary and visual representation of, 111–17
Transformational grammar
described, 81–82
Treatment programs
analysis of existing, 213–26
design in educational settings, 231–32. *See also* Context for language treatment
matrix for, 176–78
overall needs, 175–78
strengths of current programs, 226–28
weaknesses of current programs, 228–31
Treatment targets, pragmatic functions as, 178–90

Universal knowledge base for language, 22–31. *See also* Cognitive bases of language acquisition
Utterances
mean length of (MLU), 105–6, 139, 264
one-word, production of, 97–103